German Unification

Economic Issues

Edited by Leslie Lipschitz and Donogh McDonald

International Monetary Fund
Washington, D.C.
December 1990

© 1990 International Monetary Fund

Library of Congress Cataloging-in-Publication Data

German unification : economic issues / edited by Leslie Lipschitz and
Donogh McDonald.
    p.   cm. — (Occasional paper / International Monetary Fund,
ISSN 0251-6365 ; no. 75)
    "December 1990."
    Includes bibliographical references.
    ISBN 1-55775-200-1
    1. Germany (West)—Economic Policy—1974- 2. Germany
(West)—Economic conditions—1974- 3. Germany (East)—
Economic policy. 4. Germany (East)—Economic conditions.
I. Lipschitz, Leslie. II. McDonald, Donogh. III. Series: Occasional
paper (International Monetary Fund) ; no. 75.
HC286.7.G447 1990
330.943'0879—dc20   90-26503
                                     CIP

Price: US$10.00
(US$7.50 to full-time faculty members and
students)

Please send orders to:
External Relations Department, Publication Services
International Monetary Fund, Washington, D.C. 20431
Tel: (202) 623-7430   Telefax: (202) 623-7201

Contents

Tables

Charts

The following symbols or terms have been used throughout this publication:

...   to indicate that data are not available;

—   to indicate that the figure is zero or less than half the final digit shown, or that the item does not exist;

–   between years or months (e.g., 1989–90 or January–June) to indicate the years or months covered, including the beginning and ending years or months;

/   between years (e.g., 1985/86) to indicate a crop or fiscal (financial) year.

"Billion" means a thousand million.

"Trillion" means a thousand billion.

Länder are the states of the Federal Republic of Germany; DM denotes deutsche mark, the currency of the Federal Republic of Germany; M denotes marks, the currency of the former German Democratic Republic; GNP is gross national product; GDP is gross domestic product; and NMP is net material product.

Minor discrepancies between constituent figures and totals are due to rounding.

Preface

In January 1989 three of the authors of this volume were involved in the publication of a shorter paper entitled *The Federal Republic of Germany: Adjustment in a Surplus Country*. Some readers of that paper were surprised by its forthrightness. The *Financial Times* of London, noting that the IMF "pulls no punches in its criticism" and marveling at "Bonn's policy of openness" at agreeing to publication, characterized it as "a fit of glasnost" by the International Monetary Fund. In fact, the German authorities had been most helpful in the preparation of the paper and had never tried to stifle the criticism in it; neither they nor their representatives at the IMF had questioned the authors' decision to publish the paper.

The present volume comes at an even more interesting time. The papers, written initially for distribution within the IMF, afforded the authors the privilege of being close witnesses to historical changes in Germany, and forced them to try and stand apart from the euphoria of the unification process and evaluate its implications. The authors are enormously indebted to many public officials in Germany, who, despite considerably increased work loads, took great pains to enlighten and inform, to answer many questions, and to correct factual and technical errors. But the discussions with German officials did more: they transmitted to the authors some of the enthusiasm—the sanguine, almost heady, atmosphere—that was the context of German economic policymaking in 1990.

The rapid pace of developments in Germany, coupled with the inevitable time lag between preparation and publication, presents two problems. First, the data in the paper generally represent the available estimates and projections at the end of September or early October 1990—much of this will probably be out of date by the new year. The second problem is one of terminology: the area called the German Democratic Republic (GDR) became part of the Federal Republic of Germany (FRG) on October 3, 1990. In general, the designation GDR is used in referring to the pre-unification period and *east Germany* (as distinct from *west Germany*) to the post-unification period. Similar problems exist with currencies: GDR marks ceased to exist as legal tender on July 1 and deutsche mark became the sole legal tender in the FRG and the GDR. The authors take some pains to avoid confusion in these terms, but it is not always easy.

The responses to the earlier paper on Germany influenced the structure of this volume. On that occasion, in an attempt to keep the paper slim, the arguments were buttressed with references to various unpublished background notes. Many readers, however, wanted the whole picture, and were quick to request copies of these notes. For this reason the present volume is more comprehensive. While in form it resembles a conference volume (authors are listed for each paper), the extent of cooperation, review, and criticism from within the team was much greater than is apparent. In addition, the authors are indebted to Manuel Guitián (who led the 1990 IMF consultation mission to Germany) and to many other colleagues for helpful suggestions and comments, to Behrouz Guerami and Jolanta Stefanska for research assistance, to Esha Ray for editorial assistance, and to Valerie Pabst and Marie Ricasa for secretarial support. The authors bear sole responsibility for any factual errors. The opinions expressed are those of the authors and should not be construed as representing the views of the German authorities, Executive Directors of the IMF, or other members of the IMF staff.

Germany

Schleswig-Holstein

Mecklenburg-West Pomerania

Hamburg

Bremen

Brandenburg

Lower Saxony

Berlin

North Rhine-Westphalia

Saxony-Anhalt

Bonn

Hesse

Saxony

Thuringia

Rhineland-Palatinate

Saarland

Bavaria

Baden-Württemberg

| 0 | 50 | 100 | 150 | 200km |

Federal Republic of Germany and German Democratic Republic: Comparison of Selected Economic and Social Indicators in 1988

	Federal Republic of Germany	German Democratic Republic
Area and population		
Area (*1,000 sq. km.*)	249	108
Population (*millions*)	61.4	16.7
(*In percent of population*)		
Of working age	67.0[1]	65.0
Pensioners	18.5[1]	16.0
Employment		
Total employed (*millions*)	27.4	9.0
(*In percent of population*)	44.5	53.9
Female employment (*in percent of total employment*)	38.1[1]	48.6
Employment by sector		
(*In percent of total*)		
Agriculture and forestry	4.0	10.8
Mining, manufacturing, and construction	39.8	47.1
Other sectors	56.2	42.1
Household income, consumption, and saving		
Average monthly gross earnings (*DM/M*)	3,850	1,270
Household saving (*in percent of disposable income*)	12.8	7.1
Households with:		
(*In percent of total*)		
Automobiles	97	52
Color television	94	52
Telephone	98	7[2]
Production, investment, and prices		
(*Annual real growth rate, 1980–88*)		
GNP/NMP	1.7	4.2
Gross fixed investment	0.7	2.0
Of which: Machinery and equipment	2.4	5.0
Consumer prices (*annual percent rate of change, 1980–88*)	2.9	—
External trade in goods		
(*In percent of total exports*)		
Exports to state-trading countries	4.4	69.5
Imports from state-trading countries	4.7	68.7
Trade balance		
(*In percent of GNP/NMP*)	6.0	1.0
Of which: State-trading countries	0.2	1.0
Monetary accounts of households		
Household financial assets[3] (*billions DM/M*)	1,196.6	167.2
Velocity of money[4]	1.11	0.97

Sources: Statistisches Bundesamt, *Statistisches Jahrbuch der Bundesrepublik Deutschland, 1989*; Staatliche Zentralverwaltung für Statistik der DDR, *Statistisches Jahrbuch der DDR, 1989*; and Deutsche Bundesbank.

[1] 1987.

[2] 1985.

[3] Currency and bank deposits. Year-end for the FRG and year average for the GDR.

[4] Private disposable income divided by household financial assets.

I

Introduction and Overview

Leslie Lipschitz

German economic policy has become exciting again.

In the fall of 1989 the economy of the Federal Republic of Germany (FRG) seemed set to embark on its eighth year of a steady but unspectacular upswing. The principal domestic economic issue was whether, despite a stubbornly high unemployment rate, capacity constraints in certain sectors of the economy might threaten price stability. The chief international economic issues were concerned with the size of the external surplus and the process of European economic integration.

The economic statistics of the German Democratic Republic (GDR) also did not reflect the extent of incipient turmoil in the system. The GDR differed from the other member countries of the Council for Mutual Economic Assistance (CMEA) in that its entire population had a guaranteed right of access to the west. As long as emigration was prevented, the GDR was a viable economy; but the opening of Hungary's border with Austria in September 1989, coupled with political changes in the U.S.S.R., Hungary, and Poland, rendered the situation unstable.

On November 9, 1989 borders with the FRG were opened and later in the month Chancellor Helmut Kohl outlined his plan for unification. During the period January–October emigration from the GDR to the FRG had amounted to about 167,000. In the last two months of the year another 177,000 people emigrated. After continued mass emigration in the opening weeks of 1990, Chancellor Kohl, on February 6, proposed a currency union with the FRG. The "grand coalition" Government that took office in the GDR in April 1990 (after a conservative election victory in March) expressed its support for German economic, monetary, and social union (GEMSU) and rapid political accession to the FRG. The terms of GEMSU were negotiated in April–May, a State Treaty was signed in May and ratified by the legislatures in June, and GEMSU became effective on July 1, 1990. With economic unification virtually accomplished, the drive for political union accelerated: the German Unity Treaty was ratified by the parliaments

in September, and the GDR became part of the Federal Republic of Germany on October 3. The first free all-German elections since 1932 were held on December 2, 1990.[1]

Thus, the process of German unification, from the initiating events until full political union, was completed within a year. In the course of this process the GDR ceased to exist as a separate state, the basic institutions of the east German economy were essentially demolished and replaced, and the Governments of the FRG and the GDR were forced to make myriad unprecedented decisions on the structure of the economy that would influence economic policies for a long time and give rise to many new and difficult challenges.

The economics of unification will dominate the German economic policy debate for the next few years. At this early stage, however, analysis and projection are frustrated by imponderables in essential areas—for example, the viability of east German industry in a market environment—and by the absence of a statistical base covering all of Germany. The second section of this chapter discusses the economic situation in the FRG and the GDR immediately before GEMSU. The third section considers some critical aspects of policy in the process of integrating the two economies. It focuses especially on the economic implications of German unification in the period through 1991. The final section contains a brief guided tour of the following chapters and some tentative conclusions.

The Two Economies on the Eve of Unification

The Situation in the FRG

The economic performance of the FRG in 1989, the seventh year of expansion in the current cycle, exceeded

---

[1] A full chronology of political and economic events is provided in Box 1 of Chapter III.

Chart 1. Federal Republic of Germany: Developments in 1980–89

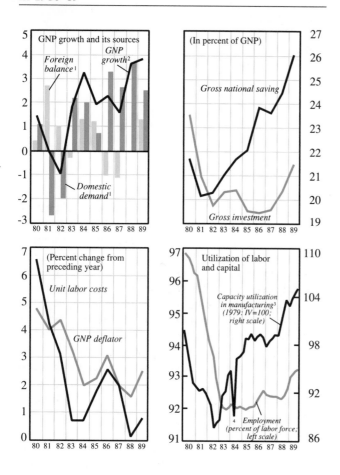

Sources: Statistisches Bundesamt, *Volkswirtschaftliche Gesamtrechnungen*; and Ifo Institute, *Schnelldienst*.
[1] Contribution in percentage points.
[2] In percent a year.
[3] The previous peak was at 100 in the fourth quarter of 1979.
[4] Affected by widespread strikes.

all expectations (Chart 1). The 4 percent increase in real GNP was the strongest thus far in the upswing. Investment accelerated in response to large profits, abundant internal company resources, strong demand, and high levels of capacity utilization. Despite a worsening of the external terms of trade, consumer price inflation remained below 3 percent and the current account surplus widened.

Real growth in 1989 exceeded conventional measures of the rate of growth of potential. Moreover, given the longevity of the upswing, most estimates showed little or no spare capacity in the economy. The strength of business investment suggests, however, that supply constraints elicited a capacity widening response. This is confirmed by developments in the labor market: in 1989 more than 370,000 jobs were created (compared with fewer than 200,000 in each of the two preceding years)

and the unemployment rate dropped sharply. But, even with the effects of large-scale immigration[2] and buoyant investment on capacity, growth at the pace achieved in 1988–89 was unlikely to be sustainable over the medium term.

The stance of macroeconomic policies in 1989 was broadly restrictive. The budget deficit of the territorial authorities[3] fell from 2½ percent to 1¼ percent of GNP, the lowest level in the current cycle. The general government accounts (which include the social security system) showed a small surplus in 1989, the first since 1973 (Chart 2). Monetary conditions were also tightened: after three years of money growth exceeding its target, in 1989 broad money (M3) grew by 4¾ percent, compared with a target of about 5 percent. Against the background of a relatively weak deutsche mark in the first three quarters of the year and high and rising capacity utilization rates, the Deutsche Bundesbank increased official interest rates on various facilities by 2½ percentage points in the course of the year; short-term money market rates rose by slightly more. With a downward tendency in U.S. dollar interest rates, the short-term differential vis-à-vis dollar rates narrowed after April and was eliminated completely by the end of the year. The deutsche mark appreciated sharply both against the U.S. dollar and in effective terms in the last quarter of 1989; thus, although on average the effective value of the deutsche mark was 1 percent lower in 1989 than in 1988, in the course of the year it appreciated by 3¾ percent.

National accounts data for the first half of 1990 showed continued rapid growth: private consumption boosted by the long-planned tax cut, further buoyant investment in both equipment and construction, and, despite some drag on the economy from a weakening foreign balance, GNP almost 4 percent above the level of the first half of 1989. Inflation (the 12-month rate of increase of the consumer price index) was 2¼ percent in June, reflecting lower import prices and little upward pressure from domestic costs.

In January 1990 the long-planned tax reduction and reform package became effective: with the lowering of gross taxes offset in part by a reduction in tax preferences, the net effect was an injection of purchasing power equivalent to 1 percent of GNP. The Government also announced its decision to abolish the stock exchange turnover tax (*Börsenumsatzsteuer*) by January 1991 and the taxes on company equity issues (*Gesellschaftsteuer*) and on bills of exchange (*Wechselsteuer*) in January 1992, measures long advocated by the financial community.

[2] In the course of 1989 the potential supply of labor was boosted by more than 700,000 immigrants—about half from the GDR and the other half ethnic Germans mainly from Poland. On average in 1989, the labor force was increased by 210,000 as a result of immigration, while almost 200,000 potential workers were enrolled in language or vocational training courses.
[3] The territorial authorities include the federal, state, and municipal governments, the Burden Equalization Fund, the European Recovery Program Fund, and the accounts of the European Community (EC).

Chart 2. Federal Republic of Germany: Indicators of Fiscal and Monetary Policy, 1980–89

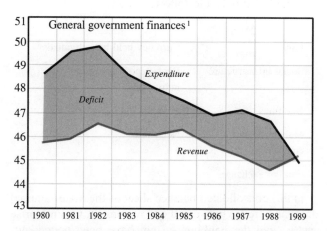

General government finances [1]

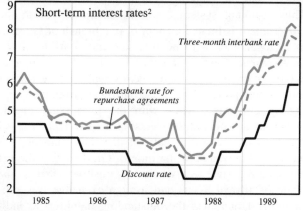

Short-term interest rates[2]

Sources: Statistisches Bundesamt, *Volkswirtschaftliche Gesamtrechnungen*; and Deutsche Bundesbank, *Monthly Report*.
[1] National accounts basis; in percent of GNP.
[2] In percent a year.

Financial conditions in the first half of 1990 reflected a continued restrictive stance of monetary policy coupled with some uncertainty about medium-term prospects. The growth of M3 was close to the lower bound of the (4–6 percent) target range and short-term interest rates were more or less stable. Bond yields, however, jumped by a percentage point in the first quarter, partly in response to developments in the GDR and the February proposal for currency union. In the first six months of the year the deutsche mark was broadly unchanged in nominal effective terms; a strong appreciation against the U.S. dollar and the Japanese yen was offset by a weakening of the deutsche mark within the exchange rate mechanism (ERM) of the European Monetary System (EMS) and against the pound sterling.

The prudent policies of the Government of the FRG through most of the period of cyclical upswing and the strength of the economy in 1988–90 provided a solid foundation for unification. Thus, the starting position for GEMSU in the FRG had many favorable aspects:

- a national saving rate that exceeded national investment by some 4½ percent of GNP;

- a considerable improvement in company profits during the previous seven years and substantial liquid company reserves for investment;

- a reformed tax system (in which taxes had been reduced by 2½ percentage points of GNP since 1985) and a balanced general government position in 1989;

- low inflation and a credible anti-inflationary stance of policies;

- net foreign assets of some US$300 billion.

Against these positive aspects one had to weigh the danger of overheating: the economy was already operating at close to full capacity and the critical question was whether the additional demand generated by GEMSU would succeed in eliciting a supply response without raising the rate of inflation. Clearly demand pressure in the FRG would be relieved to the extent that resources could be drawn in from other countries. But the flexibility of the labor market and of capacity constraints were essential considerations on which it was not easy to form a judgment.

The Situation in the GDR

It was difficult to assess the starting economic situation in the GDR. The GDR, with a population of 16½ million (a fourth that of the FRG), covered an area almost half the size of the FRG. Although the statistics on demographics and on the characteristics of the labor force and its distribution by sector were reliable, historical data on income, output, prices, and the financial situation of enterprises provided little guidance to the economic situation. The problem was fundamental: the data reflected a structure of prices set by the Government, and without a market-related set of relative prices it was impossible to come to any realistic assessment of the main economic aggregates. On the basis of the most recent estimates it appeared that the historical data presented an unrealistically positive picture of the strength of the economy and the welfare of the people. It was clear also that the economy had suffered serious setbacks during the period between the fall of 1989 and July 1, 1990.

Conventional estimates showed the following stylized facts on the GDR economy:

- a GNP some 10 percent the size of that in the FRG;

- a level of labor productivity 30–35 percent that of the FRG;

- an average gross wage about one third and net take-home pay less than half of that in the FRG;

- a heavily indebted enterprise system with considerable obsolescence in the structure of both capital and products;

- enormous environmental problems, in particular in the chemicals and energy sectors;

- a distorted structure of prices and wages coupled with an interventionist tax and subsidy system;

- a history of strict curtailment on the range of products available, with "luxury goods" largely unavailable;[4]

- more than half of external trade conducted with CMEA countries;[5]

- net foreign debt in convertible currencies of some US$16¼ billion (about one tenth of GNP) at the end of April 1990.

Successful economic integration with the FRG would entail a comprehensive privatization program, large-scale investment in public infrastructure and private productive assets, the adoption of a tax and social security system virtually identical to that in the FRG, a relinquishing of monetary control to the Bundesbank, the establishment of a market-based financial system linked with that in the West, and an incentive system that succeeded in staunching emigration and encouraging capital inflows. It would almost certainly require substantial transitional unemployment and perhaps a hardening of living conditions for some as subsidies were removed and prices of basic goods rose. A critical question was how much of GDR industry was or could be made viable in a market system. Given uncertainty about wages, input prices, actual and potential demand, and financial resources available for restructuring, it was impossible to project income even on a firm-by-firm basis.

Dismembering the State in the GDR

It may be useful to focus briefly on the most fundamental aspect of the economic reform: the dismembering of the State. In the pre-GEMSU GDR most real assets were owned by the State and the banking system consisted chiefly of the *Staatsbank* (State Bank). There was, therefore, no effective demarcation between the Government as government, the business or enterprise sector, and the banking system. The principal components of a stylized consolidated balance sheet of the State would have included only the following items:

Assets	*Liabilities*
Land	Currency held by individuals
Social infrastructure	Bank deposits held by individuals
Buildings	Foreign debt
Machinery and equipment	Net worth
Foreign exchange	

In this consolidated balance sheet of the State, internal debts and credits between the Government, the enterprise sector, and the banking system have been netted out. Thus, banking system credit to enterprises or to the Government is treated as debt of one branch of Government to another with no real influence outside of the Government. Indeed, it could be argued that internal debtor or creditor positions were chiefly a reflection of government policy. Enterprise borrowing from the banking system was always with the permission of the Government, often at the behest of the Government, and sometimes even on behalf of the Government. On balance, it appeared at the time of GEMSU that the net worth of the State as a whole was positive—that is, the value of all real assets and foreign exchange was substantially larger than the outstanding liabilities to individuals and foreigners. The fundamental institutional task facing reformers was not seen, therefore, as administering a default (as was the case in the 1948 currency reform) but rather as determining how the State's assets should be deployed in the first instance and how the Government should be separated from the banking system and the business sector. In this process of dismembering the State, decisions had to be made on how to handle internal debtor-creditor positions.

The negotiations leading up to GEMSU did not address the issue of consolidation of internal creditor and debtor positions. The enterprise system, with its debt to the banking system intact, was placed in a *Treuhandanstalt* (Trust Fund), which was given a mandate to privatize where possible, restructure potentially viable enterprises, and liquidate enterprises that were not viable. The banking system was separated from the State with its credit positions to the enterprises and the Government intact. Because, in the process of monetary unification, its assets were converted into deutsche mark at a rate different from that used for its liabilities, it required some capital infusion from Government.[6] The Government was re-

---

[4] Only about half of households in the GDR had color television sets and only 7 percent had telephones; the corresponding ratios in the FRG were 94 and 98 percent, respectively.

[5] Official statistics showed about two thirds of external trade with CMEA countries and little more than a fourth with Western industrial countries. In reality, the share of CMEA countries was smaller, as a considerable part of external trade with the convertible currency area went unreported.

---

[6] The process of monetary unification is discussed below.

constituted with a more clearly limited economic role and its outstanding debt intact (but converted into deutsche mark at a rate of M 2 = DM 1).

The separation of institutions that resulted from the dismembering of the State raised some important policy issues. A consolidation of debt that cleared enterprises' balance sheets of old debt would probably have facilitated privatization. In a situation of market imperfections and some ambiguity as to whether this debt might eventually be assumed by the Government, any uncertainties would prove counterproductive.[7] Banks would also have been better set for the future if their balance sheets could have been purged of old enterprise debt of doubtful quality. In general, the criterion governing the separation of institutions should have been the objective of providing them with the best chance of subsequent viability without recourse to special governmental assistance. The fundamental policy question was how strictly the separation of institutions would be preserved—that is, whether, and to what extent, the Government or the Trust Fund would intervene to soften budget constraints and undermine market tests and penalties. For example, if enterprises in the initial phase proved unable to borrow on their own accounts, would the Trust Fund (and ultimately the Government) guarantee such borrowing? If existing bank credits to enterprises could not be serviced or repaid, would banks be allowed to bear the consequences or would the Trust Fund or the Government come to their rescue? Would the Trust Fund be allowed to liquidate enterprises on purely market principles, or would government concerns about unemployment intrude? Would Trust Fund losses be covered (and profits be appropriated) by the Government?

In the period leading up to GEMSU, government officials were prepared to answer these questions in principle: the objective was to subject the GDR economy as quickly as possible to market forces. But it was clear from the beginning that these principles would be severely tested in the practices that would evolve during the first 18 months of GEMSU.

Economic Policies

The Process of Economic Integration

The task of building new institutions in east Germany is fundamental to the success of economic integration. Much of the institutional engineering in GEMSU was

set out in the State Treaty and the annexes to it. The architects of the Treaty on the FRG side placed particular emphasis on three themes:

First, GEMSU was a step en route to full political unification in accordance with Article 23 of the basic law of the FRG; this Article envisaged unification not as a merger of the FRG and the GDR but rather as the inclusion of the eastern Länder in the FRG. Similarly, economic integration in no way implied a mixing of the two institutional frameworks but rather the wholesale adoption by the GDR of the economic system of the FRG.

The second theme invoked the Erhardian principles that had guided the postwar economic "miracle" of the FRG. The process of unification would be guided by *Ordnungspolitik*—that is, the free play of market forces within a secure, unobtrusive, and well-understood institutional and financial framework. The objective was to establish a *Soziale Marktwirtschaft*—that is, a market economy within a social system that provided for certain basic needs such as pensions, medical services, and unemployment assistance. In a period of considerable uncertainty it was important to have a social safety net for workers. While there could be no comparable safety net for capital (i.e., firms), stable and predictable policies would reduce uncertainty and enhance the attractiveness of the GDR as a place to invest.

Third, great stress was placed on German unification not being in conflict with the FRG's commitments to Europe and the rest of the world: German unification was seen as a "contribution to European unification"; its external aspects would take cognizance of the role of the four postwar occupation powers; GEMSU was seen as consistent with the principles of free trade and, indeed, it was hoped that the extra demand generated would elicit imports from the rest of the world; and Germany's financial commitments to Eastern Europe and the developing countries would not be lessened.

Clearly, economic integration in Germany will dominate the domestic policy debate for many years. Foreigners, moreover, will be concerned about the international—and, so-called, systemic—implications of the process. In this context it is helpful that the German authorities have committed themselves to principles such as open markets, free trade, and *Ordnungspolitik*.

The numerical medium-term scenarios used to illustrate the orders of magnitude involved in the reconstruction of the east German economy and to gauge its domestic and international effects (Chapters IV–VI) underscore the importance of these principles. The resource requirements of reconstruction will be enormous. Insofar as productive capacities are fully employed, accommodating these requirements will necessitate a crowding-out of other activities. Because financial markets are closely linked across countries, especially within the EMS, this

---

[7] Uncertainties about property rights—that is, the right of enterprises (old or new) to their real estate assets in the face of legal challenges by previous owners who had lost their property to government expropriation—proved an even stronger disincentive to prospective investors.

crowding-out process will not be limited to Germany. However, its negative influence on output and employment in other countries will be offset by the positive effects of additional exports to Germany. The balance of these effects will depend on the openness of German markets to foreign goods and services and the ability of other countries to capitalize on the growth of demand in Germany. Overall the international implications appear to be relatively small.

For Germany itself, even the most sanguine scenarios envisage substantial transitional difficulties—in particular, large-scale unemployment and migration from east to west. In this context it is necessary that the "social" part of *Soziale Marktwirtschaft* be strictly limited and that these limits be widely understood. Without *Ordnungspolitik* as a basic tenet of the social and economic consensus, governments may be tempted to adopt short-term palliative policies which prove detrimental over the longer run.

Monetary Union

It is convenient to start with a discussion of monetary union and the banking system in the GDR.[8] On July 1, 1990,

- the deutsche mark became the sole legal tender in the GDR and the Deutsche Bundesbank the sole monetary authority;[9]

- a market-based banking system was introduced in the GDR with unrestricted capital flows and freely determined interest rates;

- wages, salaries, rents, and other recurrent payments were converted into deutsche mark at a rate of M 1 = DM 1;

- residents of the GDR were entitled to convert marks into deutsche mark at parity in amounts of up to 2,000 marks for those under 14 years of age, up to 4,000 marks for those between 14 and 58, and up to 6,000 marks for those 59 or more years of age;

- other domestic financial assets and liabilities were convertible at a rate of M 2 = DM 1;[10]

- assets in marks of nonresident persons or institutions acquired before the end of 1989 could be converted at a rate of M 2 = DM 1, and those acquired after December 31, 1989 at a rate of M 3 = DM 1.

These aspects of the monetary conversion coupled with decisions on conversion rates for the other items on the balance sheet of the banking system meant that the assets of the banking system were converted into deutsche mark at an average exchange rate of about M 2 = DM 1, while the liabilities were converted at a lower rate. Clearly this would mean a substantial reduction in the net worth of the banking system.

Two measures were adopted to deal with this problem. First, a fund, which was derived from the difference between the official exchange rate and the commercial exchange rate on hard-currency trade and which was deposited with the State Bank, was written down to zero.[11] Second, it was decided that, after adding up all the assets and liabilities of each banking institution and converting net worth into deutsche mark at M 1 = DM 1, each institution's assets would be increased to the extent necessary to balance the books by issuing "equalization claims"—that is, assets that pay interest at the Frankfurt interbank offer rate (FIBOR). This meant simply that the GDR Government would top up the assets of the banking system as a whole by issuing government paper (at FIBOR) to the banks. The stock of government debt and future interest obligations would thus be increased, but no increase would be shown in the government deficit as normally measured in flow terms.

Besides these "accounting" problems, there were serious questions raised about the quality of bank assets and the likely official response to the emergence of substantial nonperforming assets. Insofar as the quality of credits to the enterprise sector (about half of all assets) and housing credits (almost a fourth of all assets) was questionable, the potential for defaults on a very large scale relative to banks' equity could not be ignored. The officials of both the FRG and the GDR envisaged a significant taking-over of enterprise debt by the Trust Fund or the Government itself. A large part of enterprise debt had been incurred for noncommercial reasons and the Government might be seen as liable for this debt. In

---

[8] The State Treaty, after a preamble and a discussion of some basic principles covers monetary union (Chapter II and Annex I), economic union (Chapter III), social union (Chapter IV), and the government budget and finances (Chapter V). The Treaty is discussed in detail in Chapter III below.

[9] There was, however, no provision for GDR representation on the Bundesbank Council.

[10] The conversion rate was a matter of intense debate. In effect, based on the (end-May) consolidated balance sheet of the banking system, the average conversion rate was M 1.8 = DM 1, not very different from that proposed amidst much controversy by the Bundesbank. In the view of the author, the effective conversion rate was sufficiently depreciated to absorb excess (and potentially inflationary)

monetary balances in the GDR. The relationship between the conversion rate and real wages is tenuous. As is clear from developments in the first few weeks of GEMSU, real wages are determined in the market; and the nominal conversion rate can exert, at most, a very temporary influence on them. These issues are examined in greater depth in Chapter X.

[11] The difference between the official and the commercial rate of exchange could be seen as a tax on importers and a subsidy for exporters. Because imports exceeded exports, the fund for these taxes and subsidies was in surplus and this surplus—seen by the Government as a contingent liability to future exporters—was deposited with the State Bank. As the exchange rate system was changed with GEMSU, this liability of the State Bank was simply written down to zero.

any event, the whole of the existing stock of enterprise debt would in effect be guaranteed by the Government directly or indirectly through the Trust Fund. In the opening months of GEMSU the banks would be asked to extend working capital loans to enterprises. As it would be still too early to assess the soundness of these enterprises, these credits would in effect be guaranteed by the Trust Fund. It was intended, however, that after these transitional arrangements, the risks associated with new credits would be borne by the banks themselves.

The stock of bank credits for housing was seen as less of a problem as the collateral value of the real estate exceeded the debt. Initially, however, with rents held down, there might be difficulty in servicing these debts, and the Government envisaged substantial contributions to the servicing of housing debt in 1990–91. Subsequently, as rents were allowed to rise, the housing sector would be able to service its debt without government assistance.

In effect, since July 1, 1990 the major west German banks have played a large role in the banking system of east Germany. Some banks have entered into joint ventures with the commercial banking arm of the State Bank and have taken over the operations of many branches; others have started their own operations *de novo*. The banking law is identical to that of west Germany and therefore subject in effect to directives of the European Community (EC) on banking and solvency;[12] thus banks operate as universal banks and the system is open to participation by foreign institutions.

Since east German banks do not have assets of the quality required to engage in securities repurchase operations or to draw on the discount or Lombard facilities, they have been allowed transitional access to the Bundesbank's discount window (up to quota limits) and the Lombard facility against equalization claims or "single signature paper" (i.e., banks' own IOUs). In effect, the latter paper has been used in the opening stages because the issue of equalization claims has had to await final resolution of banks' opening balance sheets.

As is evident from this description, the separation between the State, the enterprise sector, and the banking system, while clear in principle, was not an entirely clean break in practice. After July 1, enterprises needed liquidity loans to meet current obligations while banks were not yet in a position to evaluate enterprises' creditworthiness. To keep the enterprises afloat, therefore, the Government authorized the Trust Fund to guarantee short-term bank loans. In each of the three months through September, loans amounting to almost DM 10 billion were processed in this way. It appears

that this mechanism of guaranteeing bank loans will continue during the remainder of 1990 and into the first quarter of 1991, but that the allocation of credits will be more conditional on the viability of the enterprises. To the extent that loan guarantees were granted to moribund enterprises—a not insignificant amount especially in the first phase—the net worth of the Trust Fund was diminished or, alternatively, the stock of government debt increased. It is clear that the Government wishes its involvement in the banking system to be limited to correcting past errors and easing transitional difficulties; but it is unclear how long, in practice, the transition will last.

The Enterprise System, the Trust Fund, and the Real Economy

The dismantling of the economic arm of the State left the GDR Government in a net debtor position and the banking system with a small and precarious net worth; thus, the public assets of the GDR were, by and large, taken over by the Trust Fund.[13] The State Treaty on GEMSU envisaged the financial resources of the Trust Fund being used, first, to restructure viable enterprises; second, to help consolidate the GDR Government's financial position; and, third, to the extent that resources remained, to compensate savers for the losses they suffered as a result of converting their savings into deutsche mark at a rate of M 2 = DM 1 rather than at M 1 = DM 1. Thus, much of the net worth of the State was to be deployed in the first instance to cover the costs of economic integration and development. The Trust Fund would have three sources of financing: (1) capital income—that is, the proceeds of privatization; (2) operating income distributed by its constituent companies; and (3) borrowing—up to DM 7 billion in 1990 and DM 10 billion in 1991.[14] The borrowing was seen as essentially a transitional means of financing Trust Fund operations pending the realization of funds from privatization; these funds would then be used to amortize loans.

---

[12] However, in certain circumstances, the Banking Supervisory Office in the FRG has discretion to grant exemptions from the banking law to east German banks.

[13] The State Treaty required that an inventory of all publicly owned assets be taken. A substantial amount of real estate, both land and housing, would remain outside the Trust Fund. The land being used by enterprises in the Trust Fund would be considered part of the assets of these enterprises and, consequently, fall under the aegis of the Trust Fund. The question of land ownership was a difficult one because of the various waves of government expropriations after World War II. In some cases, land could be returned to its original owners. In others, the land was now committed to an alternative use and only financial compensation would be possible. Still other cases would be tied up by competing claims. It was likely that these matters would take quite some time to be resolved in the courts.

[14] The borrowing limit was raised in the Unity Treaty to DM 25 billion for 1990–91. Borrowing of DM 12 billion was envisaged in 1990. It was not clear whether the ceiling would have to be increased again to accommodate the borrowing need in 1991.

The pre-GEMSU discussion of the Trust Fund left many unanswered questions. The first related to the value of its assets. In the past these assets had generated a substantial part of national income and most of the GDR Government's revenue. The great imponderable of the entire reform process was the value of these real assets and their income-generating capacity in a free and open market. This would be a major determinant of income, employment, and the duration and hardship of the transitional phase of economic integration. Most analysts were relatively pessimistic on this score; it was thought that perhaps 30 percent of GDR industry was viable in a market economy, another 40 percent could be restructured with reasonable chances of success, and 30 percent was probably beyond redemption. The most pervasive problem was an obsolescent structure of production and capital—the products were not of sufficient quality (at given production costs) to compete with those in the west, and the machinery and equipment were not up to the task of upgrading product standards. In some sectors—most importantly chemicals and energy—environmental concerns were also a major cause for pessimism; given the new environmental code, many plants would simply have to be shut down and a costly cleanup would be required.[15]

The second major question related to the precise mandate of the Trust Fund: was it intended that the Trust Fund behave like a private investment fund with the narrow objective of maximizing the market value of its assets on behalf of its shareholders (in effect the people of the GDR), or like an agency charged also with some social function (for example, limiting unemployment) so as to ease the transition to a market system? There were instructive examples from other countries of public sector industrial holding companies that had been used as an instrument of employment policy at substantial cost to the economy at large. In most cases it had been difficult to put the operations of such institutions under independent management and to separate pure market considerations from those of politics and social policy. In the particular case of the GDR, where a wholesale restructuring of the economy was envisaged, there was a danger that a departure from pure value-maximizing criteria might entail uneconomic cross-subsidization—that is, employing the profits of viable enterprises to keep hopeless ones afloat. It was not difficult to imagine how mismanagement might squander the net worth of the Trust Fund. Moreover, the issue of whom the managers were responsible to was clouded by the lack of clarity about the ownership of the Trust Fund. In any

event, wasteful management of the Trust Fund would leave the people of the GDR, and ultimately all Germans, worse off.

The third important set of questions related to the feasibility of the Trust Fund's task. The sheer magnitude of the operation—in effect the privatizing and restructuring of the entire industrial sector of the economy—was daunting. Where would managers be found to undertake such a task, at what pace would markets be able to absorb share sales, and, without an independent, high-quality management team, might not the Trust Fund begin to take on the appearance of an industrial planning ministry with considerable monopoly power in some segments of industry?

It was widely accepted that the initial phase of GEMSU would see a period of "creative destruction": many companies would be restructured, others would be liquidated, and unemployment would rise sharply. This was seen as a necessary step in the weeding out of obsolete economic structures so as to provide a solid foundation for future growth. Although the new social security system would be able to cushion some of the impact, this would be a painful period.

Within official circles there were different perceptions about how, in practice, the operations of the Trust Fund might be conducted. On the one hand, there was the conventional pyramid structure—top management would initiate most of the decisions on the basis of information culled from lower levels and from the market. In this view, the task for management was, indeed, enormous, and the feasibility of rapid restructuring and privatization had to be questioned. On the other hand, there was a more grassroots view—that is, managers of companies within the Trust Fund would themselves seek out partners for joint ventures or buy-outs; these deals would then be proposed to top management who would seek simply to ensure that shares or assets were sold at reasonable prices. In this latter view, which envisaged much greater reliance on grassroots entrepreneurship as individual companies sought to safeguard their existence, the tasks of the privatization program were spread more widely and appeared more feasible.[16]

In other areas of the real economy the changes expected were also radical. The services sector was underdeveloped; many parts of it would have to be built from the ground up. Public infrastructure was sorely inadequate and massive investment would be required in activities such as telecommunications. The agricultural sector in

---

[15] Article XVI (2) of the State Treaty stipulates that new plant and equipment in east Germany has to conform to the safety and environmental standards prevailing in the west. Existing plant and equipment will have to be adjusted over a period of time to fulfill the same requirements.

[16] The law establishing the Trust Fund (*Treuhandgesetz*) envisages the privatization program being conducted through a family of smaller funds. Each fund is responsible for privatizing, restructuring, or liquidating the companies in its portfolio; its decisions are to be based on economic considerations and are to be taken in consultation with banks and private financial consultants. It remains unclear whether in practice the Government will be able to influence decisions through the managers of the funds.

east Germany would have to adapt to the Common Agricultural Policy of the EC to ensure common producer prices; transitional adjustment mechanisms would be adopted. In signing the State Treaty, the Government of the GDR undertook to make available sufficient land to provide adequate facilities for foreign investors in industry, trade, and services.[17]

In the first three months of GEMSU all of the doubts raised in the pre-GEMSU discussion of the Trust Fund proved to be well-founded:

- First, estimates of the proportion of GDR enterprises that would be viable in a market economy were revised downward.

- Second, while registered unemployment had risen to 445,000 (5 percent of the labor force) by September, the number of short-time workers (in most cases disguised unemployment) had reached nearly 1¾ million. Together, unemployed and short-time workers constituted almost one fourth of the labor force.

- Third, output declined sharply: in August industrial production was only one half of its level 12 months earlier. At the same time, extravagant wage demands were acceded to—a 60 percent increase in construction and a 25 percent increase in metal, electro-technical and chemicals industries—perhaps in the expectation of a government bailout.

- Fourth, liquidation of uneconomic firms and privatization and restructuring of others did not take off. The Trust Fund—notably, for example, in the mining and chemicals industries—has been loath to take responsibility for a course of action that would entail a massive reduction in the workforce of any single large enterprise.

- Fifth, besides the difficulty of pricing east German companies, investment and takeovers from the west were slowed down by the need, in each case, to allocate responsibility between the Trust Fund and the would-be investor in four critical areas: (1) property rights—who would be responsible for settling claims by previous owners; (2) clearing up the environment— who would bear the cost; (3) shedding surplus labor— new owners would be bound by costly restraints on large-scale dismissals in the German labor law; and (4) old company debt—who would pay this. Also, investors were concerned about the adequacy of supporting infrastructure for production and distribution.

- Finally, the Trust Fund became enmeshed in the short-

term financial problems of its enterprises; the debate about guarantees for short-term bank loans diverted attention from longer-term objectives.

The task facing the Trust Fund involves liquidating or restructuring and privatizing some 8,000 enterprises with 4 million employees, a substantial debt burden, tight liquidity constraints, and, in some areas, dire environmental problems. All in all, such an undertaking looks even more daunting now than it did before GEMSU.

The Government and the Social Security System

The State Treaty required that the structure of public sector budgets in the GDR be adapted to conform with that in the FRG. Starting in the second half of 1990, the government budget would exclude the social security system (which would be budgeted for separately as in the FRG), business enterprises (which would become independent legal entities under the Trust Fund), and the railways and postal service (which would be constituted as separate entities with their own budgets). The social security system of the GDR would be adopted by and large from that of the FRG. Within the framework of general budgetary aid from the FRG to the GDR, it was envisaged that some start-up financial assistance would be given to the new unemployment and pension insurance schemes of the GDR.

In order to limit deficits and foster market mechanisms, the territorial authorities in the GDR would cut subsidies on goods (including food and agriculture generally), gradually reduce subsidies on housing, transportation, and energy, and undertake a substantial reduction in expenditure on personnel. All elements of expenditure would be scrutinized to determine their legal basis and the real need for them. The income tax laws of the FRG would be adopted,[18] property and indirect taxes would be the same as in the FRG, and the GDR would adopt the customs laws, border taxes, and duties of the EC.

The institutional arrangements envisaged in the State Treaty did not anticipate full political unification by October; as a result, fiscal policy prescriptions for the GDR as a separate state were spelled out for 1990 and 1991. Quantitative limits were set on borrowing by the GDR Government on its own account and on borrowing by the Trust Fund. The size of transfers from the FRG to the GDR, for general budgetary support and social security assistance, was specified. Moreover, all decisions on public debt, borrowing, and equalization claims in the GDR were made subject to agreement between the GDR and the FRG.

---

[17] In some cases land sale prices may be made subject to renegotiation after a sufficient period has elapsed to allow an effective real estate market to have developed.

[18] Annexes II–IV to the State Treaty, which list changes to the law of the GDR required to effect GEMSU, give some sense of the extent to which GEMSU entailed a wholesale adoption by the GDR of the FRG's legal framework for the economy.

The Stance of Policies

Fiscal Policy

In midyear, the territorial authorities in the FRG envisaged expenditure equivalent to 30½ percent of GNP in 1990 and a deficit of DM 53 billion (2.2 percent of GNP). This represented a doubling of the 1989 deficit; it reflected an acceleration in expenditures (to 6 percent, double the medium-term target rate) and a sizable tax cut (1 percent of GNP net of subsidy reductions), offset by the positive influence of faster-than-expected growth. In 1991 the deficit was projected to be virtually unchanged.

In the GDR borrowing by the territorial authorities was not to exceed DM 10 billion in 1990 (effectively the second half of the year) and DM 14 billion in 1991. Besides these figures, the total amount of government financing included the borrowing of the *Fonds Deutsche Einheit* (German Unity Fund)[19]—DM 20 billion in 1990 and DM 31 billion in 1991—and potential borrowing by the Trust Fund—DM 7 billion in 1990 and DM 10 billion in 1991.

On July 22, the parliament in the GDR passed a budget for the second half of 1990 which was consistent with the financing constraints laid out in the State Treaty on GEMSU. By September, however, it had become clear that budget financing requirements would be a great deal larger than initially envisaged.

First, the social insurance funds would require substantial additional financing. Payment of unemployment benefits would be far above budget, both because of higher unemployment—the budget had assumed an unemployment level of 270,000 with an additional 160,000 short-time workers[20]—and because of higher benefit levels owing to wage increases. The costs of medical services had risen more quickly than anticipated—doctors' fees had increased and more expensive drugs from the FRG had replaced local products—so that the medical insurance system would require additional financing. Also, there were likely to be some delays and shortfalls in social security receipts because of administrative difficulties, problems faced by illiquid enterprises in remitting payroll taxes, and lower employment.

Second, difficulties had also arisen in the budget of the Central Government itself. Receipts had been adversely influenced by some of the same factors affecting the social insurance funds. On the expenditure side it appeared that the principal overruns would be in transfers and subsidies. Energy and transportation subsidies would be larger owing to greater consumption than anticipated in the budget and higher oil prices. Subsidies to support exports to the CMEA countries might also be significantly larger than budgeted[21] and the difficulties in the agricultural sector might result in increased budgetary support. Also, an across-the-board expenditure cut (of DM 3½ billion) contained in the budget estimates seemed unlikely to be fully realized.

Although the fiscal situation in the GDR was turning out much weaker than budgeted, it was decided not to produce a revised budget as, with political unification, the central government functions in the GDR would be absorbed into their FRG counterparts. Instead, at the end of September, the FRG introduced a third supplementary federal budget that provided DM 26 billion in additional borrowing, of which DM 24 billion was related to the GDR. Similarly, although the State Treaty provided a framework for fiscal policy in the GDR in 1991 (in the form of a borrowing limit for the GDR Government and specified transfers from the FRG to the GDR), there would not now be any separate budget for east Germany in 1991. The magnitude of the fiscal imbalance in the country as a whole and the extent of the revisions in the budgetary outlook are summarized in Table 1.

There are a number of caveats with respect to these estimates.

First, the figures in the table are current services estimates—that is, they make no allowance for any discretionary changes in expenditure or taxation. It is not unlikely, however, that the authorities will introduce significant expenditure cuts, thereby reducing the overall deficit.

Second, the figures exclude the capital infusion to the banking system by the GDR Government—perhaps some DM 26 billion in 1990—which, while not in the budget as conventionally measured, will add to the (still relatively modest) outstanding stock of government debt.

Third, the operations of the Trust Fund will influence the financial position of the public sector. Successful privatization will produce capital receipts and viable enterprises that are not privatized will produce income. On the other hand, there are bound to be additional Trust Fund

---

[19] The German Unity Fund was set up to help finance unification. It will provide DM 115 billion over five years. Each year a certain (relatively small) amount will be financed directly out of the federal budget of the FRG and the rest will be borrowed in the market. The interest and amortization payments on these loans will be borne half by the Federal Government of the FRG and half by the state and municipal governments. At the time of GEMSU it was envisaged that in 1990, DM 22 billion would be transferred to the GDR by the Unity Fund; of this, DM 2 billion would be from the federal budget. In 1991, DM 35 billion would be transferred, including DM 4 billion from the Federal Government.

[20] The direct cost of each additional 100,000 unemployed workers in the second half of 1990 would amount to DM 500 million. The cost of additional short-time workers would depend upon the proportion of time that they were out of work; payment would then be determined by the normal unemployment insurance rules (i.e., 63–68 percent of net wages). In addition, some employers would pay supplements under wage contracts for the nonworking period.

[21] The currency conversion from GDR marks to deutsche mark involved a substantial real appreciation vis-à-vis the transferable ruble because of the deutsche mark nominal rate being set higher against the transferable ruble while wages were initially converted at the rate of M 1 = DM 1. Budgetary subsidies were, therefore, necessary in order to maintain supplies to CMEA countries.

Table 1. Germany: Borrowing Requirement of the Public Sector[1]

(In billions of deutsche mark)

	1990[2]		1991	
	Original (June)	Revised (Sept.)	Original (June)	Revised (Sept.)
Borrowing by the FRG Government	53	} 94	53½	} 145
Borrowing by the GDR Government	10		14	
Borrowing by the Unity Fund	20	20	31	31
Borrowing by the Trust Fund[3]	7	12	10	13
Total	90	126	108½	189
Total in percent of all-German GNP	3½	4¾	3¾	6½

Source: IMF staff current services estimates—that is with unchanged tax rates and expenditure programs.

[1] Including the Unity Fund and the Trust Fund, but excluding the social security system.

[2] For the GDR the figures refer only to the second half of the year.

[3] The revised figures for the Trust Fund reflect the limit set in the Unity Treaty.

liabilities to the banks related to guarantees of short-term bank borrowing by enterprises. To the extent that enterprises with such loan guarantees are liquidated, the Trust Fund will have to assume the liabilities. In principle, it would seem that the vast physical assets of the Trust Fund should be capable of earning substantial income—historically enterprise profits were the principal source of government revenue—but recent developments do not augur well for the earnings of the Trust Fund and call into question the net worth of the Fund.

Fourth, it is not inconceivable that part of the large stock of old debt of GDR enterprises and some of the old housing debt might be assumed by the Government. This, of course, would increase the stock of government debt and future debt service would raise budget expenditures.

However one analyzes these projections, it is clear that the first 18 months of economic integration will witness a sizable increase in government borrowing in the deutsche mark area. The question arises therefore as to how this should best be financed. The Government has indicated an aversion to increasing taxes to finance unification. While one might be loath to endorse a pledge of no new taxes, decisions on the appropriate method of financing would depend upon the duration and composition of the additional demands for public resources. An argument against tax increases would be strengthened to the extent that:

- The large deficits are likely to be temporary—that is, they are projected to decline quickly after peaking in 1991.

- The deficits are linked to public investment—that is, expenditures aimed at increasing the potential output of the economy—rather than to current expenditures aimed simply at easing the transition.

- There is room for a substantial restructuring of expenditures in west Germany. For example, the Government estimates the cost of its support for the inner-German border areas and West Berlin at about DM 40 billion in 1990.[22]

- Strict limitations on the scope for new taxation, combined with a rigorous antipathy for deficits, will help to contain subsidies. Ideally, subsidies in east Germany should be limited to self-correcting transitory support (e.g., unemployment benefits); subsidization of employment or investment will quickly be reflected in factor prices, embedded in investment decisions, and thus entrenched.

- It is possible to extrapolate from the historical (econometric) evidence for the FRG, which shows that some 60 percent of any increase in public saving from higher taxes would be offset in the short run by a drop in private saving.

- The external current account remains in surplus so that German saving continues to help finance investment abroad.

Clearly the case against taxation involves a great many conditions. There is a danger that the sequence of developments will influence the composition of public expenditure. Large public works programs that are necessary in their own right would also help to absorb unemployed labor; but initiating such programs will require many decisions at the state and local government levels and it may take some time before this decision-making apparatus is put in place. Without such programs concerns about prolonged unemployment might elicit costly and wasteful subsidies that subsequently prove difficult to remove. Moreover, a dearth of supporting public infrastructure will discourage private investment. The case against new taxation is critically contingent on the composition of government expenditure, as well as on the magnitude of financing required.

It is not difficult to envisage changes in the structure of taxation that would yield short-run revenue gains and would nevertheless be consistent with the medium-term thrust of German tax policy toward a more efficient system. There is scope for raising indirect taxes in a way that would be compatible with the process of harmonization within the EC. The benefits of such action would have to be weighed against the unfavorable temporary impact on prices.

Monetary Policy

In 1989 the restrictive stance of monetary policy was supported by a sizable reduction in the government

[22] The rationale for these subsidies should disappear with the lifting of the inner German border. Subsidy reductions in other areas would also help to contain deficits while exerting beneficial supply-side effects. Savings could also result from reductions in defense outlays.

deficit; nevertheless, real growth proved robust and interest rates rose. In 1990, even without the effects of GEMSU, fiscal policy would have eased, wage costs would have increased more rapidly, and capacity utilization rates would have risen—thus the task of containing inflation would have become more difficult. Given the added effects of GEMSU, the environment for monetary policy will be even more demanding.

In the FRG, the 18 months before GEMSU had seen pre-emptive monetary policy actions that had helped sustain the favorable economic performance. Growth of the monetary aggregates had been brought back into line with that of potential real output and an inflation rate of about 2 percent. There was some concern about the pace of growth of residents' holdings of short-term bank bonds and Euromarket deposits—although these assets are less liquid than those included in M3—which would probably have argued for holding the growth of M3 (for FRG residents) to the lower end of the target range of 4–6 percent. In the second half of 1990, the Bundesbank intended to continue to maintain separate data for the FRG and the GDR as constituted before unification, and to target M3 in the (old) FRG.[23]

The currency conversion part of GEMSU was accomplished without disruption. The consolidated balance sheet of the banking system in the GDR for the end of June was not available for some time after the currency unification, and it was therefore not possible to quantify the effects of the currency conversion on the balance sheets of the banks or on the money supply with great precision. Equalization claims to compensate GDR banks for the asymmetric nature of the currency conversion would only be issued after the final resolution of opening balances.[24] In the interim, the Bundesbank conducted its money market operations in the GDR primarily against single signature paper issued by the banks (i.e., bank IOUs). Given the favorable interest rate charged on discount operations, the initial discount quota (DM 25 billion) granted to the banks in the GDR was quickly utilized. Some banks also had recourse to the Lombard facility. Additional liquidity to the GDR financial markets came from fiscal transfers to the GDR and from FRG banks. Deutsche mark currency outstanding (including currency held by banks) at the end of July 1990 was 10½ percent higher than 12 months earlier.

The Bundesbank recognized that monetary union would exacerbate the difficulties facing monetary policy at both a technical level and a more fundamental level. At a technical level, monetary control would be made more difficult. With a free flow of people and capital between east and west Germany and the same banks operating in both, it would

become increasingly difficult to segregate the monetary statistics. In the transition, with monetary targeting only in the west, the money supply in the east would be determined by demand. Financial flows would, therefore, accommodate sharp increases in certain prices and wages. These might be seen largely as an unwinding of relative price distortions. The eventual shift from targeting money in west Germany to targeting money in the whole deutsche mark area would involve venturing into unknown territory, since there was no history on which to base estimates of money demand in east Germany. The relative size of east Germany, however, was such that even fairly large errors in calculating money demand would not be that significant in the whole deutsche mark area.

The appropriate amount of liquidity to provide to east Germany was difficult to determine: that there was enormous potential for rapid growth from a very low base was obvious, but far from obvious were the bottlenecks that might emerge and the rate of growth that could be sustained without inciting sharp upward pressures on prices of nontraded goods. It would also be difficult to infer monetary conditions from interest rates: to the extent that returns on fixed capital investment in east Germany had risen, higher real interest rates might not dampen activity. But interest arbitrage would equalize rates over the whole deutsche mark area and (albeit less perfectly) in the ERM, and there was no clear consensus on an appropriate rise for the whole area. In these circumstances, the Bundesbank acknowledged that it would have to infer monetary conditions from a wide variety of indicators—not just the path of the monetary aggregates and interest rates, but also developments in exchange rates, wages, prices, demand, and output—and would err, if at all, on the side of restrictiveness. The credibility of the Bundesbank's aversion to inflation was seen as an important asset that ought not to be put at risk and, from this standpoint, a strong deutsche mark was seen as a key ingredient of monetary policy in the period following GEMSU.

In the area of bank supervision and oversight there were also incipient problems. Much of the stock of state enterprise debt held by banks was of doubtful quality; however, it was not unlikely that these debts would be assumed or guaranteed by the Trust Fund or the Government. In the period following GEMSU banks faced considerable difficulty in finding criteria on which to base lending decisions to Trust Fund enterprises; it was near impossible to gauge the creditworthiness of the enterprises. Short-term bank loans to enterprises were guaranteed by the Trust Fund; this relieved the banks of the need to scrutinize the financial positions and prospects of enterprises. As (at least) some enterprises proved nonviable, the guarantees would be activated and the banks' positions would have to be covered by the Trust Fund or, ultimately, the Government. This mechanism produced a soft budget constraint for enterprises that allowed a prolongation of illusions about the feasibility

---

[23] The monetary aggregates are defined in terms of residency rather than currency.

[24] Interest on these claims would be paid retroactively to July 1.

of uneconomic decisions on wages, prices, and products. It divorced certain decisions on credit from the relevant underlying economic calculations.

At the broad level of macroeconomic policy, GEMSU sparked concerns about the effect of the policy mix on the environment for monetary policy. If private investment in the GDR proceeded at the pace needed to successfully integrate the two economies and the budget turned out to be as expansionary as feared, the burden of containing inflation would fall disproportionately on monetary policy. It was difficult to tell whether this would mean higher interest rates—longer-term rates had jumped upon the announcement of currency union perhaps in anticipation of these resource demands—but even if high interest rates were warranted they would undoubtedly be unpopular. It was broadly accepted, however, that, without underutilized resources, successful integration of the GDR would have to entail some crowding out—if not by an interest rate mechanism, then via prices, taxes, or the exchange rate. The policy mix chosen would in any event have implications for exchange rate developments.

The Exchange Rate

Most scenarios envisage GEMSU eliciting more rapid growth and a more expansionary fiscal policy with continued monetary stringency. Such conditions would be consistent with higher real interest rates and some real appreciation of the deutsche mark. The appreciation would help to spread the additional demand from GEMSU to other countries and to reduce Germany's current account surplus. At the start of GEMSU, it was difficult to tell whether these changes had been fully anticipated by market participants and were, therefore, already reflected in market rates. Some argued that they had not been fully anticipated so that a further appreciation was likely, while others thought that the market might have overshot its equilibrium so that some depreciation of the deutsche mark was possible.

The FRG authorities were skeptical of this latter position. They did not believe that an effective depreciation of the deutsche mark was warranted and were firmly of the view that a strong deutsche mark would be necessary to reduce the current account surplus, channel resources to the GDR, and contain the inflationary effect of GEMSU while spreading the beneficial real effects to the rest of the world. In particular, they did not envisage a depreciation of the deutsche mark against the U.S. dollar; this, they thought, would be contrary to the objective of narrowing current account imbalances. Events since the beginning of July 1990 have vindicated this view. Between June 30 and the end of September, the deutsche mark appreciated by 7 percent against the U.S. dollar and by almost 1 percent in effective terms.

Within the ERM, the deutsche mark was initially close to the lower intervention limit[25] so that, in principle, some appreciation would have been possible without any change in central parities. Among certain participants there would be strong resistance to any change in central parities—in particular, France and the Benelux countries saw fixed central parities with the deutsche mark as essential to their macroeconomic policy stance.

A Guided Tour and Some Tentative Conclusions

A Guided Tour

Much of the foregoing material has been culled from the chapters that follow. Chapter II analyzes the economy of the FRG immediately before GEMSU. It discusses the combination of advantageous external developments and prudent policies that put the economy in an almost ideal starting position for GEMSU, but also highlights the limits to production capacity in the west that might constitute an important constraint on the process of integrating the eastern Länder. Chapter III describes the economy of the GDR before the rapid changes that began in late 1989; it also assesses the present economic situation and outlines the process of reform.

The picture of vast disparities between the western and the eastern parts of Germany that emerges from these two chapters shows economic integration to be a truly enormous undertaking. Moreover, decisions on institutions and structures that are taken in the first phase are extremely important: seemingly small details in institutional arrangements may have sizable and enduring effects.

Against this background the subsequent chapters analyze some key issues raised by the process of economic integration. Chapters IV–VI attempt to quantify some of the macroeconomic effects over the medium term. The starting point is the question: What are the investment needs of the former GDR over the next ten years? The framework developed to answer this question entails a detailed specification of the supply side of the east German economy that relates productivity growth to capital accumulation and the efficiency of the use of labor and capital. The specific quantitative path depends upon an array of assumptions, but, by undertaking a variety of numerical experiments, it is possible to get some sense of the scale of the challenge.

The investment in the east may be financed by domestic saving or by grants or loans from the west. An analysis

---

[25] To some extent this was an anomalous situation—because of a policy mix in some countries that overburdened monetary policy, the other participants were clustered together in the lower part of the band with little room to move within the band.

of the financial implications of economic integration requires a more comprehensive macroeconomic model. Such a model is developed in Chapter V and is used to examine alternative scenarios for the east German economy. In Chapter VI, to help assess how economic developments in east Germany might influence west Germany and other countries, the different scenarios for the east are used as inputs into the IMF's global MULTIMOD model. In this experiment, some alternative assumptions about policies are used to generate different scenarios.

Given that west Germany is likely to bear the brunt of the increased demand from east Germany, the question arises as to how readily resources can be made available to meet this demand. There are two aspects to this question: first, how much additional output will be generated in west Germany, and, second, how much of this increase in output will be available to support demand in east Germany? These issues are taken up in Chapters VII–IX.

Chapter VII explores the relationship between potential output, the natural rate of unemployment, and the actual level of unemployment in west Germany. Its purpose is to explain the persistence of a rate of unemployment considerably above those of the 1960s and 1970s, and to estimate the margin of spare capacity left in the economy. The calculations in the chapter suggest that output was at about the same level as "quasi potential" (a measure based on actual underlying unemployment and reflecting the existing characteristics of wage bargaining) in 1988 but that full potential output (a measure based on the estimated natural rate of unemployment) was some 2½ percentage points higher. To realize the unused potential in a sustainable fashion would require changes in the system of wage bargaining, structural policy measures to reduce the power of "insiders" in the wage bargaining process, or a favorable supply or demand shock. The implications of this analysis are sanguine: they suggest that, with appropriate structural measures, there might be more spare capacity in the economy than is conventionally estimated.

Since 1988, actual output is estimated to have risen above "quasi potential." The question arises therefore as to why more marked price inflation has not emerged. Notably, the econometric results in Chapter VII do not suggest that the capacity pressures seen thus far would have produced a substantial inflationary response. Moreover, long-term wage contracts negotiated in 1987–88 are still influencing wage developments; a number of important wage agreements reached in 1990 do indicate an uptick, though not an unmanageable one, in wage inflation. However, it is also possible that the growth of both quasi potential and full-potential output over the past few years has been greater than estimated. Increased flexibility in working arrangements may have added to the effective supply of capital in

a way not captured by conventional measures of the capital stock. Moreover, large-scale immigration may have reduced the influence of insiders in the labor market in a way that could also have not been captured by historical relationships estimated over a period when immigration was considerably smaller.

The question of immigration and the importance of the behavior of insiders is also taken up in Chapter VIII, which examines the history of immigration into the FRG, its economic effects, and its policy implications. The model experiments reported in this chapter suggest that continued rapid economic absorption of immigrants will depend very much on the nature of wage bargaining. Even if east German labor stays in the east and capital flows east to take advantage of lower costs, there are likely to be consequences for labor incomes in the west (either reduced employment or lower wages relative to some baseline)—this is the counterpart of the increased rate of return that will be required by investors. To ensure that the supply-side implications are as favorable as possible—that is, higher output rather than increased unemployment—it is important that structural policies be used to enhance the flexibility of the labor market.

Chapter IX uses a model of saving and investment in the former FRG to examine the question of how much of the additional output generated by GEMSU in the west will be available to finance development in the east. It concludes that additional income in the west will give rise to increased saving that will be available to finance capital accumulation in the east; nevertheless, rapid capital accumulation in the east will require resources that far exceed those available from additional saving in west Germany. This raises a question as to whether fiscal policy should be used to offset some of the additional excess demand. The saving equation analyzed in this chapter suggests that the influence of increased government saving on national saving might be significantly dampened on impact. The estimates imply that, in the first year, 60 percent of increased government saving is offset by reduced private saving. Over time, the offset coefficient wanes, but it is still about a quarter in the third year. These results need to be borne in mind in considering the appropriate fiscal response to demand pressures from GEMSU.

Chapters IV to IX highlight considerations that should influence the priorities in policymaking over the coming years. The subsequent chapters (X–XII) examine the roles of monetary, fiscal, and structural policies.

Chapter X takes up issues related to monetary and financial management during the transitional phase of GEMSU. Common misconceptions about the currency conversion are corrected: first, it did not, in itself, create a significant risk of inflation; second, the Bundesbank did not simply swap deutsche mark for marks, rather banks in the east had to borrow from the Bundesbank in order to supply their clients with deutsche mark, thereby increasing the seignorage revenues of the Bundesbank. The principal goal of the conversion can be interpreted as the reorganization of financial assets and liabilities in the GDR in such a way as to promote the establishment of a sound and efficient financial system subject to the constraint of an appropriate initial level of liquidity in the economy. It is against this objective that the results must be judged. At the macroeconomic level, to what extent might GEMSU threaten the integrity (that is, the real value) of the deutsche mark? At a microeconomic level, to what extent might the arrangements following GEMSU threaten the solidity of the major financial institutions?

Chapter XI describes the fiscal system that existed in the GDR prior to GEMSU and outlines how the planned reforms of the system are likely to affect government finances. Government finances will be sensitive to the evolution of the east German economy. Moreover, given a unified fiscal system and the urgent need to bring infrastructural facilities up to the level of the west, there is not much room for flexibility in fiscal policy in east Germany. Therefore, if economic growth is much less rapid than generally envisaged, the fiscal imbalances generated in the east German economy could remain large for quite some time.

Finally, Chapter XII analyzes the history of fiscal and structural policy in the FRG, and draws on this experience to evaluate alternative policy responses to GEMSU. At a microeconomic level, the guidance from the experience of the 1970s and 1980s is clear: expenditure and tax policies aimed at influencing the short-run allocation of resources and distribution of income run the risk of becoming entrenched and exerting a detrimental longer-run influence on the economy. On the other hand, the experience of the 1950s and the 1960s suggests that adjustment can occur efficiently when the Government limits its interference in the economy. The desiderata implicit in this analysis may be useful to policymakers overseeing the integration of the economies of east and west Germany.

Some Tentative Conclusions

In the discussion and debate on economic unification, the Germans have set themselves idealistically high standards. *Ordnungspolitik*—a clear institutional framework within which the free play of market forces guides the economy—is easier to describe in principle than to abide by in practice. But it is useful not to lose sight of guiding principles, to require that deviations from them be justified in each and every case as temporary aberrations, and to limit the scope and duration of such deviations.

Many untidy departures from *Ordnungspolitik* were left in the wake of the rapid process of unification. The separation of the banking system and the enterprise system from the State in east Germany was not a clean break; as a result, the delegation of responsibility in a number of areas remains ambiguous.

The banks will have on their books many old loans of dubious quality; the net worth of the banking system depends critically upon the extent to which the servicing and repayment of these loans is guaranteed by the Government.

New bank loans to enterprises have been guaranteed by the Trust Fund and, ultimately, the Government. This has relieved the banks of the responsibility of scrutinizing and assessing the viability of would-be borrowers. Moreover, to the extent that some of these loans have been made to moribund industries, the servicing and amortization obligations will eventually have to be borne by the Trust Fund or the Government.

The budgetary costs of unification will be substantially larger than initially envisaged. Moreover, if one adds to the budget (as conventionally defined) the increases in government debt related to equalization paper (issued to preserve the net worth of the banking system), a portion of the old enterprise debt on the books of the banks, some of the new debt guaranteed by the Trust Fund, and an allowance for correcting the environmental problems in parts of east Germany, the budgetary costs of unification become higher still.

To the extent that large budget deficits are a temporary phenomenon linked to the acquisition of public capital that increases productive potential, they should be acceptable. Moreover, the distinction between capital and current expenditures is not entirely clear—current expenditures to put in place certain administrative systems, for example, are in effect infrastructural investment. Nevertheless, there are grounds for concern in the present circumstances that sizable deficits could persist and that they may be related in significant part to transfers to support consumption rather than to public investment. Should these concerns prove warranted, the question of tax policy will have to be addressed. It would seem unwise to rule out categorically the possibility of tax increases; indeed, it is possible to envisage changes in the tax structure that might improve the efficiency of the tax system, help in the process of tax harmonization in the EC, and, while yielding additional revenues in the short run, allow for the possibility of future direct tax relief.

The Trust Fund has been assigned a task of enormous scope and complexity: the privatization, restructuring, and, in some cases, liquidation of 8,000 enterprises with 4 million employees. Even taking care of the short-run financial problems of these enterprises has proved daunting; the more fundamental task will be near impossible to achieve with any rapidity. It is, moreover, not clear that the Trust Fund as presently constituted is capable of taking difficult decisions on mass dismissals and liquidations. Very large post-GEMSU wage increases in a number of financially troubled industries might be taken to suggest that workers believe that their enterprises will be bailed out.

The pricing of Trust Fund enterprises for sale will entail difficult negotiations in each case that will need also to establish financial responsibility for settling claims on enterprise property, for cleaning up the environment, and for servicing and amortizing old enterprise debt. Beyond these issues, it will not be easy to privatize firms that are grossly overmanned as large-scale dismissals are very costly under German labor law. Thus, some restructuring will be required in almost all of the Trust Fund enterprises. To the extent that restructuring and liquidation is postponed, and that short-term financial mechanisms are used to maintain the status quo, the net worth of the Trust Fund will be eroded.

The mere fact that these issues are part of the public debate, of the ongoing assessment of mechanisms and modalities for economic integration, is a basis for optimism. It is important to appreciate, too, the strengths of the parties to this huge undertaking.

First, the starting point in the FRG was almost ideal: low inflation and a credible anti-inflationary policy, a balanced fiscal position, a high domestic saving ratio, a corporate sector in an unusually strong financial position, and an enormous wealth of resources (including foreign assets).

Second, the authorities have a formidable track record on fiscal discipline and generally prudent economic policies. There is also widespread political commitment to a restructuring of government expenditures so as to limit the budgetary effects of unification. One should not forget the almost legendary distaste of the general public in Germany for budget deficits or any other economic policies that threaten the integrity of financial savings.

Third, the deutsche mark is perhaps the quintessential hard currency. Given that it was precisely this access to a credible hard currency that was sought by the GDR in the currency union, it is unlikely that the Bundesbank's anti-inflationary commitment would be eroded by the process of integration.

Fourth, perhaps the greatest asset of the former GDR is its human capital. All evidence suggests that the level of general and technical education of the east German labor force is high.

Fifth, while large-scale investments and the transformation of the old state *Kombinate* into market-responsive companies might appear slow, grassroots entrepreneurship in the east is booming. Some 96,000 new businesses were registered in the first three months of GEMSU.

From an international economic perspective, it appears that the process of unification in Germany will not constitute a major shock to the system. To be sure, some German saving that would in the past have financed investment abroad will now be used for investment at home; this will mean somewhat higher interest rates. On the other hand, for many years the international community has voiced concern over the size of the FRG's current account surplus and advocated measures to reduce it. The positive demand effects from a properly managed restructuring of east Germany should elicit imports from all of Germany's trading partners and, for some countries, may help to moderate a slowdown in growth that had just begun at the start of GEMSU.

In the final analysis, the success of economic integration will depend on private initiatives: the readiness of private investors in west Germany and abroad to commit resources to east Germany and the development of home-grown entrepreneurship in the east. The great imponderables in the situation have to do with enterprises, wages, and migration: To what extent can existing enterprises be restructured so as to be viable in a market economy? Will wage demands that move ahead of productivity developments discourage investment from abroad? And will sustained wage differentials with the west elicit a resurgence of westward migration, especially of highly qualified personnel? These questions cannot be answered at this time. But it is clearly essential to the success of economic integration that capital flow east rather than labor flowing west, and that income growth and new opportunities are sufficient to meet reasonable aspirations on the part of the residents of east Germany. In seeking to realize these objectives, the Government should avoid ad hoc policy interventions in response to short-term problems; it should hold instead to policies based firmly on market principles and be willing to accept some transitional roughness in the passage to longer-term goals.

II

Economic Developments in the Federal Republic of Germany

Thomas Mayer, Donogh McDonald, Garry J. Schinasi, and Günther Thumann

The Real Economy

Overview

In 1989, for the second year in a row, the pace of economic growth in the Federal Republic of Germany (FRG) exceeded most projections.[1] Real GDP rose by 3¼ percent, and, with an unusually fast rise in investment income from abroad, real GNP grew by 4 percent, the highest rate seen in a decade (Table 1, and Chart 1 in Chapter I). The principal source of stimulus was strong foreign demand, particularly from European trading partners. Despite an acceleration of investment, domestic demand expanded less quickly than in 1988, as consumption growth slowed noticeably. Indeed, the increase in investment in 1989, although markedly stronger than in any other year since 1979, was exceeded by the rise in national saving; as a result, the excess of national saving over investment, the mirror image of the external current account surplus, widened by ½ of 1 percentage point of GNP to 4½ percent. Despite continued rapid growth of demand, underlying inflationary pressures remained moderate, with economy-wide unit labor costs rising by less than 1 percent; the rate of increase of consumer prices did double in 1989 to 2¾ percent, but this was due principally to indirect tax measures introduced at the beginning of the year and a deterioration in the terms of trade. There was a notable improvement in labor market conditions—job creation far exceeded the expansion of the labor force resulting from higher immigration—and the unemployment rate fell by ¾ of 1 percentage point.

Data for the first half of 1990 indicated continued strong growth and, for the year as a whole, GNP is expected to rise by about 4½ percent, spurred by the increased demand

Table 1.   Federal Republic of Germany: Indicators of Economic Performance

(Percent change from previous year)

	1987	1988	1989	1990
Real GDP	1.7	3.7	3.3	4½
Real GNP	1.6	3.7	3.9	4½
Real domestic demand	2.8	3.7	2.7	4¾
Unemployment (percent of labor force)	7.9	7.7	7.1	6½
Consumer price index	0.2	1.3	2.8	2¾
Current account (percent of GNP)[1]	4.1	4.2	4.6	3¼

Sources: Statistisches Bundesamt, *Volkswirtschaftliche Gesamtrechnungen*; Deutsche Bundesbank, *Monthly Report*; and authors' estimates.

[1] Before July 1, 1990 defined as the current account balance of west Germany vis-à-vis areas other than east Germany. From July 1, 1990 defined as the current account of the entire deutsche mark currency area.

emanating from German economic, monetary, and social union (GEMSU). The unemployment rate is projected to fall by a further ½ of 1 percentage point in 1990 despite rapid growth in the labor force. Although the rise in oil prices has boosted consumer prices in the second half of the year, consumer price inflation is expected to be about the same as in 1989 (2¾ percent). A significant decline in the current account surplus is likely, reflecting the diversion of part of west Germany's saving surplus from foreign use to financing the resource needs in the area formerly constituting the German Democratic Republic (GDR).

Aggregate Demand

Real Domestic Demand

In 1989, final domestic demand rose by 2¼ percent, somewhat slower than the 3 percent rate of increase over the previous three years (Table A1). This reflected weaker

---

[1] This chapter deals with developments in the area within the boundaries of the FRG prior to unification with the GDR on October 3, 1990.

growth of private consumption and a decline in public consumption; gross fixed investment, on the other hand, picked up steam.

The relative weakness of private consumption was a response to the slower expansion of real disposable income: although nominal disposable income increased at about the same pace as in 1988, growth of real disposable income was almost halved as a result of higher consumer price inflation (Tables A2 and A3).[2] The effect on consumption of the slower real income growth was moderated, however, by a fall in the household saving rate.

Real public consumption declined in 1989, reflecting reductions in health care expenditure in response to the 1989 health reform. The fall in medical expenses was in part a technical reaction to the surge in the demand for health services that had occurred in the previous year in anticipation of cuts in entitlements under the 1989 reform. The modest nominal increase in civil service wages and salaries (2½ percent) also restrained public consumption.

Business fixed investment was boosted by a number of factors. Among these, the high degree of capacity utilization in manufacturing, accelerator effects related to strong export growth, the favorable liquidity situation,[3] and positive profit expectations (related in part to the single market program of the European Community—EC) were important. Machinery and equipment investment grew particularly rapidly (9¾ percent), but business construction, which benefited from a mild winter, also expanded at a strong pace (5¾ percent).

Nonbusiness investment, which is almost entirely construction, also picked up steam in 1989. Residential building responded to housing shortages in the major urban areas, the strong real income and savings positions of households and, perhaps, also to expectations of a rise in mortgage interest rates;[4] higher rates of household formation and the large influx of ethnic Germans from the countries of Eastern Europe may also have played a role.[5] As a result, the number of dwellings completed rose by 14½ percent and the number of residential building permits by 29 percent. Public construction recorded its fastest growth rate since 1986 (3¾ percent), reflecting favorable financing conditions at the state and local government levels.

Inventory investment contributed ½ of 1 percentage point to the rate of growth of GNP in 1989. It should be noted that this category of expenditure also includes statistical discrepancies—in the FRG the output measure of GNP is statistically better founded than the expenditure measure. Thus, a comparatively high contribution to growth from stockbuilding could reflect an underestimation of one or more of the other expenditure components.[6]

Data for the first half of 1990 indicated an acceleration of domestic demand. Private consumption grew at an annualized rate of 7 percent after relatively slow growth (2 percent) in the course of 1989. Important factors were the boost to disposable income from the tax cut which took effect in January 1990, the falling out of the inflation effects of the indirect tax increase of 1989, and spending by immigrants and visitors from the GDR.[7] Investment growth was even stronger, particularly in the first quarter of 1990, when the mild winter allowed construction expenditure to expand at an extraordinarily fast rate. For 1990 as a whole, the growth of final domestic demand is projected to be twice that of 1989. Most of the increase reflects an acceleration of private consumption, after its sluggish expansion in 1989, but public consumption and fixed investment are also expected to contribute to faster demand growth.

Foreign Balance

In 1989, for the first time since 1985, the real foreign balance made a significant contribution to real GNP growth (amounting to 1¼ percentage points). Half of this resulted from an unusually large increase in the surplus on real net factor services from abroad,[8] reflecting the rise in net foreign assets, a higher rate of return on foreign assets,[9]

---

[2] The sources of the rise in nominal disposable income were somewhat different than in 1988. Income from employment and distributed profits accelerated. However, these factors were offset by a slower expansion of social transfers to private households and a quicker growth of personal income taxes. The latter reflected the resumption of fiscal drag after the tax cuts of 1988.

[3] In 1989, enterprises financed 88 percent of gross investment out of retained earnings, depreciation, and net capital transfers; in 1988, this ratio had been even higher at 97 percent. Retained earnings in 1988–89 averaged 4½ percent of national income at factor prices, compared with 3 percent in 1986–87 and ½ of 1 percent in 1984–85.

[4] Mortgage interest rates rose by more than 1½ percentage points during 1989.

[5] The influx of GDR citizens was concentrated in the last three months of the year and therefore had little effect on the average level of construction activity in 1989.

[6] In 1988, for instance, a year with a similarly high contribution to growth from stockbuilding, there were indications that the size of the foreign balance was underestimated because of problems with a new foreign trade reporting system that had been introduced in January 1988.

[7] Spending on consumer goods in the FRG by GDR residents should, conceptually, have been accounted for as FRG exports to the GDR. However, statistical coverage of such purchases was no longer feasible after the fall of the Berlin wall. As a consequence, private consumption expenditure in the FRG in 1990 has been to some extent overestimated and exports correspondingly underestimated.

[8] Exports of real factor services surged by 27 percent, while factor payments abroad rose by only 10 percent in real terms.

[9] The rise in the rate of return in 1989 was due principally to higher short-term interest rates. The increase in short-term interest rates was particularly notable for deutsche mark denominated assets but this also benefited the net investment income account as, at the end of 1988, 40 percent of the FRG's net short-term external asset position was denominated in deutsche mark. At the long end, interest rate movements were less favorable to the investment income account as changes in yield differentials favored the deutsche mark (U.S. dollar yields actually declined) and the FRG is a substantial net long-term debtor in deutsche mark denominated assets. However, interest movements at the long-end were less marked than at the short-end and, moreover, get reflected in the existing stock of assets only with substantial lags.

and the depreciation of the deutsche mark.[10] Real net exports of goods and nonfactor services gained strongly, too, reversing part of the decline that occurred in 1986–87. The rate of growth of exports of goods and nonfactor services jumped from 5½ percent in 1988 to 9¾ percent in 1989, owing to strong foreign demand (in particular from European countries) and the real effective depreciation of the deutsche mark in 1988 and the first half of 1989. Despite the depreciation of the deutsche mark and slower growth of GDP, imports of goods and nonfactor services quickened, rising by 8¾ percent in 1989 compared with 5¾ percent in the previous year.

In the balance of payments, the rise in the real foreign balance more than offset a deterioration in the terms of trade, and the current account surplus widened by DM 16 billion to DM 104 billion (Table A4). About two fifths of the increase reflected a higher trade surplus (Table A5).[11] The services balance improved even more, from a deficit of DM 8½ billion in 1988 to a surplus of DM 7 billion in 1989, largely due to the rise in net factor incomes (Table A6). Partially offsetting these gains, the deficit on supplementary items and transfers widened by DM 6½ billion.

In the first half of 1990, the real foreign balance provided a stimulus to growth (amounting to ½ of 1 percent of GNP), but this was not sufficient to offset the decline in the foreign balance that took place in the second half of 1989; the real foreign balance was thus below the level in the first six months of 1989. For 1990 as a whole, the real foreign balance is expected to be broadly unchanged. However, with a terms of trade gain, the nominal surplus on goods and services, on a national accounts basis, is likely to rise. This increasing surplus of the western part of Germany (on a national accounts basis) masks a notable shift in composition, with a significant surplus vis-à-vis the eastern part of Germany (compared with small deficits in the past) concealing a decline in the surplus against other areas.[12] Excluding transactions between the western and eastern parts of Germany,[13] the external surplus is likely to decline in 1990 as the pace of domestic expansion, higher capacity utilization, and a real appreciation of the deutsche mark boost imports and discourage exports. Furthermore,

---

[10] For a given rate of return on foreign currency assets, a depreciation of the deutsche mark results in higher earning valued in terms of deutsche mark.

[11] Table A5 provides a geographical breakdown of the trade account. The trade surplus widened by DM 15½ billion vis-à-vis European countries, but fell by DM 8 billion vis-à-vis the United States.

[12] In the past, there have been two approaches to recording the external transactions of the FRG. The national accounts incorporated all external transactions, including those with the GDR, whereas the external trade and balance of payments data excluded transactions with the GDR. This had little material effect on the quantification of the FRG's external trade and current account position as the balance on transactions between the FRG and the GDR was, until 1990, relatively small.

[13] This corresponds to the basis of calculation that had previously been used in the trade and balance of payments accounts (see the previous

Chart 1. Federal Republic of Germany: Immigration from the German Democratic Republic and Eastern Europe, First Quarter 1986–Second Quarter 1990

(In thousands)

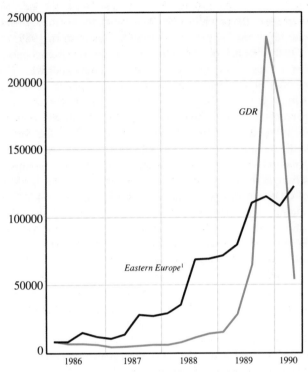

Source: Bundesanstalt für Arbeit, *Arbeitsmarkt in Zahlen*.
[1] Ethnic Germans from Eastern Europe (*Aussiedler*).

looking at the transactions of what now constitutes the deutsche mark currency area, the decline will be even greater—from over DM 100 billion in 1989 to about DM 80 billion in 1990.[14]

Employment, Wages, and Prices

Over the past three years, the labor force in the FRG has been boosted by high immigration from Central and Eastern Europe. Chart 1 shows that the number of immigrants rose notably from mid-1987. Initially, this was due to the inflow of ethnic Germans (*Aussiedler*) from Eastern Europe but, from the summer of 1989, also reflected the surge in GDR citizens moving to the FRG (*Übersiedler*). In 1989, 377,000 ethnic Germans and 344,000 GDR citizens migrated to the FRG;[15] the cor-

---

footnote). As of July 1, 1990, the balance of payments data cover the entire deutsche mark area.

[14] This calculation assumes that the balance of the GDR on transactions with areas other than the FRG was relatively small in 1989 and the first half of 1990.

[15] In addition, about 200,000 asylum seekers were recorded.

responding numbers for 1988 were 203,000 ethnic Germans and 40,000 GDR citizens. Despite the sharp increase in immigration, however, the growth of the labor force in 1989 (½ of 1 percent) was a little slower than in 1988 (Table A7).[16] Employment, on the other hand, grew by 1½ percent in 1989, almost twice the rate of increase of the previous year. As a result, the unemployment rate fell from 7¾ percent in 1988 to 7 percent in 1989.

In the first half of 1990, employment growth strengthened. On average, the number of people employed was 2½ percent higher than in the corresponding period of 1989. Although the labor force also rose markedly (by 1½ percent), reflecting the large immigration of ethnic Germans in 1989 and of GDR citizens after the fall of the Berlin wall, the unemployment rate was about ½ of 1 percentage point lower than a year earlier.[17] Immigration remained strong in the first six months of 1990: the cumulative inflow of GDR citizens and ethnic Germans amounted to 470,000 adding, over time, a potential ¾ of 1 percent to the FRG labor force. The inflow of GDR citizens was concentrated in the early months of the year and fell off significantly after March 1990 as the political outlook in the GDR improved in the wake of the general election and as prospects for GEMSU became clearer. In January–March, 184,000 people moved from the eastern part of Germany to the west, but only 55,000 migrated over the next three months.[18] The number of ethnic Germans immigrating into the FRG from Eastern Europe (232,000) was, however, more evenly distributed over the six-month period.

Despite the strong economy in 1988 and 1989, cost pressures remained subdued. In 1988, the rise in hourly earnings (3¼ percent) was almost matched by the rise in productivity, with the result that unit labor costs remained virtually stable. In 1989, unit labor costs rose by almost 1 percent, reflecting faster growth of hourly earnings (3¾ percent) and slower productivity growth (2¾ percent). The relatively small rise in unit labor costs in 1988–89 allowed profit margins to widen and, thus, the decline in the labor share of national income since the beginning of the 1980s continued (Chart 2).[19] In 1989, the labor share was sharply lower than in the 1970s when it had been historically high;

---

[16] Of the 720,000 immigrants, only a comparatively small proportion were in the labor force in 1989. First, many of the immigrants of working age underwent some form of retraining. Second, the large surge in immigration from the GDR in the second half of 1989 had a relatively small effect on the average labor force for the year. Finally, a sizable number of ethnic Germans from Eastern Europe started learning the German language. The number of participants in German language courses rose from 32,000 in mid-1988 to 63,000 at the end of 1988 and to 109,000 at the end of 1989; almost all were ethnic Germans.

[17] Despite continued large-scale immigration, the number of unemployed immigrants fell from 261,000 in December 1989 to 231,000 in September 1990.

[18] From July 1, 1990, data on migration from the GDR to the FRG have not been collected.

[19] The measure used in Chart 2 adjusts the conventional national accounts measure of the labor share (which incorporates only labor income earned by employees) for shifts between dependent and self-employment.

Chart 2. Federal Republic of Germany: Labor Share of Net National Product, 1955–89[1]

(In percent)

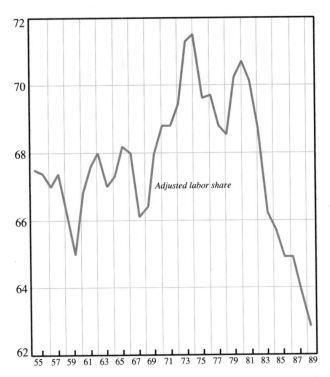

Source: Statistisches Bundesamt, *Volkswirtschaftliche Gesamtrechnungen.*

[1] Adjusted for changes in the composition of employment between dependent employment (employees) and self-employment; measured as the share of employee compensation in net national product, holding the distribution of employment between dependent employment and self-employment constant at the level of 1970.

indeed, since 1986, the labor share has been beneath the low level of 1960.

The fall in the labor share in the 1980s was related to market pressures for an unwinding of the excessive increase of the labor share in the 1970s[20] and the conciliatory stance in successive wage rounds taken by the trade unions; for most of the 1980s, the unions put greater emphasis than previously on a reduction in the statutory number of hours worked per week and less on wage demands. In 1988–89, the strength of the economy, in conjunction with the prevalence of moderate multiyear wage agreements, reached when the outlook was less buoyant, seems to have been an important factor behind the further decline in the labor share.

More recently, however, it appears that the wage climate has been changing, albeit not radically. Whereas, in 1989, the major sectors of the economy remained covered under

---

[20] Various studies showed the emergence of a significant wage gap (the difference between the prevailing wage level and that needed to ensure full employment) in the FRG in the 1970s (see, for example, Leslie Lipschitz, "Wage Gaps, Employment, and Production in German Manufacturing" (unpublished; International Monetary Fund, 1986)).

multiyear wage agreements, contracts covering 11 million of the 18 million private sector employees expired in 1990. In the new agreements replacing these expiring ones, there has been a return to one-year contracts; further reductions in the work week have been delayed; and pay increases have been less moderate. The new agreements implied a rise in tariff wages and salaries of 6 percent on average for 1990.[21] Multiyear agreements covering 7 million private sector workers have remained in effect in 1990; the average increase implicit in these contracts amounted to 3 percent. With government sector workers also covered by a multiyear agreement, earnings per employee are expected to rise by close to 5 percent in 1990, compared with 3 percent in 1989, and unit labor costs to increase by 2½ percent (after a 1 percent rise in 1989).

Consumer price inflation, at 2¾ percent, was higher on average in 1989 than in any other year since 1983 (Chart 3). However, excluding the effects of the increase in excise taxes and postal prices at the beginning of 1989, the rise in the consumer price index (CPI) was about 2 percent, compared with 1¼ percent in 1988 and ¼ of 1 percent in 1987. This acceleration in the CPI (after adjusting for increased taxes) mainly reflected a 4½ percent increase in import prices in 1989. However, from the middle of 1989, import prices fell, owing to a strengthening of the deutsche mark and declining international commodity prices. As a result, the 12-month rate of increase of the CPI came down from 3 percent in the final quarter of 1989 to 2¼ percent in the second quarter of 1990. The downward trend in import prices came to an end in June 1990 and the subsequent increase in oil prices is expected to add ¾ of 1 percentage point to the level of the CPI in the last few months of the year. For 1990, on average, the CPI is expected to increase by 2¾ percent with about ¼ of 1 percentage point reflecting the influence of higher oil prices.

The moderate domestic price environment has been reflected in sectoral statistics. In July 1990, before increased oil prices began to affect statistics, industrial producer prices were only 1½ percent higher than 12 months earlier and agricultural producer prices in the first half of the year were actually lower than in the corresponding period of 1989. The only significant exception to this picture was in the construction sector. Reflecting excess demand, prices for residential construction have been accelerating since early 1988. In 1989, they rose by 3½ percent and in August 1990 they exceeded their year-earlier level by 6½ percent.[22] It should be noted that, historically, construction prices have tended to lead inflationary developments in the FRG (Chart 4).

---

[21] The new agreements were generally not in effect for the full calendar year; thus, on a full-year basis, they implied a somewhat larger rise in wages.

[22] Demand pressures in this sector were also reflected in a new wage agreement in the construction sector, reached in the second quarter of 1990, which provided for an effective increase in wages of about 8 percent.

Chart 3. Federal Republic of Germany: Inflation, 1984–90

(Annualized rate in percent)

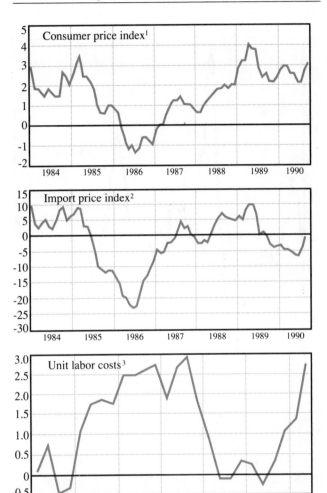

Source: Deutsche Bundesbank, *Monthly Report, Supplement 4*.

[1] The increase over the previous six months of the seasonally adjusted consumer price index, converted to an annual rate.

[2] The increase over the previous six months of the seasonally adjusted import price index, converted to an annual rate.

[3] Moving average of unit labor costs (in the total economy) in the current and in the previous quarter relative to the corresponding calculation for the previous year.

Potential Output and Capacity Utilization

Most estimates of economy-wide potential output in the western part of Germany suggest that the output gap which opened up in the course of the 1981–82 recession will have been closed in 1990. A new study, presented in Chapter VII, confirms the impression that capacity utilization is high. Indeed, the study finds that, adjusted for institutional rigidities in the labor market, output in

Chart 4. Federal Republic of Germany: Construction Prices and Consumer Prices, First Quarter 1961– Third Quarter 1990

(Percent change from the corresponding quarter of the previous year)

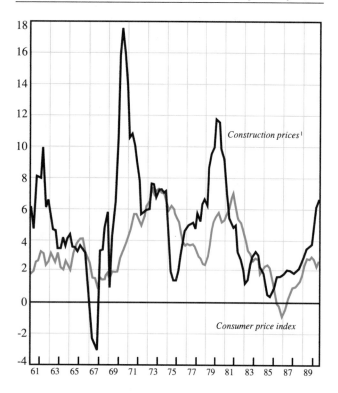

Construction prices[1]

Consumer price index

Sources: Deutsche Bundesbank, *Monthly Report*; and International Monetary Fund, Data Fund.
[1] Residential construction.

1988 was at about its potential level.[23] Sectoral data present a similar picture. Demand pressures in the construction sector have already been noted. In manufacturing, pending capacity limits are suggested by order backlogs, overtime worked, reported shortages of skilled labor, and the Ifo Institute's indicator of capacity utilization.[24] Historical experience would suggest that, in such an environment, inflation pressures are likely to emerge. Chart 5 illustrates that the joint trajectory of inflation and the output gap has tended to take the form of backward bending loops since the early 1960s.[25] While

the chart does suggest that, in the last three years, inflationary pressures have increased in line with historical experience, caution needs to be exercised in such an interpretation as the picture is distorted by the low inflation rate in 1986–87 related to the large terms of trade gain. As already observed, the underlying inflationary pressures in the economy, with the exception of the construction sector, were relatively moderate.

In these circumstances, what can explain the rapid growth of output in conjunction with limited price pressure? It is true that the strong immigration into the FRG in conjunction with the higher level of investment has boosted potential output growth. Moreover, the analysis in Chapter VII suggests that, based on past experience, the inflationary pressures of recent years have not been inconsistent with measured levels of capacity utilization. But even taking these factors into account, the supply elasticity in the FRG in 1988–90 has surprised many. In part, price pressures may have been delayed by multiyear wage agreements. There are grounds for believing, however, that potential growth has been faster than measured by increases in potential labor and capital inputs. First, greater flexibility in working arrangements (e.g., shift working) has boosted the available supply of capital services in a way not captured by measures of the capital stock based on investment data. Second, the downward movement of the labor share has lowered the "equilibrium" level of unemployment and the high level of immigration may have had a significant effect on the bargaining power of unions. The growth pattern in the present upswing (Chart 6) would seem to support the view that supply conditions have improved in the last few years.[26]

Developments in Money and Financial Markets

Overview

Money market conditions were tightened considerably in the FRG during 1989. As a result, and despite the buoyant economy, the expansion of M3 slowed to a growth rate of 4¾ percent during the year (fourth quarter to fourth quarter), compared with an increase of 6¾ percent in the course of 1988. Thus, in 1989, after three years of overshooting, the Deutsche Bundesbank met its monetary target (M3 growth of about 5 percent).

---

[23] In Chapter VII, the level of potential output, after taking account of institutional rigidities in the labor market, is denoted the quasi-potential output level.

[24] See Chart 1 in Chapter I.

[25] Analytically, such counterclockwise movements in inflation-output space can be explained by models incorporating rational expectations and sluggish price-wage adjustments. Taking 1961 as a starting point, three of these counterclockwise movements in inflation-output space can be identified. The first loop stretched from 1961 to about 1969. Its diameter was comparatively small, centered on a high degree of capacity utilization and a low rate of inflation. The second loop extended from 1970 to 1979, with a much larger diameter, and its center at a higher inflation rate and

smaller capacity utilization. Whereas the first and second loops took about a decade to complete, the third loop is longer-lived. Its diameter is similar to that of the second loop, but its center is characterized by a much lower inflation rate.

[26] Growth cycles have tended to be M-shaped with the second "peak" of the "M" somewhat lower than the first. In the present cycle, however, the second peak indicates a strengthening in the later part of the upswing.

Chart 5. Federal Republic of Germany: Inflation-Output Loops, 1961–89[1]

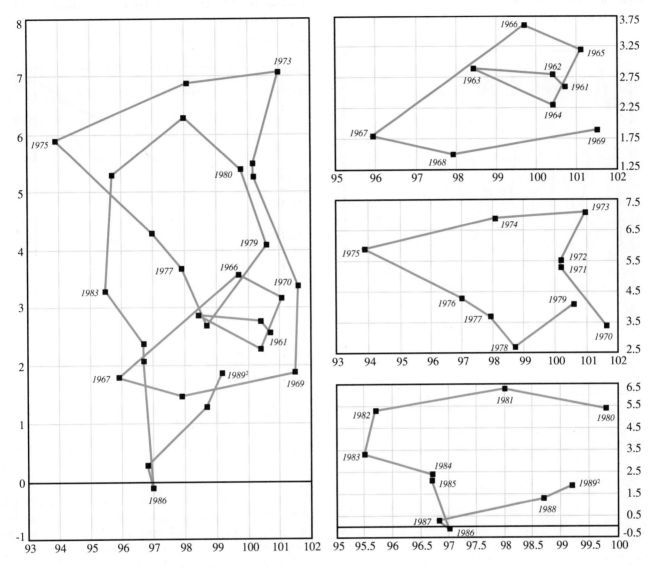

Sources: International Monetary Fund, Data Fund; and authors' calculations.
[1] The vertical axes show the percent change in the consumer price index and the horizontal axes show actual GDP in percent of potential.
[2] Inflation rate excluding the effects of the 1989 increase in indirect taxes.

Despite the tighter monetary stance, the deutsche mark lost value in the first half of 1989, as adverse sentiment in the foreign exchanges was reflected in large long-term capital outflows. In the second half of the year, with the abolition of the withholding tax on interest (which had come into effect in January 1989) and prospects of higher real yields on investments in Germany, the long-term capital account turned around and the exchange rate recovered. On balance, the deutsche mark gained in value during the course of 1989 (December to December), by ¾ of 1 percent against the U.S. dollar and by 3¾ percent in nominal effective terms.

In the first nine months of 1990 monetary growth continued to be restrained and short-term money-market rates rose gradually. There was, however, a sharp rise in long-term interest rates, particularly in response to the announcement in early February of plans for German economic and monetary union. In September, the external value of the deutsche mark was about ½ of 1 percent higher in nominal effective terms than in December 1989, with appreciations against the U.S. dollar and the yen largely offset by a weakening against currencies participating in the exchange rate mechanism of the European Monetary System, the Swiss franc, and the pound sterling.

Chart 6. Federal Republic of Germany: Pattern of Growth Cycles, 1967–90

(Percent change of GDP)

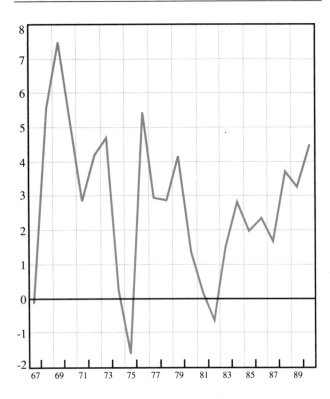

Sources: International Monetary Fund, Data Fund; and authors' projection for 1990.

Chart 7. Federal Republic of Germany: Monetary Targets and Monetary Developments, January 1985– September 1990

(In billions of deutsche mark)[1]

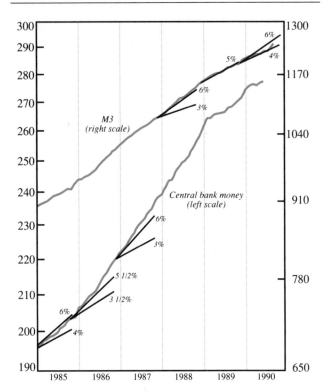

Source: Deutsche Bundesbank, *Monthly Report, Supplement 4*.
[1] Log scale.

Monetary Aggregates

In December 1988, the Central Bank Council of the Bundesbank announced a target for growth of M3 of around 5 percent from the fourth quarter of 1988 to the fourth quarter of 1989. As in the previous year, it used M3 as its monetary target, but it deviated from its usual practice of announcing a target range.[27]

During the early months of 1989, money growth was faster than targeted: in the first quarter, M3 was 6 percent (at an annual rate) above the target base (Table A8). Monetary growth in January was affected by a shift out of longer-term financial assets into monetary assets and currency in particular; this, apparently, was influenced by the withholding tax on interest.[28] The demand for

currency abated after the announcement in April that the withholding tax would be abolished on July 1. Reflecting this and the influence of interest rate increases by the Bundesbank, monetary growth slowed and, by June, M3 was below its target path. From June to December, M3 grew at a rate of a little under 5 percent and, in the final quarter of 1989, it stood 4¾ percent above the target base (Chart 7). However, an extended M3 aggregate, taking into account, in addition, the deutsche mark deposits of German nonbanks on the Euromarkets and holdings of short-term bank bonds, grew by 8¼ percent over this period.[29]

In December 1989, the Central Bank Council announced its monetary target for 1990. The underlying assumptions

---

[27] Before the announcement of monetary targets in December 1987, the targeted monetary aggregate had been central bank money (CBM). Between 1979 and 1988 the target had been announced in the form of a range of growth rates. Box 1 in Chapter X contains a discussion of monetary policy instruments and procedures in the FRG. See also Leslie Lipschitz and others, *The Federal Republic of Germany: Adjustment in a Surplus Country*, IMF Occasional Paper, No. 64 (Washington: International Monetary Fund, January 1989), pp. 8–9.

[28] It is likely that the imposition of the withholding tax increased the demand for liquid assets as investors deliberated on how to place funds

withdrawn from longer-term assets. It is, however, less easy to explain why the withholding tax would have encouraged currency holdings of German residents to grow faster than other liquid components of broad money. Investor misunderstanding as to the nature of the withholding tax may have been responsible. For example, some investors may have feared that the confidentiality of their holdings with financial institutions was threatened.

[29] The faster growth of extended M3 was reflected particularly in a sharp jump in Euromarket deposits of companies. It is not clear how the "moneyness" of these deposits compares with the components of M3.

of the target (which, as usual, was set in a medium-term context) were an expansion of about 2½ percent in productive potential, an increase of 2 percent in the price level, and a trend reduction in velocity of ½ of 1 percent. On this basis, M3 was targeted to grow in the range of 4–6 percent; thus, the midpoint of the range corresponded to the target that had been set in the previous year. From July 1, 1990—the effective date of the currency union with the GDR—the Bundesbank has controlled monetary policy for the entire deutsche mark currency area. As of October 1990, however, no official pronouncement had been made as to how this would affect the design and implementation of monetary policy. Meanwhile, the Bundesbank has continued to publish separately monetary data for the western part of Germany.[30] On this basis, M3 in September was 5 percent (at an annual rate) above the target base and thus in the middle of the target path. The extended M3, however, continued to grow somewhat faster than M3.[31]

Financial Market Developments

Interest Rate Developments

Following its restrictive policy stance in the second half of 1988, the Bundesbank continued to push interest rates to higher levels through 1989. The discount and Lombard rates were increased on four occasions, in three steps of 50 basis points in the first half of the year (January 20, April 21, and June 30) and by a further 100 basis points later in the year (October 6); at the end of 1989, the discount and Lombard rates stood at 6 percent and 8 percent, respectively (Table A9 and Chart 8). The rate on repurchase transactions—the Bundesbank's principal tool for managing the money markets on a week-to-week basis—rose by a similar amount during the year, with the increase more evenly spread.

Market forces were also generating upward pressure on interest rates. The economy was growing at a rapid pace and there were fears of inflationary pressures related to the rising capacity utilization, the upcoming wage round, and the weakness of the deutsche mark in the first half of the year. The three-month interbank rate increased by almost 3 percentage points between December 1988 and December 1989, ending the year at just over 8 percent.

Meanwhile, the rise in long-term bond yields was more moderate; in December 1989, the yield on public authority bonds with maturity of nine–ten years was less

---

[30] In producing these data, it has been necessary to estimate currency holdings, since the geographical distribution of currency holdings cannot be identified from the raw data.

[31] In August, the extended M3 was 5¼ percent above the target base at an annual rate, compared with 4¾ percent for conventional M3.

Chart 8. Federal Republic of Germany: Interest Rate Developments, January 1985–September 1990

(In percent a year)

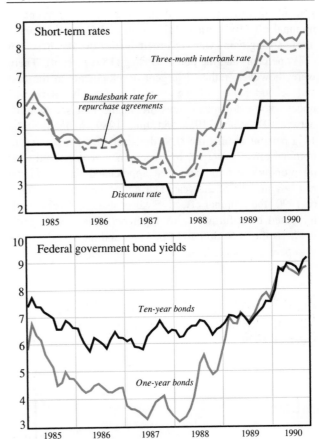

Sources: Deutsche Bundesbank, *Monthly Report* and *Monthly Report, Supplement 2*.

than 1 percentage point above its level one year earlier. The increase was concentrated in the latter part of 1989, apparently influenced by developments in Eastern Europe, particularly in the GDR. Reflecting the sharper increase in short-term rates, the yield curve became inverted in the middle of 1989 and remained so for the rest of the year.

In the first nine months of 1990 there were no changes in the discount or Lombard rates. The Bundesbank's repurchase rates and short-term money-market rates rose at a more moderate pace than in 1989; in September 1990 they were about ½ of 1 percentage point above their levels in December 1989. Long-term rates, however, rose quite sharply with yields on nine–ten year bonds jumping by 1¾ percentage points over the same time period. Much of this increase occurred in February, after the announcement of Chancellor Kohl's proposals for economic and monetary union with the GDR.

Exchange Market Developments

Over the 12-month period ending in December 1989, the value of the deutsche mark appreciated by ¾ of 1 percent against the U.S. dollar and by 3¾ percent in nominal effective terms (Table A10 and Chart 9). Particularly strong gains were recorded against the Japanese yen (17¼ percent) and the pound sterling (15½ percent). There were, however, rather divergent developments in the first and second halves of the year. The deutsche mark was under strong downward pressure in the first six months: between December 1988 and June 1989, it declined by 11½ percent against the U.S. dollar and by 1½ percent in nominal effective terms. In the summer, it fluctuated with no pronounced trend and then appreciated sharply in the last few months of the year. During the first three quarters of 1990, the nominal effective value of the deutsche mark increased by a further ½ of 1 percent. There were gains vis-à-vis the U.S. dollar (11 percent) and the Japanese yen (7¼ percent), while losses were recorded against the pound

Chart 9. Federal Republic of Germany: Exchange Rate Developments, First Quarter 1980–Third Quarter 1990

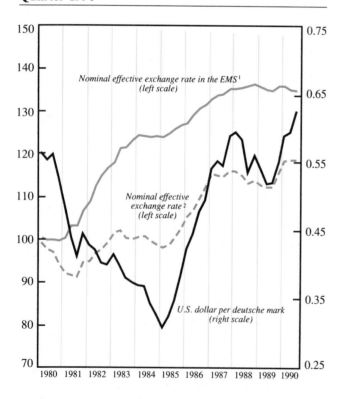

Sources: International Monetary Fund, Data Fund; and Deutsche Bundesbank, *Monthly Report.*

¹ Vis-à-vis countries participating in the exchange rate mechanism of the European Monetary System; January 1980 = 100; includes Spain from June 1989.

² Vis-à-vis industrial partner countries; January 1980 = 100.

Chart 10. Federal Republic of Germany: Bilateral Exchange Rates and Interest Rate Differentials vis-à-vis the Deutsche Mark, January 1987–October 1990¹

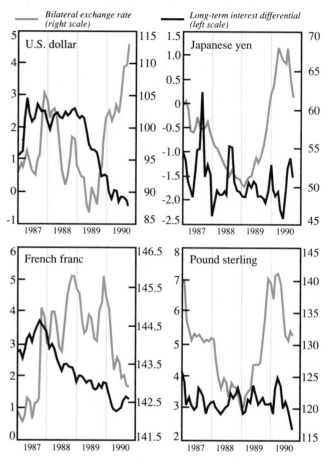

Sources: International Monetary Fund, Data Fund; and Deutsche Bundesbank, *Monthly Report.*

¹ Exchange rate data are in terms of the units of the currency specified per deutsche mark and are expressed in index form with January 1980 = 100. Long-term interest differentials are calculated as the interest rate for the currency specified minus the deutsche mark interest rate.

sterling (6 percent) and the currencies participating in the ERM (1 percent).

The short-run time pattern of exchange rates is often difficult to explain with reference to contemporaneous developments in goods and financial markets. For example, changes in interest rate differentials can spark exchange rate changes or may themselves be a market reaction to changes in sentiment in the foreign exchange markets; Chart 10, for example, illustrates that the relationship between long-term interest differentials and exchange rates has varied considerably across countries. Broadly speaking, the weakness of the deutsche mark in the first half of 1989, which was relatively minor compared with the strength over the preceding three years, can probably be attributed to adverse sentiment related to the coming into effect of the interest withholding tax and concerns about higher inflation resulting from the booming economy and the forthcoming wage round. In the second half of the year, investors moved back into assets denominated in deutsche mark, as the tight stance of monetary policy moderated inflation fears, the withholding tax was abolished, interest rates continued to rise in the FRG, and developments in Eastern Europe, particularly in the GDR, strengthened profit expectations for German industry. Thus, while there had been a large outflow of long-term capital in the early part of 1989, the improved sentiment in favor of the deutsche mark was seen in sizable long-term capital inflows in the last quarter of the year (Table A11). In 1990, the debate over GEMSU and the fears of inflation that it rekindled created some uncertainties in the financial markets. Indeed, there was a sizable long-term capital outflow in the first quarter of the year, but any adverse influence on sentiment in the foreign exchange markets appears to have been more than offset by prospects for higher real yields.

Fiscal Policy and Structural Reform

Overview

After an expansionary stance in 1988, fiscal policy turned restrictive in 1989. This was the result of fiscal drag and of discretionary policy measures—an earlier planned increase in indirect taxes took effect. The withdrawal of fiscal stimulus from the latter had an unintended, but not unwelcome anticyclical effect. The interaction between fiscal policy and the real economy has been, perhaps, less fortunate in 1990. As a consequence of a large cut in direct taxes, enacted in 1987, and strong expenditure growth, fiscal policy has been expansionary, at the same time as economic growth, already strong, has been boosted by GEMSU. Meanwhile, there seems to be little spare capacity in the economy. Some important structural measures taken in recent years, in particular the three-stage reform of direct taxation, have put the supply side of the economy in a better position to respond to the increased demand, but much remains to be done in the areas of subsidies and government regulation of the economy.

Given the concerns that exist over the high degree of capacity utilization in the economy, questions arise as to how fiscal and structural policy measures might be used to alleviate any adverse consequences of the increased pressure on demand resulting from GEMSU. The remainder of this section reviews recent developments in the areas of fiscal and structural policy as background to an analysis of the role for these policies in the coming years. This latter question is taken up in Chapters I and XII.

Budgetary Developments in 1989

The budget deficit of the territorial authorities declined by more than DM 25 billion to DM 26½ billion (1¼ percent of GNP) in 1989 and reached its lowest level during the present upswing (Table A12 and Chart 11).[32] The favorable budgetary developments were primarily the result of strong growth of tax revenue (Table A13). This growth had three main sources: first, several excise taxes were raised at the beginning of the year;[33] second, a withholding tax on interest income was in effect for the first six months of the year;[34] and, third, the buoyant economy reinforced the effects of fiscal drag and contributed to a strong rise of income and corporation taxes. As a result, tax revenue of the territorial authorities rose by 9½ percent. Other current revenue, after declining in 1988, increased by 9 percent as profit transfers from the Bundesbank recovered from their low level of 1988.[35] The increase in total revenue, at close to 9 percent, was a little slower than that of current revenue as the rise in current receipts was in part offset by a drop in capital revenue, which reflected the winding down of the Federal Government's privatization program (see below).

Expenditure growth in 1989 (1¼ percentage points above the medium-term target rate of 3 percent) was buoyed by capital spending and current transfers. Investment at the municipality level was encouraged by favorable revenue developments and by an investment incentive program launched by the Federal Government in 1988.[36] The Länder also raised their investment spending, in response to the DM 2½ billion transfer to "structurally weak" states from the Federal Government.[37] The rise in current transfers of

---

[32] The term territorial authorities refers to the Federal and Länder Governments, the municipalities, the Burden Equalization Fund, the European Recovery Program Fund, and the EC's accounts.

[33] The mineral oil tax, the tobacco tax, and the insurance tax were increased and a tax on natural gas was introduced. Additional revenue from these tax changes was estimated at DM 8 billion.

[34] The 10 percent withholding tax took effect on January 1, 1989 and was abolished, after a heated debate about its effects on capital markets, with effect from July 1, 1989.

[35] Bundesbank profits were sharply reduced in 1987 as assets denominated in U.S. dollars were written down in value. At the end of December 1987, the U.S. dollar reached its lowest point, to that date, against the deutsche mark (US$1 = DM 1.5815). As a result, profit transfers to the Federal Government in 1988 were small (DM 250 million). With profits returning to a more normal level in 1988, the Bundesbank transferred DM 10 billion to the Federal Government in 1989. Of this, DM 5 billion was counted as current revenue and the rest was used to retire federal debt. This meant that half of the Bundesbank profit transfer was included below the line as a financing item in the federal budget.

[36] Against the background of the drop in stock prices and the turbulence in the foreign exchanges, the Federal Government decided in December 1987 to take fiscal measures to support economic growth. The package included DM 15 billion in additional loans to municipalities over 1988–90, with interest subsidies from the federal budget of DM 200 million annually over a ten-year period (at a total estimated budgetary cost of about DM 2½ billion).

[37] This represented in 1989 the first installment of a DM 24½ billion investment support program for "needy" Länder. Disbursements were to be in equal installments over a ten-year period.

the territorial authorities reflected increased federal transfers to the Labor Office[38] and higher social spending, including support of immigrants.[39]

The budgetary outcome for the social security system was even more favorable than for the territorial authorities. On a national accounts basis, the budgetary surplus increased by about DM 15 billion to DM 16 billion (¾ of 1 percent of GNP). This was largely the result of an improvement in the finances of the health insurance system,[40] but the accounts of the unemployment insurance system also strengthened as a result of more favorable labor market conditions.[41]

Reflecting the smaller deficit of the territorial authorities and the larger surplus of the social security system, the financial balance of the general government (on a national accounts basis) improved by some DM 50 billion and, for the first time since 1973, the general government accounts were in surplus (Chart 11 and Tables A14 and A15).[42] The share of general government expenditure in GNP dropped by almost 2 percentage points, with one half of this decline on account of a lower ratio for public consumption, while the share of revenue rose by about ½ of 1 percentage point. Among revenue items, the increase in direct taxes was particularly notable; the rise in indirect taxes as a proportion of GNP was considerably smaller, despite the increase in excise taxes, reflecting the relatively slow growth of consumption in 1989.

Budgetary Developments in 1990

The federal budget for 1990, which was passed by parliament in December 1989 foresaw an increase in

---

[38] After budgetary surpluses in 1984–85, the Federal Labor Office experienced deficits in 1986–89. In 1988, the financial reserves of the Labor Office were exhausted and since then the current deficits have had to be covered by the Federal Government.

[39] In midyear, a supplementary budget was passed authorizing, inter alia, an additional DM ½ billion in social expenditures. Of this, about one half was for the support of ethnic German immigrants.

[40] The medical insurance reform that took effect in 1989 led to a drop in expenditures of the health insurance system by 3½ percent. In substantial part, this reflected genuine expenditure savings (estimated at DM 5½ billion in 1989), but there was also a shift in expenditures from 1989 to 1988 (estimated at DM 2½ billion) in anticipation of the cutback in insurance coverage of medical services.

[41] The decline in unemployment compensation, however, was in part offset by an increase in payments to ethnic German immigrants receiving language training.

[42] In addition to differences in coverage (principally, the treatment of the social security funds, and, from 1990, the German Unity Fund), the general government finances on a national accounts basis differ from those of the territorial authorities (on an administrative basis) owing to accounting conventions. For example, the national accounts are on an accrual basis while the administrative accounts are close to a cash basis; lending is treated as an expenditure in the administrative accounts but as a financing transaction in the national accounts; and, while only part of the Bundesbank's profit transfer has been counted as revenue in the administrative accounts for 1989–90, it has all been recorded as revenue in the national accounts.

Chart 11. Federal Republic of Germany: Selected Indicators of Fiscal Policy, 1950–89

(In percent of GNP)

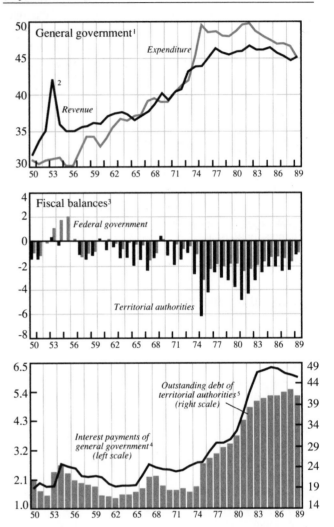

Source: Statistisches Bundesamt.
[1] National accounts basis.
[2] The sharp jump in revenue in 1953 reflects the recording of a large capital transfer from abroad as foreign loans were converted into grants.
[3] Administrative basis.
[4] In percent of expenditure.
[5] In 1953 debt increased despite the recording of a surplus in the accounts of the territorial authorities. This was due to the inclusion in the debt statistics of liabilities related to war reparation and pre-1945 external debts, as agreed in the London Debt Agreement of 1953.

expenditure of 3 percent in line with the Government's medium-term target. Additional demands on federal outlays, however, required three supplementary budgets. The first supplementary budget (DM 6.8 billion) was passed by parliament in March 1990, the second (DM 4.8 billion) in May, and the third (DM 25.8 billion) in October. The additional borrowing needs resulted primarily from developments in east Germany. But, even

Table 2.   German Unity Fund: Transfers to Eastern Germany and Their Financing[1]

(In billions of deutsche mark)

	1990	1991	1992	1993	1994	1990–94
Total transfers to GDR	22	35	28	20	10	115
Financed from the federal budget	2	4	4	5	5	20
Borrowing requirement	20	31	24	15	5	95
Debt service[2]	—	2	5.1	7.5	9	23.6
Paid by:						
Federal Government	—	1	2.6	3.8	4.5	11.9
Länder	—	0.6	1.5	2.3	2.7	7.1
Municipalities	—	0.4	1.0	1.5	1.8	4.7

Source: Bundesministerium der Finanzen.
[1] As laid out in the State Treaty on GEMSU.
[2] Based on a 30-year repayment schedule. The annuity after 1994 will be DM 9.5 billion.

excluding transfers to the GDR, expenditure of the Federal Government is expected to rise by about 5½ percent. Expenditure of the Länder and municipalities is expected to rise at an even faster rate. On the other hand, revenue collections of the territorial authorities in 1990 have been influenced by the third stage of the 1986–90 tax reform, which provided net tax relief of some DM 25 billion (about 1 percent of GNP) with effect from the beginning of the year (Table A16). Thus, despite strong economic growth, tax revenue is projected to increase by only 2 percent.

Reflecting these developments, the deficit of the territorial authorities, including all GDR-related expenditure in the three supplementary budgets of the Federal Government, is expected to widen by about DM 58 billion to DM 84 billion (3½ percent of GNP). In addition, the German Unity Fund (see below) is expected to raise about DM 20 billion on the financial markets. As part of the increase in the territorial authorities' deficit reflects lending activities and as the surplus of the social security funds is likely to widen, the deterioration in the financial position of general government is expected to be of the order of DM 75 billion (including the Unity Fund). Incorporating all GDR-related borrowing of the Federal Government, the general government is expected to record a deficit of some DM 70 billion (3 percent of GNP) in 1990, compared with a surplus of DM 5½ billion in 1989.

Fiscal Implications of GEMSU

From a fiscal policy point of view, unification of the two German economies came at a favorable time. Owing to stronger-than-expected economic growth, the tax estimates prepared by a group of experts[43] in May 1990

produced a substantial upward revision in revenue projections—accumulating, between 1990 and 1993 to DM 115 billion (compared with the May and November 1989 estimates).[44] It was recognized, however, that this would not be sufficient to cover all the additional expenditure related to GEMSU, and that, despite a reduction in other expenditure (in particular for regional subsidies),[45] borrowing would be larger than anticipated in earlier budgetary plans.

To undertake the additional borrowing associated with GEMSU, the Federal Government and the Länder agreed, in April 1990, to establish an off-budget fund (the so-called German Unity Fund). The total endowment of the Unity Fund was set at DM 115 billion. Of this, DM 95 billion would be raised in the capital market, with the remaining DM 20 billion to come from the federal budget.[46] The Federal Government would bear half of the debt service costs of the Fund, with the remainder paid by the Länder and municipalities (see Table 2). Transfers from the Unity Fund were intended to finance a significant part of the deficits of the territorial authorities in east Germany, with government units in the east financing the remainder on the capital markets. Thus,

[43] Official tax estimates in the FRG are prepared by a group of experts (*Arbeitskreis Steuerschätzungen*), which includes officials of the federal, state, and municipal governments and the Bundesbank, and representatives of the five major economic research institutes and the Council of Economic Advisors.

[44] The projection period was 1990–94 but the calculation of the upward revision relates to 1990–93, as the previous round extended only to 1993. The additional revenue estimated was DM 8 billion for 1990, DM 28 billion for 1991, DM 35 billion for 1992, and DM 44 billion for 1993. Projections were based on nominal GNP growth of 7 percent in 1990, 6.5 percent in 1991, and 5.5 percent a year in 1992–94. Despite the stronger revenue growth, the ratio of taxes to GNP was projected to decline from 23.7 percent in 1989 to 23.2 percent in 1994, owing to the income tax cut that took effect at the beginning of 1990.

[45] The German authorities have estimated the budgetary "costs of division" at DM 40 billion a year, reflecting the Federal Government's support to the State Government in Berlin (DM 13 billion); subsidies to the border areas and Berlin (DM 14 billion); social transfers (DM 5½ billion); and spending for various other purposes (DM 7½ billion). With the rationale for this support disappearing, the authorities envisage phasing out a significant part of these subsidies and transfers during the coming years.

[46] The contribution from the federal budget was expected to be financed by reductions in expenditures from planned levels of DM 2 billion in 1990, DM 4 billion a year in 1991–92, and DM 5 billion a year in 1993–94.

Table 3. German Unity Fund and Supplementary Federal Budgets: Additional Borrowing Related to East Germany

(In billions of deutsche mark)

	1990
From the first supplementary budget	6.0
Of which:	
Transfer to the German Unity Fund	*2.0*
From the second supplementary budget	2.8
Transfer to pension system	0.8
Transfer to unemployment insurance	2.0
From the third supplementary budget	24.2
Of which:	
Expenditure increases in east Germany[1]	*17.7*
Revenue shortfalls in east Germany[1]	*6.5*
German Unity Fund	20.0
Total	53.0
(In percent of GNP in west Germany)	*2.2*

Source: Bundesministerium der Finanzen.
[1] Relative to the budget passed by the GDR's parliament in July 1990. See Chapter XI for details.

Table 4. Germany: Public Sector Borrowing Requirement, 1990

(In billions of deutsche mark)

	1990
Territorial authorities, FRG[1]	84.0
Territorial authorities, GDR[2]	10.0
German Unity Fund	20.0
Trust Fund[3]	12.0
Total (gross)	126.0
Social security system, FRG	−18.0
Off-budget Bundesbank transfers[4]	−3.0
Total (net)	105.0
(In percent of combined GNP)	4

Source: Authors' estimates.
[1] See Table A12.
[2] Includes only borrowing after July 1, 1990. The State Treaty on GEMSU granted a borrowing authority of DM 10 billion.
[3] Does not include guarantees on commercial bank credits to enterprises.
[4] The federal budget for 1990 includes DM 7 billion in profit transfers from the Bundesbank. The actual transfer was DM 10 billion and the difference is being used to retire federal debt.

the establishment of this off-budget fund would allow continuation of the existing system of financial relations between the Federal Government and the Länder until the end of 1994 in that the agreement excluded the Länder of the east from the revenue sharing arrangements existing between the Länder of the western part of Germany and the Federal Government.

In the months after GEMSU took effect, it became apparent that the budgetary costs would be much higher than previously expected. However, it was decided not to make any changes in the budget of the German Unity Fund, particularly since the accelerated path to political unification fundamentally changed the prospective nature of financial relations between the Federal Government and government units in eastern Germany. The Unification Treaty stipulated that 85 percent of the resources of the German Unity Fund would be directed to the Länder governments in the former area of the GDR, with the remainder going to the Federal Government; the additional budgetary costs at the federal level would be borne directly by the budget of the FRG. As already noted, a third supplementary budget became necessary to cover the additional budgetary costs in 1990. Borrowing related to the eastern part of Germany in 1990 that was incorporated in the three supplementary federal budgets for 1990 or that was to be undertaken by the Unity Fund is shown in Table 3. Table 4 presents the public sector borrowing requirement for 1990 for all of Germany, that is, including also the borrowing authority granted to the Government of the GDR.[47]

Structural Reforms[48]

In the area of "qualitative fiscal consolidation,"[49] the completion of the 1986–90 tax reform represented a considerable achievement. Attention has now begun to focus on the reform of business taxation. With a view to undertaking such a reform during the next legislative period, the Government appointed, at the end of 1989, an expert commission (consisting of members of the academic, business, and political communities) with the mandate to publish recommendations for reform in early 1991. Debate has centered on how marginal tax rates relate to those in other countries and on the existence of taxation unrelated to company profitability.[50] The authorities believe, in addition, that some net reduction in the tax burden of businesses is warranted. But the size of the cut and the timing of the reform have become more uncertain owing to the fiscal costs of GEMSU. Agreement, however, has been reached on the abolition of the stock exchange turnover tax (*Börsenumsatzsteuer*) in 1991 and of the company tax (*Gesellschaftsteuer*) and the bills of exchange tax (*Wechselsteuer*) in 1992.[51] The

---

[47] Under the State Treaty on GEMSU, the amount that could be borrowed by the GDR Government was limited to DM 10 billion.

[48] A detailed review of structural policies in the FRG is given in Leslie Lipschitz and others, *The Federal Republic of Germany: Adjustment in a Surplus Country*, IMF Occasional Paper, No. 64 (Washington: International Monetary Fund, January 1989), Section IV.

[49] In the Federal Government's medium-term fiscal strategy, the term "qualitative consolidation" denotes the restructuring of government revenue and expenditure with a view to improving the supply side of the economy, while "quantitative consolidation" refers to the reduction of expenditure and borrowing in relation to GNP.

[50] The trade tax (*Gewerbesteuer*) is in part levied independently of company profits. However, since it is the main independent source of revenue for municipalities, resistance to its abolition is strong.

[51] The stock exchange turnover tax is levied on secondary market transactions in equities, bonds, and other financial instruments, the

Federal Government has also largely completed its privatization program.[52]

In contrast to the improvements on the revenue side, however, only limited progress has been made in the area of expenditure. Subsidies, in particular, fell only moderately in relation to output in the period 1980–89 (Tables A17–A18).[53] While some further progress was made in 1990 with the phasing out of a number of tax exemptions, plans to subsidize investment and support the restructuring of enterprises in the eastern part of Germany are likely to put upward pressure on subsidy expenditure.

Some steps have been taken in the area of deregulation. A reform of the postal system, decided in 1989, went into full effect in 1990; although the reform involved some opening up of the telecommunications sector to private suppliers, a considerable part of the telecommunications market remains under the monopoly of the Deutsche Bundespost.[54] There has been a limited liberalization of shop opening hours: Shops may now remain open on Thursday evenings provided they cut opening hours on Saturday afternoon (Saturday afternoon opening is allowed once a month) so that the total weekly opening time does not change. There have also been some reforms in the area of financial markets (see above), but altogether deregulation seems not to have gained any noticeable momentum. The long-awaited report of the Deregulation Commission is now scheduled to be released in 1991, although the Commission has recently published recommendations on the deregulation of the insurance and transportation industries.[55]

In the area of competition policy, the Cartel Law has been revised. The major changes, which went into effect in early 1990, were (1) stricter competition rules in the retail sector with a view to providing small and medium-sized companies better protection against large companies; (2) extension of the Cartel Law to cover previously excluded areas, for example, the banking, insurance, transportation, and utilities sectors; and (3) stricter control of mergers and acquisitions.

---

company tax on new equity issues, and the bills of exchange tax on the issue of these bills. These taxes have hindered the development and distorted the structure of financial markets in Germany. The abolition of these taxes was part of a law (*Finanzmarktförderungsgesetz*), passed by parliament in March 1990; the law also abolished some existing restrictions on the issuing of financial paper, and gave mutual funds more autonomy (in particular, access to the German Futures Exchange and the option of investing in money market paper).

[52] However, significant scope for privatization still exists at the level of the Länder and municipalities.

[53] The FRG has tended to fall toward the middle in international comparisons of subsidy levels (Tables A19 and A20).

[54] About 85 percent of the revenue accruing to Telekom, the Deutsche Bundespost company providing telecommunications services, is estimated to come from that market segment where the public monopoly remains.

[55] A final report with recommendations for deregulation was originally scheduled for 1990, but, in January 1990, the Federal Government extended the mandate of the Commission for another year so that recent developments in the eastern part of Germany could be taken into account. At the same time, it was agreed that the Commission would submit an advance report on insurance and transportation, areas of particular relevance for the single European market. For the insurance industry, the Commission recommended a liberalization of prices (with the exception of the health insurance) and less regulation of contract terms with a view to opening up the market to competition from abroad. For the transportation industry, the Commission recommended a reform and restructuring of the railways; a liberalization of prices and an abolition of quotas for road transport; fewer restrictions on bus services, in particular for long-distance services; an abolition of quotas and a liberalization of prices for taxi services; and price liberalization and an opening-up to foreign competition in sea and air transport.

Appendix

Statistical Tables

Table A1. Federal Republic of Germany: Aggregate Demand

	1989		1985	1986	1987	1988	1989	1989[1]				1990[1]	
	At current prices		At 1980 prices					I	II	III	IV	I	II
	(In billions of deutsche mark)	(In percent of GNP)	(Percent change from previous period)[2]										
Private consumption	1,211.3	53.6	1.4	3.4	3.3	2.7	1.7	0.4	0.5	—	1.0	2.7	0.6
Public consumption	419.0	18.5	2.1	2.6	1.6	2.3	−0.9	−1.8	−0.1	—	−1.0	2.9	−0.5
Gross fixed investment	458.4	20.3	0.1	3.3	2.2	5.1	7.1	9.3	−3.8	−1.4	3.0	13.8	−7.2
Construction	250.8	11.1	−5.6	2.7	−0.3	3.3	5.1	15.3	−10.2	−2.6	2.2	20.2	−12.8
Residential	119.1	5.3	−10.0	−1.1	−1.5	3.5	5.1	. . .	. . .	. . .	. . .	. . .	. . .
Business	88.8	3.9	−0.9	5.1	1.3	3.8	5.7	. . .	. . .	. . .	. . .	. . .	. . .
Public	42.9	1.9	−1.6	8.2	−0.2	1.7	3.8	. . .	. . .	. . .	. . .	. . .	. . .
Machinery and equipment	207.6	9.2	9.4	4.1	5.6	7.5	9.7	2.0	5.0	—	3.8	6.6	—
Final domestic demand	2,088.7	92.4	1.2	3.2	2.7	3.1	2.3	1.9	−0.6	−0.3	1.0	5.2	−1.5
Stockbuilding	29.2	1.3	−0.4	0.3	0.1	0.6	0.4	−1.4	1.2	−0.4	2.4	−3.5	1.6
Total domestic demand	2,117.8	93.7	0.8	3.5	2.8	3.7	2.7	0.4	0.6	−0.7	3.6	1.5	0.2
Exports of goods and services	787.1	34.8	6.8	—	0.9	5.7	11.5	7.0	4.2	−2.5	−0.4	8.6	−3.1
Imports of goods and services	643.7	28.5	3.7	3.5	4.8	6.0	8.8	1.5	6.0	−3.8	7.0	2.6	−0.3
Foreign balance	143.5	6.3	1.2	−1.0	−1.1	0.1	1.2	2.0	−0.4	0.3	−2.4	2.2	−1.1
Gross national product	2,261.3	100.0	1.9	2.3	1.6	3.7	3.9	2.3	0.2	−0.4	1.0	3.6	−0.9
Memorandum item:													
Gross domestic product	2,235.6	98.9	2.0	2.3	1.7	3.7	3.3	. . .	. . .	. . .	. . .	. . .	. . .

Sources: Statistisches Bundesamt, *Volkswirtschaftliche Gesamtrechnungen*; and Deutsche Bundesbank, *Monthly Report, Supplement 4*.

[1] Seasonally adjusted, but not annualized.

[2] Data for stockbuilding and the foreign balance are contributions to real GNP growth in percentage points.

Table A2. Federal Republic of Germany: Distribution of Income

	1970	1980	1988	1989	1985	1986	1987	1988	1989
	(Share of net national product)[1]				*(Percent change from previous year)*				
Net national product	**100.0**	**100.0**	**100.0**	**100.0**	**4.6**	**6.3**	**3.7**	**5.6**	**6.0**
Gross income from employment	68.0	73.5	68.1	67.2	3.9	5.1	4.0	3.9	4.5
Direct taxes	6.8	9.8	10.0	10.2	7.4	3.1	8.3	2.0	8.3
Social security contributions	16.2	21.3	21.5	21.2	4.8	5.6	4.3	4.3	4.2
Employer	9.9	13.4	13.3	13.0	4.4	5.4	4.3	3.8	3.9
Employee	6.2	7.9	8.2	8.1	5.6	5.9	4.1	4.9	4.8
Net income from employment	45.0	42.4	36.6	35.8	2.4	5.3	2.8	4.3	3.6
Gross income from entrepreneurial activity and property	32.0	26.5	31.9	32.8	6.2	9.1	2.9	9.4	9.1
Direct taxes	6.1	5.4	4.6	5.1	12.4	2.0	−5.6	9.6	18.0
Net income from entrepreneurial activity and property	25.9	21.1	27.3	27.7	5.0	10.5	4.5	9.4	7.6
Distributed to private households and nonprofit organizations	21.0	22.2	25.0	25.1	5.5	1.6	5.3	3.9	6.7
Government[2]	0.4	−1.0	−2.4	−1.7	...	...	...	...	...
Retained profits[2]	4.4	−0.1	4.8	4.3	...	...	...	...	...
Household disposable income	**80.7**	**83.9**	**80.1**	**79.0**	**3.4**	**3.9**	**4.3**	**4.3**	**4.5**
Sources:									
Net wages and salaries	45.0	42.4	36.6	35.8	2.4	5.3	2.8	4.3	3.6
Distributed profits and property income	21.0	22.2	25.0	25.1	5.5	1.6	5.3	3.9	6.7
Net transfers	17.1	21.8	20.8	20.5	2.7	4.3	5.3	4.6	4.6
Of which:									
Transfers from governments	*16.6*	*22.0*	*21.1*	*20.7*	*2.3*	*3.8*	*5.1*	*4.7*	*3.8*
Less:									
Unrecorded payments[3]	2.4	2.5	2.3	2.5	2.2	3.7	0.8	4.1	14.8

Source: Statistisches Bundesamt, *Volkswirtschaftliche Gesamtrechnungen*.

[1] In percent.

[2] Figures fluctuate around small bases, giving rise to extreme growth rates.

[3] Includes unrecorded tax payments, social contributions of the self-employed, net casualty insurance payments, and international private transfers.

Table A3. Federal Republic of Germany: Household Income and Consumption

(Percent change from previous year)

	1982	1983	1984	1985	1986	1987	1988	1989
Real private consumption	−1.3	1.7	1.5	1.4	3.4	3.3	2.7	1.7
Real household disposable income	−2.5	−0.5	2.3	1.3	4.1	4.0	2.9	1.7
Nominal disposable income	2.6	2.8	4.7	3.4	3.9	4.3	4.3	4.5
Consumer price inflation	5.2	3.3	2.4	2.0	−0.1	0.2	1.3	2.8
Nominal interest rate[1]	9.0	7.9	7.8	6.9	5.9	5.8	6.1	7.0
Unemployment rate[2]	6.7	8.1	8.1	8.2	7.9	7.9	7.7	7.1
Personal saving ratio[3]	12.8	10.9	11.4	11.4	12.2	12.6	12.8	12.5

Sources: Deutsche Bundesbank, *Monthly Report*; and Statistisches Bundesamt, *Volkswirtschaftliche Gesamtrechnungen*.

[1] Nominal yield on outstanding public bonds with a remaining maturity of more than three years, in percent per annum.

[2] In percent of total labor force, based on microcensus data.

[3] Household saving as a percent of household disposable income, national accounts definition.

Table A4.   Federal Republic of Germany: Balance of Payments Summary

(In billions of deutsche mark)

	1985	1986	1987	1988	1989
Current account	**48.3**	**85.8**	**82.1**	**88.3**	**104.1**
Foreign trade[1]	73.4	112.6	117.7	128.0	134.6
Exports (f.o.b.)	537.2	526.4	527.4	567.7	641.0
Imports (c.i.f.)	463.8	413.7	409.6	439.6	506.5
Supplementary trade items and transit trade	−1.3	−1.5	−1.8	0.6	−3.0
Services	5.4	1.7	−5.0	−8.4	7.1
Receipts	144.3	143.6	146.6	154.5	188.7
Expenditure	138.9	141.9	151.6	162.9	181.5
Transfer payments	−29.1	−27.1	−28.9	−31.9	−34.6
Of which:					
Remittances of foreign workers	*−8.0*	*−7.5*	*−7.3*	*−7.4*	*−7.5*
Payments to the EC (net)	*−8.3*	*−8.2*	*−10.4*	*−13.0*	*−13.4*
Capital account (net capital exports: −)	**−54.6**	**−82.6**	**−38.9**	**−127.1**	**−128.2**
Long-term capital	−12.9	33.4	−23.1	−86.9	−22.7
German investment abroad	−61.7	−55.4	−62.5	−97.9	−92.2
Foreign investment in Germany	48.8	88.9	39.5	11.0	69.4
Short-term capital	−41.7	−116.0	−15.8	−40.3	−105.5
Financial institutions	−27.7	−59.0	−6.1	−20.0	−56.7
Enterprises	−14.1	−56.7	−11.0	−22.0	−44.5
Official	0.1	−0.3	1.4	1.7	−4.3
Balance of unclassifiable transactions (balancing item)	8.1	2.7	−2.0	4.1	5.2
Change in the net external assets of the Bundesbank (increase: +)[2]	1.8	6.0	41.2	−34.7	−19.0

Source: Deutsche Bundesbank, *Monthly Report, Supplement 3.*

[1] Excluding supplementary trade items.

[2] At transactions values.

Table A5. Federal Republic of Germany: Regional Breakdown of Foreign Trade[1]

	Exports (f.o.b.)				Imports (c.i.f.)				Trade Balance		
	1987	1988	1989	1989	1987	1988	1989	1989	1987	1988	1989
	(Percent change from preceding period)			*(Percent of share in total)*	*(Percent change from preceding period)*			*(Percent of share in total)*	*(In billions of deutsche mark)*		
Western industrial countries	1.8	8.1	12.5	85.6	0.1	7.2	15.0	82.7	111.7	124.0	130.2
EC countries	3.9	10.9	14.4	55.0	−0.2	5.5	13.8	51.1	62.3	80.8	94.0
Of which:											
Belgium-Luxembourg	*4.5*	*8.2*	*9.4*	*7.2*	*−0.4*	*7.0*	*12.2*	*6.9*	*9.7*	*10.9*	*11.0*
Denmark	*−8.6*	*1.0*	*7.3*	*1.9*	*0.1*	*8.0*	*11.6*	*1.8*	*3.5*	*3.0*	*2.9*
France	*2.1*	*12.0*	*18.3*	*13.1*	*0.8*	*11.7*	*13.9*	*11.9*	*16.1*	*18.2*	*23.9*
Italy	*7.4*	*12.2*	*15.8*	*9.3*	*2.9*	*2.6*	*12.4*	*8.9*	*6.8*	*11.4*	*14.6*
Netherlands	*1.4*	*6.7*	*10.6*	*8.5*	*−6.0*	*1.1*	*14.3*	*10.2*	*1.2*	*3.8*	*2.5*
United Kingdom	*4.6*	*13.4*	*12.3*	*9.3*	*−1.2*	*3.6*	*13.9*	*6.8*	*17.2*	*22.4*	*24.7*
Other European countries	1.8	6.5	10.9	18.4	1.9	7.1	13.3	15.7	34.4	36.3	38.5
Of which:											
Austria	*1.0*	*12.2*	*10.7*	*5.5*	*5.6*	*9.4*	*11.0*	*4.1*	*11.1*	*12.9*	*14.3*
Sweden	*7.4*	*5.1*	*10.2*	*2.9*	*—*	*7.7*	*19.0*	*2.5*	*5.9*	*5.9*	*5.6*
Switzerland	*3.5*	*7.2*	*10.8*	*5.9*	*2.6*	*3.6*	*8.1*	*4.2*	*13.2*	*14.8*	*16.9*
Non-European countries	−5.4	−0.1	6.5	12.2	−1.0	13.6	21.0	15.9	15.0	6.9	−2.4
Of which:											
Japan	*21.1*	*24.3*	*16.5*	*2.4*	*5.1*	*12.4*	*13.3*	*6.3*	*−14.7*	*−15.3*	*−16.9*
United States	*−9.6*	*−8.4*	*2.1*	*7.3*	*−4.7*	*13.6*	*31.5*	*7.6*	*24.3*	*16.6*	*8.4*
Developing countries (excluding OPEC)	−0.5	1.8	17.9	7.1	−1.3	12.4	13.6	9.8	−1.2	−5.4	−4.5
OPEC countries	−20.2	8.2	6.1	2.6	−16.1	−2.5	14.2	2.4	3.2	4.6	4.0
State-trading countries	−11.2	7.5	18.5	4.6	−8.0	5.1	22.9	5.0	3.5	4.3	4.2
Total[2]	0.2	7.7	13.0	100.0	−1.0	7.4	15.2	100.0	117.7	128.0	134.6

Source: Deutsche Bundesbank, *Monthly Report, Supplement 3.*

[1] Excluding supplementary trade items.

[2] Including trade with unspecified countries.

Table A6. Federal Republic of Germany: Services Account

(In billions of deutsche mark)

	1982	1983	1984	1985	1986	1987	1988	1989
Tourism	−24.4	−23.2	−23.1	−23.7	−25.4	−27.9	−28.9	−29.1
Receipts	9.7	10.8	12.2	14.0	13.7	13.8	14.9	16.3
Payments	34.1	33.9	35.4	37.7	39.0	41.7	43.8	45.4
Transportation	10.5	9.3	9.7	10.9	9.1	8.1	8.9	10.8
Investment income	−2.8	4.2	10.3	9.3	9.0	7.3	9.1	22.1
Receipts	32.2	34.5	41.6	43.8	47.2	51.7	57.8	79.3
Payments	35.1	30.3	31.3	34.5	38.2	44.3	48.7	57.2
Government payments[1]	13.5	14.8	17.7	20.3	19.6	19.2	18.0	19.6
Other	−10.4	−11.7	−9.9	−11.4	−10.6	−11.7	−15.4	−16.3
Balance on services	−13.7	−6.6	4.7	5.4	1.7	−5.0	−8.4	7.1

Source: Deutsche Bundesbank, *Monthly Report, Supplement 3*.

[1] Balance on payments among official institutions which are not included elsewhere in the balance of payments accounts; reflects mainly receipts of the German Government for deliveries of goods and services to foreign military posts in Germany.

Table A7. Federal Republic of Germany: Earnings, Employment, and Productivity

(Percent change from previous year)

	1984	1985	1986	1987	1988	1989
Labor force	0.2	0.8	1.0	0.7	0.8	0.6
Dependent employment	0.2	0.9	1.5	1.0	0.9	1.6
Unemployment (in percent of labor force)[1]	8.1	8.2	7.9	7.9	7.7	7.1
Hourly earnings[2]	2.8	3.4	4.1	3.8	3.3	3.7
Labor productivity[3]	3.0	2.0	1.8	1.9	3.1	2.7
Unit labor costs[4]	0.7	1.7	2.6	2.1	0.1	0.9

Sources: Statistisches Bundesamt, *Volkswirtschaftliche Gesamtrechnungen*; and Deutsche Bundesbank, *Monthly Report*.

[1] Unemployment in percent of the total labor force excluding the armed forces, based on microcensus data.

[2] Tariff wages and salaries on an hourly basis. Actual earnings differed owing to wage drift.

[3] Real GDP per hour worked.

[4] Based on actual earnings and thus there are discrepancies with calculations based on hourly earnings reported above.

Table A8. Federal Republic of Germany: Growth of the Main Monetary Aggregates[1]

(Period averages)[2]

	Dec. 1989 Level[3]	1985	1986	1987	1988	1989	1989[3] I	II	III	IV	1990[3] I	II	Memorandum Items Growth from 1987:IV–1988:IV	1988:IV–1989:IV
	(In billions of deutsche mark)	*(Percent change from preceding period at annual rate)*												
Central bank money stock[4]	271.7	4.6	6.4	8.1	8.2	7.3	11.3	3.7	2.6	4.7	7.3	1.8	8.4	5.5
Narrow money, M1	423.8	4.4	8.4	9.0	9.7	6.3	11.8	-2.0	4.5	4.8	4.9	0.9	9.8	4.7
Of which:														
Currency outside banks	*143.3*	*3.6*	*6.9*	*9.2*	*11.7*	*9.0*	*17.3*	*0.2*	*0.9*	*2.7*	*2.2*	*-3.0*	*13.0*	*5.0*
Demand deposits	*280.5*	*4.8*	*9.2*	*9.0*	*8.8*	*4.9*	*9.1*	*-3.1*	*6.4*	*6.0*	*6.3*	*3.0*	*8.1*	*4.5*
Broad money, M2	741.9	4.5	5.3	6.7	6.3	9.0	11.4	7.1	10.0	11.9	18.4	9.6	7.3	10.1
Of which:														
Time deposits with maturities less than four years	*318.1*	*4.7*	*1.3*	*3.6*	*1.4*	*13.3*	*10.8*	*22.1*	*18.4*	*22.5*	*38.9*	*21.2*	*3.7*	*18.4*
M3 (M2 plus savings deposits at statutory notice)	1215.0	5.1	5.7	7.1	6.4	5.6	6.1	4.4	4.0	4.0	5.1	2.8	6.7	4.7
Of which:														
Savings deposits at statutory notice	*473.1*	*5.9*	*6.3*	*7.6*	*6.4*	*0.9*	*1.5*	*-2.9*	*-2.7*	*-5.4*	*-12.8*	*-8.9*	*6.1*	*-2.4*
Monetary capital formation	1481.2	7.5	7.2	6.3	3.5	4.4	1.5	6.7	9.0	11.9	15.6	11.7	2.7	7.2
Of which:														
Savings deposits and savings bonds	*422.4*	*6.9*	*10.6*	*6.4*	*1.0*	*-1.9*	*-9.5*	*0.3*	*4.8*	*7.0*	*6.7*	*7.5*	*-0.7*	*0.5*
Time deposits with maturities as of four years or more	*492.1*	*11.3*	*11.4*	*11.2*	*12.0*	*9.5*	*10.5*	*8.1*	*7.5*	*8.5*	*9.3*	*6.7*	*11.5*	*8.6*
Bank bonds outstanding[5]	*409.7*	*4.7*	*2.7*	*0.8*	*-3.5*	*4.0*	*0.9*	*10.9*	*15.9*	*19.8*	*35.6*	*23.7*	*-4.2*	*11.7*
Bank loans outstanding to domestic nonbanks	2448.6	6.2	4.1	3.5	5.4	6.0	7.4	5.8	4.4	5.6	9.6	6.2	5.6	5.8
Public authorities	542.9	6.0	1.7	3.1	8.8	4.3	6.0	2.1	-2.0	-1.5	3.6	4.1	8.6	1.1
Private nonbanks	1905.6	6.3	4.8	3.6	4.4	6.5	7.8	6.9	6.4	7.8	11.4	6.8	4.7	7.2
Short-term[6]	368.4	4.8	-0.2	-4.8	-0.2	7.7	10.4	10.6	10.9	8.4	17.2	8.7	2.2	10.1
Long-term	1537.2	6.8	6.3	6.0	5.5	6.2	7.2	6.1	5.3	7.6	10.0	6.4	5.3	6.5

Source: Deutsche Bundesbank, *Monthly Report*, and *Monthly Report, Supplement 4.*

[1] From December 1985, the published data are not comparable with earlier data because of extended coverage; to construct this table, the pre-December and post-December 1985 series have been spliced together based on the December 1985 values under the old and new coverage.
[2] For series other than central bank money and the quarterly data for M3, data are averages of end-of-month levels.
[3] Seasonally adjusted.
[4] Currency held by nonbanks plus minimum reserve requirements on domestic bank liabilities (at constant reserve ratios of January 1974).
[5] Other than bank holdings.
[6] Up to one year.

Table A9. Federal Republic of Germany: Interest Rates

(In percent a year)

| | Bundesbank Rates[1] | | | Money Market Rate[2] | Government Bond Yields[2] | | Memorandum Items[2] | |
| | | | | | | | Eurodollar Three-month LIBOR | U.S. Government 10-year bonds |
	Discount rate	Securities repurchase rate[3]	Lombard rate[4]	Three-month rate	Average yield[5]	Long-term bonds[6]		
1979 December	6.0	. . .[7]	7.0	9.6	7.9	7.9	14.7	10.4
1980 December	7.5	9.5	9.0	10.2	8.9	8.8	19.6	12.8
1981 December	7.5	10.3	10.5	10.8	9.7	9.7	13.4	13.7
1982 December	5.0	5.9	6.0	6.6	7.9	8.0	9.6	10.5
1983 December	4.0	6.0	5.5	6.5	8.2	8.4	10.2	11.8
1984 December	4.5	5.5	5.5	5.8	7.0	7.2	9.1	11.5
1985 December	4.0	4.6	5.5	4.8	6.5	6.6	8.1	9.3
1986 December	3.5	4.6	5.5	4.8	5.9	6.1	6.4	7.1
1987 December	2.5	3.3	4.5	3.7	6.0	6.5	8.0	9.0
1988 December	3.5	4.8	5.5	5.3	6.3	6.5	9.4	9.1
1989 January	4.0	5.1	6.0	5.7	6.7	6.5	9.3	9.1
February	4.0	5.8	6.0	6.4	6.9	6.9	9.7	9.2
March	4.0	6.0	6.0	6.6	6.9	7.0	8.7	9.4
April	4.5	5.9	6.5	6.4	6.9	6.9	10.1	9.2
May	4.5	6.3	6.5	7.0	7.1	7.0	9.7	8.7
June	5.0	6.6	7.0	7.0	6.9	6.8	9.3	8.3
July	5.0	6.6	7.0	7.0	6.8	6.7	9.0	8.0
August	5.0	6.7	7.0	7.0	6.8	6.8	8.9	8.1
September	5.0	6.9	7.0	7.4	7.1	7.0	8.9	8.2
October	6.0	7.4	8.0	8.1	7.3	7.1	8.7	8.0
November	6.0	7.5	8.0	8.2	7.6	7.4	8.5	7.9
December	6.0	7.4	8.0	8.1	7.6	7.3	8.4	7.8
1990 January	6.0	7.8	8.0	8.3	7.9	7.7	8.3	8.2
February	6.0	7.8	8.0	8.3	8.7	8.5	8.4	8.5
March	6.0	7.9	8.0	8.4	8.9	8.8	8.5	8.6
April	6.0	7.8	8.0	8.2	8.9	8.7	8.6	8.8
May	6.0	7.8	8.0	8.3	8.9	8.7	8.5	8.8
June	6.0	7.8	8.0	8.3	9.0	8.8	8.4	8.5
July	6.0	7.9	8.0	8.3	8.7	8.6	8.2	8.5
August	6.0	8.0	8.0	8.5	9.0	8.9	8.1	8.8
September	6.0	8.0	8.0	8.5	9.1	9.1	8.2	8.9
Memorandum items[8]								
1986 average	3.6	4.4	5.5	4.6	5.9	6.1	6.9	7.7
1987 average	3.0	3.7	4.9	4.0	5.8	6.2	7.2	8.4
1988 average	3.0	3.9	4.8	4.3	6.1	6.5	8.0	8.9
1989 average	4.9	6.6	6.9	7.1	7.0	7.0	9.3	8.5

Sources: Deutsche Bundesbank, *Monthly Report*, and *Monthly Report, Supplement 2*; and International Monetary Fund, Data Fund.

[1] End of period for the discount rate and the Lombard rate; period average for the rate on securities repurchase transactions.
[2] Period average. After June 1990, reflects a change in the definition of the series.
[3] Unweighted average of rates during the period; for American style tenders, calculated on the basis of the low rate accepted.
[4] Interest rate on special Lombard loans during the suspension of the general Lombard facility, from February 20, 1981 to May 6, 1982.
[5] Average yield on public authority bonds with remaining maturities of three years or more.
[6] Average yield on public authority bonds with remaining maturities of nine–ten years.
[7] No transactions.
[8] Averages of end-of-month rates for the discount rate and the Lombard rate.

Table A10. Federal Republic of Germany: Exchange Rates

(Percent change from end of previous period)[1]

	1985	1986	1987	1988	1989	1989 I	1989 II	1989 III	1989 IV	1990 I	1990 II	1990 III	Memorandum Items 1989[2]	Memorandum Items Dec. 1989–Sept. 1990
													(Percent change)	
Effective exchange rates														
Nominal														
All countries[3]	5.5	9.2	3.5	−2.8	3.8	−1.1	−0.3	0.2	5.0	0.5	−0.7	0.6	−0.9	0.4
EMS[4]	2.9	3.7	2.9	0.3	0.3	−0.5	−0.2	−0.5	1.5	−0.9	−0.6	0.4	−0.6	−1.1
Real														
All countries (ULC based)[5]	7.7	9.6	5.8	−1.0	3.6	−1.2	0.4	−0.7	5.6	2.3	0.4	−0.8	−0.2	1.8
All countries (CPI based)[6]	2.9	5.7	1.6	−4.5	2.1	−1.2	−0.9	−0.1	4.4	−0.2	−1.3	0.3	−2.4	−1.2
Bilateral exchange rates[7]														
U.S. dollar	23.3	26.3	21.9	−7.0	0.8	−5.9	−5.8	1.5	12.1	2.1	1.2	7.3	−6.7	10.9
French franc	−0.2	7.3	3.3	0.7	—	−0.8	0.1	−0.5	1.2	−1.2	−0.3	−0.4	—	−2.0
Pound sterling	1.2	27.3	−4.3	−6.8	15.4	0.2	4.1	0.3	10.4	0.3	−3.8	−2.4	1.6	−5.9
Japanese yen	1.0	1.1	−3.6	−10.5	17.3	−0.7	4.1	2.2	10.9	8.9	1.7	−3.2	0.5	7.2

Sources: Deutsche Bundesbank, *Monthly Report*; and International Monetary Fund, Data Fund.

[1] Unless otherwise noted; based on monthly average data. Positive figures indicate appreciation of the deutsche mark.
[2] Annual average percent change.
[3] Based on exchange rates vis-à-vis 16 other industrial countries.
[4] As calculated by Bundesbank for countries participating in the ERM. Calculations for 1989 and 1990 include Spain, which joined the ERM on June 19, 1989. Calculations for 1985–88 exclude Spain.
[5] Based on normalized unit labor costs (ULC) in manufacturing and exchange rates vis-à-vis 16 other industrial countries.
[6] The consumer price based index uses a wider range of countries in its weighting scheme—35 other countries, compared with 16 other countries used for the unit labor cost based calculation.
[7] Units of foreign currency per deutsche mark.

Table A11. Federal Republic of Germany: Long-Term Capital in the Balance of Payments Accounts[1]

(In billions of deutsche mark)

	1983	1984	1985	1986	1987	1988	1989	1989 I	1989 II	1989 III	1989 IV	1990 I	1990 II
German investment abroad	**−36.5**	**−45.0**	**−61.7**	**−55.4**	**−62.5**	**−97.9**	**−92.2**	**−31.8**	**−15.7**	**−25.5**	**−19.2**	**−37.7**	**−21.6**
Direct investment	−8.1	−12.5	−14.1	−20.9	−16.4	−19.8	−25.3	−4.9	−5.2	−5.8	−9.4	−9.5	−6.7
Advances and loans of enterprises	−0.8	−1.7	0.3	0.2	−0.8	−0.0	−4.3	−3.3	−0.3	−0.4	−0.3	−1.9	−0.7
Portfolio investment	−10.4	−15.7	−31.5	−21.3	−24.9	−72.9	−49.8	−23.0	−6.9	−16.5	−3.4	−8.9	−8.1
Of which:													
Foreign currency bonds	*−5.3*	*−14.0*	*−20.2*	*−9.5*	*−21.5*	*−42.4*	*−26.2*	*−10.9*	*−1.9*	*−12.0*	*−1.4*	*−1.6*	*−3.2*
Deutsche mark bonds	*−0.5*	*−1.7*	*−7.2*	*−6.9*	*−3.3*	*−12.2*	*−14.3*	*−6.6*	*−2.6*	*−2.6*	*−2.5*	*−7.9*	*−4.0*
Equities	*−4.6*	*—*	*−4.1*	*−4.9*	*−0.1*	*−18.2*	*−9.3*	*−5.4*	*−2.4*	*−2.0*	*0.5*	*0.6*	*−1.0*
Advances and loan of banks	−8.4	−6.8	−8.4	−6.3	−13.8	2.2	−5.2	0.8	−1.5	−0.9	−3.6	−15.1	−4.4
Official[2]	−6.8	−6.9	−6.3	−5.3	−5.0	−5.6	−5.6	−0.9	−1.4	−1.4	−2.0	−1.8	−1.1
Real estate investment	−1.3	−1.0	−1.0	−1.0	−1.0	−1.2	−1.2	−0.3	−0.3	−0.3	−0.3	−0.3	−0.3
Other	−0.8	−0.4	−0.7	−0.7	−0.6	−0.7	−0.8	−0.2	−0.2	−0.3	−0.1	−0.3	−0.3
Foreign investment in Germany	**29.5**	**25.2**	**48.8**	**88.9**	**39.5**	**11.0**	**69.4**	**−0.8**	**16.2**	**20.0**	**34.1**	**2.9**	**7.4**
Direct investment	4.5	1.6	1.7	2.6	3.4	2.4	11.2	2.9	1.5	1.8	5.0	0.3	3.3
Advances and loans of enterprise	1.3	0.5	−0.0	0.7	2.8	1.9	−0.4	−0.0	0.8	−0.4	−0.8	0.6	3.8
Portfolio investment	25.5	21.7	36.3	69.1	21.2	−3.2	40.6	−7.4	8.3	14.2	25.5	−4.5	−2.4
Of which:													
Bonds	*10.8*	*13.8*	*31.5*	*59.1*	*35.0*	*2.1*	*22.5*	*−7.6*	*8.4*	*9.7*	*12.0*	*−11.4*	*2.9*
Official borrowers' note	*11.9*	*4.3*	*−2.0*	*−5.0*	*−12.0*	*−10.9*	*−5.2*	*−2.3*	*−1.7*	*−1.5*	*0.2*	*−0.5*	*−0.4*
Advances and loans to banks	−1.6	1.5	10.9	16.6	12.1	10.1	18.2	3.8	5.6	4.4	4.4	6.7	2.6
Other	−0.2	−0.0	−0.1	−0.1	−0.1	−0.2	−0.1	−0.0	−0.0	−0.0	−0.1	−0.1	−0.1
Balance on long term capital account	**−7.0**	**−19.8**	**−12.9**	**33.4**	**−23.1**	**−86.9**	**−22.7**	**−32.6**	**0.5**	**−5.6**	**14.9**	**−34.7**	**−14.2**

Source: Deutsche Bundesbank, *Monthly Report, Supplement 3.*

[1] Outflows of funds have a negative sign.

[2] Includes share contributions to international organizations.

Table A12. Federal Republic of Germany: Territorial Authorities' Finances[1]

(Administrative basis)

	1989 Actual	1990 Estimate[2]	1987	1988	1989	1990 Estimate[2]
	(In billions of deutsche mark)		(Percent change from preceding period)			
Total expenditure	**699.6**	**749.5**	**3.6**	**3.0**	**4.3**	**7.1**
Current expenditure	593.7	636.8	4.0	3.6	3.9	7.3
Wages and salaries	219.6	231.0	4.3	2.5	2.4	5.2
Goods	111.2	116.6	2.7	1.2	4.7	4.8
Interest	61.0	65.9	1.4	3.2	1.1	7.5
Current transfers	201.9	223.6	5.3	6.4	6.0	10.7
Capital expenditure	105.9	112.7	1.6	−0.8	6.9	6.4
Investment	59.5	64.3	2.8	0.1	7.7	8.0
Capital transfers	25.2	25.7	−0.9	−6.1	13.7	1.8
Loans	21.1	22.7	1.4	2.9	−2.3	7.6
Total revenue	**673.0**	**689.4**	**2.4**	**3.0**	**8.8**	**2.4**
Current revenue	652.5	669.9	2.1	3.0	9.5	2.7
Taxes	535.1	545.2	3.5	4.3	9.6	1.9
Other	117.4	124.7	−3.4	−2.4	8.9	6.2
Capital revenue	20.5	19.5	10.7	3.7	−8.5	−4.9
Financial balance	**−26.6**	**−60.1**	...	...	...	...
(In percent of GNP)	−1.2	−2.4	−2.5	−2.5	−1.2	−2.4
Memorandum items:						
Financial balance, including in 1990 GDR-related items in the third supplementary budget of the Federal Government	−26.6	−84.3	...	...	...	...
(In percent of GNP)	−1.2	−3.5	−2.5	−2.5	−1.2	−3.5
Expenditure, excluding in 1990 GDR-related items in the first and second supplementary budgets of the Federal Government[3]	699.6	740.7	3.6	3.0	4.3	5.9

Sources: Bundesministerium der Finanzen; and authors' estimates of September 1990.

[1] Including the Federal Government, the Länder, the municipalities, the Burden Equalization Fund, the European Recovery Program Fund, and the European Community's accounts.

[2] Excludes the German Unity Fund but includes the contribution of the Federal Government to the Fund (DM 2 billion in 1990). Following the official presentation, the accounts for west Germany include GDR-related expenditure in the first and second supplementary budgets of the Federal Government (DM 8.8 billion including the contribution to the German Unity Fund) but exclude GDR-related items in the third federal supplementary budget. The latter gave rise to additional borrowing of DM 24.2 billion, which is incorporated in an adjusted balance reported as a memorandum item.

[3] See Table 3 in the text for details.

Table A13. Federal Republic of Germany: Territorial Authorities—Tax Revenue[1]

(Cash basis)

	1970	1975	1980	1985	1989	1989	1986	1987	1988	1989
						(In billions of DM)				
		(In percent of total)					*(Percent change over preceding period)*			
Total tax revenue	**100.0**	**100.0**	**100.0**	**100.0**	**100.0**	**535.5**	**3.5**	**3.6**	**4.1**	**9.7**
By type of tax										
Personal income tax	34.5	41.9	41.8	41.7	43.2	231.3	4.3	6.6	3.3	10.4
Corporation tax	5.7	4.2	5.8	7.3	6.4	34.2	1.5	−15.5	9.9	13.9
Wealth tax	1.9	1.4	1.3	1.0	1.1	5.8	2.5	23.3	2.4	4.0
Trade tax[2]	7.0	7.4	7.4	7.0	6.9	36.7	4.0	−1.7	9.6	6.5
Value-added tax[3]	24.7	22.3	25.6	25.1	24.6	131.5	1.2	6.9	3.8	6.6
Petroleum tax	7.5	7.1	5.8	5.6	6.2	33.0	4.6	1.9	3.4	21.9
Tobacco tax	4.2	3.7	3.1	3.3	2.9	15.5	0.2	0.2	0.3	6.6
Motor vehicle tax	2.5	2.2	1.8	1.7	1.7	9.2	27.3	−10.6	−2.3	12.2
Other taxes	12.1	9.9	7.3	7.3	7.2	38.5	3.6	3.2	4.9	8.0
By level of government										
Federal Government[4]	55.2	50.1	48.7	47.6	46.6	249.8	1.3	3.9	1.8	12.2
Länder[5]	32.7	33.7	34.4	34.9	35.3	189.2	5.0	4.0	3.9	9.4
Municipalities[6]	11.8	13.7	14.0	14.1	13.7	73.6	3.8	1.6	6.2	6.9
European Community[7]	—	2.5	2.9	3.5	4.3	22.8	18.2	2.1	29.2	−3.7
Memorandum item:										
Tax revenue *(In percent of GNP)*	22.8	23.5	24.6	23.7	23.7	23.7	23.3	23.2	23.0	23.7

Sources: Deutsche Bundesbank, *Monthly Report*; and Bundesministerium der Finanzen.

[1] Data in this table are calculated on a cash basis and may differ from data reported in Table A12, which are on an administrative basis.

[2] Tax based on capital stock of businesses and on return to capital.

[3] Including turnover tax on imports.

[4] Including Burden Equalization Fund.

[5] Excluding municipal taxes in Berlin, Bremen, and Hamburg.

[6] Including municipal taxes in Berlin, Bremen, and Hamburg.

[7] The EC's share of tax collections.

Table A14. Federal Republic of Germany: General Government—Revenue and Expenditure

(National accounts basis)

	1989 Actual	1990 Estimate[1]	1987	1988	1989	1990 Estimate[1]
	(In billions of deutsche mark)		*(Percent change from preceding period)*			
Total expenditure	**1,015.6**	**1,099.0**	**4.1**	**4.3**	**2.5**	**8.2**
Expenditures on goods and services	471.5	497.3	3.7	3.6	2.2	5.5
Public consumption	419.0	439.9	3.9	3.8	1.5	5.0
Public investment	52.5	57.4	2.4	1.8	7.5	9.2
Transfer payments	544.1	601.7	4.5	5.0	2.7	10.6
Social benefits	358.3	377.6	4.9	4.5	4.5	5.4
Subsidies	45.4	45.6	8.3	6.5	−4.7	0.5
Interest	60.4	63.2	1.0	3.6	0.9	4.6
Other	80.0	115.3	2.9	6.8	0.9	44.1
Total revenue	**1,021.0**	**1,053.3**	**2.8**	**3.7**	**7.9**	**3.2**
Tax revenue	560.0	566.5	3.9	4.3	9.2	1.2
Indirect taxes	278.2	296.5	3.9	4.7	8.1	6.6
Direct taxes	281.8	270.0	3.8	3.9	10.3	−4.2
Social security contributions	383.4	406.4	3.9	4.6	4.6	6.0
Other revenue	77.6	80.4	−8.3	−4.7	16.5	3.6
			(In percent of GNP)			
Financial balance	**5.5**	**−45.7**	**−1.9**	**−2.1**	**0.2**	**−1.9**
Of which:						
Territorial authorities	*−10.9*	*−43.7*	*−2.2*	*−2.2*	*−0.5*	*−1.8*
Social security system	*16.3*	*18.0*	*0.3*	*0.1*	*0.7*	*0.7*
German Unity Fund	*. . .*	*−20.0*	*. . .*	*. . .*	*. . .*	*−0.8*
Memorandum items:						
Financial balance, including in 1990 GDR-related items in the third supplementary budget of the Federal Government	5.5	−69.9	−1.9	−2.1	0.2	−2.9
			(Percent change from preceding period)			
Expenditure, excluding in 1990 GDR-related items in the first and second supplementary budgets[2]	1,015.6	1,090.2	4.1	4.3	2.5	7.3

Sources: Bundesministerium der Finanzen; and authors' estimates of September 1990.

[1] Including the German Unity Fund. See footnote 2 of Table A12 for the coverage of data for the territorial authorities.

[2] See Table 3 in the text.

Table A15. Federal Republic of Germany: Selected Indicators of the Size of the General Government[1]

(In percent of GNP)

	1950	1955	1960	1965	1970	1975	1980	1981	1982	1983	1984	1985	1986	1987	1988	1989
Revenue	31.8	35.0	35.9	36.5	39.3	43.9	45.7	45.9	46.6	46.1	46.1	46.3	45.6	45.2	44.6	45.2
Of which:																
Indirect taxes	12.9	14.3	13.8	13.6	13.2	12.7	13.0	12.8	12.6	12.8	12.8	12.5	12.1	12.2	12.1	12.3
Direct taxes	8.1	8.7	9.2	10.0	10.8	12.0	12.6	12.2	12.1	11.9	12.0	12.5	12.2	12.2	12.0	12.5
Social security																
* contributions*	8.5	8.6	10.3	10.6	12.6	16.3	16.7	17.4	17.8	17.3	17.2	17.4	17.3	17.4	17.3	17.0
Other	2.2	3.3	2.6	2.4	2.8	2.9	3.3	3.5	4.0	4.1	4.0	4.0	3.9	3.5	3.1	3.4
Expenditure	31.1	30.3	32.9	37.2	39.1	49.5	48.6	49.6	49.8	48.6	48.0	47.5	46.9	47.1	46.7	44.9
Of which:																
Public consumption	10.3	10.5	13.3	15.2	15.8	20.4	20.1	20.6	20.4	20.0	19.8	19.8	19.7	19.7	19.4	18.5
Public gross investment	2.1	2.7	3.2	4.6	4.6	3.9	3.6	3.2	2.8	2.5	2.4	2.3	2.4	2.4	2.3	2.3
Interest payments	0.6	0.8	0.7	0.7	1.0	1.4	1.9	2.3	2.8	3.0	3.0	3.0	2.9	2.9	2.8	2.7
Transfer payments	10.2	16.3	15.6	16.7	17.7	23.8	23.1	23.5	23.8	23.1	22.8	22.3	21.9	22.1	22.1	21.4
Of which:																
Social transfers	11.8	11.1	12.5	12.8	13.0	17.9	16.8	17.5	18.0	17.3	16.7	16.3	16.1	16.3	16.1	15.8
Subsidies	0.5	0.2	0.8	1.3	1.7	2.0	2.1	1.9	1.8	1.9	2.0	2.1	2.1	2.2	2.2	2.0
Other current																
* transfers*	4.5	4.1	0.7	0.9	1.1	1.6	2.0	2.0	2.0	2.1	2.2	2.1	2.1	2.1	2.2	2.1
Capital transfers	1.3	0.9	1.6	1.7	1.9	2.2	2.2	2.0	2.0	1.9	1.9	1.8	1.6	1.6	1.5	1.4
Financial balance	0.6	4.7	3.0	−0.6	0.2	−5.6	−2.9	−3.7	−3.3	−2.5	−1.9	−1.1	−1.3	−1.9	−2.1	0.2
Current receipts	...	...	35.1	35.8	38.4	42.7	44.6	44.8	45.5	45.0	45.0	45.3	44.6	44.2	43.5	44.2
Current expenditures	...	...	28.1	30.9	32.6	43.3	42.8	44.3	45.0	44.2	43.7	43.4	42.9	43.2	42.9	41.2
Saving	3.1	7.4	7.0	4.9	5.8	−0.6	1.8	0.5	0.4	0.7	1.3	2.0	1.7	1.1	0.7	3.0

Sources: Bundesministerium der Finanzen; and Statistisches Bundesamt, *Volkswirtschaftliche Gesamtrechnungen.*

[1] National accounts basis. The general government comprises the Federal Government, the Länder governments, municipalities, the social security system, the Burden Equalization Fund, the European Recovery Program Fund, and the European Community's accounts.

Table A16.   Federal Republic of Germany: Financial Implications of Tax Reform

(In billions of deutsche mark)

	1986	1988	1990	1986–90	*(In percent of total gross tax reduction)*
Reduction in taxes due to:					
Changes in tax rate schedule	5.7	12.9	31.9	50.5	79.8
Basic deduction	2.1	1.4	5.9	9.4	14.9
Entry rate	. . .	. . .	6.2	6.2	9.8
Reduction of progressivity	3.6	11.5	18.7	33.8	53.4
Top rate	. . .	. . .	1.1	1.1	1.7
Changes in family allowances	5.2	0.3	2.4	7.9	12.5
Child allowance	4.8	. . .	1.8	6.6	10.5
Other family deductions	0.4	0.3	0.4	1.1	1.7
Job promotion in private households	. . .	. . .	0.2	0.2	0.3
Other measures	. . .	0.5	4.4	4.9	7.7
Special depreciation allowances for small and medium-sized companies	. . .	0.5	. . .	0.5	0.8
Higher special deductions	. . .	. . .	0.6	0.6	0.9
Lower corporate tax rate	. . .	. . .	2.5	2.5	4.0
Doubling of savings deduction	. . .	. . .	0.6	0.6	0.9
Higher depreciation allowances for rental properties	. . .	. . .	0.5	0.5	0.8
Other	. . .	. . .	0.2	0.2	0.3
Total gross tax reduction	10.9	13.7	38.7	63.3	100.0
Reduction in tax exemptions	. . .	. . .	14.0	14.0	. . .
Total net tax reduction	10.9	13.7	24.7	49.3	. . .

Source: Bundesministerium für Wirtschaft, *Aktuelle Beiträge zur Wirtschafts- und Finanzpolitik*, No. 4/1990 (January 10, 1990).

Table A17.   Federal Republic of Germany: Subsidies[1]

(In billions of deutsche mark)

	1970	1975	1980	1985	1986	1987	1988	1989[2]
Federal Government								
Payments	7.8	10.1	12.5	11.9	12.4	12.4	12.3	14.5
Preferential								
tax treatment	6.2	9.7	12.1	15.7	15.7	15.9	16.9	16.9
Total	14.0	19.8	24.6	27.6	28.1	28.3	29.2	31.4
(In percent of GNP)	2.1	1.9	1.7	1.5	1.4	1.4	1.4	1.4
Länder and municipalities								
Payments[3]	6.8	8.3	13.1	13.1[4]	11.8	12.4	12.1	12.9
Preferential tax								
treatment	6.6	11.7	14.2	18.4	18.5	19.2	20.5	21.1
Total	13.4	20.0	27.3	31.5	30.3	31.6	32.6	34.0
(In percent of GNP)	2.0	1.9	1.8	1.7	1.6	1.6	1.5	1.5
ERP payments[5]	1.1	1.3	2.7	2.9	3.2	3.1	3.5	3.7
EC payments	2.9	2.2	6.2	8.0	9.4	8.3	10.2	10.5
Total subsidies	31.4	43.3	60.8	70.0	71.0	71.3	75.5	79.6
(In percent of GNP)	4.6	4.2	4.1	3.8	3.7	3.5	3.6	3.5

Sources: Bundesministerium der Finanzen; and authors' estimates.

[1] In the definition of the Government's biannual subsidy report; excluding rent subsidies for low-income households.

[2] Subsidy payments according to budgets.

[3] Data for municipalities are estimates.

[4] In 1985, DM 0.8 billion in subsidies for housing were permanently shifted from the Länder to the Federal Government.

[5] Loan subsidies, mainly to small and medium-sized enterprises, related to lending by the European Recovery Program Fund.

Table A18. Federal Republic of Germany: Fiscal Assistance and Tax Relief of the Federal Government[1]

(In billions of deutsche mark)

	1970	1975	1980	1985	1986	1987	1988	1989
Agriculture and forestry[2]	4.8	4.2	3.7	4.7	4.9	4.9	5.2	5.3
(*In percent of value added*)	21.8	14.7	12.1	14.7	14.7	16.4	16.1	14.9
Enterprises (excluding transport)	3.7	5.6	9.2	11.1	11.0	12.0	13.5	15.1
(*In percent of value added*)	1.3	1.4	1.7	1.7	1.6	1.7	1.8	2.0
Of which:								
Mining	*0.5*	*1.0*	*2.6*	*1.6*	*2.0*	*3.0*	*3.2*	*3.9*
Energy and raw materials	—	*0.4*	*0.3*	*0.4*	*0.4*	*0.3*	*0.2*	*0.3*
Technology and innovation	*0.2*	*0.1*	*0.5*	*0.9*	*1.0*	*0.8*	*0.7*	*0.6*
Sectoral aid	*0.2*	*0.4*	*0.7*	*1.3*	*0.6*	*0.5*	*1.0*	*1.7*
Shipbuilding	—	*0.1*	*0.3*	*0.1*	*0.1*	*0.1*	*0.3*	. . .
Aircraft	*0.2*	*0.3*	*0.4*	*0.4*	*0.4*	*0.4*	*0.8*	. . .
Steel	—	—	—	*0.7*	*0.1*	—	—	. . .
Regional measures	2.1	3.0	4.2	5.4	5.7	5.8	6.4	6.6
Other measures	0.8	0.7	0.8	1.5	1.4	1.6	1.9	2.0
Transport	0.9	1.4	2.5	1.7	1.7	1.7	1.7	1.6
(*In percent of value added*)	2.4	2.3	2.9	1.6	1.5	1.5	1.4	1.3
Construction[3]	1.3	2.7	3.9	5.3	5.3	5.3	5.0	5.1
(*In percent of value added*)	2.5	4.2	3.9	5.6	5.4	5.2	4.5	4.3
Saving and capital formation	2.7	5.1	4.0	3.3	3.1	2.8	2.3	2.7
(*In percent of business sector value added*)	0.5	0.6	0.3	0.2	0.2	0.2	0.1	0.1
Other	0.6	0.9	1.5	1.6	2.0	1.5	1.6	1.4
Total	14.0	19.8	24.6	27.6	28.1	28.3	29.2	31.4
(*In percent of business sector value added*)	2.4	2.3	2.0	1.8	1.7	1.7	1.6	1.7
Memorandum item:								
EC payments for agricultural price support	2.9	2.2	6.2	8.1	9.5	8.4	10.2	. . .
(*In percent of value added*)	13.1	7.6	20.5	25.1	28.3	28.0	31.7	. . .

Source: Bundesministerium der Finanzen; and authors' estimates.

[1] In the definition of the Government's biannual subsidy report.

[2] Including the effect of changes in the value-added tax for inputs in agriculture.

[3] In 1985, DM 0.8 billion in subsidies for housing were permanently shifted from the Länder to the Federal Government; excluding rent subsidies for low-income households.

Table A19.   Comparison of Subsidies in the European Community, 1981–86, Average

(In percent of value added)

	Belgium	Denmark	France	Federal Republic of Germany	Greece[1]	Ireland	Italy	Luxembourg	Netherlands	United Kingdom	EC-10
Agriculture	7.3	8.0	12.1	9.8	...	13.2	8.6	12.0	7.2	14.1	...
Manufacturing	6.4	2.8	4.9	3.0	12.9	12.9	16.7	7.3	4.1	3.8	6.2
Of which:											
Steel	*40.4*	*18.0*	*58.3*	*8.6*	...	*107.2*	*71.4*	*14.6*	*4.3*	*57.6*	...
Shipbuilding	*27.7*	*33.8*	*56.6*	*12.3*	...	...	*34.2*	—	*10.7*	*21.6*	...
Railways	70.0	15.0	38.0	37.0	...	...	49.0	181.0	22.0	18.0	...
Total											
(In percent of GDP)	4.1	1.3	2.7	2.5	2.5	5.3	5.7	6.0	1.5	1.8	3.0
ECU per employee	1,113	353	792	761	278	1,036	1,357	1,562	444	396	771

Source: European Community, quoted in Bundesministerium der Finanzen, *Zwölfter Subventionsbericht*, 1989, pp. 54–55.
[1] Estimated.

Table A20.   International Comparison of Subsidies, 1979–87[1]

(In percent of GDP)

	1979	1980	1981	1982	1983	1984	1985	1986	1987[2]
Belgium	1.7	1.4	1.5	1.4	1.4	1.5	1.4	1.4	1.4
Germany	2.2	2.1	1.9	1.8	1.9	2.1	2.1	2.1	2.2
Denmark	3.2	3.2	3.0	3.2	3.3	3.3	3.0	2.9	3.0
France	2.0	1.9	2.2	2.2	2.1	2.4	2.3	2.3	2.4
United Kingdom	2.3	2.5	2.6	2.1	2.1	2.4	2.0	1.6	1.6
Italy	2.6	2.4	2.5	3.0	2.5	2.7	2.8	3.0	2.6
Japan	1.3	1.5	1.5	1.4	1.4	1.3	1.1	1.1	1.1
Canada	2.0	2.7	2.7	2.5	2.5	2.8	2.4	2.0	2.3
Netherlands	1.3	1.5	1.6	1.7	1.8	1.9	1.9	1.8	1.8
Norway	7.0	7.0	6.7	6.5	6.1	5.7	5.4	5.8	5.7
Austria	2.9	3.0	3.0	3.0	3.0	2.8	2.9	3.1	3.0
Sweden	4.3	4.3	4.7	5.0	5.2	5.0	4.9	4.8	4.8
Switzerland	1.4	1.4	1.2	1.3	1.4	1.4	1.4	1.4	1.4
United States	0.4	0.4	0.4	0.5	0.7	0.6	0.6	0.6	0.6

Source: Organization for Economic Cooperation and Development, quoted in Bundesministerium der Finanzen, *Zwölfter Subventionsbericht*, 1989, p. 18.
[1] National accounts basis; general government.
[2] Partly estimated.

III

German Democratic Republic

Background and Plans for Reform

Thomas Mayer and Günther Thumann

Political Situation

East Germans had been disenchanted with their country's economic and political system for many years, but opposition was suppressed. Following major political changes in the U.S.S.R. and reforms in Poland and Hungary, opposition in the German Democratic Republic (GDR) came into the open during 1989. A sizable number of GDR citizens voted with their feet, that is, they emigrated to western Germany; many of those who stayed held mass demonstrations.[1] In October 1989, under the pressure of these developments and lacking support from the U.S.S.R., the Secretary General of the Socialist Unity Party (SED) and chief of state Erich Honecker resigned. In an attempt to defuse the crisis, the borders to the west were opened on November 9, paving the way for a massive wave of emigration.[2]

After the opening of the border, the pace of events quickened. In the GDR, a new government was constituted in mid-November with reform-communist Hans Modrow as prime minister while, later in the month, Chancellor Kohl proposed a ten-point plan for eventual unification of the two parts of Germany (see Box 1). Although it initially met considerable skepticism from both the GDR Government and opposition groups, Kohl's plan—and the idea of unification—gained popularity in the GDR after revelations of widespread corruption among the former leadership and the subsequent resignation of party chief Krenz together with the Politburo and Central Committee of the SED in early December. The Modrow Government was not affected by this shakeup, but serious difficulties arose in early January 1990 when it was revealed that Prime Minister Modrow had retained about three fourths of the state security forces (*Stasi*), despite promises that he would disband

the organization and establish a new state security agency before the elections scheduled for May. Toward the end of January, the political and economic situation became more fragile. Emigration was running at a daily rate of 1,500 to 3,000 people, output was declining, and government authority was vanishing. In order to avoid political and economic collapse, Modrow broadened his government by including eight representatives of the major opposition groups and advanced the date of the elections from May 6 to March 18.[3]

With the political and economic situation in the GDR deteriorating rapidly, the Government of the FRG decided in early February to offer economic and monetary union between the two German economies at a much earlier stage than originally envisaged in the ten-point plan. The run-up to the March parliamentary elections was heavily influenced by the debate on this offer. Although all the parties were in favor, there were considerable differences about the speed with which economic and monetary union should be achieved. In contrast to the other parties, the conservative Alliance for Germany (consisting of the CDU—one of the old block parties—as well as the newly founded German Social Union and Democratic Awakening) favored a quick path. The election victory of the CDU, which had received large-scale support from its sister party in the FRG, was seen as a clear endorsement by the GDR electorate of early adoption of the FRG's offer. And, indeed, shortly after the formation of a new government in mid-April with CDU chairman Lothar de Maizière as Prime Minister, agreement was reached with the Bonn Government on the basic conditions for German

---

[1] A chronology of recent events is provided in Box 1.

[2] See Chart 1 in Chapter II and the accompanying text.

[3] The enlarged cabinet consisted of 16 communist party members; 11 members of the so-called block parties (the previously existing parties, i.e., the Christian Democrats (CDU), the Liberal Democrats (LPDP), the National Democrats (NPDP), and the Farmers' Party); and 8 new ministers without portfolio from eight newly formed opposition groups, including the Social Democratic Party, the Democratic Awakening, and the New Forum.

Box 1.   A Chronology of the Dissolution of the German Democratic Republic

1989

Phase I—The Dictatorship Comes to an End

August–September: Large numbers of GDR citizens occupy FRG embassies in several Eastern European countries in order to obtain permission from the GDR Government for emigration.

September 10: Hungary opens its border with Austria to GDR citizens, suspending a 1968 agreement with the GDR Government that required Eastern European countries to block travel of GDR citizens to the West.

September 11–14: More than 13,000 GDR citizens leave Hungary en route to the FRG via Austria—the largest exodus from the GDR to the West since the Berlin wall was built in 1961. The GDR closes its border with Hungary.

September 30: With permission from the GDR Government, more than 17,000 refugees from the GDR emigrate to the FRG via Czechoslovakia and Poland.

October 3: The GDR closes its border with Czechoslovakia.

October 7: Fortieth anniversary of the founding of the GDR. Soviet President Gorbachev visits East Berlin and draws cheers from demonstrators.

October 9: Seventy thousand people demonstrate in Leipzig. General Secretary Honecker orders the demonstration to be stopped, if necessary by force, but security forces do not intervene.

October 16: About 100,000 people demonstrate in Leipzig, the largest unauthorized demonstration in the GDR since 1953.

October 18: Erich Honecker is replaced by Egon Krenz as General Secretary of the ruling SED.

October 24: Egon Krenz is elected Chairman of the State Council (*Staatsrat*), the second governing body of the GDR.

November 7: The Council of Ministers (*Ministerrat*), the de facto GDR Government, resigns.

November 9: Borders with the FRG open for all GDR citizens. After 167,000 emigrants in January–October 1989, another 177,000 emigrate to the FRG in November–December, bringing the total for the year to 344,000. In 1988, 40,000 people had emigrated to the FRG.

November 13: Hans Modrow is elected Prime Minister. He proposes a "treaty community" between the FRG and the GDR.

November 18: A new government is sworn in.

November 23: Tighter customs and currency controls and buying restrictions on foreigners in the GDR are announced, triggered by activities of "arbitrageurs" who bought highly subsidized GDR goods for resale in the FRG and Poland.

November 28: Chancellor Kohl proposes a ten-point plan for unification. Its main elements are as follows:

- Providing humanitarian aid to the GDR, in particular for the health sector where severe shortages emerged after the emigration of a great number of doctors and nurses.

- Establishing a DM 2.9 billion currency fund (with a DM 2.2 billion contribution by the FRG) allowing GDR citizens, with effect from January 1, 1990, to acquire deutsche mark against marks for travel purposes once a year, at exchange rates of DM 1 = M 1 for the first DM 100 and at DM 1 = M 5 for the second DM 100.

- Undertaking joint projects with a view to reducing pollution, improving the railway system, and modernizing the telecommunications system in the GDR.

- Establishing linkages in all areas of public life based on intergovernmental treaties after free elections had taken place in the GDR.

- Developing confederative structures between the FRG and the GDR.

- Creating a FRG-GDR confederation in the context of European integration and in line with the Helsinki agreements on human rights.

December 1: The parliament (*Volkskammer*) in the GDR deletes the guarantee of a "leading role for the SED" from the Constitution of the GDR.

December 3: After revelations of widespread corruption among the former SED leadership, party chief Krenz resigns, together with the Politburo and the Central Committee of the SED. General elections are scheduled for May 6, 1990.

December 9: Gregor Gysi, a lawyer who had defended dissidents, is elected SED chairman.

December 20: Chancellor Kohl visits the GDR and an agreement is reached on economic cooperation in several areas.

1990

Phase II—On the Road to Free Elections

January 12: The GDR Constitution is changed to allow the establishment of a market-oriented economy. Specifically, in addition to state, cooperative, and mixed ownership, private ownership of production facilities and joint ventures with foreign companies are made possible (although many restrictions apply).

Box 1 (*Continued*).   A Chronology of the Dissolution of the German Democratic Republic

End-January: Emigration continues at a rate of 1,500–3,000 people a day. The Modrow Government, fearing economic and political collapse, advances the date of elections to March 18 and includes members of the major opposition groups in a grand coalition.

February 1: Prime Minister Modrow proposes a plan for German unity after talks in Moscow.

February 6: Chancellor Kohl offers negotiations on a currency union of the FRG with the GDR.

February 12: Talks involving the two German states and the four Allied powers with rights in Germany (France, the United Kingdom, the United States, and the U.S.S.R.), the so-called 2 + 4 talks, begin in Ottawa.

March 18: In the parliamentary elections, the Conservative Alliance for Germany wins a surprise victory with 48 percent of the vote (CDU—41 percent; German Social Union (DSU)—6 percent; and Democratic Awakening (DA)—1 percent). The Social Democratic Party (SPD) receives 22 percent, the Party of Democratic Socialism (PDS, formerly SED) 16 percent, and the Liberal Party 5 percent of the vote.

Phase III—Establishing Economic, Monetary, and Social Union

April 2: The Bundesbank publishes its proposal for a conversion law to become part of a treaty on German economic, monetary, and social union (GEMSU) between the FRG and the GDR. The proposal consists of six basic points.

- On the designated day, all domestic liabilities in the GDR and payments for current transactions (e.g., wages and pensions) would be converted into deutsche mark at a rate of M 2 = DM 1. Wages and pensions would, however, be adjusted to compensate losses of purchasing power as a result of price reform prior to conversion. Preferential treatment would be given to individual bank accounts of up to M 2,000 a person, which would be converted at a rate of M 1 = DM 1.

- In light of the less favorable treatment for accounts larger than M 2,000, the Government of the FRG would suggest in negotiations with the GDR that savers be guaranteed a stake in assets held by the State in trust for the people.

- The accord between the FRG and the GDR would also guarantee that in regard to monetary policy in the GDR, only the Bundesbank law and Bundesbank regulations would apply. Moreover, the Bundesbank would be able to implement in the GDR all monetary policy decisions made by its central council.

- To fulfill its responsibilities, the Bundesbank would open a provisional administrative office in East Berlin and about 15 other branch offices in the GDR.

- The commercial banking law of the FRG would be introduced in the GDR, allowing FRG banks and foreign commercial banks to open offices. Regulations on interest rates and foreign exchange limits in the GDR would be removed.

- Borrowing by the GDR public authorities would be limited.

April 12: A grand coalition government between the CDU, SPD, DSU, DA, and the Liberals is formed in the GDR with Lothar de Maizière (CDU) as Prime Minister. The Government opts for economic, monetary, and social union (GEMSU) with the FRG by mid-1990 and political accession, at a later date, under Article 23 of the FRG's Basic Law.

April 23: The FRG Government publishes its proposal for the terms of GEMSU. Savings of up to M 4,000 a person (M 2,000 for those under 14 years of age and M 6,000 for those above 58 years of age) would be converted at parity to the deutsche mark; savings exceeding these limits and other financial assets and liabilities would be converted at DM 1 = M 2. Wages and other current payments would also be converted at parity. Pensions would be linked to net wages, with a pension after 45 years of employment typically reaching 70 percent of average net income.

May 18: The Finance Ministers of the FRG and the GDR sign the State Treaty establishing GEMSU.

June 22: The State Treaty is ratified by the parliaments of the FRG and the GDR.

July 1: GEMSU takes effect.

Phase IV—Approaching Political Union

July 15–16: A meeting in the Caucasus between President Gorbachev and Chancellor Kohl results in approval from the U.S.S.R. for German unification, with the united Germany a member of the North Atlantic Treaty Organization (NATO).

August 3: An election treaty is signed, stipulating accession of the GDR to the FRG before all-German elections on December 2, 1990.

August 31: The Unity Treaty is signed, providing the legal basis for unification and the transition rules.

September 12: The 2 + 4 talks end; a treaty is signed terminating the rights of the Allied powers in Germany.

October 3: The five GDR states—Brandenburg, Mecklenburg-West Pomerania, Saxony, Saxony-Anhalt, and Thuringia—accede to the FRG under Article 23 of the FRG Constitution; the GDR ceases to exist.

economic, monetary, and social union (GEMSU). The legislative process was accelerated so that the agreement could take effect on July 1, 1990.

The deep-rooted economic problems that became more apparent after GEMSU took effect, as well as other political and administrative difficulties, added further momentum to the unification process. In the summer, the two Governments agreed to advance political unification of the two parts of the country to October 3, 1990. A Unification Treaty was agreed in August and ratified by the parliaments of the FRG and the GDR in September, stipulating among a host of transition and other regulations[4] that the five Länder[5] of the GDR would accede to the FRG under Article 23 of the FRG's Constitution.

Economic Background

Until 1989, official statistics painted a rosy picture of the GDR economy. According to these statistics, net material product (NMP—broadly equivalent to net domestic product but excluding part of the services sector)[6] increased in real terms at an average annual rate of 4 percent in 1980–88. Net investment grew by 2 percent a year and real per capita disposable income by 4½ percent a year. Prices were stable, the external accounts generally in surplus, unemployment nonexistent, and government accounts in balance.

Economic performance, in fact, was much worse.[7] This poor performance can be attributed to several factors. First, the increased emphasis on central planning since the early 1970s rendered the already inflexible economic system even less able to adjust to the external shocks of the 1970s and 1980s, to the emergence of new technologies, and to changing consumer tastes. Second, the pursuit of economic autarky resulted in a lack of integration into the world economy that deprived the GDR economy of the impulses that result from external competition. Third, the concentration of investment in a few selected technology-intensive areas[8] led to a deterioration of the capital stock in many other areas, most notably in the consumer durables industry and the public infrastructure.[9] Fourth, increased reliance on lignite coal instead of mineral oil for energy production enabled the authorities to avoid measures to increase efficiency in the use of energy and contributed to severe air pollution.[10] Fifth, the all-pervasive regulation of the labor market, the rigid wage structure with little wage differentiation (Table A1), and the low sectoral and regional mobility of labor added to the inefficiencies. Last, but not least, the rising gap in living standards between the GDR and the FRG, as well as the unresponsiveness of the leadership to the emerging problems (and its harsh rejection of reforms), contributed to a declining morale in the workforce.

As a result, productivity in the GDR lagged far behind that in the FRG. The magnitude of the productivity gap has been the subject of much debate. Based on production data and input-output relationships published by the GDR authorities and prices in the FRG, the Deutsches Institut für Wirtschaftsforschung (DIW) estimated the productivity gap in the industrial sector at about 50 percent on average in 1983.[11] However, a more recent analysis suggested that, for the economy as a whole, productivity was about 40 percent of the FRG level.[12] In a study based on a different methodology, the DIW estimated that in the GDR about three times as many workers as in the FRG were needed to achieve a given level of export revenues in convertible currency.[13] Comparisons of GNP per capita were less unfavorable to the GDR, as the ratio of the labor force to population was much higher in the GDR, reflecting, in particular, higher participation rates.

Given the dubious quality of the data base and the methodological problems, these various estimates can only serve as broad, backward-looking benchmarks. For exam-

---

[4] Sections I and II of the Unification Treaty laid out the principles under which political unification would take place. Section II also contained a set of rules that would initially govern the system for allocating revenue among the federal and state governments. The implications of unification for domestic laws and international treaties were spelled out in Sections III and IV. Matters concerning public administration, especially those relating to the administration of the states, were covered in Section V. Section VI contained the principles under which public assets and liabilities would be administered. A variety of other issues, including labor laws, social welfare, and science and education policies were dealt with in Sections VII–IX.

[5] Brandenburg, Mecklenburg-West Pomerania, Saxony, Saxony-Anhalt, and Thuringia.

[6] Value added in the banking, insurance, professional services, and government services sectors is not included in NMP. Recent figures published by the Statistical Office of the GDR put net domestic product at M 294 billion in 1988, compared with M 268 billion for NMP, reported in the GDR Statistical Yearbook for 1989.

[7] This is apparent even from official data: use of NMP (for either consumption or investment) grew at a rate of a little over 2 percent in 1980–88, some 2 percentage points less than the growth of production, implying a substantial terms of trade loss.

[8] For example, in the "Economic Strategy for the 1980s," adopted at the tenth Party Congress of the SED in 1981, microelectronics was singled out as a high-priority investment sector.

[9] In automobile production, for example, many machines predated World War II. The highways and the rail system were in poor repair and the telecommunications system was outdated. Overall, the capital-output ratio—according to official data—exceeded 4.5, a value much higher than in the FRG or other Western industrial countries.

[10] The lignite found in east Germany has a large sulfur content which, because of insufficient filtering, causes severe air pollution in the process of generating electricity. Power plants are inefficient and subsidization of electricity at the producer and consumer level has encouraged waste.

[11] Reported in Deutscher Bundestag, *Materialien zum Bericht zur Lage der Nation im geteilten Deutschland, 1987*, November 1987. Estimates based on output per working hour tended to show a gap a couple of percentage points larger, as hours worked per worker are higher in the GDR compared with the FRG.

[12] See Deutsches Institut für Wirtschaftsforschung, *Wochenbericht 26/90* (Berlin), June 28, 1990, pp. 341–56. GDP per employed person was estimated at about 40 percent of the west German level.

[13] See Deutsches Institut für Wirtschaftsforschung, *Wochenbericht 14/90* (Berlin), April 5, 1990, pp. 172–74.

ple, measures of productivity based on physical production data are limited by difficulties in taking account of quality differences—the studies mentioned above evaluated GDR production at prices prevailing in the FRG. The approach focusing on export earning power, too, suffers from weaknesses, as, in contrast to a market-oriented economy, the GDR did not necessarily export products in which it enjoyed a comparative advantage. Autarky was a major economic policy objective and areas for exporting seem to have been identified with little regard for their economic returns. More important, estimates of past productivity are not useful indicators of potential productivity with the prevailing capital and labor supplies. It has been suggested, for instance, that productivity could be improved quickly by 20–30 percent if certain inefficiencies arising from interruptions of input supply, absenteeism, and in-house production of inputs were removed.[14] On the other hand, much of the output produced prior to the opening up of the GDR economy might not be marketable in an open trading environment. Thus, in the initial months of GEMSU, with the output level falling under pressure from external competition, and some shelter still provided for employment, productivity as measured by the official statistics has been declining.

Although average monthly gross wages in the GDR in 1988 amounted to only a third of west German wages when converted at parity, differences in taxation seem to have narrowed the gap for net wages to about 60 percent.[15] But the purchasing power of wages in the GDR was affected by the unavailability of certain goods. Although the supply of basic consumer goods was satisfactory and housing was cheap,[16] the supply of consumer durables was limited: only about half of households owned a car or a color television set, which are almost standard possessions in west German households. Moreover, it is doubtful that prices were as stable as officially proclaimed. The basket used for the computation of the consumer price index included low-priced goods that were no longer produced. In addition, companies appear to have been able to raise prices by declaring minor alterations of products as improvements in quality.[17] There also seems to have been suppressed inflation that gave rise to a monetary overhang, reflected in the drop in the velocity of money (Table A2).

Apart from suppressed inflation, the GDR economy

suffered from a severely distorted price structure, with low prices for basic consumer goods and high prices for "luxury" goods (Table A3). In order to support low prices for basic consumer goods, the Government spent about M 50 billion in 1988, equivalent to 18½ percent of NMP (Table A4). Given the vast differences in relative prices, comparisons of purchasing power of the mark and the deutsche mark depended heavily on the assumed consumer basket. The more the basket was tilted toward basic products, the more favorable was the purchasing power of the mark compared with that of the deutsche mark. Thus, computed purchasing power parities ranged from M 1 : DM 1.45 for a two-person pensioner household with a GDR consumption pattern to M 1 : DM 0.89 for a four-person wage earner household with a west German consumption pattern (Tables A5–A6). Moreover, these calculations overstated the relative purchasing power of the mark owing to the limited availability of certain goods in the GDR and differences in quality.

The mark was only valid for transactions in the GDR and could not be exported or imported legally. External trade data were denominated in valuta marks (VM). Each valuta mark was equivalent to one deutsche mark. The official conversion rate for trade in convertible currencies was M 1 = VM 1 but, in effect, a more depreciated rate was used, which was adjusted from time to time. In 1989 this latter rate was M 4.4 = VM 1.[18] Trade with member countries of the Council for Mutual Economic Assistance (CMEA) was denominated in the transferable ruble (TR), which was converted into marks at a rate of TR 1 = M 4.667.[19] Until recently, the official exchange rate for tourists was M 1 = DM 1. As of the beginning of 1990, the tourism rate was devalued to M 3 = DM 1.[20] The free

---

[14] See Deutsches Institut für Wirtschaftsforschung, *Wochenbericht 26/90* (Berlin), June 28, 1990, pp. 341–56.

[15] In 1988, the take-home pay in the GDR and the FRG averaged M 925 and DM 2,070, respectively.

[16] Rents were kept artificially low—in 1985 a new two-room efficiency apartment cost only M 75 a month, compared with DM 390 in the FRG—but the housing stock was old and deteriorating. In 1989, about 26 percent of apartments and houses did not have an indoor toilet and 19 percent did not have a bath or a shower. More than half of the apartments and houses were built before 1945 and about one third were built before 1919. See Ifo Institute, *Schnelldienst* (Munich), Vol. 43, No. 15 (May 21, 1990), pp. 9–25.

[17] Price increases because of improvements in quality do not enter inflation calculations.

[18] In order to reconcile the official exchange rate with that for external trade, a special fund (*Rückstellungen für Richtungskoeffizienten* or RIKO fund) was established at the State Bank. When goods worth DM 100 were exported to the convertible currency area, the exporter obtained the equivalent valued at the external trade exchange rate, for example, M 440 if the transaction took place in 1989. Of this, he received M 100 (the value of the exports at the official exchange rate) directly from the foreign trade company responsible for the transaction and the balance (i.e., M 340, if the transaction took place in 1989) from the special fund. Similarly, an importer importing goods worth DM 100 paid M 100 to the foreign trade company and M 340 to the special fund. See also the discussion in Chapter X, section on "Mechanics of the Conversion."

[19] The transferable ruble is the common unit of account used by the International Bank for Economic Cooperation (IBWZ) of the CMEA countries. The foreign currency value of the transferable ruble is determined through a currency basket that contains the currencies of the major Western trading partners of the CMEA countries. The exchange rate of the transferable ruble is regularly adjusted by the IBWZ.

[20] The tourism rate applied without limitation to purchases of marks. In the first half of 1990, sales of marks by GDR residents were limited to M 200 a year (M 100 for children) and were subject to two exchange rates. Half of the total amount could be exchanged into deutsche mark at parity and the other half at DM 1 = M 5. To maintain the official rate, a currency fund of DM 2.9 billion was established with contributions from the FRG and the GDR amounting to DM 2.2 billion and DM 0.7 billion, respectively.

market rate in West Berlin was about M 9 = DM 1 in October 1989. After the opening of the border it fell temporarily but by January 1990 had recovered to M 7 = DM 1. Following the decision to introduce the deutsche mark in the GDR, the free market rate appreciated considerably.

Contrary to official statistics, it seems that the government budget in the GDR experienced small deficits over the years. According to the financial accounts for 1989, released by the State Bank (*Staatsbank*) in early 1990, gross domestic liabilities of the Central Government to the banking system amounted to M 50 billion (18 percent of NMP) at the end of 1989 (Table A7).[21] Including the housing sector, public liabilities amounted to M 158 billion (57 percent of NMP). Since capital markets did not exist in the GDR, these liabilities reflected the debt that had been created through bank financing of deficits and construction investment. In addition, the indebtedness of the state-owned enterprises had risen to high levels—94 percent of NMP—as profits had been largely used to bolster government revenue.

At the end of 1989, net external indebtedness of the GDR to the non-state-trading area was M 32 billion or about $18.5 billion (see Table A7). This was partly offset by net assets vis-à-vis state-trading countries in the amount of M 10 billion.[22] The relatively favorable external debt situation seems consistent with official trade data, which reported moderate external surpluses through most of the 1980s (Table A8). Calculations based on partner country information obtained from the IMF's *Direction of Trade Statistics* confirm external surpluses of the GDR with IMF member countries for most of the period 1982–86, but indicate the emergence of deficits in 1987–89 (Table A9). Trade was heavily focused on investment and intermediate goods, with trade in consumer goods particularly small on the import side (Table A10). According to official statistics, about two thirds of external trade was conducted with state-trading countries and only a little more than one fourth with Western industrial countries. In reality, however, the share of state-trading countries was considerably lower, as a significant part of external trade with the convertible currency area went unreported and valuation practices further distorted the picture. Trade in goods between the FRG and the GDR was broadly balanced over the years, but there was a substantial infusion of foreign exchange into the GDR through the net export of services to the FRG as well as through transfers and capital flows (Tables A11–A12).

---

[21] In part, this debt reflected credit extended by the State Bank to the Government, as a result of the need to replenish the RIKO fund (described in footnote 18) after devaluations of the commercial rate of exchange between the mark and the valuta mark that applied in trade in convertible currencies.

[22] The foreign currency value of these assets is difficult to establish since they were presumably denominated in nonconvertible currencies.

Recent Economic Situation

Economic developments in 1989 were heavily influenced by political turbulence. Reflecting the wave of emigration, the labor force declined by 220,000 (2½ percent) during the year. While NMP rose in real terms by 2 percent on average in 1989, output fell in the final quarter of the year. Emigration of skilled workers seems to have contributed to structural unemployment as, at the end of 1989, there were 50,000 unemployed but 250,000 officially recorded vacancies.

The traces of the political turmoil were particularly visible at the sectoral level. While industrial production increased by 2½ percent for the year as a whole, it declined after the opening of the Berlin wall, and in December was 3 percent below its level of December 1988. Similarly, construction output was broadly unchanged in the annual average but, in December, was about 8 percent below the level of a year earlier. At the same time, demand for transportation and communications services soared; for example, toward the end of 1989, there were 1.2 million unfilled orders for telephone installations.

While aggregate supply weakened through the year in 1989, demand strengthened. Although retail sales rose by only 3½ percent on an annual average basis, there was a private consumption boom toward the end of the year. To finance these purchases, consumers withdrew deposits from savings accounts—M 900 million during the month of November alone—and household savings accounts increased by only M 8 billion during 1989, compared with M 10 billion in 1988; as a result, the household saving rate declined from 7 percent of net money income to 6¼ percent.

The deteriorating economic situation resulted in a weakening of the financial position of enterprises and a decline in profit transfers to the government budget. Reflecting this, the budget was officially reported in deficit to the extent of M 6 billion (2 percent of NMP). The economic difficulties also led to larger increases in the official price index than had been typical in the past—the consumer price index rose by 2 percent in 1989. With wages increasing by about 3 percent, real wages rose (officially) by about 1 percent.

The decline of GDR industry gathered momentum during 1990 with industrial output falling, relative to the corresponding period of the previous year, by 4½ percent in the first quarter and by 9½ percent in the second quarter. In August 1990, the second month in which the GDR economy was fully open to competition, industrial output was 50 percent lower than in the same month of 1989. Construction activity also slumped; in July 1990 it was 15 percent below the level of a year earlier. As a result, unemployment soared. In September, 2.2 million people (one fourth of the labor force) were either registered as unemployed or on short-time work.

Wage developments in 1990 have been clearly out of

line with productivity developments. Shortly after GEMSU took effect, wage increases ranging from 25 percent (metals industry) to 60 percent (construction) were granted, often on top of sizable awards in the first half of 1990.[23] Moreover, the duration of the new contracts was limited—in most cases to less than six months. These wage developments put further pressure on the financial situation of enterprises as prices became subject to market forces. The July consumer price index was 5½ percent lower than a year earlier.[24] Basic goods became more expensive, partly reflecting the abolition of consumer price subsidies, but prices of many durable goods declined as the high excise taxes levied on them no longer applied and pressure of competition from Western goods intensified.

Plans for Reform

Shortly after the opening of the borders, a broad political consensus emerged in the GDR that the command economy could not be repaired. What was needed was radical economic reform. However, the reform steps undertaken by the Modrow Government (Box 2) appeared to be half-hearted and not far-reaching enough. In addition, views differed on how to implement the reform program. While initially the thinking in official and academic circles had been overwhelmingly in favor of a gradual approach to reform in the GDR with economic and monetary union with the FRG being the crowning result of a long restructuring process, the rapidly deteriorating economic situation and increasing political dissatisfaction created pressures for prompt economic unification. It was against this background that, on February 6, 1990, Chancellor Kohl, in a surprise move, offered currency union through introducing the deutsche mark in the GDR.

Currency union, of course, implied that the economic system of the GDR would be subject to international competition and, hence, would have to be reshaped fundamentally. In particular, it would require (1) replacing central planning by decentralized decision making, open markets, and competition; (2) allowing private ownership of land, housing, and production facilities by domestic residents and foreigners; (3) a reform of the banking system (including the central bank); (4) a redefinition of the role of government and a restructuring of the social security system; (5) a phasing out of consumer price subsidies and a freeing of prices (including wages); and (6) a liberalization of external trade. To accomplish these tasks, the Governments of the FRG

and the GDR in May 1990 concluded a State Treaty that specified the reforms required in the GDR and set out the terms of GEMSU.

The first chapter of the State Treaty stipulated that the union, which was to go into effect on July 1, 1990, would be based upon the principles of the social market economy, that is, private property, competition, free prices, free movement of labor, capital, goods, and services, as well as labor legislation and a social security system in line with these principles. Chapter II specified the terms of the currency union, particularly the currency conversion rates. Chapter III dealt with several aspects of economic union—external and domestic trade, structural adjustment of GDR enterprises, agricultural policy, and environmental protection. Chapter IV contained the provisions for social union, including the new structure of the social security system and regulations for the unemployment, pension, health, and accident insurance funds. Finally, Chapter V described the fiscal reform and provided for transfers from the FRG to the GDR budget as well as stipulating limits on borrowing by the GDR public authorities. By and large, the State Treaty extended the economic and social system of the FRG to the GDR. Below, the institutional arrangements existing in the GDR prior to GEMSU are described and the implications of the reform process discussed.

Systemic Reforms

The replacement of the centrally planned economy of the GDR by a social market economy had far-reaching implications for economic decision making, property rights, and the price formation process.

Reform of the Economic Decision-Making Process

Economic decision making in the GDR revolved around the establishment and implementation of the central plan (see Appendix II for a brief history of central planning in the GDR). The top decision-making body was the Politburo or, in a somewhat wider context, the Central Committee (ZK) of the Socialist Unity Party (SED).[25] The overall framework and the major guidelines for economic policy were determined by the Politburo. Within these guidelines, the Ministerial Council formulated, issued, and controlled a variety of economic plans, the details of which were worked out by the Planning

---

[23] In May, wages in industry were 17 percent higher than in May 1989.

[24] Measured inflation rates in the GDR in the initial months of GEMSU have to be interpreted carefully because of difficulties in allowing for the sharp shift in the availability and quality of goods.

[25] The ZK, whose members were elected by the party congress, acted as the legislative and executive body of the SED. Its day-to-day operations were conducted by the so-called Secretariat (Sekretariat des ZK der SED). The ZK elected the members of the Politburo who formed the most powerful group within the SED.

Box 2. Selected Economic Reforms, November 13, 1989–April 11, 1990

- *Amendment of the Constitution:* Private, cooperative, semipublic, and mixed ownership, including joint ventures with foreign investors, were given the same legal status as state ownership.
- *Abolition of certain restrictions on private companies:* The limitations on employment by private crafts and retail companies, as well as special levies on investment goods imported by these enterprises, were abolished.
- *Reorganization of the Kombinate: Kombinate* were allowed to pursue foreign trade directly; the number of ordinances governing business of the *Kombinate* was greatly reduced; and companies were given greater independence.
- *Abolition of price subsidies:* Subsidies for children's

clothing were abolished and child support payments raised.
- *Reorganization of the banking sector:* The State Bank was given the status of an independent central bank and a commercial bank was created to take over the other functions previously held by the State Bank.
- *Establishment of a trust for the management of public property (Volkseigentum): Kombinate*, companies, and other entities were to be transformed into joint-stock companies with shares held by the trust.
- *Workers' rights:* A bill was passed in parliament giving extensive rights to workers' representatives in companies.
- *Reduction of taxes:* Tax relief for private enterprises and self-employed was given and taxes on certain "luxury" items were reduced.

Commission.[26] The plans set by the command sphere were passed on in disaggregated form to the operating units of the economy. Instructions were in the form of legal directives and hence binding on the companies concerned. A complicated system of accounts was needed to make plans operational, to coordinate them, and to monitor the results. Although the planning institutions and operating units interacted in various ways, decision making was predominantly top-down. Entrepreneurial activities at the company level were hence discouraged, and consumers remained largely passive at the receiving end of the line of command.

GEMSU necessitated a complete revamping of this authoritarian economic system. Chapter I of the State Treaty required that central planning be abolished and replaced by a system of free enterprise, competition, and open markets, that is, by a system based on individual economic decision making. The role of the State was to be limited to the provision of public goods and the maintenance of an economic and social order in line with the principles of the social market economy as it existed in the FRG.

An effective competition policy was seen to be particularly important during the process of restructuring. In the area of traded goods, this could be achieved through the maintenance of an open trading system and the avoidance of government subsidies to specific industries. Strong antitrust laws were needed, however, to

prevent the survival or the emergence of monopolistic market structures in the area of nontraded goods. Under the State Treaty, the GDR adopted the FRG's cartel law with the modification that the GDR cartel office could permit mergers deemed to be in the "general economic interest" even though market dominance might result. Since political unification, the FRG's cartel law has applied in its entirety in areas formerly part of the GDR.

Privatization

Expropriation began in the eastern part of the defeated Germany in 1945 when the Soviet military administration confiscated property of the German Reich, the German military administration, the Nazi party, and prominent members of this party. In the early postwar years, a large segment of the industrial sector was nationalized—part was converted into "Soviet joint-stock companies" and part into "people's companies" (*Volkseigene Betriebe*)—so that in 1950 nationalized industries accounted for 75 percent of industrial production.[27] In agriculture, there was a land reform in 1945 in which farms of 100 hectares and more were expropriated, followed by collectivization in 1952–60 that resulted in the nationalization of 90 percent of all arable land. The process of nationalization was completed in 1972 with the incorporation of the remaining private or semiprivate industrial enterprises into the sector of state-owned companies. Thus, in 1988, virtually all industrial employment was

---

[26] Formally, the Planning Commission had the rank of a ministry. In addition to the preparation of economic plans, the Planning Commission was responsible for the analysis and projections of economic developments and the control and supervision of other planning institutions, for example, the planning commissions of the regional and local levels of government. Under the Modrow Government, the planning commission became the economic commission, but its function remained essentially unchanged.

[27] A large part of the assets of Soviet joint-stock companies was transferred to the U.S.S.R. as war reparations. The remainder was returned to the GDR in 1952–53, in part against payment. See Deutsches Institut für Wirtschaftsforschung, *Handbuch DDR Wirtschaft* (Berlin, 1985).

accounted for by the state sector (Table A13). Similarly, almost all transportation companies, banks, and insurance companies had been nationalized. In the agricultural, construction, and retail sectors, there was a mixture of state and cooperative ownership; the latter, however, did not entail any private ownership rights for the members of the cooperative. Only in the handicraft and housing sectors was there still considerable private ownership; about 72 percent of the labor force in the handicraft sector worked in private companies and a significant part of the existing housing stock was in the hands of private owners.[28] However, private ownership was predominant in the prewar housing stock, while most new residential structures were owned by the State.

Public ownership of the means of production was considered by the SED to be the most important element of the economic system and was guaranteed in Article 9 of the GDR Constitution.[29] In Article 10, socialist ownership was defined to comprise public ownership, common property of cooperatives, and property of "certain groups of society" (i.e., political parties and social and cultural bodies). Public ownership was never seen as entailing any property rights for individuals. Public ownership rights lay exclusively with the State, which meant in effect the top echelons of the SED and the government bureaucracy. This dogmatic approach to the question of ownership explains why the GDR Government consented so late—much later than, for example, Hungary or Poland—to joint ventures, and why—under the Modrow Government—private participation in enterprises was limited to 49 percent.

Private ownership was essentially confined to small-scale retail businesses, restaurants, and craft shops. Private companies were permitted to exist only if they were "predominantly based on personal labor" (Article 14(2) of the Constitution). According to official statistics, private businesses produced less than 4 percent of NMP in the 1980s. They faced extremely unfavorable conditions, including very high marginal tax rates and frequent changes in regulations.

The most fundamental difference between a centrally planned and a market economy is the distribution of property rights. It is, therefore, not surprising that privatization of state-owned property turned out to be one of the most contended issues in the reform of the GDR's economy. Although private property rights were mentioned in Chapter I of the State Treaty as one of the principles on which GEMSU was based, the treaty was rather short on the specifics of privatization. Appendix IX to the treaty stipulated only that the GDR would

ensure a sufficient supply of land for private investors and that the assets of the state-owned enterprises that were to be transformed into joint-stock companies would include the land they occupied. In order to clarify the position, the Governments of the FRG and the GDR subsequently published an additional agreement on the principles of privatization and the *Volkskammer* of the GDR passed a law on the privatization and reorganization of state-owned property (*Treuhandgesetz*).

The agreement between the two Governments stipulated that the following principles would guide the privatization process.

- Expropriations undertaken by the Soviet Military Government in 1945–49 would not be reversed, but an all-German parliament would have the right to determine appropriate compensation.

- Expropriated or state-administered land and real estate would in principle be returned to the previous owners or their heirs.[30] If, however, land or real estate had been used for other than its original purpose and could not be returned, compensation would be paid. This applied also to cases where the property has been legally acquired in good faith by citizens of the GDR.

- Companies or participations expropriated after 1949 would, in principle, be returned to their previous owners. For companies expropriated between 1949 and 1972, compensation might be paid in lieu of restoration of ownership rights.

- The GDR authorities would establish an extrabudgetary fund to finance compensation payments.[31] Applications for the return of property or compensation would have to be submitted within a time period to be specified; this deadline would be no later than six months after the effective date of GEMSU. The authorities would ensure that no land or real estate, the property rights to which were unclear, would be sold before the expiration of the application period.

The modalities of the privatization of state-owned enterprises were regulated in the *Treuhandgesetz*, which went into effect on July 1 together with the State Treaty.[32] Under this law, state-owned enterprises were transformed into joint-stock or limited liability companies and a public trust fund for the administration of state property (*Treu-*

---

[28] In 1989, 19 percent of apartments and 87 percent of one- and two-family houses were privately owned. See Ifo Institute, *Schnelldienst* (Munich), Vol. 43, No. 15 (May 21, 1990), pp. 9–25.

[29] Constitution of 1968 as amended in 1974.

[30] This stipulation was later found to be one of the major deterrents to private investment in the GDR. In the Unification Treaty it was changed so as to limit claims of previous owners to monetary compensation.

[31] It has been suggested that this fund be financed from revenue derived from privatization.

[32] Agriculture and forestry were covered by separate regulations that took account of the specific characteristics of these sectors.

handanstalt) took temporary ownership. The Trust Fund was established as a public corporation under the supervision of the Prime Minister of the GDR.[33] Its objective was to create competitive enterprises and to privatize them. The State Treaty stipulated that revenue from privatization was to be used primarily to restructure the state-owned enterprises; it might also be used to improve the financial position of the Government and to cover operational expenses of the Trust Fund.[34] Should any assets remain after the needs of the ailing enterprises and the budget had been satisfied, they could be used to compensate those GDR citizens whose savings had been devalued by the currency conversion.

The Trust Fund was to conduct the privatizations through a family of smaller funds to which it would transfer ownership rights in the joint-stock and limited liability companies.[35] The funds were to be responsible for the closing or restructuring and privatization of the companies in their portfolio, and they were required by the law to take their decisions on the basis of economic considerations, with advice from banks and management consultants.

Price Reform

In the central planning system of the GDR, prices served several purposes. First, they were used as a unit of measurement in the plan; second, they were used to set economic incentives; and third, they served as instruments for changing the distribution of income. Prices did not reflect relative scarcities and were not meant to do so. In principle, factory prices were established by production costs and a markup, while deviations of retail prices from the factory prices for consumer goods were financed through the government budget. Thus, prices in the GDR would not have differed much from what would have resulted in a market economy if costs had reflected relative scarcities of the inputs into the production process and indirect taxes and subsidies had been of a moderate size and structured rationally. In practice, however, factor costs were not aligned with shadow prices. In general, capital was underpriced—the basic interest rate on credits to enterprises was 5 percent

(Table A14)[36]—and profit margins were set to reward socially desirable production. Similarly, since wages were fixed primarily with a view to social considerations, the wage costs embedded in the factory price tended not to reflect the scarcity value of different skills and wage differentials were narrow (see Table A1). In particular, manual labor tended to be overvalued and other labor undervalued.

Since the factory prices resulting from these costs and markups did not in general coincide with the politically desired final sales prices, there was an elaborate system of product-specific taxes and subsidies. In 1988, product taxes amounted to M 43 billion (16 percent of NMP) and product price subsidies to M 50 billion (18½ percent of NMP). Of the latter, M 32 billion (12 percent of NMP) was used to subsidize agricultural products.

The size of subsidies for food products resulted from the extraordinarily high agricultural producer prices. In the 1980s, the level of agricultural producer prices far exceeded that in the FRG. This reflected the greater emphasis put on price policy as a tool to influence production in the agricultural sector than in other sectors of the economy and was justified by the high costs and low yields of east German agriculture. Agricultural price policy was also guided by the objective of equalizing living standards of the rural and urban population.

As a result of currency union and price reform, the FRG's price structure emerged for all traded goods. Initial distortions, in the form of excessive prices for a number of Western goods in certain areas of the GDR, were eliminated quickly through competition. The system of taxes and subsidies also came into line with that of the FRG, with the exception of rents, household energy use, and public transport. Subsidies in these latter areas will be reduced, starting in 1991.[37]

Monetary Reform

According to socialist economic theory, a one-bank system is desirable for a centrally planned economy. Although the GDR never fully reached this "ideal," the state banking monopoly and the dominant position of the State Bank ensured that banking activities were tied into the system of planning that governed the real economy. The State Bank acted as the central bank of the GDR, as a commercial bank for industry, construc-

---

[33] It was to be headed by an executive board (*Vorstand*) consisting of a president and four directors, who were to be appointed by the supervisory council (*Verwaltungsrat*). The latter would monitor and support the operations of the board of directors. The supervisory council would consist of a chairman and 16 members. The chairman and seven council members were to be appointed by the GDR Government and the remaining members by the GDR parliament.

[34] Originally, the Trust Fund was given authority to borrow DM 7 billion in 1990 and DM 10 billion in 1991 in anticipation of revenues from privatization. Later, in the Unity Treaty, the borrowing authority was raised to DM 25 billion in 1990–91.

[35] Allocation of shares would be determined by the supervisory council of the Trust Fund.

[36] In addition, interest subsidies and surcharges were used to orient investment decisions toward the objectives of the plan.

[37] Rents in the GDR were so low that they did not cover capital and maintenance costs of the housing stock. The State Treaty on GEMSU, however, foresaw that rents would increase in line with wages and salaries so that these costs would gradually be taken over by the private sector. It has already been announced that rents are to double at the beginning of 1991. In cases of social hardship, there will be direct income support from the Government.

tion, wholesale and retail trade, transportation, and tourism, and as the bank of the Government. In this latter function, the State Bank automatically financed the government budget deficit. Special banks for agriculture and the food industry and for foreign trade, a cooperative bank for small businesses, and a large number of postal and savings banks all fell under the direct control of the State Bank.

There was no money or capital market in the GDR. Credit and interest rates were used solely as central planning instruments. Bank credit to enterprises was regulated according to administrative credit plans. To facilitate fulfillment of these plans, enterprises were obliged to hold accounts with specific banks. Payments between enterprises had to be effected through transfers so as to minimize the need for cash.

Interest rate policy, which was introduced as an important economic lever during the reform period of the 1960s, retained its role as an instrument of indirect control of business activities in the 1970s and 1980s: interest rates were a cost element in the determination of prices; they were used to evaluate investment projects; and enterprises had to pay ''punitive'' interest rates when they ran arrears on loan repayments (see Table A14). However, while higher interest payments reduced company profits and hence payments of wage premiums to managers and workers, the lack of an effective threat of bankruptcy[38] limited the use of interest rates as an instrument of control.

While it was relatively easy to control credit developments, influence on private holdings of cash was much more difficult. A monetary overhang appears to have accumulated during periods when the central plan forced growth of capital goods at the cost of consumer goods, resulting in an excess demand for consumption goods. Because of the rigid consumer prices, the overhang of purchasing power did not produce open inflation.

The problem of a monetary overhang can be illustrated by the developments of a number of economic indicators during the 1960–88 period. First, the share of cash in total money (consisting of cash and savings deposits) fell during this period by 11 percentage points to 9½ percent (see Table A2). Second, the velocity of money (defined as the ratio of disposable income to money) declined by two thirds,[39] from over 2½ to less than 1, largely on account of the rise in savings deposits.[40] Third, the household savings rate rose markedly. Thus, past efforts to

eliminate the overhang had not been completely successful.[41] The actual amount of the overhang that existed prior to GEMSU is difficult to estimate since it depended on the (unknown) velocity of money that would have existed in a market system.[42] It seems likely, however, that the overhang was eliminated by the terms of the currency conversion.[43]

Chapter II of the State Treaty on GEMSU spelled out the terms of currency union and monetary reform in the GDR. All responsibility for monetary policy in the union would be with the Deutsche Bundesbank and the Government of the FRG would remain the sole issuer of coins. In order to create the conditions necessary for an effective conduct of monetary policy, the GDR would introduce a market-oriented credit system and reform the commercial banking system. Regarding the terms of currency union, which was to take effect on July 1, 1990, the State Treaty stipulated that

- wages, salaries, scholarships, rents, and leases, as well as other recurrent payments would be converted at parity into deutsche mark;[44]

- all other claims and liabilities would, in principle, be converted at a rate of M 2 = DM 1;

- permanent residents of the GDR could, however, exchange at parity the following amounts:[45] under 14 years of age up to M 2,000; between 14 and 58 years of age up to M 4,000; and above 58 years of age up to M 6,000;

- deposits of nonresidents that existed on December 31, 1989 would be converted at M 2 = DM 1, while deposits made at a later date would be converted at M 3 = DM 1;[46]

- all businesses would, in due course, issue an opening balance sheet in deutsche mark.

The terms of the currency conversion implied that on average the assets of the banking system (consisting mainly of claims on Government, enterprises, and the housing sector) were converted at a less favorable rate than the

---

[38] Enterprise losses were financed through bank credit or out of the government budget. There was never an effective bankruptcy threat for any of the state-owned companies.

[39] By comparison, the velocity of broad money in the FRG declined by only one third during the same period, despite a much more rapid expansion of the range of financial instruments.

[40] The velocity of cash in circulation declined by only 18 percent during this period.

[41] In 1967, the overhang was reduced by a forced cut in private cash holdings (a mini currency reform).

[42] See Chapter X, section on ''The Implications of the Conversion Rate.''

[43] On the basis of deposits at the end of May, the terms for currency conversion (see text below) reduced the amount of cash and sight and savings deposits held by households by 32 percent from M 182 billion to the equivalent of M 123 billion (evaluated at parity between the mark and the deutsche mark). See Chapter X for further discussion.

[44] For wages and salaries, contractual payments in effect on May 1, 1990, were used as the base for the conversion.

[45] The State Treaty allowed for the possibility, sometime in the future, of compensating those whose savings were devalued with proceeds from the privatization of previously state-owned enterprises.

[46] The mark was devalued to M 3 = DM 1 with effect from January 1, 1990 and it was presumed that financial transactions of nonresidents after that date took account of the new official exchange rate.

liabilities (consisting mainly of deposits by the Government, enterprises, and private households, as well as foreign liabilities and equity).[47] The State Treaty therefore foresaw allocation to the banking system of claims on a newly established equalization fund (*Ausgleichsfonds*).[48] Net liabilities of this fund were to be balanced by claims on the GDR Government. The total amount of equalization claims would be determined by (1) the conversion of the book values of banks' assets and liabilities at conversion day; (2) any devaluation of the converted assets that might become necessary after the establishment of deutsche mark opening balance sheets of businesses; and (3) any additional amounts needed to ensure appropriate capitalization of banks.

The conversion of banks' assets created a rather arbitrary distribution of debt between the Government and the enterprise sector and among enterprises. In the past, enterprises often borrowed on behalf of the Government or for purposes unrelated to their main activities. As a consequence, government debt was relatively light after conversion, while enterprise debt was rather heavy. A future reallocation of debt from enterprises to the Trust Fund or the Government is therefore likely to take place in cases where enterprises suffer from an undue debt burden and in cases of bankruptcy.[49]

Reform of the External Trade System and Structural Adjustment

Consistent with the principle of central planning, external trade was subject to a state monopoly by constitutional law.[50] Monopoly power was traditionally exercised by the Ministry of Foreign Trade and its subsidiaries, although it was weakened in the 1980s with the Ministry of Foreign Trade having to share control over exports and imports with the *Kombinate*.[51] Foreign trade activities were assigned to special foreign trade companies (*Aussenhandelsbetriebe*). Detailed plans determined domestic prices and quantities of exports and imports. In addition to domestic requirements,[52] obli-

gations vis-à-vis the other CMEA countries, in particular the U.S.S.R., had to be taken into account.

Trade with Western economies took place mostly under bilateral treaties at world market prices. Prices in trade with CMEA countries were, in more recent years, linked to developments in world market prices, albeit with significant lags. Intra-German trade was subject to a special treaty (*Berliner Abkommen* 1951, which was revised in 1960), which stipulated lists of products that could be exchanged, as well as the modalities for payment. As a rule, only goods of German origin could be traded; prices were market prices in deutsche mark; valuation was, however, in conversion units (*Verrechnungseinheiten*) each equivalent to one deutsche mark; and payments were effected through accounts at the Deutsche Bundesbank and the State Bank. Under the *Berliner Abkommen*, there was an interest-free overdraft facility (the "Swing") with a limit that was adjusted from time to time; between 1986 and 1990, it amounted to 850 million conversion units.

Chapter III of the State Treaty on GEMSU abolished the arrangements for intra-German trade and introduced a free external trading system in line with regulations of the European Community (EC). Existing contracts and trade relations with CMEA partners were, however, given special protection. In the area of agricultural production and trade, the GDR would adopt a price support scheme in line with the EC's Common Agricultural Policy. In trade of agricultural products between the two German economies, quantitative restrictions would be allowed until the full integration of the GDR's agricultural sector into the EC market.[53] The GDR was also given authority to support structural adjustment of enterprises during the transition to a market economy.[54]

Reform of the Fiscal and Social Security System[55]

As explained above, the public sector was in effect the owner of most of the national capital stock. As a

---

[47] Preliminary calculations on the basis of data as of May 30, 1990, indicated that the converted assets of the banking system would fall short of liabilities (including equity) by some DM 26 billion, allowing a conversion rate for equity of M 1 = DM 1. See Chapter X, section on "The Mechanics of the Conversion" for further details.

[48] When after conversion the assets of a bank exceeded its liabilities (including equity), the equalization fund received a claim in that amount on this bank. Interest on equalization claims was set at the three-month Frankfurt interbank offer rate (FIBOR).

[49] Since the Trust Fund, as a public corporation, is backed by the Government, there is little difference between the two alternatives.

[50] Article 9(5) of the 1968 Constitution.

[51] *Kombinate* were large conglomerates. Their creation is described in Appendix II.

[52] The GDR economy depended on raw materials and energy imports from the U.S.S.R. and on imports of technologically advanced products from the industrial countries.

[53] In midyear, the GDR introduced a system of import prohibitions and quotas for a range of agricultural products. The FRG abolished export restitution payments and import levies in agricultural trade with the GDR, but left quotas on imports intact. Subsequently, restrictions on agricultural trade between the FRG and the GDR were abolished.

[54] The GDR Government decided to give financial support to investors in the amount of 12 percent of investment undertaken between July 1, 1990 and June 30, 1991 and 8 percent of investment undertaken between July 1, 1991 and June 30, 1992. In addition, since political unification, regional assistance premiums have been available for investment in the former area of the GDR under the regional policy program of the FRG. Premiums granted under the two schemes cannot, in sum, exceed 33 percent of the investment expenditure. However, investment spending in the east benefits in addition from special depreciation rates that allow write-offs of 50, 30, and 20 percent, respectively, in the first, second, and third year of the investment.

[55] A more detailed description is provided in Chapter XI.

consequence, government revenue and expenditure were dominated by transfers to and from industry and agriculture. In 1988, about one third of total expenditure was accounted for by transfers to these sectors that included, inter alia, production subsidies and reinvested profits of the state enterprises (see Table A4). A considerable part of the remaining expenditure was devoted to social purposes, in particular to social security (20 percent of the total) and to consumer price subsidies (18½ percent). As the most important landlord in the country, the Government also allocated 11 percent of its expenditure to housing. Revenue was largely determined by transfers from industry and agriculture, accounting for more than three fourths of the total in 1988. Social security contributions and taxes each accounted for about 7½ percent of total revenue.

Direct taxes in the GDR consisted essentially of taxes on labor income (wage and social security taxes) and, to a rather limited extent, on income from small private companies and self-employment (company taxes). The top marginal tax rate on labor income (20 percent) was much lower than in the FRG (where the top rate was reduced from 56 percent to 53 percent in 1990). Moreover, it was only levied on regular wage income, while supplementary payments and premiums were tax free. Thus, in 1988 wage taxes accounted for only 8½ percent of gross income of wage earners (compared with 14½ percent in the FRG). Social security contributions from wage earners accounted for another 7 percent of gross wage income (12 percent in the FRG), bringing the total average direct tax burden to 15¾ percent (26½ percent in the FRG). Company taxes were highly progressive with top rates reaching 90 percent for all companies and for the self-employed who did not benefit from preferential tax rate schedules.[56]

Chapters IV and V of the State Treaty on GEMSU contained stipulations breaking down the existing public sector into the territorial authorities, the social security system (consisting of pension, unemployment, health, and accident insurances), and private and public enterprises (e.g., railways and the postal system). These chapters also stated that, with a view to promoting social union, the social security system of the FRG be introduced in the

GDR. Thus, regulations for unemployment compensation and pension payments were to be harmonized with those in the FRG;[57] the generous special social benefits previously granted to GDR immigrants by the FRG were eliminated shortly before GEMSU became effective.[58] In the area of health insurance and services, a gradual transition to the FRG system and standards was envisaged. Contributions to the social security system were introduced at the same rates as in the FRG.

Regarding fiscal reform, the expenditure and revenue side of the GDR Government accounts were to be completely restructured. On the expenditure side, the budget would be substantially reshaped by the altered relationship between the Government and the enterprises and by the elimination of most consumer subsidies. On the revenue side, the State Treaty stipulated the adoption of the tax system of the FRG by the GDR. Indirect taxes were to be introduced on July 1, while the full system of direct taxes would be introduced in January 1991. For the second half of 1990, a simplified system of income and corporate taxation was adopted.[59]

In addition to specifying expenditure and revenue reforms, the State Treaty on GEMSU provided a financial framework for fiscal policy in the GDR in 1990 and 1991, in the form of borrowing limits for the GDR Government and provision for fiscal transfers from the FRG to the GDR. This framework was, however, overtaken by events, as the much weaker-than-expected economic situation in east Germany in the second half of 1990 was reflected in the government finances and the earlier-than-expected political union fundamentally changed the institutional framework. As far as central government functions are concerned, they have been absorbed, from October 3, 1990, by the federal government budget, and the new Länder and the local authorities in the eastern part of Germany will have their own budgets. Recent budgetary developments in east Germany are discussed in Chapter XI.

---

[56] Preferential tax treatment was given to several groups of self-employed. Highly preferential rates applied to scientists, artisans, and writers (with a top marginal rate of 30 percent). Other groups benefiting from preferential rates were other professionals (top marginal rate of 60 percent) and retail traders (top marginal rate of 70 percent).

[57] Unemployment benefits would amount to 65 percent or 68 percent of net wages in previous employment, depending on the marital status of the worker. After 45 years of work, pensioners would receive, on average, 70 percent of the average GDR net wage.

[58] These benefits included special assistance in finding jobs and housing as well as settling-in grants. In addition, GDR immigrants had full access to the FRG's social security system as if they had paid regular contributions.

[59] In the second half of 1990, wage taxes were to be levied on the basis of Tax Class I of the west German tax code which normally only applies to unmarried persons without children. Companies were to pay taxes according to the GDR tax code for the remainder of the year.

Appendix I

Statistical Tables

Table A1.   German Democratic Republic: Average Monthly Gross Wage Income by Sector

(In marks)

	1970	1975	1980	1985	1987	1988	1989
Agriculture and forestry	710	886	1,000	1,076	1,156	1,197	1,242
Industry	770	895	1,039	1,147	1,253	1,292	1,324
Construction	833	949	1,041	1,158	1,255	1,287	1,310
Trade	668	798	905	1,021	1,104	1,134	1,168
Transportation	806	990	1,127	1,241	1,378	1,405	1,436
Post and telecommunications	653	818	928	1,075	1,136	1,185	1,206
Average[1]	740	889	1,007	1,120	1,214	1,250	1,281
Standard deviation	74	74	82	78	102	98	97

Source: Statistisches Bundesamt, *DDR 1990–Zahlen und Fakten*, 1990.

[1] Unweighted.

Table A2.   German Democratic Republic: Income and Money in Circulation

(In millions of marks)

	1960	1970	1975	1980	1985	1986	1987	1988	1989
Cash	4,543	7,407	10,139	12,250	13,651	14,330	15,014	15,623	17,022
(*In percent of money*)	20.6	12.4	11.9	10.9	9.9	9.8	9.6	9.3	9.6
Savings deposits	17,498	52,149	75,315	99,730	124,577	132,315	141,851	151,590	159,671
(*In percent of money*)	79.4	87.6	88.1	89.1	90.1	90.2	90.4	90.7	90.4
Money[1]	22,041	59,556	85,454	111,980	138,228	146,645	156,865	167,213	176,693
Disposable income	57,500	79,400	101,100	120,900	141,600	149,500	156,500	162,600	166,800
Velocity of money[2]	2.61	1.33	1.18	1.08	1.02	1.02	1.00	0.97	0.94

Source: Staatliche Zentralverwaltung für Statistik der DDR, *Statistisches Jahrbuch der DDR 1989*; and Statistisches Bundesamt, *DDR 1990–Zahlen und Fakten*, 1990.

[1] Excluding deposits of Government and enterprises and life insurance deposits of private households.

[2] Disposable income divided by money.

**Table A3.   German Democratic Republic and Federal Republic of Germany:
Selected Consumer Prices, 1985**

Product or Service	Price in GDR (*In marks*)	Price in FRG (*In deutsche mark*)	GDR Price in Percent of FRG Price
Food, beverages, and tobacco			
Potatoes (5 kg)	4.05	5.32	76
Tomatoes (kg)	4.40	2.10	210
Apples (kg)	1.40	2.15	65
Canned pineapple (½ kg)	18.50	4.10	451
Beef (kg)	9.80	19.45	50
Eggs (10)	3.40	2.39	142
Butter (kg)	9.20	8.76	105
Rye bread (1½ kg)	0.93	4.54	21
Noodles (½ kg)	1.40	1.99	70
Sugar (kg)	1.59	1.72	92
Chocolate (100 g)	3.85	0.89	433
Coffee (250 g)	25.00	5.25	476
Beer (0.33 liter)	0.98	0.66	149
White wine (0.7 liter)	7.80	3.98	196
Cigarettes (20)	3.20	3.47	92
Textiles			
Men's jeans	135.00	59.90	225
Men's leather jackets	1,690.00	259.00	653
Men's shirts	41.00	20.00	205
Pantyhose	15.80	2.99	528
Men's shoes	218.00	89.90	242
Bed linens	119.50	39.35	299
Consumer durables			
Bedroom furniture	4,728.00	1,870.00	241
Living room furniture	4,275.00	1,495.00	286
Kitchen range	815.00	389.50	209
Refrigerator	1,435.00	369.50	388
Washing machine	2,750.00	869.50	316
Radio-cassette recorder	1,160.00	199.95	580
Pocket calculator	123.00	9.95	1,236
Color television	5,650.00	1,199.00	471
Camera	2,530.00	429.00	588
Car (Lada Nova)	24,500.00	10,210.00	240
Quartz wrist watch	260.00	25.00	1,040
Housing			
Rent (two-room apartment)	75.00	390.00	19
Electricity (75 kwh)	7.50	29.30	26
Gas (1,000 m³)	38.00	95.40	40
Lignite coal (50 kg)	3.51	19.40	18
Services			
Railway ticket (50 km)	4.00	9.20	43
Commuter ticket (per month)	20.00	96.00	21
Children's day care (per month)	7.00	140.00	5
Men's haircut	1.90	11.25	17
Permanent wave	9.90	45.00	22
Suit cleaning	7.20	12.35	58
Restaurant meal (pork steak)	4.60	7.50	61
Two-week vacation package in Romania	1,960.00	926.00	212

Source: Deutsche Bundesbank.

Table A4.   German Democratic Republic: Government Revenue and Expenditure

(In billions of marks)

	1980	1985	1987	1988
Total expenditure	160.3	234.4	260.2	269.5
Of which:				
Housing	*17.4*	*27.1*	*29.1*	*30.2*
Social security	*39.7*	*45.7*	*51.5*	*54.1*
Consumer price subsidies	*16.9*	*40.6*	*49.3*	*49.8*
Transfers to industry	*39.4*	*64.6*	*74.5*	*84.5*
Transfers to agriculture	*12.1*	*11.3*	*10.8*	*9.4*
National defense	*9.4*	*13.0*	*15.1*	*15.7*
Total revenue	160.7	235.5	260.4	269.7
Of which:				
Transfers from industry	*115.2*	*176.8*	*188.3*	*193.5*
Transfers from agriculture	*5.9*	*12.7*	*13.8*	*12.5*
Company taxes	*5.3*	*7.7*	*8.9*	*9.2*
Wage tax	*6.8*	*8.5*	*9.6*	*10.0*
Other taxes	*1.4*	*1.5*	*1.6*	*1.7*
Social security contributions	*16.5*	*18.9*	*20.1*	*20.6*
Balance	0.4	1.1	0.3	0.2

Source: Staatliche Zentralverwaltung für Statistik der DDR, *Statistisches Jahrbuch der DDR*, 1989.

Table A5.   German Democratic Republic and Federal Republic of Germany: Consumption of Private Households, 1985

(In percent of total)

	German Democratic Republic		Federal Republic of Germany	
	Four-person employee household	Two-person pensioner household	Four-person employee household	Two-person pensioner household
Food, beverages, and tobacco	41.0	51.1	26.6	32.3
Food	27.0	34.4	17.8	23.9
Beverages and tobacco	9.8	13.3	5.3	5.2
Consumption in restaurants	4.2	3.4	3.5	3.2
Manufactured goods	41.8	30.4	35.4	22.4
Textiles and clothing	11.1	9.1	6.9	6.2
Shoes	3.2	1.9	1.8	0.9
Other	27.5	19.4	26.7	15.3
Services and repairs	14.7	16.9	34.4	43.3
Rents	3.4	4.3	17.7	24.0
Utilities	1.8	2.4	4.8	7.3
Transportation	1.2	2.4	3.0	4.6
Repairs and other services	8.3	7.8	8.9	7.4
Taxes, insurances, and contributions	2.5	1.6	3.6	2.0
Total	100.0	100.0	100.0	100.0

Source: Deutscher Bundestag, *Materialien zum Bericht zur Lage der Nation im geteilten Deutschland 1987*, 1987, p. 510.

Table A6. German Democratic Republic: Purchasing Power of the Mark

(Purchasing power of the deutsche mark = 100)

	1972[1]	1977[2]	1981[2]	1983[2]	1985[2]
	Four-person employee household				
Consumption basket of FRG	88	88	83	88	89
Consumption basket of GDR	101	112	120	125	124
Average	95	100	102	107	107
	Two-person pensioner household				
Consumption basket of FRG	105	104	98	111	110
Consumption basket of GDR	125	126	130	143	145
Average	115	115	114	127	128

Source: Deutscher Bundestag, *Materialien zum Bericht zur Lage der Nation im geteilten Deutschland 1987*, 1987, p. 517.
[1] End 1972–beginning 1973.
[2] Midyear.

Table A7. German Democratic Republic: Consolidated Balance Sheet of the Credit System as of December 31, 1989

(In billions of marks)

Assets		Liabilities	
Domestic credit	**421.4**	**Domestic deposits**	**238.4**
Enterprises	260.4	Enterprises	48.3
Housing	108.5[1]	Housing	12.3
Consumers	2.9	Households	174.4[2]
Government	49.6[3]	Government	3.4
Foreign assets	**47.1**	**Foreign liabilities**	**68.3**
State-trading		State-trading	
countries	11.5	countries	1.0
Other	35.6	Other	67.3
		Currency in circulation	**17.0**
		Other liabilities	**144.8**
		Equity	50.9
		RIKOs[4]	93.9
Total	**468.5**	**Total**	**468.5**

Source: Staatsbank, *Jahresbericht 1989*, March 1990.
[1] Of this, M 10.4 billion were used for public construction (hospitals, schools, kindergartens, etc.).
[2] Of this, M 90.7 billion were in savings accounts, M 69 billion in sight deposits, and M 14.7 billion in term deposits.
[3] Of this, M 31.9 billion were loans to the Government. The remainder reflected shares and participations of the State Bank in public property.
[4] RIKOs (*Richtungskoeffizienten*) reflect the cumulated balance of the special fund described in footnote 18.

Table A8. German Democratic Republic: External Trade[1]

(In billions of valuta mark)

	1970	1980	1985	1986	1987	1988
Exports	19.2	57.1	93.5	91.5	89.9	90.2
State-trading countries	14.2	39.7	60.8	61.1	61.9	62.7
Of which: U.S.S.R.	...	*20.0*	*34.8*	*33.5*	*33.0*	*32.3*
Other countries	5.0	17.4	32.7	30.4	28.0	27.5
Imports	20.4	63.0	86.7	90.5	86.6	87.2
State-trading countries	14.1	40.1	58.2	61.5	60.0	59.9
Of which: U.S.S.R.	...	*22.6*	*35.2*	*37.1*	*35.5*	*34.2*
Other countries	6.2	22.9	28.5	28.9	26.7	27.3
Trade balance	−1.1	−5.8	6.8	1.0	3.3	3.0
State-trading countries	0.1	−0.4	2.6	−0.4	1.9	2.8
Of which: U.S.S.R.	...	*−2.5*	*−0.4*	*−3.6*	*−2.5*	*−1.9*
Other countries	−1.2	−5.5	4.2	1.5	1.3	0.3

Source: Staatliche Zentralverwaltung für Statistik der DDR, *Statistisches Jahrbuch der DDR*, 1989.

[1] Trade data of the former GDR substantially underestimated trade with non-CMEA countries. Accordingly, it is likely that these data will be revised.

Table A9. German Democratic Republic: External Trade with IMF Member Countries

(In millions of U.S. dollars)

	1982	1983	1984	1985	1986	1987	1988	1989
Exports	5,005	5,128	4,830	4,756	5,342	5,581	5,853	6,095
To industrial countries	2,140	2,181	2,123	2,097	2,241	2,324	2,414	2,638
To developing countries	2,865	2,947	2,707	2,660	3,101	3,257	3,438	3,457
Imports	4,685	5,052	4,844	4,404	5,237	6,404	6,800	7,291
From industrial countries	1,864	2,169	1,983	1,624	2,066	2,721	3,202	3,454
From developing countries	2,821	2,883	2,861	2,780	3,171	3,682	3,597	3,837
Trade balance	320	76	−14	353	106	−823	−947	−1,196
With industrial countries	276	12	140	473	176	−398	−788	−816
With developing countries	44	64	−154	−120	−70	−425	−159	−380

Source: International Monetary Fund, *Direction of Trade Statistics*.

**Table A10. German Democratic Republic:
External Trade by Major Products**

(In percent of total)

	1970	1980	1987	1988
Exports				
Machinery, equipment, and vehicles	51.7	51.3	48.0	47.6
Fuels, minerals, and metals	10.1	14.8	16.7	15.1
Other raw materials, semifinished				
goods, and food products	7.4	6.4	6.8	7.0
Consumer goods	20.2	14.8	16.0	16.4
Chemical products, fertilizers,				
rubber, construction material,				
and other products	10.6	12.7	12.5	13.9
Imports				
Machinery, equipment, and vehicles	34.2	30.8	34.1	37.0
Fuels, minerals, and metals	27.6	36.7	38.0	33.5
Other raw materials, semifinished				
goods, and food products	28.1	18.9	13.1	14.1
Consumer goods	4.5	5.0	5.7	5.7
Chemical products, fertilizer,				
rubber, construction material,				
and other products	5.6	8.6	9.1	9.7

Source: Staatliche Zentralverwaltung für Statistik der DDR, *Statistisches Jahrbuch der DDR*, 1989.

**Table A11. German Democratic Republic: Payments Received from the Public Sector of
the Federal Republic of Germany**

(In billions of deutsche mark)

	1971–75	1976–80	1981	1982	1983	1984	1985	1986	1987	1988
Payments from federal budget	**1.2**	**3.4**	**1.0**	**1.0**	**0.7**	**0.7**	**0.6**	**0.7**	**0.6**	**0.6**
Lump-sum payment for transit										
traffic	0.9	2.2	0.6	0.6	0.6	0.6	0.6	0.6	0.5	0.5
Other[1]	0.2	1.2	0.5	0.4	0.2	0.1	—	0.1	0.1	—
Payments from other public budgets	**0.4**	**0.4**	**0.1**	**0.1**	**0.2**	**0.2**	**0.2**	**0.2**	**0.2**	**0.3**
Payments for services supplied										
to Berlin	0.2	0.4	0.1	0.1	0.1	0.1	0.1	0.1	0.2	0.2
Federal Post Office and										
Railways	0.2	0.1	—	—	0.1	0.1	0.1	0.1	—	0.1
Total	**1.6**	**3.9**	**1.1**	**1.1**	**1.0**	**0.9**	**0.8**	**0.9**	**0.8**	**0.9**

Source: Deutsches Institut für Wirtschaftsforschung, *DDR–Wirtschaft im Umbruch*, 1990.
[1] Includes capital transfers to improve traffic with Berlin, reimbursement of visa fees, etc.

Table A12.   Balance of Payments of the Federal Republic of Germany with the German Democratic Republic

(In billions of deutsche mark)

	1975–88[1]			
Item	Total	In units of accounts	In free currency	1988[1]
Transactions in goods and services	**−7.4**	**2.8**	**−10.2**	**−0.4**
Goods	0.2	−4.4	4.6	0.2
Exports to GDR	77.4	72.8	4.6	6.5
Imports from GDR	77.2	77.2	0.0	6.4
Services	−7.6	7.2	−14.8	−0.6
Receipts	20.9	15.9	5.0	1.9
Expenditure	28.5	8.7	19.8	2.5
Of which:				
Transportation				
Receipts	7.3	7.3	—	0.6
Expenditure	1.4	1.4	—	0.2
Travel				
Receipts	2.7	—	2.7	0.5
Expenditure	16.1	—	16.1	1.2
Post Office lump-sum payment				
Expenditure	1.8	1.8	—	0.2
Transfer payments	**−15.0**	**−0.1**	**−14.9**	**−1.3**
Private sector	−2.9	−0.1	−2.9	−0.2
Transfers from GDR	1.5	—	1.5	0.1
Transfers to GDR	4.4	0.1	4.3	0.3
Public sector	—	—	—	—
Transfers from GDR	12.0	—	12.0	1.2
Transfers to GDR	12.0	—	12.0	1.2
Of which:				
Transit lump-sum payment	6.6	—	6.6	0.5
Payments to visitors from GDR	2.0	—	2.0	0.4
Balance on current account[2]	**−22.4**	**2.7**	**−25.1**	**−1.8**
Balance on capital account[2]	**−2.0**	**−2.2**	**0.2**	**0.6**
Of which:				
Swing credit of Deutsche Bundesbank	0.7	0.7	—	0.4
Balance on current and capital accounts[2]	**−24.4**	**0.5**	**−24.9**	**−1.2**

Source: Deutsche Bundesbank, *Monthly Report*, January 1990.

[1] Cumulative.

[2] Minus sign indicates deficit of the FRG.

Table A13.   German Democratic Republic: Employment[1] by Sector and Type of Ownership, 1988

	Socialist		Private	
	In thousands	In percent	In thousands	In percent
Industry	3,389	99.9	2	0.1
Crafts (excluding construction)	78	27.6	205	72.4
Construction	563	92.3	47	7.7
Agriculture and forestry	955	98.5	15	1.5
Transportation and postal services	660	97.8	15	2.2
Trade	829	90.0	92	10.0
Other productive sectors	263	98.8	3	1.2
''Nonproductive'' sectors	1,770	94.9	95	5.1
Total	8,506	94.7	473	5.3

Source: Staatliche Zentralverwaltung für Statistik der DDR, *Statistisches Jahrbuch der DDR, 1989.*
[1] Including apprentices.

Table A14.   German Democratic Republic: Interest Rates as of End-1989

(In percent)

On credits to finance fixed investment	
Basic rate	5.0
Interest rate deductions up to	1.8
Interest rate surcharges up to	8.0
On credits to finance working capital	
Basic rate	5.0
Interest rate deductions up to	1.8
Interest rate surcharges up to	8.0
Overdraft	12.0
Penalty rate	12.0
On credits to state or cooperative institutions for housing construction	4.0
On consumer credit	
Basic rate	6.0
For families with many children	3.0
For special cases	—
On household savings deposits	3.25
On short-term deposits of state-owned companies, cooperatives, and private enterprises	1.0
On long-term deposits of cooperatives and private enterprises	
12–23 months	2.0
24–35 months	3.0
36 months and more	4.0

Source: Deutsches Institut für Wirtschaftsforschung, *DDR–Wirtschaft im Umbruch*, 1990.

Appendix II

A Brief History of Central Planning in the German Democratic Republic

The constitution of the GDR (Article 9) mandated a socialist planned economy. Accordingly, production, employment, investment, price formation, money and credit creation, and, though less directly, private consumption, were in one way or another subject to central planning. The approach to central planning in the GDR was changed on several occasions because of dissatisfaction with the results. These changes manifested themselves in the relationship between the command and the operational spheres of the economy. Broadly, three phases can be identified:

- strict central planning (1945–62)
- reform period under General Secretary Ulbricht (1963–70)
- recentralization under General Secretary Honecker (1971–89)

Central planning in the first phase was very crude, with complete dominance of the command sphere. Production, distribution, and investment at the plant level were controlled directly and output volumes were specified in detail. Capital investment, particularly in heavy industries took precedence over satisfying consumer demand. This rigid approach to planning led to severe difficulties resulting in low economic growth, pervasive bottlenecks, and structural imbalances between supply and demand[1] and triggered a comprehensive reform of the planning system in the early 1960s.[2] The new economic system (*Neues Ökonomisches System der Plannung und Leitung der Volkswirtschaft* or *NÖS*) was adopted by the Ministerial Council in 1963. Its main characteristic was a partial shift of responsibilities from the command sphere to the operational sphere, giving companies more freedom in decision making. So-called "economic levers" (*Ökonomische Hebel*) were introduced, reducing substantially the number of quantitative indicators and targets. Profitability and premium wages were given greater emphasis. In addition, a price reform

was carried out, starting with capital goods prices and later extending to inputs for industry. The prices of consumer goods, however, were adjusted only to a small extent, because stable consumer prices remained an important political objective. The measures adopted were, however, partial, and following some early successes of the economic reform program, severe difficulties re-emerged in the late 1960s.

Under a new party leader, Erich Honecker, the eighth party congress of the SED brought the reform era to an abrupt end and shifted economic policy back to a more direct system of central planning. Under external pressures (oil price shocks in 1973 and 1979 and a drying-up of credit from Western banks in 1982), this system was modified several times, and some elements of the earlier reform program were reintroduced. In particular, the system of targets and indicators was changed frequently. In 1984, net profits and other efficiency criteria were again used as important measures of company performance. The principle of "creating own funds for investment" was revived, giving back to companies some freedom in making independent investment decisions. Frequent attempts were also made to improve the functioning of the rigid price system.[3] Success was limited, however, because of the partial nature of the reforms. For example, in 1979–80 many smaller and medium-sized companies with similar production and marketing characteristics were merged into the so-called *Kombinate* in order to facilitate central planning and control.[4] The return to the strict command economy in the early 1970s followed by the subsequent partial reintroduction of reform elements was not successful: the gap in living standards between east and west Germany widened further, sowing the seeds for the demise of central planning at the end of the 1980s.

---

[1] Economic difficulties had been exacerbated by the mass exodus of GDR citizens to west Germany before the erection of the Berlin wall in 1961 (see Chapter VIII for details), frictions in intra-German trade relations, and a bad harvest in 1961.

[2] Interestingly, the reform movement began in the U.S.S.R., spurred by a series of articles in *Pravda*. General Secretary Ulbricht propagated these ideas in the GDR and the SED Politburo adopted them in 1962. The sixth party congress of the SED accepted a comprehensive economic reform program in 1963.

[3] In June 1976, industrial producer prices were adjusted in the wake of the first oil price shock and new rules for determining consumer prices were introduced (constant prices for basic goods; cost determined prices for more advanced products). In the 1984 reform of agricultural prices, the principle of cost determined prices was extended to agriculture. Also in 1984, pricing rules for new products were introduced and a new price system for capital goods was initiated.

[4] In 1988, there were altogether 173 centrally controlled and 143 locally controlled *Kombinate*, which together accounted for close to 50 percent of overall employment in the GDR. The majority of enterprises merged into the *Kombinate* (about 60 percent) were small and medium-sized companies (up to 500 employees); only 21 enterprises with more than 10,000 employees were part of the mergers.

IV

Investment Needs in East Germany

Donogh McDonald and Günther Thumann

The events of the past year have focused attention on the troubled state of east Germany's economy. At the same time, the prospect of a fast pace of integration of the two German economies has raised the question of what is needed to bring labor productivity in east Germany close to that prevailing in the western part of the country. In this chapter, a framework for analyzing the supply side of east Germany's economy is developed, in which productivity growth is linked to capital accumulation and improvements in the efficiency with which labor and capital services are utilized. This is then used to provide illustrative calculations for the investment needs based on assumptions relating to the initial conditions in east Germany, the behavior of factor efficiency, and the speed with which the productivity gap between east and west Germany is narrowed.

The approach is, thus, a macroeconomic one. It involves estimating the capital required to achieve a specified productivity level relative to west Germany and comparing this with an estimate of the current capital stock in east Germany. Some examples of the former calculation are easily given. Assuming the same potential supply of services per unit of labor and capital as in west Germany, the achievement of a productivity level in east Germany on par with that in the west would require a similar capital-labor ratio and elimination of inefficiencies in the economic system. Actually, this would probably overstate the capital requirements, as capital in east Germany would be on average much newer than in the west. A lower productivity target would, of course, reduce the capital needed and indeed, more than proportionately, given the ability to substitute labor for capital in the production process. Estimates of the present value of the capital stock in east Germany are more difficult, since they involve evaluating current output in terms of what can be sold in open markets. They also depend on the extent to which productivity can be increased with a more efficient use of existing resources. Illustrative calculations are provided for initial produc-

tivity levels of 30 percent and 35 percent of the west German level, and a range of values for the efficiency of factor use in east Germany at the time of German economic, monetary, and social union (GEMSU).

Given the nature of the calculations, it is necessary first to map out a scenario for the economy of west Germany; this is provided in the next section. Then the supply framework for east Germany is discussed in greater detail. These two sections form the basis for the numerical illustrations of the investment requirements in east Germany. The calculations show that the investment needs are large but also rather sensitive to the assumptions made. Assuming an initial productivity level in east Germany that is 30 percent of the level in west Germany, net investment of some DM 1,100 billion (in terms of 1990 prices) would be required over the period 1991–2000, under the central scenario, in order to reach a productivity level that is 80 percent of the west German level by the year 2001. This net investment would amount to about 60 percent of net national product in west Germany in 1990 and involve an increase in the net capital stock in the east of about 170 percent from its end-1990 level, compared with an assumed increase in west Germany's net capital stock of about 40 percent over the same period. To close the productivity gap with the west completely would require, perhaps, an additional DM 600 billion in net investment.

Supply Conditions in West Germany

Initial Conditions

It is assumed that value added in west Germany is determined according to a CES (constant elasticity of substitution) production function:

$$V = [p_L \cdot LS^{-\lambda} + p_K \cdot KS^{-\lambda}]^{-1/\lambda} \qquad (1)$$

where V is real (net) value added, KS and LS are the supplies of capital and labor services, p_K and p_L are constants,[1] and λ is $\sigma/(1 - \sigma)$ with σ being the elasticity of substitution between capital and labor services. Technical change is assumed to be labor augmenting and is incorporated in LS; there is therefore no need in equation (1) for a variable denoting total factor productivity. Supplies of factor services at time (t) can be characterized as follows:

$$KS_{Wt} = K_{Wt} \tag{2}$$

$$LS_{Wt} = TA_{Wt} \cdot TK_{Wt} \cdot L_{Wt} \tag{3}$$

$$TA_{Wt} = (1 + \epsilon_A)^t \tag{4}$$

$$TK_{Wt} = \{1 + f \cdot [(KL_{Wt}/KL_{W0}) - 1]\} \tag{5}$$

TA_{Wt} and TK_{Wt} are terms describing technical change; technical change is assumed to be, in part, exogenous (TA_{Wt}) and, in part, related to the speed with which the capital-labor ratio increases (TK_{Wt}), where K/L denotes the capital-labor ratio. Purely as a normalization convenience, 1990 is designated t_0 and KS_W and LS_W in 1990 are set equivalent to the actual levels of capital (K) and labor (L).[2] The production function (1) is parameterized so as to make it consistent with supply conditions in the west German economy in 1990. It is assumed that the elasticity of substitution between KS and LS is 0.5,[3] that firms are profit maximizing, and that the labor market is in equilibrium (in the sense that the marginal product of labor is equal to the real wage). On this basis, information on factor shares in net national product can be used to derive the parameter values in (1). A profile of key supply-side elements for the west German economy in 1990 is provided in Table 1.

Medium-Term Assumptions

The next step is to construct a scenario for the evolution of the supplies of labor and capital services so as to provide a picture of production conditions in the west German economy in 2001. The broad outlines of the scenario are as follows. The labor force is assumed to rise in total by 4½ percent, with most of this occurring in

Table 1. West Germany: Key Supply-Side Data[1]

(Evaluated at constant 1990 prices)

	1990	2001
Net domestic product, factor cost *(In billions of deutsche mark)*	1,856	2,555
Net capital stock[2] *(In billions of deutsche mark)*	7,205	10,250
Total employment *(In millions)*	28.2	29.6
Of which: dependent employment *(In millions)*	25.2	26.4
Gross income per employee *(In thousands of deutsche mark)*	50	66
Total labor income[3] *(In billions of deutsche mark)*	1,404	1,955
Compensation of capital *(In billions of deutsche mark)*	452	600
Rate of return[4] *(In percent)*	6.3	5.9

[1] Authors' estimates for 1990 and model calculations for 2001. The estimates for 1990 were made in the summer of 1990. Later revisions, which are shown in Table 1 of Chapter II, have not been incorporated here or in the modeling exercises in Chapters V–VI. If the more recent estimates had been incorporated, the effects on the calculations of capital requirements presented in this chapter or on the scenarios presented in the next two chapters would have been negligible.

[2] Beginning of the year; includes residential structures and public infrastructure.

[3] Assuming that the average labor income of the self-employed is the same as that for employees.

[4] Compensation of capital relative to the net capital stock, including public infrastructure and residential property.

the first half of the scenario under the influence of immigration from east Germany and Eastern Europe; the increase in employment is a little larger, as the unemployment rate falls from 6½ percent in 1990 to 6 percent in 2001. With respect to the capital stock, the key consideration is what happens to the rate of return to capital. In the scenario adopted, the rate of return to capital declines by about ½ of 1 percentage point, implying an increase in the capital-output ratio. The fall in the rate of return is founded on the premise that in 1990, based on real interest rates prevailing prior to the announcement of GEMSU, the rate of return is above equilibrium, that is, the capital stock in 1990 has not yet adjusted fully to the sharp unexpected decline in the labor share (rise in the profit rate) that occurred in 1987–90.[4] This disequilibrium has probably been offset, at least in large part, by the rise in real interest rates associated with GEMSU. In later years (as the effect of GEMSU on the cost of capital recedes), the disequilibrium would re-emerge in the absence of a rise in the capital-output ratio. The final element needed to complete the picture of supply conditions in west Germany in 2001 is the behavior of

---

[1] The parameters p_K and p_L reflect the feasible technology for combining KS and LS and the units in which KS and LS are denominated. KS is related to the capital stock at the beginning of the year.

[2] K is the net capital stock in terms of 1990 prices and L is the labor force in millions of workers.

[3] Artus found elasticities of substitution ranging from 0.5 to 0.8 in the major industrial countries (see Jacques R. Artus, "The Disequilibrium Real Wage Rate Hypothesis—An Empirical Evaluation," *Staff Papers*, International Monetary Fund (Washington), Vol. 31 (June 1984), pp. 249–302). Lipschitz estimated an elasticity of substitution in the region of one half in the manufacturing sector of the FRG (see L. Lipschitz, "Wage Gaps, Employment, and Production in German Manufacturing" (unpublished; Washington: International Monetary Fund, 1986)). Econometric evidence presented in Chapter IX also suggests an elasticity of substitution in the region of one half.

[4] Recent developments in the labor share in west Germany are discussed in Chapter II, section on "Employment, Wages, and Prices."

technical change. It is assumed that autonomous labor-augmenting technical change takes place at the rate of 1 percent a year (i.e., in equation (4), $\epsilon_A = 0.01$) and that labor services per unit of labor input respond to changes in the capital-labor ratio with an elasticity of one half (i.e., $f = 0.5$).[5] This implies that, if there was no change in the capital-output ratio,[6] labor productivity would grow at 2 percent a year; half of this productivity growth would reflect exogenous forces and the other half be induced by capital accumulation. In the medium-term scenario adopted here, labor productivity rises somewhat faster (2½ percent a year) owing to the increase in the capital-output ratio. Incorporating the assumed growth in the labor force, output grows at an annual rate of 3 percent and the net capital stock at 3¼ percent.

A Supply-Side Framework for East Germany

In analyzing supply conditions, it is assumed that the production function in east Germany is the same as in west Germany; lower productivity levels in the east reflect, first, a poorer endowment of resources, which results in a lower potential output per worker than in west Germany and, second, inefficiencies in production practices, which lead to a below-potential economic performance. The lower potential output per worker in the east is due, in part, to the mix of factor resources (less capital per worker) but also to the assumption that labor-augmenting technical change is embodied to some extent in capital accumulation; the latter assumption implies there are fewer labor services potentially available per man-hour of work effort than in west Germany. The below-potential performance of the eastern economy is also viewed as having two sources: general inefficiency in the economy, affecting both capital and labor, and labor-specific inefficiency. The first of these can be attributed to poor management and the absence of a well-functioning system of factor allocation. Labor-specific inefficiency is likely to comprise in large part of labor hoarding—lowering the physical quantity of labor used does not lower output as retained labor can be used more efficiently.[7] More generally, to the extent that systemic inefficiencies in the economy are not neutral in their effects on the effective supply of capital and labor services, a factor-specific inefficiency term is necessary in the modeling of production. In the context of the modeling approach used here, it seems likely that this

nonneutrality term should be attached to labor services both because of the believed importance of labor hoarding and because labor is more mobile.[8] These elements are reflected in the following characterization of the supply of factor services in east Germany:

$$k_E = g \cdot k_W \qquad (6)$$

$$l_E = h \cdot g \cdot \{1 + f \cdot [(KL_E/KL_W) - 1]\} \cdot l_W \qquad (7)$$

Equation (6) relates k_E, the supply of capital services (KS) per unit of capital (K) in east Germany, to a general efficiency factor (g) and the amount of capital services provided by a unit of capital in the west (k_W).[9] Equation (7) states that l_E, labor services (LS) per unit of labor (L) in east Germany, depends on the availability of labor services per physical unit of labor in the west (l_W),[10] the capital-labor ratio in the east relative to the west (KL_E/KL_W),[11] the general efficiency parameter (g), and the labor-specific efficiency parameter (h). The supply of factor services per unit of factor input can be broken into two components: first, what is potentially available and, second, the degree to which this potential is used. In the case of capital services, the potential availability per physical unit of capital is the same as in west Germany[12] but actual use of capital services per unit of capital is lower due to the general inefficiencies in the economy ($g < 1$). In the case of labor services, the potential availability of labor services per man-hour $\{1 + f \cdot [(KL_E/KL_W) - 1]\} \cdot l_W$ is lower than in west Germany (l_W) because of the lower capital-labor ratio. This potential is less than fully used due to the general inefficiency in the economy and to inefficiencies related specifically to labor ($h < 1$). Thus, the key factors influencing productivity in the east relative to that in the west are changes in the efficiency parameters (h and g) and the relative paths of employment and the capital stock in the two areas.

Initial Conditions in East Germany

In characterizing the initial supply position in the east German economy, the objective is to produce a picture of conditions at the start of GEMSU, that is, before any factor reallocation has taken place. Official data of the German Democratic Republic (GDR) suggested that, in 1988, economy-wide labor productivity was close to half

---

[5] The implications of alternative assumptions for the parameter f are discussed in the final section.

[6] This is equivalent to assuming no change in the ratio of KS to LS.

[7] Indeed in the framework used here, there is a positive output effect as labor dishoarding enhances the potential supply of labor services from those remaining in employment, given the assumed link between the capital-labor ratio and labor-augmenting technical change.

[8] Inappropriate allocation of capital can be less easily rectified and, to this extent, is reflected in the valuation of capital and not in an inefficiency term.

[9] As a normalization convenience, k_W is set at 1; see equation (2). For simplicity, the time subscript has been dropped.

[10] The parameter l_W increases over time as a result of labor-augmenting technical change in the west.

[11] This reflects the assumption that labor-augmenting technical change is partially embodied in the capital-labor ratio.

[12] Capital in the east is evaluated in terms of capital in the west.

Table 2. East Germany: Initial Production Conditions Based on 35 Percent Relative Productivity Level

(West Germany = 1)

	I	II	III
Labor share in net national product	0.65	0.675	0.70
Gross wage per employed person	0.30	0.31	0.32
Effective LS per employed person (l_E)	0.41	0.39	0.38
Effective KS per employed person ($g \cdot k_E$)	0.24	0.26	0.28
Case A. General factor efficiency (g)—75 percent			
Potential KS per employed person (k_E)	0.33	0.35	0.38
Potential LS per employed person $\{1 + f \cdot [(KL_E/KL_W) - 1]\}$	0.66	0.67	0.69
Labor efficiency per employed person ($h \cdot g$)[1]	0.62	0.58	0.55
Labor-specific efficiency factor (h)	0.82	0.78	0.73
Starting capital stock (*In billions of 1990 deutsche mark*)	721	777	842
Case B. General factor efficiency (g)—80 percent			
Potential KS per employed person (k_E)	0.30	0.33	0.36
Potential LS per employed person $\{1 + f \cdot [(KL_E/KL_W) - 1]\}$	0.65	0.66	0.68
Labor efficiency per employed person ($h \cdot g$)[1]	0.62	0.59	0.56
Labor-specific efficiency factor (h)	0.78	0.74	0.70
Starting capital stock (*In billions of 1990 deutsche mark*)	676	728	789
Case C. General factor efficiency (g)—85 percent			
Potential KS per employed person (k_E)	0.29	0.31	0.33
Potential LS per employed person $\{1 + f \cdot [(KL_E/KL_W) - 1]\}$	0.64	0.65	0.67
Labor efficiency per employed person ($h \cdot g$)[1]	0.63	0.60	0.57
Labor-specific efficiency factor (h)	0.75	0.71	0.67
Starting capital stock (*In billions of 1990 deutsche mark*)	637	686	743

[1] Calculated as effective LS per employed person divided by potential LS per employed person.

of the level in the Federal Republic of Germany (assuming a 1:1 conversion rate between marks and deutsche mark). All indications are, however, that the underlying position was considerably less favorable. In the months running up to GEMSU, estimates of east German productivity tended to lie in the range of 30–40 percent of the west German level. Developments in the months after GEMSU took effect would suggest that this range should be lowered somewhat.

The approach adopted here is to identify alternative sets of the parameters g, h, and K that would be consistent with the assumed relative productivity level and the employment prevailing in the GDR on the eve of GEMSU. As the notion of productivity being used is based on economic efficiency in the production of a given level of output, the answer depends on relative factor prices. Calculations are made for three different assumptions on the relative factor prices that would result from marginal product pricing; for any level of output, this determines the values of LS and KS. From equations (6) and (7), this leaves two equations in three unknowns (g, h, and K); choosing one of these variables is sufficient to tie down the other two. Tables 2 and 3 show, for

various levels of g and of the labor share in national output, the combinations of h and K that would be consistent with productivity at 30 percent and 35 percent of that in west Germany.[13]

To illustrate the calculations, assume an output per worker that is 35 percent of the level in west Germany, broadly in line with perceptions at the time of GEMSU. Consider case B.II in Table 2, where general factor efficiency is only 80 percent of potential, and the labor share 67½ percent of net national product (which corresponds to a gross wage of 31 percent of the west German level, assuming all workers were employed). With producers maximizing profits, labor services per person employed are 39 percent of the western level and capital services per person employed 26 percent of the western level. Reflecting the assumption that, as a result of general inefficiency, actual factor use is only 80 percent of potential factor use, potential capital services per employed person are one fourth

---

[13] An alternative approach would have been to start from assumed values of g and h; these would have been sufficient to determine K and the warranted factor shares. The calculations resulting from this approach would have been entirely consistent with those described above.

Table 3. East Germany: Initial Production Conditions Based on 30 Percent Relative Productivity Level

(West Germany = 1)

	I	II	III
Labor share in net national product	0.65	0.675	0.70
Gross wage per employed person	0.26	0.27	0.28
Effective LS per employed person (l_E)	0.35	0.34	0.32
Effective KS per employed person ($g \cdot k_E$)	0.21	0.23	0.24
Case A. General factor efficiency (g)—75 percent			
Potential KS per employed person (k_E)	0.28	0.30	0.33
Potential LS per employed person $\{1 + f \cdot [(KL_E/KL_W) - 1]\}$	0.64	0.65	0.66
Labor efficiency per employed person ($h \cdot g$)[1]	0.55	0.52	0.49
Labor-specific efficiency factor (h)	0.73	0.69	0.65
Starting capital stock (*In billions of 1990 deutsche mark*)	618	667	721
Case B. General factor efficiency (g)—80 percent			
Potential KS per employed person (k_E)	0.26	0.28	0.30
Potential LS per employed person $\{1 + f \cdot [(KL_E/KL_W) - 1]\}$	0.63	0.64	0.65
Labor efficiency per employed person ($h \cdot g$)[1]	0.55	0.52	0.50
Labor-specific efficiency factor (h)	0.69	0.66	0.62
Starting capital stock (*In billions of 1990 deutsche mark*)	580	624	676
Case C. General factor efficiency (g)—85 percent			
Potential KS per employed person (k_E)	0.25	0.26	0.29
Potential LS per employed person $\{1 + f \cdot [(KL_E/KL_W) - 1]\}$	0.62	0.63	0.64
Labor efficiency per employed person ($h \cdot g$)[1]	0.56	0.53	0.50
Labor-specific efficiency factor (h)	0.66	0.63	0.59
Starting capital stock (*In billions of 1990 deutsche mark*)	546	588	637

[1] Calculated as effective LS per employed person divided by potential LS per employed person.

higher at 33 percent of the west German level. The lower potential of capital services per employed person than in the west means that the potential labor services per employed person are only 66 percent of the west German level, as labor-augmenting technical change is partially embodied in capital accumulation. Actual use of labor services is only 59 percent of this potential;[14] this in part reflects the general inefficiency in factor use ($g < 1$) but it also involves significant labor-specific inefficiency ($h < 1$). The level of the capital stock implied by these calculations is DM 728 billion,[15] of which DM 582 billion (80 percent) is being effectively used; over time, as the general efficiency of the economy improves, the difference between the potential capital stock and the effective capital stock disappears.

By way of comparison, consider a relative productivity of 30 percent, which seems more in line with recent developments. Case B.II in Table 3 uses the same assumptions on the labor share and general efficiency as in the example just discussed. Since relative factor prices determine the mix of factor services that is efficiently used in production, for any level of g the levels of K and h are proportionately reduced (i.e., they are 86 percent (30 divided by 35) of the level in the example described above); thus, the value of K would be DM 624 billion.

The numerical illustrations in Tables 2 and 3 produce a wide range of estimates for the initial capital stock in east Germany; the calculations assuming a lower general efficiency parameter or higher labor share than in the examples used above produce larger capital stock estimates, while assumptions of higher general efficiency or a lower labor share produce smaller estimates of K. All of these estimates are, however, considerably less than official capital stock data of the GDR.[16] This reflects the objective of measuring the capital stock with a view to what is usable in the new environment, with the valuation based on the value of capital in west Germany. The calculations in the remainder of this chapter and in the next chapter narrow the range of estimates by starting from the premise that underlying productivity in east Germany at the time of GEMSU was about 30 percent of the level in west Germany. While

[14] This is derived by dividing effective labor services by potential labor services.

[15] This estimate includes residential structures and public infrastructure.

[16] The official data put the total net value of the capital stock in 1988 at M 1,685 billion, expressed in terms of 1986 prices, about three quarters of this being in "productive" sectors. However, these estimates excluded residential capital and public infrastructure.

Table 4. East Germany: Capital Requirements in 2001[1]

	Net Capital Stock (In billions of 1990 deutsche mark)	Capital-Labor Ratio (West Germany = 1)
A. Target labor productivity—100 percent of west German level		
1. No factor efficiency advantage	2,580	1.00
2. 5 percent factor efficiency advantage	2,380	0.92
3. 10 percent factor efficiency advantage	2,200	0.85
B. Target labor productivity—80 percent of west German level		
1. No factor efficiency advantage	1,770	0.69
2. 5 percent factor efficiency advantage	1,620	0.63
3. 5 percent factor efficiency disadvantage	1,930	0.75
C. Target labor productivity—80 percent of west German level		
1. $f = 0.5$	1,770	0.69
2. $f = 0.35$	1,630	0.63
3. $f = 0.2$	1,470	0.57
4. $f = 0.0$	1,250	0.48

[1] Beginning of the year.

significant differences remain depending on the assumptions used, these differences are relatively small when compared with the investment needs in east Germany.

The Capital Stock in 2001

In illustrating the capital needs of east Germany in the year 2001, two scenarios for labor productivity are examined: in the more ambitious one, net domestic product (NDP) per worker reaches the same level as in west Germany; in the other, NDP per worker rises to 80 percent of the western level over this period. The narrowing of the productivity gap is achieved in three ways. First, potential productivity rises faster than in west Germany owing to quicker capital accumulation, which also results in a more rapid rate of labor-augmenting technical change. Second, reduction of inefficiencies in factor use closes the gap between actual and potential output. Finally, favorable "vintage" effects on productivity can be expected as a result of the lower average age of the capital stock in the east.

Consider first the capital stock needed to equalize labor productivity by 2001. Leaving aside vintage effects, for the moment, and assuming that over the next ten years inefficiencies in the use of labor and capital are eliminated, that is, g and h reach the same level as in the west ($g = h = 1$), the equalization of productivity would require that capital-labor ratios be the same in the two areas at the beginning of 2001.[17] The actual level

of the capital stock will depend also on employment developments. In what follows, it is assumed that the labor force declines on average at a rate of 1 percent a year and unemployment falls to 6 percent of the labor force.[18] On these assumptions, a net capital stock of DM 2,580 billion would be required in east Germany at the beginning of the year 2001 (case A.1 in Table 4). In this calculation, however, 85 percent of the capital stock in the east would be less than ten years old in 2001, but this would apply to only 55 percent of the capital stock in west Germany.[19] Hence, some favorable vintage effects are to be expected in the east and two alternatives are illustrated in the table: in the first of these, effective labor and capital services per physical unit of factor input are 5 percent higher in east Germany than in the west by 2001 (i.e., $g = 1.05$) while, in the second, the assumed vintage effect is 10 percent ($g = 1.1$). As can

---

[17] It is assumed that there is no change in west Germany in the parameters g and h. Structural measures to improve the allocation of resources in west Germany would increase g and h. The associated increase in profitability would boost the demand for capital in west Germany. Thus even if these increases in g and h were matched in

east Germany, the investment requirements would be larger than calculated in this chapter. It is unlikely, however, that the effects of structural policy measures would significantly affect the broad picture presented here; for example, a 5 percent increase in the estimate of the terminal capital requirements in east Germany would be relatively small in relation to the rise in the capital stock needed over the next decade.

[18] The underlying demographic projections are based on Deutsches Institut für Wirtschaftsforschung, *Wochenbericht, 23–24/90* (Berlin), Vol. 57, June 14, 1990. Net emigration is assumed to decline to 100,000 in 1991, 50,000 in 1992, 20,000 in 1993, and zero thereafter. Migration to west Germany is assumed to be higher, offset by immigration of ethnic Germans from Eastern Europe. A decline of the female participation rate, which is presently much higher in east Germany than in west Germany, is also assumed. An alternative scenario for migration and the labor force is considered in Chapter V.

[19] These calculations include in the new capital stock both net investment in 1991–2000 and replacement investment (depreciation) related to the pre-1990 capital stock. The difference in the average age of the capital stocks would be less marked for machinery and equipment, which has a shorter economic life than structures.

be seen, there is a significant influence on the capital stock needed to equalize productivity levels.

The implications of cutting the target productivity to 80 percent of the west German level are also illustrated in Table 4. Case B.1 examines the situation of no factor efficiency advantages in the east. The reduction of the target productivity level has a more than proportional effect on the capital stock requirements; the sharper reduction in the terminal capital stock than in the target productivity reflects the ability to substitute between capital and labor (and a similar supply of man-hours under the two scenarios, assuming that labor supply is not responsive to wage rates). Indeed, the decline in the estimate of capital needed would have been even greater were it not for the assumption that technical progress is to some extent embodied in capital accumulation. Again, for this scenario, one must consider vintage effects. However, the vintage effects here are likely to be smaller than in the case where the productivity target is 100 percent; with lower capital accumulation in east Germany, the gap between the average age of the capital stock in east and west Germany would be less favorable to the east than in the calculations for case A. Moreover, offsetting these vintage effects, one must consider the possibility that the gap between productive potential and output has not yet been fully closed by 2001.[20] Accordingly, Table 4 presents calculations for the cases of a 5 percent efficiency advantage in the GDR and a 5 percent efficiency disadvantage.

The calculations thus far have assumed that the elasticity of labor services with respect to the capital-labor ratio (the parameter f in equation (7)) is 0.5. The final part of Table 4 illustrates the implications when the degree to which technical progress is embodied in capital accumulation is lower. A striking feature of these calculations is that east German productivity levels could be remarkably close to those in west Germany with production considerably less capital intensive in the east. While there is no firm basis for setting the parameter f at 0.5, it is clear that a number closer to half seems more reasonable than one close to zero.

Investment Needs

The analysis of the previous two sections can be used to illustrate the magnitude of the investment needs in east Germany over the next decade. Taking case B.II in Table 3 as a starting point (a relative productivity level of 30 percent in east Germany and a starting capital stock of DM 624 billion), and assuming net investment of DM 25–30 billion in the second half of 1990, the broad conclusion is that to achieve output per worker similar to that in the west by 2001 would require a net investment of DM 1,500–1,900 billion (in 1990 prices) over the period 1991 to 2000. Moderating the target to 80 percent of west German productivity levels reduces the needed net investment to the range DM 1,000–1,300 billion. One should, of course, bear in mind that, in addition to the assumptions on terminal conditions, the scale of the investment requirement is sensitive to the estimate of the initial capital stock; it is however easy to adapt the calculations to different estimates of the initial capital stock as, in the framework used here, the terminal capital stock is independent of the initial capital stock in the east for a given set of terminal assumptions.

The question arises as to how much of this investment is likely to occur in the public sector. As a guide, one can take the current distribution of the fixed capital stock in west Germany, where about 20 percent is in the general government sector, and assume that the public infrastructure in east Germany is in no worse a state than the capital stock in the remainder of the east's economy; this would suggest that about 20 percent of the net investment requirements would need to be undertaken by general government. Such an estimate would not include investment by public bodies outside of general government (telecommunications and railways, for example), whose investment will presumably be financed in part by capital transfers from the Government.[21] Moreover, the calculations do not take into account expenditures to rectify deterioration of the environment.

---

[20] The existence of an efficiency gap would seem to be more likely the larger the shortfall of east German productivity from the west German level.

[21] Of course, the fact that some activity has been in the public sector in west Germany does not necessarily imply that it will need to be financed by government funds in east Germany. For example, there has been recent discussion on the construction of privately financed toll roads in the east.

V

East Germany
The New *Wirtschaftswunder?*

Donogh McDonald and Günther Thumann

Introduction

The regional imbalances that characterize many advanced industrial economies have long frustrated economic policymakers. The large gaps in our understanding of these imbalances prompt the question: Will the evolution of the east German economy over the next decade reveal a new economic miracle—*Wirtschaftswunder*—or the emergence of another regional problem within the European Community? On the one hand, the saving surplus in west Germany provides a large pool of resources from which the investment needs of east Germany can be financed. Moreover, the tradition of enterprise in the eastern part of the country was strong before World War II and it may be possible to revive this tradition quickly, despite its long suppression by the system of central planning. On the other hand, given the present dearth of capital in east Germany, it will be some time before west German wage levels can be supported in the east without large-scale subsidies or substantial unemployment. This creates obvious tensions. While a slow closing of the earnings gap might result in a migration of the most skilled to the west, a premature narrowing of the gap could well discourage investment; either might endanger the process of economic recovery in the east.

To highlight some of these issues, this chapter presents scenarios for east Germany during the first 11 years of unification (1991–2001) under alternative assumptions as to how quickly the productivity gap between east and west Germany is narrowed.[1] The scenarios take as their starting point a profile of the economic situation in east Germany in the second half of 1990, incorporating official fiscal projections and the assumption that, immediately prior to German economic, monetary, and social union (GEMSU), underlying labor productivity in the east was about 30 percent of the level in west Germany. The growth rates required in the east to narrow the productivity gap over the next decade depend not only on the size of the initial gap but also on the increase in labor productivity

in west Germany; it is assumed that labor productivity in west Germany will increase at about 2½ percent a year or cumulatively by close to one third between 1990 and 2001.[2]

To provide some perspective on the present size of the productivity gap, Table 1 contains information on productivity differences between regions of the Federal Republic of Germany (FRG) in 1987.[3] The Länder in the FRG are arranged into three groups, ranked according to output per capita and productivity levels. The third ranked group (comprising Rhineland-Palatinate, Lower Saxony, and Schleswig-Holstein), which had a population of some 13 million in 1987, had an average productivity level about 13 percent below that of the FRG as a whole and 18 percent below that in the other eight Länder.

Against this background, two scenarios for east Germany are illustrated (see Chart 1).[4] In *scenario A* rapid growth boosts productivity levels in east Germany to 80 percent of the west German level by the year 2001. Unemployment is initially high—one fourth of the labor force in 1991—but falls rapidly and by the end of the scenario is at about the same level (6 percent) as in the baseline scenario for west Germany. The investment needs in this scenario are large: In 1991–92 gross investment averages DM 110 billion a year (43 percent of GDP).[5] This investment is financed entirely by external resources (i.e., resources from outside east Germany, including fiscal transfers from west Germany); indeed, external resources amount to about 150 percent of net investment. Over the period 1991–2001 as a whole, total net investment is of the order of DM 1¼ trillion, equivalent to two thirds of west Germany's net national product in 1990, with three fourths of this net investment financed from outside east Germany.[6] The

---

[1] The duration of the simulation was chosen to allow ten years of investment to influence the terminal productivity level. Investment in 2001 is assumed to have no influence on productivity in 2001.

[2] Further details of the underlying assumptions are given in Chapter IV, section on "Supply Conditions in West Germany."

[3] Of course, to the extent that these productivity differences were due to structural weaknesses in the poorer Länder, they reflected problems one might hope to avoid in restructuring the east German economy.

[4] The model used is described in the following section.

[5] All deutsche mark figures are in terms of 1990 prices. Unless otherwise indicated, all ratios to GDP relate to GDP in east Germany.

[6] The calculation of the investment needs to reach a relative productivity level of 80 percent by 2001 reported in Chapter IV was

Table 1. Federal Republic of Germany: Regional Profile of Output and Employment, 1987

	GDP	Population[1]	Employment[1]	Unemployment Rate[1]	Output per Capita	Output per Worker
	(In billions of deutsche mark)	*(In millions)*		*(In percent)*	*(FRG = 100)*	
Hamburg	91.7	1.6	0.7	11.6	175	178
Bremen	27.5	0.7	0.3	12.8	127	135
Berlin (West)	76.2	2.0	0.9	9.2	115	110
Hesse	203.4	5.5	2.5	5.7	112	109
Baden-Württemberg	322.5	9.3	4.4	4.6	106	99
Bavaria	361.3	10.9	5.1	5.1	101	95
North Rhine-Westphalia	524.4	16.7	6.9	8.8	95	101
Saarland	30.2	1.1	0.4	11.2	87	98
Rhineland-Palatinate	105.7	3.6	1.6	6.7	89	90
Lower Saxony	196.1	7.2	3.0	8.7	83	86
Schleswig-Holstein	70.1	2.6	1.1	8.8	83	84
Total	2009.1	61.1	26.9	7.2	100	100
Top four Länder	398.8	9.8	4.4	7.9	124	122
Middle four Länder	1238.4	38.0	16.8	6.7	99	99
Bottom three Länder	371.9	13.3	5.7	8.1	85	87

Source: Statistisches Bundesamt, *Statistisches Jahrbuch, 1989.*

[1] Population and labor market data as of May 25, 1987.

declining recourse to external saving over time reflects, in part, falling investment requirements in relation to output, but, more important, a rising saving rate. Private saving increases, but the principal source of the stronger external position is the improvement in the government accounts. The general government deficit in the east is initially very large (50 percent of GDP in 1991), principally on account of substantial government dissaving. Over time, the deficit drops steadily, with a small overall deficit and a primary budget surplus by the end of the scenario.[7]

Scenario B is less optimistic, with productivity in 2001 only 60 percent of that in west Germany and migration from east to west occurring on a much larger scale. The weaker economic performance results from lower investment and a slower reduction of inefficiencies in the use of labor and capital. Net investment in 1991–92 is only 60 percent of that in scenario A, and this relative weakness of investment persists throughout the scenario as the initial hesitancy of investors is reinforced by aggressive wage demands and by ingrained structural weaknesses in the economy. The fiscal imbalance declines more slowly than in scenario A as low growth restrains revenue and boosts social expenditure relative to GDP; by the end of the

scenario the primary fiscal deficit in east Germany is of the order of 9 percent of GDP. Larger accumulated deficits also increase interest payments.[8] Given these fiscal developments, the imbalance in the external accounts throughout the scenario is also much larger than in scenario A.

Scenarios A and B are discussed in greater detail in the following sections. In interpreting these scenarios, one should bear in mind the uncertainties surrounding the initial conditions in east Germany, the likely response of foreign investors, prospective migration patterns, the ability of east Germany to absorb large-scale investment (particularly in the initial years of GEMSU), the policy and institutional framework, and the behavior of economic agents. Moreover, as noted above, there are large gaps in our knowledge of the factors that promote rapid growth in some less developed regions but allow others to languish alongside rich neighbors. Thus, it is important to look at scenarios A and B not as projections but as providing a consistent framework within which issues related to GEMSU can be explicitly examined. Some of these issues are brought up as details of the scenarios are presented, with a more wide-ranging discussion following in the final section of the chapter.

While the two illustrative scenarios produce what are in many respects quite different outlooks, a common feature is that they both imply rapid growth rates; in scenario A, output grows at a rate of 10½ percent a year and labor productivity at a rate of 11½ percent, while in scenario B

---

lower as it did not include investment in the year 2001. The share financed by external resources is sensitive to the assumption on fiscal transfers from west Germany. In this chapter, it is assumed that fiscal transfers cover government dissaving in the east. See footnote 26 for further discussion.

[7] For analytical purposes, fiscal operations in east Germany have been separated from those in west Germany. It is also assumed that there are no changes in tax rates or in the rules governing the operations of the social insurance funds.

[8] Given the assumption on fiscal transfers from west Germany, larger interest payments resulting from greater government dissaving in east Germany are recorded in the fiscal accounts of west Germany.

Chart 1. Scenarios for East Germany, 1991–2001

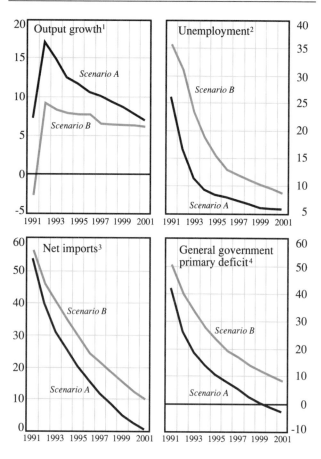

[1] Percent change in real net domestic product. For 1991, growth is measured using output in the second half of 1990 as a measure of the underlying value of output for all of 1990. See footnote 23 in the text.

[2] In percent of the labor force; including the effective period of unemployment for those on short-time work.

[3] Net imports of goods and nonfactor services, in percent of GDP, at 1990 prices.

[4] Overall deficit, excluding interest payments, in percent of GDP, at 1990 prices.

the output and productivity growth rates are 6½ percent and 9 percent, respectively.[9] The challenge over the next ten years is clearly formidable; in Box 1, it is put in a historical context.

The Model

The supply side of the model has already been outlined in Chapter IV (see section on "A Supply-Side Framework for East Germany"). As discussed there, the key elements are capital accumulation, improvements in the general and labor-specific efficiency parameters (g and h), and

changes in employment. In scenarios A and B, all but one of these variables are used as inputs into the model, the exception being employment, which is determined interactively with wages. The model is structured so as to allow wage levels to reflect profit maximization in an environment of well-functioning factor markets; that is, for a given level of employment, there is a warranted real wage. However, in the early years, wage income is allowed to exceed this notional equilibrium. This might be the result of employers being off their profit maximizing labor demand schedules;[10] alternatively, institutional factors might provide those employed in certain sectors with substantial protection from the operation of competitive forces. There is no explicit link in the model between labor markets in the eastern and western parts of Germany. However, the two scenarios presented differ in the scale of migration, with larger westward migration in the less optimistic scenario.[11]

The assumptions on labor income outlined above are a key element in the development of household disposable income. The extent to which income from capital is distributed is also of importance. In broad terms, the distribution rate is set low initially, reflecting the high degree of public ownership and the need to retain earnings to finance investment and restructuring expenditures. Over time, the distribution rate increases but still remains below the west German level at the end of the scenario. Taxation and social transfers are determined within the legal framework adopted under the State Treaty on GEMSU. Given the relatively low initial level of income in east Germany, the average tax rate on wage income is significantly less than that in west Germany; it rises quickly with income growth but remains lower than in the west as long as wage levels are lower. Transfer payments to households are related to caseload (e.g., number of unemployed) and, for unemployment and pension benefits, wage levels in east Germany.

In addition to fiscal operations that take place within the usual framework of the general government accounts, it is important also to consider the operations of the public Trust Fund (*Treuhandanstalt*). The calculations of the Trust Fund's financial balance are on a national accounts basis incorporating dividend receipts, interest payments, and capital transfers to enterprises. Asset transactions related to privatization, the amortization of

[9] The larger gap between output and productivity growth rates in scenario B reflects the assumed scale of westward labor migration, lower labor force participation, and higher unemployment in this scenario.

[10] One can imagine a number of reasons for this. For example, much of the economy will remain in public or cooperative ownership and this may moderate the extent to which profit maximizing criteria are used. Employers in new enterprises may also be willing to pay above the "going wage" to engender good labor relations or, in the case of investors from outside of east Germany, because of pressure from unions at the home base of the investor.

[11] The underlying trend of the labor force in east Germany is based on demographic projections (see Deutsches Institut für Wirtschaftsforschung, *Wochenbericht*, 23–24/90, June 14, 1990, pp. 315–21), and the assumption that the female labor force participation rate, presently significantly above the rate in west Germany, will decline.

Box 1.   The Scenarios in Historical Context

To help place the challenges facing east Germany in some historical context, the table below presents data for key macroeconomic aggregates in the FRG in the 1950s. Between 1950 and 1960, real net domestic product in the FRG grew at an annual rate of 8¼ percent, and with employment growing at about 2¼ percent, the annual growth of labor productivity was just under 6 percent. While these figures are impressive, it is noteworthy that the growth of output and labor productivity in scenario A is much larger. However, one should be careful when making such comparisons. First, labor hoarding and general inefficiency in factor use in the FRG in 1950 may not have been as large as those believed to prevail in east Germany at the time of GEMSU. For example, unemployment in the FRG was 11 percent of the dependent labor force in 1950 and declining, whereas in east Germany, prior to GEMSU, there was hardly any open unemployment but the underlying unemployment rate was some 25–35 percent of the labor force according to scenarios A and B. Improving the efficiency of factor use in the east German economy is expected to be an important source of productivity gain in the coming years.

Second, the investment ratio in the FRG in the 1950s was not unusually large. On average, gross fixed investment was 22 percent of GNP, sustaining a rate of growth of the net capital stock of 7¾ percent a year. These investment ratios do not suggest that the FRG's economy was reaching the limits of its ability to physically absorb capital; investment ratios were higher in the FRG in the 1960s as they were in many other industrial countries. Nor was the FRG straining its investable resources in the 1950s: the FRG ran an external surplus which averaged 4 percent of GNP (on a national accounts basis) over the period.

It is worth noting that with higher investment, the Japanese economy grew at an average rate of 9 percent over the period 1955–73. In the 1960s, growth in Japan was even faster at 10½ percent on average with labor productivity rising at a rate of 8¾ percent. Moreover, these latter growth rates were, presumably, achieved from a base (1960) that was not characterized by the scale of inefficiency in factor use that presently prevails in east Germany.

Historical experience, however, is unable to give clear guidance on the scale of investment that can be absorbed in relation to output. While the proximity of suppliers of capital goods as well as the general slack in east Germany's economy might be expected to enhance its ability to absorb investment, the investment ratios envisaged in scenario A in the initial years of GEMSU are quite large—in Japan, gross fixed investment was close to one third of GNP, on average, over the period 1960–80, with a peak investment ratio of 36 percent in 1973. More generally, one needs to be cautious in using historical comparisons given that the political and economic circumstances of east Germany are so different. Indeed, the situation in east Germany is unique in many respects. First, the political imperative to close the productivity gap between west and east Germany would seem to favor the prospects for large investments in the east. Second, expectations of rapid income gains may influence wage demands and investment incentives; more modest expectations undoubtedly prevailed in the FRG in the 1950s and in Japan in the 1960s. Furthermore, the system of social protection in east Germany over the next decade is likely to be more comprehensive than that in the FRG in the 1950s.

Federal Republic of Germany: Selected Data from the 1950s

	Real Net Domestic Product	Employment	Labor Productivity	Real Net Capital Stock	Real Wages[1]	Foreign Balance[2]	Gross Fixed Investment	Household Saving Rate[3]	Unemployment Rate[4]
	(Annual changes in percent)					(In percent of GNP)[5]		(In percent)	
1950	...	...	...	...	...	2.0	18.9	4.3	11.0
Period averages:									
1951–60	8.3	2.3	5.8	7.7	5.7	4.2	22.1	7.7	5.7
1951–55	9.8	2.8	6.8	7.0	6.5	4.9	20.8	6.7	8.3
1956–60	6.8	1.8	4.9	8.4	4.9	3.5	23.4	8.6	3.1

Sources: Deutsche Bundesbank, *40 Jahre Deutsche Mark: Monetäre Statistiken, 1948–1987* (1988); and Statistisches Bundesamt, *Volkswirtschaftliche Gesamtrechnungen.*

[1] Nominal wages deflated by the consumer price index.
[2] National accounts basis; excludes transfers.
[3] Bundesbank definition.
[4] In percent of the dependent labor force.
[5] In current prices.

Table 2. East Germany: Key Supply-Side Elements of Scenario A

	Relative to FRG (FRG = 1)		Growth Rates[1]					
	1990[2]	2001	1991[3]	1992–94	1995–97	1998–2000	2001	1991–2001
Net domestic product at factor cost[4]	0.09	0.20	7	15	11	8½	7	10½
Employment[5]	0.29	0.25	−15½	2½	—	—	−½	−1
Labor force	0.29	0.25	−2½	−1	−½	−½	−½	−1
Unemployment rate[6]	...	...	17½	11	8	6½	6	...
Adjusted unemployment rate[7]	...	...	26½	12½	8	6½	6	...
Net emigration (in thousands)	...	...	100	23	—	—	—	...
Output per worker[4]	0.31	0.80	27	12	11	9	7½	11½
Net capital stock[4]	0.09	0.17	4½	11½	11	10	9	10
Net capital per worker[4]	0.29	0.69	24	9	11	10	9½	11
Gross compensation per worker[4]	0.44	0.76	8	6½	7½	9½	8½	8
General efficiency factor (g)	0.80	1.00	5	2½	2	1½	½	2
Labor-specific efficiency factor (h)	0.67	1.00	12	5½	2½	1½	1	3½

Source: Authors' calculations.

[1] In percent a year, rounded to the nearest ½ of 1 percent; except for the unemployment rate, which is the annual average for the period specified, in percent of the labor force, and migration, which is the annual average in thousands.

[2] Second half of the year at an annual rate.

[3] Relative to the second half of 1990, with data for the second half of 1990 on an annualized basis. See footnote 23 in the text.

[4] In constant 1990 prices.

[5] Including those on short-time work.

[6] In percent of the labor force; includes only full-time unemployed.

[7] Adjusted to incorporate the degree to which part-time workers are unemployed.

debt, and compensation of the former owners of property expropriated by the Government of the GDR, are included "below the line"; they, thus, do not influence the financial balance but do affect the gross financial debt of the Trust Fund. The Trust Fund is assumed to have an initial net worth of DM 100 billion.[12]

On the demand side, private consumption is related to developments in disposable income and the behavior of the household saving rate. Government consumption is assumed to decline relative to GDP over time, in light of its very high initial level. Investment is determined by the path for the capital stock, which in turn is related to the productivity target. The difference between supply and domestic demand represents the net foreign balance on goods and nonfactor services.

An important question is how the demand and supply sides of the model are made consistent. Over the medium to long term, with east German producers likely to be

price takers in the larger German and European markets, output will be determined by supply-side conditions. For the initial years of the scenarios, however, this is not a reasonable assumption. A feature of the demand pattern that has just been discussed is that relative prices play no explicit role in the model in allocating domestic and foreign demand between domestic output and foreign output. This is not because relative prices are believed to be irrelevant but rather that the large market disequilibria that are likely to exist in the initial stages of GEMSU and the marked shifts in the composition of supply and demand make it extremely difficult to judge what the degree of substitutability might be. Implicitly, it is assumed that, in the initial stages, output and demand elements of the scenarios have been made consistent by a combination of relative price adjustment and disequilibrium quantity adjustment. This issue is discussed further below; taking note of it at this stage serves to underline the illustrative nature of the scenarios.

---

[12] The initial endowment of the Trust Fund is based on the estimate of the capital stock in the economy, using sectoral shares for west Germany to distribute the east German capital across sectors—only the industrial sector is attributed to the Trust Fund. It is assumed that most of the initial debt of the enterprises is offset by the value of land holdings. Initially the value of the endowment is below potential owing to the general inefficiencies in the economy. Over time, the efficiency of the enterprises in the Trust Fund does not increase as fast as that of the economy as a whole, as the firms experiencing the largest efficiency gains are privatized.

Starting Conditions

The base for the scenarios is the second half of 1990. Key elements of the starting position are presented in Tables 2–4, with all data for 1990 referring to the second half of the year on an annualized basis. On the supply

Table 3. East Germany: Demand Pattern Under Scenario A

(Period averages)

	1990[1]	1991[2]	1992–94	1995–97	1998–2000	2001
	(In billions of deutsche mark)	*(Percent change a year)*				
GDP[3]	216	9	14½	11	8½	7
Domestic demand	332	9	7	6½	5½	5
Private consumption	180	4	5½	6½	5½	5
Government consumption	78	−8½	4½	3	2½	2½
Gross fixed investment	73	40	11	8½	7	6
Household disposable income	190	2½	6½	7½	7	6
(Saving rate)	5	3½	4½	7	10½	12½
		(In billions of 1990 deutsche mark)				
Foreign balance on goods and nonfactor services	−116	−127	−101	−71	−31	−5
(In percent of east German GDP)	−54	−54	−33	−16	−6	−1
Current account[4]	−23	−51	−66	−72	−74	−70
(In percent of east German GDP)	−11	−22	−21	−17	−13	−11
Gross national saving[5]	−44	−25	22	74	138	184
(In percent of east German GDP)	−20	−11	7	17	24	28
Gross investment	74	104	130	168	208	234
(In percent of east German GDP)	34	44	42	38	37	36
Fiscal transfers from west Germany	95	78	42	23	−3	−19
(In percent of east German GDP)	44	33	14	5	−1	−3
Net external liabilities[6]	33	84	214	426	647	789
(In percent of east German GDP)	15	35	67	97	114	120
Memorandum items (in percent of east German GDP):						
Current account						
(Excluding fiscal transfers)	−55	−55	−35	−22	−13	−8
Sectoral financial balances						
Households	4	3	3	4	6	7
Enterprises[7]	−9	−13	−15	−14	−14	−14
General government	−50	−45	−23	−12	−4	−1

Source: Authors' calculations.

[1] Second half of 1990 on an annualized basis.

[2] Percent changes are relative to the second half of 1990, with the second half of 1990 expressed on an annualized basis. See footnote 23 in the text.

[3] Differences between GDP growth and the growth of net domestic product in Table 2 reflect principally the influence of the changing share of net indirect taxes in GDP.

[4] Including balances on transfers and investment income. The balance on investment income includes all property income (net of tax) attributable to nonresidents, including retained earnings of enterprises owned by nonresidents.

[5] Excludes fiscal transfers from west Germany.

[6] End of year, or average of end-of-year data for groups of years; represents the initial debt level plus the cumulation of the external current account deficit.

[7] All investment income attributable to nonresidents is treated as an outlay, including retained earnings of enterprises owned by nonresidents.

side of the economy, it is assumed that, on the effective date of GEMSU, productivity in east Germany was 30 percent of the west German level, in terms of output that could be profitably sold in open markets. The factor inputs and factor efficiency underlying this output level are taken from Table 3 in Chapter IV, using the central case (B.II) from that table. According to those calculations, capital per worker in east Germany was 28 percent of the level in west Germany but, owing to a general 20 percent inefficiency in the use of factor services, effective capital services per worker were lower. Labor was also inefficiently used; apart from the below potential use of labor services due to the general economy-wide inefficiency, labor services were also effectively reduced by large labor-specific inefficiencies.

The above characterizes the supply-side position on the eve of GEMSU. For the second half of 1990, it is assumed that there is no increase in the underlying value of output[13] but labor productivity rises as some dishoarding of labor occurs. Wages are considerably higher than warranted by supply conditions, owing in part to recent large wage awards,[14] and absorb 90 percent of net domestic product.

The base for the demand projections is derived from the assumptions made about labor income and investment

[13] Output as measured by official statistics is likely to fall substantially. See Chapter III, section on "Recent Economic Situation," for a discussion of output developments after GEMSU took effect.

[14] See Chapter III, section on "Recent Economic Situation," for a discussion of wage developments in the early months of GEMSU.

Table 4. East Germany: Government Finances Under Scenario A

(In percent of GDP in east Germany, period averages)

	1990[1]	1991	1992–94	1995–97	1998–2000	2001
General government balance[2]	− 50	− 45	− 23	− 12	− 4	− 1
Revenue	39	41	41	39	39	39
Tax revenue	39	40	39	37	37	37
Income and corporate taxes	3	4	5	7	9	10
Social security taxes	16	18	19	17	16	16
Indirect taxes	19	18	15	13	12	11
Nontax revenue	1	1	2	2	2	2
Expenditure	90	86	64	51	43	41
Current expenditure	83	74	54	43	38	36
Consumption	36	30	25	20	16	15
Social transfers	35	34	22	17	15	15
Unemployment	13	12	4	3	2	2
Pensions	11	12	10	9	9	9
Other	10	10	7	6	5	4
Interest	2	2	3	3	4	4
Other	9	7	4	3	3	3
Capital expenditure	7	12	10	7	6	5
Fixed investment	5	9	8	6	5	4
Transfers	2	3	2	2	1	1
Trust Fund balance	− 9	− 13	− 1	—	—	—
Fiscal transfers from west Germany	44	33	14	5	− 1	− 3
General government debt[3]	26	36	47	56	62	64
Trust Fund debt[3]	9	32	16	4	—	—
Memorandum items:						
Total interest, including interest in west German fiscal accounts[4]	2	4	8	10	10	9
General government balance, including interest in west German fiscal accounts	− 50	− 46	− 28	− 18	− 11	− 7
General government debt, including debt registered in west German fiscal accounts[3,5]	48	89	118	134	131	123

Source: Authors' calculations.

[1] Second half of the year on an annualized basis.

[2] National accounts basis; excluding fiscal transfers from west Germany.

[3] At year-end, or average of end-of-year data for groups of years.

[4] Interest in the west German accounts related to financing fiscal transfers to east Germany.

[5] Debt incurred in the west German fiscal accounts related to financing fiscal transfers to east Germany and the associated interest costs. The debt level at the end of 1990 reflects the initial debt level assumed for July 1, 1990 and the borrowing requirement in the second half of 1990 (i.e., at half of the annual rate implicit in the column for 1990).

and from official projections for the government finances. Private disposable income is initially high relative to GDP, reflecting the size of the labor share, large social transfers, and the low rate of direct taxation. Assuming a household saving rate of 5 percent, private consumption absorbs about 83 percent of GDP, compared with 54 percent in west Germany. Government consumption is also assumed to be higher than in the west (36 percent of GDP compared with 18 percent).[15] Thus, in total, consumption expenditure represents 120 percent of GDP and an even larger percentage of national income. The assumed value of investment is about the same (on an annual basis) as in 1989 (converted at an exchange rate

of DM 1 = M 1), though this involves a significant increase in quality. Moreover, given that the underlying value of output is much lower than implied by official estimates of production under the former economic system, this level of investment represents a substantial share of GDP (34 percent). The high levels of consumption and investment relative to output result in a large external deficit in the second half of 1990 financed in part by fiscal transfers from west Germany. The decomposition of this imbalance shows that it is mostly accounted for by the general government deficit.

In the construction of the scenarios, it has been assumed for analytical purposes that east Germany retains a full range of government institutions, including those absorbed by the Federal Government at the time of political unification. This separation of fiscal accounts can be

[15] The assumptions on government finances are discussed in greater detail below.

seen as a device that facilitates the examination of the effects of the integration process on the combined fiscal position of east and west Germany. The starting fiscal situation in the east is constructed so as to be consistent with official projections for the fiscal effects of GEMSU in the second half of 1990.[16] A central feature of the unification process is that the legal and institutional structures governing social expenditures and taxes in west Germany have been adopted in the east. However, given the differences in the level of income, in the composition of demand, in infrastructural needs, and in the previous budgetary systems, the structure of the government budget in the east is quite different from that in the west. On the revenue side, total receipts relative to GDP are about 4 percentage points lower than in the west. The yield from income and profit taxes in the east is limited as a result of the interaction of lower wage levels with a progressive tax structure and exemption levels attuned to west German income levels. Offsetting this, however, collections of indirect taxes relative to GDP are greater in the east, given the high initial consumption level.[17] Potential social security tax receipts are also above those in west Germany, owing to the large share of labor income in output in east Germany; collections are, however, well below this potential as many companies with liquidity problems do not remit either their own contributions or workers' contributions withheld from wages.[18]

Thus, differences between east and west Germany on the spending side are at the center of the government fiscal imbalance in the east; the ratio of expenditure to GDP is double that in the west in the second half of 1990.[19] In part, this reflects higher expenditure on infrastructure and capital transfers to enterprises. However, the principal difference lies in current expenditure: public consumption reflects the high employment levels that characterized the government sector of the GDR and the high cost, relative to GDP, of health services in east Germany under the influence of the higher drug prices and medical fees that prevail in the west; and social transfers are boosted by heavy expenditure on unemployment insurance and pension payments.[20]

The outcome of these assumptions is a general government deficit (on a national accounts basis) equivalent to one half of GDP in east Germany in the second half of 1990. In addition, the Trust Fund runs a deficit of 9 percent of GDP, as a result of transfers made to enterprises to promote structural adjustment. It is assumed that the general government authorities in the east borrow to finance capital expenditures, with current deficits financed by transfers from west Germany.[21] The Trust Fund finances its activities by borrowing.

Scenario A

Supply Developments

Table 2 illustrates how key supply-side variables might look in the year 2001 with east German productivity having reached 80 percent of the west German level. A basic premise is that inefficiencies in factor use will have been eliminated.[22] Over the 11-year period, output grows at 10½ percent a year and productivity at about 11½ percent a year. Improved efficiency in factor use accounts for a large part of the growth rate differential vis-à-vis west Germany, with the narrowing of the gap in the capital-labor ratio being the other important factor.

In this scenario, output growth quickly rises to a peak and then falls back gradually.[23] The important factors

---

[16] See Chapter II, section on ''Fiscal Implications of GEMSU.''

[17] Actual collections in east Germany have, however, been adversely affected by the extent to which east German residents have made their purchases in west Germany. This has been ignored here as it has had no effect on the fiscal situation in Germany as a whole.

[18] In principle, slow payment should not affect revenue as recorded in the national accounts, as the latter are on an accrual basis. But to the extent that the firms experiencing liquidity difficulties are not likely to survive, and, thus, unlikely to make payment, this revenue should be excluded. Accordingly, social security receipts are set at about 80 percent of potential in the second half of 1990.

[19] The figures that follow on the composition of government expenditure are illustrative; information on the structure of government spending in east Germany is, as yet, relatively limited.

[20] The large size of unemployment expenditures results from the high level of unemployment (including part-time unemployment) and the assumption that almost all the unemployed are eligible for either benefits or retraining programs. Pension benefits are larger in relation to average incomes than in the west as female pensioners receive pensions closer to those received by male pensioners, reflecting the high female participation rate that has prevailed in the east.

[21] This assumption is in line with the general principle governing finances in the FRG that government borrowing should not be greater than capital expenditure. Of course, given that central government operations in east Germany are within the budget of the Federal Government, many of these transfers will take the form of internal accounting transfers as the Federal Government collects much less in revenue from east Germany than it spends there. This assumption on the financing of government expenditure in the east has little implication for the measurement of the economic situation in Germany as a whole. It does over time affect the distribution of the government deficit between east and west Germany, as a substantial part of the interest expenditure related to accumulated deficits in east Germany appears in the fiscal accounts in west Germany. The size of these interest payments recorded in the west German fiscal accounts is indicated in Tables 4 and 7. See also footnote 26.

[22] There is no allowance for a positive vintage effect on production; see Chapter IV, section on ''The Capital Stock in 2001'' for further discussion.

[23] In interpreting output growth for 1991, one should bear in mind that it is calculated using the second half of 1990 as base, with output in the second half of 1990 taken as a measure of the underlying value of output (i.e., output marketable in an open trading environment). Assuming that the underlying value of output was broadly similar in the first half of 1990, the growth figure for 1991 can also be interpreted as indicating the rise in output relative to the average level of marketable output in all of 1990. In contrast to the calculations shown here, the official data for 1991 will almost inevitably show a decline in output in 1991, as a result of the large negative statistical carry-over from the second half of 1990. Output in the second half of 1990 has fallen sharply in reaction to the competitive pressures resulting from GEMSU. For some details of output developments in 1990, see Chapter III, section on ''Recent Economic Situation.''

determining this pattern are as follows. First, over the initial four years, the general efficiency of factor use rises markedly, particularly in 1991–92. Labor dishoarding occurs even more rapidly owing to the competitive pressures generated by GEMSU. The growth of the capital stock in 1991, which reflects investment in 1990, is only 4½ percent, but then jumps to a 11½ percent rate of increase in 1992–94. The front-loaded growth of the capital stock seen in Table 2 is due to the assumption that major public expenditures on infrastructure occur at an early stage as a prerequisite for profitable private investment and that considerations related to profitability and strategic positioning induce large up-front private investment. Among the factors that would be expected to encourage private foreign investment are lower land prices and an abundant trained labor force, which for a number of years is expected to be less expensive than that in the west.[24]

As regards employment, the dishoarding of labor is initially only partially offset by increased demand for labor services induced by economic growth, with the result that the unemployment rate is about one quarter of the labor force in 1991—about two thirds of this is assumed to be open unemployment with the remainder being in the form of short-time employment. Despite the high unemployment rate, real wages rise, though at a much lower pace than productivity. Over the next few years, wages continue to grow less rapidly than productivity under the influence of high unemployment and the initial excessive share of labor income in output. Net wages increase more slowly than gross wages, as the progressive tax structure boosts average tax rates. With the high investment rate feeding into the capital stock, profitability rising and domestic output becoming more substitutable with foreign output, labor market conditions improve and the unemployment rate begins a steady decline.

Demand Developments

Following a strong growth of consumption in the second half of 1990, investment expenditure surges in 1991 (Table 3). The increase in private consumption in 1991, on the other hand, is more restrained than that of output, owing to the relatively moderate growth of household income. While gross wage rates rise by 8 percent, this is offset by a decline in the number of people employed, and a fall in disposable income is prevented by increases in pension payments and unem-

ployment compensation. Government consumption expenditure drops notably in 1991, as a result of economies in the demand for goods and a reduction in employment. On balance, total domestic demand grows at about the same pace as GDP in 1991; the external deficit on goods and services, although higher in terms of deutsche mark, is unchanged in relation to GDP. The stability of the external imbalance conceals shifts in sectoral financial balances; in particular, the government balance improves relative to the period July–December 1990, while the sharp increase in private investment is only partially financed by improved company profits.

Over the first half of the 1990s, household income expands at a much slower pace than output, reflecting a smaller rise in wages than in productivity, increasing average tax rates, and reduced growth of social transfers (principally due to lower unemployment payments). As a result, the share of private consumption in GDP falls markedly. In the second half of the decade, with wages moving more in line with productivity, a rising household saving rate restrains the growth of private consumption relative to GDP. Public consumption also increases more slowly than GDP, as economies are made in employment and other current expenditure. Investment growth gradually declines through the scenario (reflecting the assumed time pattern for the growth of the capital stock), but remains the leading factor in the growth of domestic demand.

The external imbalance on goods and nonfactor services in east Germany, which is 5 percent of west German GDP in 1990–91, declines steadily throughout the scenario, as demand grows more slowly than output. The foreign imbalance that remains in 2001 essentially reflects net income payments to foreign investors. From a saving-investment perspective, the fall in the external deficit is due in part to the declining investment demand in relation to GDP, but the principal source is an increase in the national saving rate. In 2001, the net national saving rate (19 percent of NDP, excluding fiscal transfers from west Germany) is above the level in the west (17 percent) and is still rising; although the productivity gap has been narrowed significantly, a large difference remains in the wealth-income ratios of the two regions.[25] It should be noted, however, that this estimate of the saving rate in east Germany is sensitive to the assumption on fiscal transfers from the west.[26]

---

[24] The question of absorptive capacity is, however, difficult to judge and might affect the distribution of investment in the early years of GEMSU. The broad time pattern of investment would nevertheless be expected to be similar to that in Table 2. Specifically, over the longer run, an important consideration in the time profile of output and the capital stock is that, as productivity conditions in the two economies converge, rates of growth of important macroeconomic variables such as the capital stock and output should also converge.

[25] The higher saving rate in east Germany is reflected in enterprise saving, used to finance the still high investment ratio.

[26] The interest costs on the borrowing to finance fiscal transfers to east Germany are reflected in the fiscal accounts in west Germany. Assuming lower fiscal transfers from west Germany would be equivalent to incorporating the corresponding interest costs in the east German fiscal accounts. This would reduce national saving in east Germany as a result of higher external interest payments. From a longer-run perspective, one might want to estimate fiscal transfers and the distribution of the interest costs between east and west Germany on the basis of who will ultimately pay. Reducing expenditure in west

Fiscal Developments

The basic premise of the scenario is that the major differences in the fiscal structures of east and west Germany will be eliminated over the next decade. In east Germany, the fiscal imbalance (DM 110 billion in 1991)[27] declines rapidly relative to GDP, almost entirely because of a falling expenditure ratio. Government consumption expands less quickly than output as manning levels are reduced and the growth of wages is slower than that of production; by the end of the scenario the government consumption ratio is assumed to be 3 percentage points lower relative to GDP than that in west Germany, due to economies of scale in public administration (for example, in defense and in foreign relations), which are assumed to be reflected entirely in the east German accounts. After 1991, social transfers also drop sharply as the unemployment rate falls. Government investment expenditures are assumed to rise markedly in 1991–92; after 1993 they stay constant in real terms and thus decline steadily relative to GDP. Over the entire scenario, net fixed investment of the Government accounts for one fifth of the economy-wide total, broadly in line with the share of the west German capital stock located in the general government sector. Interest payments, on the other hand, rise in relation to GDP. Indeed, the rise is much larger if one includes interest payments made by the fiscal sector in west Germany related to the financing of transfers to east Germany (see the memorandum item in Table 4).

On the revenue side, collections of indirect taxes fall notably relative to GDP over the scenario as consumption grows more slowly than output. The underlying trend in the ratio of social security contributions to GDP is also downward as the share of labor income in national income declines; initially, this is not apparent in actual receipts as collection efficiency rises with the improved liquidity situation of enterprises. Falling shares of indirect taxes and social security contributions are only partially offset by rising direct tax collections relative to GDP. At the end of the scenario, the tax ratio is about 3 percentage points lower than in west Germany, reflecting lower income levels and a higher saving ratio.[28]

By 2001, the imbalance in the general government accounts has been almost entirely eliminated. Thus, net saving by the Government covers most of its net investment. However, incorporating also interest payments

recorded in west Germany's fiscal accounts, fiscal operations in east Germany still represent a drain on government saving.

Table 4 also contains an illustrative scenario for the finances of the public Trust Fund. Over time, the Trust Fund finances its operation through privatization and dividends from the subsidiary holding companies. These receipts are used to service the Trust Fund's debt, make capital transfers to enterprises, and pay into a compensation fund.[29] In 1991, it is assumed that the Trust Fund makes DM 15 billion in capital transfers to enterprises for restructuring purposes, with a further DM 15 billion in transfers to banks as guarantees on liquidity loans made in the second half of 1990 are called. In subsequent years, outlays above the line are solely in the form of interest payments; these are largely covered by dividends received, with the result that the deficit drops rapidly.[30] Below the line, as the privatization process gets under way, receipts are directed to reducing the debt of the Trust Fund and making compensation payments. By the late 1990s, all assets have been privatized, the debt of the Trust Fund has been redeemed, and substantial payments have been made to the compensation fund, but no funds have been applied to reducing the debt of the general government.[31]

Scenario B

Supply Developments

This scenario takes the same starting point as scenario A. However, the development of key supply-side variables soon sets the path of the economy on a lower trajectory. Investors are more reluctant to commit themselves than under scenario A,[32] and this reluctance is exacerbated by aggressive wage demand—real wages grow by 21 percent in 1991 (Table 5), compared with 8 percent in scenario A. These developments are compounded by a slower rate of improvement in the efficiency parameters in the economy.

In contrast to scenario A, output at factor cost declines in 1991, and the relatively large increase in labor

---

Germany would, for example, have a different incidence than servicing the increased debt through cuts in expenditure affecting all of Germany or through increased tax rates.

[27] This would correspond to a borrowing requirement of about DM 150 billion for the territorial authorities in all of Germany (including the German Unity Fund).

[28] Lower income levels interacting with the progressive tax structure result in a smaller direct tax ratio, while the higher saving ratio reduces indirect tax collections relative to GDP.

[29] It is assumed that resources of the compensation fund are used to compensate those who suffered financial losses as a result of the nationalization of private property in the GDR.

[30] It is assumed that, after 1991, transfers to enterprises for restructuring purposes are handled by the subsidiary holding companies and do not appear on the books of the Trust Fund.

[31] Given the many uncertainties surrounding the financial situation and prospects of the Trust Fund and also the need for compensation payments, it is extremely difficult to anticipate either the financial resources that will be available to the Trust Fund or the extent to which these could be directed to reducing general government debt. Here, for simplicity, it has been assumed that no funds are available for this latter purpose.

[32] This could reflect, for example, unresolved questions of property rights, a slow unwinding of institutional rigidities left over from central planning, and a more cautious view on expected profits.

Table 5. East Germany: Key Supply-Side Elements of Scenario B

	Relative to FRG (FRG = 1)		Growth Rates[1]					
	1990[2]	2001	1991[3]	1992–94	1995–97	1998–2000	2001	1991–2001
Net domestic product at factor cost[4]	0.09	0.13	−2½	8½	7½	6½	6	6½
Employment[5]	0.29	0.22	−23	½	1	−½	−½	−2
Labor force	0.29	0.23	−2½	−2	−1½	−1½	−1½	−2
Unemployment rate[6]	. . .	. . .	25	21	13½	10½	9	. . .
Adjusted unemployment rate[7]	. . .	. . .	36	24½	13½	10½	9	. . .
Net emigration (in thousands)	. . .	. . .	100	207	136	108	90	. . .
Output per worker[4]	0.31	0.60	26½	8	6½	7	7	9
Net capital stock[4]	0.09	0.12	4½	7	7	7	6½	6½
Net capital per worker[4]	0.29	0.57	35½	6½	6½	7½	7½	9
Gross compensation per worker[4]	0.44	0.57	21	½	3	6	7	5
General efficiency factor (g)	0.80	0.90	3½	1	½	½	½	1
Labor-specific efficiency factor (h)	0.67	0.90	6	3	2	2	2	2½

Source: Authors' calculations.

[1] In percent a year; rounded to the nearest ½ of 1 percent except for the unemployment rate, which is the annual average rate for the period specified, in percent of the labor force, and migration, which is the annual average in thousands.

[2] Second half of the year at an annual rate.

[3] Relative to the second half of 1990, with data for the second half of 1990 on an annualized basis. See footnote 23 in the text.

[4] In constant 1990 prices.

[5] Including those on short-time work.

[6] In percent of the labor force; includes only full-time unemployed.

[7] Adjusted to incorporate the degree to which part-time workers are unemployed.

productivity is the mirror image of the sharp fall in employment. In the following few years, wage developments respond to market forces and real wages stay broadly unchanged, encouraging some recovery in investment and stimulating employment but output growth is slower than in scenario A. In the second half of the scenario, the economy settles into a pattern of steady expansion at 6–7 percent a year. With the labor force declining more rapidly than in scenario A, owing principally to increased westward migration, the unemployment rate falls for a number of years but then levels out at a rate of about 9 percent toward the end of the scenario. The high unemployment is a reflection of structural rigidities that are assumed to become ingrained in the economy. These rigidities are also apparent in the path of the efficiency factors, which by 2001 are still considerably below levels in west Germany.

Demand Developments

Demand rises more slowly in 1991 than under scenario A, but, with output growth also weaker, the external deficit on goods and services is not much lower (Table 6). Investment expenditure falls, but this decline is to a large extent offset by a faster rate of expansion of private consumption. Despite the higher unemployment, labor income grows more quickly than in scenario A, owing

to rapid wage growth, and disposable income is further raised by unemployment benefits. Over the remainder of the scenario, investment rises at quite a respectable rate, but both its level and growth rate are much lower than under scenario A. After its initial surge, private consumption is restrained by slow growth of disposable income. Government consumption also rises more slowly than in scenario A after 1991, reflecting, inter alia, lower wage growth and the declining population.

Over the entire scenario, the reduction in output relative to scenario A is only partially compensated by lower demand, with the result that the external imbalance on goods and nonfactor services declines more slowly and still represents 10 percent of GDP by the end of the simulation period. From a saving-investment perspective, the weaker external position reflects a smaller national saving rate under scenario B; this is partially offset by a decline in the investment ratio. The drop in saving is mirrored in the higher government deficit.

Fiscal Developments

Because of less buoyant economic conditions, the fiscal situation in scenario B is considerably weaker than that under scenario A (Table 7). The rise in the deficit in 1991 reflects a higher expenditure ratio as government consumption and investment absorb larger shares of

Table 6. East Germany: Demand Pattern Under Scenario B

(Period averages)

	1990[1]	1991[2]	1992–94	1995–97	1998–2000	2001
	(In billions of deutsche mark)	*(Percent change a year)*				
GDP[3]	216	—	8½	7	6½	6
Domestic demand	332	2	3½	3½	3½	3½
Private consumption	180	6	1½	3	3	3
Government consumption	78	−6	3	2½	2	1½
Gross fixed investment	73	−½	8	6	5½	5½
Household disposable income	190	5½	1½	3	4	4½
(Saving rate)	5	4½	4½	5½	7	9
		(In billions of 1990 deutsche mark)				
Foreign balance on goods and nonfactor services	−116	−122	−103	−81	−59	−43
(In percent of east German GDP)	−54	−56	−41	−25	−16	−10
Current account[4]	−23	−29	−37	−38	−38	−34
(In percent of east German GDP)	−11	−13	−14	−12	−10	−8
Gross national saving[5]	−44	−49	−20	14	47	73
(In percent of east German GDP)	−20	−23	−8	4	12	17
Gross investment	74	74	88	106	125	139
(In percent of east German GDP)	34	34	34	33	32	32
Fiscal transfers from west Germany	95	94	71	53	41	33
(In percent of east German GDP)	44	44	28	17	11	8
Net external liabilities[6]	32	62	133	249	363	433
(In percent of east German GDP)	15	28	51	77	94	100
Memorandum items (in percent of east German GDP):						
Current account						
(Excluding fiscal transfers)	−55	−57	−42	−29	−20	−15
Sectoral financial balances						
Households	4	4	4	4	5	6
Enterprises[7]	−9	−8	−9	−8	−8	−8
Government	−50	−53	−37	−24	−17	−13

Source: Authors' calculations.

[1] Second half of 1990 on an annualized basis.

[2] Percent changes are relative to the second half of 1990, with the second half of 1990 expressed on an annualized basis. See footnote 23 in the text.

[3] Differences between GDP growth and the growth of net domestic product in Table 5 reflect principally the influence of the changing share of net indirect taxes in GDP.

[4] Including balances on transfers and investment income. The balance on investment income includes all property income (net of tax) attributable to nonresidents, including retained earnings of enterprises owned by nonresidents.

[5] Excludes fiscal transfers from west Germany.

[6] End of year, or average of end-of-year data for groups of years; represents the initial debt level plus the cumulation of the external current account deficit.

[7] All investment income attributable to nonresidents is treated as an outlay, including retained earnings of enterprises owned by nonresidents.

national output and social transfers are boosted by the increased unemployment rate. Surprisingly, the ratio of revenue to GDP is also greater in scenario B as collections, relative to GDP, of indirect taxes and social security are raised, respectively, by the surge in consumption expenditure already noted and the higher share of labor income in national income. In subsequent years, the deficit declines, albeit at a more gradual rate than in scenario A. As in scenario A, most movement occurs in the expenditure ratio. While government consumption grows more slowly in this scenario, it is not sufficient to compensate for weaker output growth, and thus by the end of the simulation period, the ratio of government consumption to GDP is considerably above that in scenario A. The burden of social transfers also remains

greater under scenario B, owing to the larger unemployment and the higher dependency ratio in the economy.[33] Capital expenditure, on the other hand, is only slightly higher relative to GDP than in scenario A as real outlays are lower. Over the entire scenario, however, government net fixed investment represents one fourth of total net fixed investment, a higher share than under scenario A (one fifth). Interest payments rise relative to GDP throughout the scenario; the increase is particularly fast if one takes into account interest payments reflected in the west German fiscal accounts.

The financial position of the Trust Fund is also weaker under this scenario. The principal difference is below

[33] Migrants are disproportionately from the working-age groups.

Table 7. East Germany: Government Finances Under Scenario B

(In percent of GDP in east Germany, period averages)

	1990[1]	1991	1992–94	1995–97	1998–2000	2001
General government balance[2]	−50	−53	−37	−24	−17	−13
Revenue	39	44	44	41	41	41
Tax revenue	39	43	41	39	38	38
Income and corporate taxes	3	4	5	7	8	9
Social security taxes	16	19	19	17	16	16
Indirect taxes	19	20	17	15	14	13
Nontax revenue	1	1	2	3	3	3
Expenditure	90	97	81	66	58	54
Current expenditure	83	87	71	57	51	47
Consumption	36	34	30	26	23	21
Social transfers	35	41	31	22	19	18
Unemployment	13	19	10	5	3	3
Pensions	11	13	13	11	10	10
Other	10	10	8	7	6	5
Interest	2	2	3	4	5	5
Other	9	9	6	4	4	4
Capital expenditure	7	10	10	9	7	7
Fixed investment	5	7	7	7	6	5
Transfers	2	4	3	2	2	2
Trust Fund balance	−9	−14	−2	−1	−1	−1
Fiscal transfers from west Germany	44	44	28	17	11	8
General government debt[3]	26	35	49	67	79	85
Trust Fund debt[3]	9	40	24	13	9	9
Memorandum items:						
Total interest, including interest in west German fiscal accounts[4]	2	4	11	17	20	21
General government balance, including interest in west German fiscal accounts	−50	−55	−45	−37	−32	−29
General government debt, including debt registered in west German fiscal accounts[3,5]	48	101	167	232	271	287

Source: Authors' calculations.

[1] Second half of the year on an annualized basis.

[2] National accounts basis; excluding fiscal transfers from west Germany.

[3] End of year, or average of end-of-year data for groups of years.

[4] Interest in the west German accounts related to financing fiscal transfers to east Germany.

[5] Debt incurred in the west German accounts related to financing fiscal transfers to east Germany and the associated interest payments. The debt level at the end of 1990 refects the initial debt level assumed for July 1, 1990 and the borrowing requirement in the second half of 1990 (i.e., at half of the annual rate implicit in the column for 1990).

the line, however. The less buoyant economy results in lower receipts from privatization for the Trust Fund.[34] Thus, when privatization has been completed, and assuming the same payments to the compensation fund as under scenario A, a significant debt remains on the books of the Trust Fund.

Issues Arising from the Scenarios

The illustrative scenarios presented in the previous two sections demonstrate, at the very least, the degree of uncertainty that surrounds developments in east Germany over the next decade. The two scenarios, thus, provide a useful background for discussing a range of issues related to GEMSU.

---

[34] In addition, it is assumed that the Trust Fund takes on an extra DM 10 billion in debts owed by companies that are liquidated.

Supply Issues

Investment plays a key role in the supply side not only by providing additional capital services but also as an important vehicle for technical change. The capital needs to bring productivity levels in east Germany close to those in west Germany over the next decade are clearly enormous. The belief that capital will be quickly forthcoming is based on a presumption that the potential rate of return in the east is much higher than in the west. However, there are a number of factors that might create uncertainties about the prospective rate of return and generate a weaker response from investors such as illustrated in scenario B. It is important, for example, that the legal and institutional structure be supportive. Three key questions arise here: Will the issue of property rights, related, for example, to past nationalizations, be resolved quickly enough to give investors confidence that legal complications will not arise? How will the costs of the environmental cleanup be allocated? And how promptly will the new administrative structure in the east be able to make the change from a planning system to one more oriented to market requirements?[35] Then there is the question about the adequacy of the economic infrastructure; this issue arises not only because provision of complementary public services is important for enterprise efficiency but also because it affects the absorptive capacity of the east. Absorptive capacity is of course a wider concern; one can imagine machinery and equipment being largely imported and construction activities being able to draw on a large pool of unemployed workers. But bottlenecks could emerge in areas such as the transportation of investment goods or the availability of specialized construction skills. Investors are also likely to be sensitive to the stance that unions take in wage bargaining; large wage demands may scare off investors. More generally, there are important gaps in our knowledge of the reasons why some underdeveloped regions attract capital and grow quickly while others get relegated to the economic periphery. In this context, tradition may favor east Germany: before World War II, industry in the southern part of east Germany, in particular, was strong. This suggests that, if the other factors mentioned above are, on balance, favorable, there are good prospects for the east's economy.

Scenarios A and B, as well as the calculations in Chapter IV, illustrate the importance of assumptions on the degree of inefficiency in the economy and the speed with which this can be removed. These inefficiencies affect the rate of return and hence the level of investment. Moreover, eliminating inefficiencies is likely to be the most important source of supply response in the first year or two of the economic integration process. It is difficult, however, to get a sense of the scale of these inefficiencies or the speed with which they could be eliminated. For example, if substantial migration of highly skilled workers to west Germany continues, what would be the implications for the potential productivity of workers remaining in the east? The nature of inefficiencies is also quite important. The existence of general factor inefficiency is more favorable to the size of the initial supply response. In the case of labor dishoarding, on the other hand, the released labor finds a shortage of capital with which it can be combined.

Next we turn to the link between wages and employment. A notable feature of scenario A is that wages grow rapidly (as does productivity) for a number of years despite high unemployment.[36] Why would there not be

higher employment and lower wage growth? Clearly, this trade-off exists in principle, but in the short run, the coexistence of rapid wage growth with high unemployment would not be particularly surprising. First, rapid wage growth is a means of breaking free of the compression of the wage range that has characterized the former GDR and seems particularly likely for highly skilled workers for whom the option of migration to the west is greatest. Meanwhile, the social safety net will limit downward pressure on the wages of those who have been relatively overpaid.[37] Second, unemployment rates tell little about the match of skills of the unemployed to the emerging work opportunities; this may well be an important issue in the initial years of the transition, when some skills are likely to be in particularly short supply and others in large surplus. Moreover, offering labor services at reduced wages in an area in which effective demand is not perceived as being readily forthcoming may not be a strong encouragement to employers to boost employment or for unions to be more moderate in their wage demands.[38] Finally, linkages between labor markets in east and west Germany can be expected to develop quickly, especially in areas close to the former border between the GDR and the FRG and in the market for skilled labor.[39] This said, the response of wage growth to market conditions does play an important role in the scenarios. In both scenarios, the initial large labor share is unwound as wages grow more slowly than productivity for a number of years. Moreover, in scenario B, in

---

[35] While federal government functions no longer exist separately in east Germany, important questions affecting businesses are dealt with at the level of the Länder and community governments.

[36] It is interesting to note that significant real wage growth coincided

with high unemployment in the FRG in the 1950s, when a less developed social safety net than assumed for east Germany in these scenarios would have been expected to strengthen the negative relationship between unemployment and wage growth (see Box 1).

[37] Most workers in east Germany are likely to be eligible for compensation, on average, at 67 percent of the last net wage. In west Germany, only one half of the unemployed receive full benefits.

[38] Where domestic production is a good substitute for imports or where export markets have been developed, the increased output might be absorbed through changes in the foreign balance: relative prices could, in principle, move to encourage the appropriate shift in demand, with the relative price shift needed not being particularly large in a small economy well integrated in the world economy. However, in the environment such as that likely to exist in east Germany in the first year of GEMSU, with large changes in the composition of demand and supply, major institutional developments, and substantial market disequilibria, questions arise as to what degree of downward pressure on wages would be necessary to encourage employers to increase employment. Effective labor supply, at the margin, may not be easily transformed into goods that are in demand due to the skill composition of the unemployed, the areas in which capital is concentrated, or because of problems with informational flows.

[39] Such links are already obvious, for example, in Berlin. In the context of these links, some may find puzzling the persistence of low real wages relative to west Germany in scenario B. This aspect of the scenarios can be interpreted in two ways. First, the migration that occurs on a larger scale in scenario B is principally of highly skilled workers, and this lowers the average productivity of those remaining, who have less opportunity to migrate. Second, the low relative wage level can be interpreted as an indication of the tensions that might arise in the system, leading, for example, to pressures for higher government subsidies.

response to the particularly large jump in unemployment in 1991, wages stagnate for a few years.

Demand Issues

Developments on the demand side are likely to play an important role in influencing initial supply conditions. While a large increase in demand in east Germany is to be expected, it is not clear to what extent this will fall on domestic products. Investment in machinery and equipment and consumption spending, for example, are both likely to have a large import content. This pattern of demand may pose a problem for realizing the potential response of supply to improved efficiency in the initial stages of GEMSU, when the options of boosting exports or displacing imports may well be perceived as limited. Of the various components of demand, output is likely to be most responsive to increases in construction demand, underlining the importance of a favorable investment climate for short-term output developments as well as for the long-term supply response. Over the medium to long term, however, marketing goods should be less of a problem as new investment comes on line producing goods oriented to a market environment, and a prominent role of foreign investors could further ease placement of goods in external markets.

A second uncertainty on the demand side revolves around consumption behavior. Initially, a key question is the degree of financial dissaving that can be expected and the extent to which such behavior has already occurred, given the greater availability of consumer goods since the opening of the border between east and west Germany. Moreover, the general uncertainty and high unemployment may initially engender more cautious consumption behavior on the part of those who remain in their jobs. Nevertheless, household saving is likely to be low for a number of years, reflecting pent-up demand for consumer goods and the large share of income support payments in disposable income. In scenario A, with rapid growth in household incomes, the household saving rate subsequently rises quickly toward the level in west Germany. In scenario B, lower income levels and higher unemployment restrain the rise in the saving rate.[40]

Fiscal Issues[41]

The government finances are likely to be used as a barometer for developments in the overall economy. Already in the early months of GEMSU, there has been concern about reports that the fiscal situation in the second half of 1990 is worse than was, perhaps optimistically, projected. That the budget has deviated from projections is not, however, particularly surprising; the scenarios illustrated the uncertainties about the fiscal situation and how vulnerable it is to weakening in economic conditions.

On the revenue side, apart from concerns about the vulnerability of revenue collections to less favorable economic developments, questions arise as to the extent of administrative difficulties in levying taxes in the early stages of GEMSU. There are also issues related to uncertainties about the prospective size of receipts from privatization and the financial position of the Trust Fund.

On the expenditure side, the finances of social expenditure programs are vulnerable to adverse developments in the economy. Moreover, the fiscal burden that might arise from providing west German standards of health care in the east is not yet fully apparent. Uncertainty also surrounds the needed scale and the timing of public infrastructural expenditure.[42] Perhaps even more important, however, than the total investment needs of the Government is the scale of government investment in the initial years of GEMSU; this will be important, both for encouraging private investment and limiting social (and migration) problems associated with high unemployment. A further unknown is the initial level and growth path of government consumption; important considerations here are the level of government employment that existed in the former GDR, the scope for its reduction and for improving efficiency in other areas of government consumption, and the economies of scale in public expenditure that might come from the process of economic integration. Finally, the scenarios and scenario B in particular, highlight tensions that are likely to give rise to pressures for subsidies to support employment and wages.

One of the more controversial issues facing fiscal policy is how deficits resulting from fiscal operations in east Germany should be financed. As mentioned above, these deficits are already looming much larger than had been projected earlier by the authorities. The considerations bearing on the question of financing were outlined in Chapter I (section on ''The Stance of Policies''). There, the degree to which higher deficits would be a temporary phenomenon was judged a key element. A comparison of Tables 4 and 7 underlines the extent to which this will depend on the success in revitalizing the economy of east Germany.[43]

---

[40] Data on household saving behavior in the FRG in the 1950s can be found in Box 1.

[41] Fiscal issues related to GEMSU are discussed also in Chapters I, VI, XI, and XII.

[42] In west Germany, about 20 percent of the net capital stock is in the hands of the general government and in scenario A about 20 percent of the cumulative net investment is assumed to be carried out by the general government. This does not include capital transfers to public bodies outside general government (e.g., the post office or the railways).

[43] The implications of these scenarios for the fiscal accounts of all of Germany can be seen in Table 4 of Chapter VI.

VI

Domestic and International Macroeconomic Consequences of German Unification

Paul R. Masson and Guy Meredith

Introduction

German economic, monetary, and social union (GEMSU) is likely to have major implications in a number of areas, both for Germany and for its neighbors. The most dramatic effects are likely to occur in the economy of eastern Germany—the former German Democratic Republic (GDR)—and a proper analysis requires detailed microeconomic information and assessment of the transition from a planned to a market economy.[1] But western Germany will also be affected in a major way, through higher government deficits and increased exports to the east. The purpose of this chapter is not to quantify the effects of unification on the east itself, nor to quantify induced increases in government spending. Instead, taking as given estimates of those variables, the macroeconomic consequences for western Germany and other industrial countries are analyzed from a global perspective.[2]

The second section starts by considering the additional demand on world saving coming from increased investment and higher social spending in the east. The shift of the former GDR economy to a market economy will have favorable supply-side effects over and above those that result from capital accumulation, since productivity should rise as a result of improved management, greater work incentives, and the transfer of modern technology. However, increases in productivity will also require increased government spending (for instance, on infrastructure) and substantial private capital accumulation (in order to replace obsolete equipment and to reorient production for Western markets) and the increases in

productivity from these sources will materialize only over time. An initial effect of GEMSU would therefore be to increase global investment relative to saving. Thus, in the first instance GEMSU would take the form mainly of a positive demand shock; in the medium to long run, in contrast, the supply effects should strengthen, and there is no reason to expect a permanent drain on global saving.

With a rise in global investment relative to saving, it is to be expected that real interest rates will rise in all countries to some extent. Some numerical estimates of effects on interest rates and exchange rates are given, using a simple global saving-investment model. GEMSU is also likely to increase the demand for German output relative to that of other countries. Much of the investment in eastern Germany will probably be undertaken by firms from western Germany, because of former business ties, common language, and physical proximity. In addition, because western Germany has a comparative advantage in the machinery and equipment that is needed to retool the economy of eastern Germany, a good part of the investment demand is likely to be directed to western Germany, though no doubt imports of goods from other countries will also increase. In these circumstances, the relative price of German output (its real exchange rate) can be expected to increase initially compared to the value it would otherwise have taken—at least on the presumption that goods from different countries are not perfectly substitutable and that output in western Germany is constrained by existing capacity. Expected real exchange rate changes would affect the distribution of real interest rate increases, which would likely be initially higher in Germany than elsewhere.

Another aspect of German unification is migration from the east to the west. Migration occurred on a large scale in the latter months of 1989 and early in 1990 (see Chapter II for details) and is expected to continue, albeit at a much reduced rate. Migration increases potential

---

[1] See Chapter V.

[2] Other model simulation studies using a similar methodology include Alexander and Gagnon (1990), McKibbin (1990), and Netherlands, Central Planning Bureau (1990). The effects of German unification are also discussed in the Organization for Economic Cooperation and Development's 1989/1990 OECD Survey for Germany.

output in western Germany and eases capacity pressures there. The third section presents estimates of the effects on potential output of projected migration.

The fourth section considers other factors that may be important for a complete analysis of the macroeconomic impacts of German unification. The above discussion ignored monetary phenomena and inflation—real variables were assumed to be independent of monetary policies and output to equal capacity output. Prices, however, are not perfectly flexible, and capacity limits not perfectly inflexible; thus, the stance of monetary policy will influence the response of output and inflation in western Germany to increased demand from the east. In this section, simulations of the IMF's macroeconomic model, MULTIMOD, are presented; this model includes effects of monetary policies and estimates of the degree of price stickiness.

The model used for these simulations thus incorporates several additional mechanisms compared with the saving-investment model discussed in the second section. In MULTIMOD, there is no absolute constraint on output in the short run because the capacity limit is unlikely ever to be reached, barring exceptional circumstances, such as wartime. Additional demand can be satisfied by increasing the intensity of use of existing capacity, for example through overtime and additional shifts. However, the higher is demand relative to normal capacity output, the greater are inflationary pressures. The interaction of monetary policy and inflation stickiness has important effects not only on the size of real interest rate and real exchange rate changes induced by GEMSU, but also on whether they are achieved through nominal interest rate and exchange rate movements or through price level effects.

Net demand from eastern Germany and migration to western Germany are simulated under two scenarios: in the more optimistic scenario, investment in the east is sufficient to raise output per worker to 80 percent of the level in the west by 2001; in the less optimistic scenario, investment is lower, output per worker only reaches 60 percent of that level, and migration to the west is considerably higher. The MULTIMOD simulation of the more optimistic scenario takes as given an increase in net imports of goods and services by eastern Germany from the rest of the world (including western Germany) of about DM 60 billion in 1990 and DM 130 billion in 1991, declining gradually thereafter. The MULTIMOD simulation of the effects of this demand shock suggests that it might increase the level of output in western Germany by about 2 percent in the short term (by 1991), and temporarily raise inflation by ½ of 1 percentage point. By 2001, the combined output of eastern and western Germany would rise by 14½ percent relative to a baseline without unification. These effects would be associated with an initial rise in real long-term interest rates of about ¾ of

1 percentage point, an exchange rate appreciation of about 4 percent against the U.S. dollar, and a reduction of the combined German current account surplus by about 2½ percentage points of GNP for several years. In the more pessimistic scenario, combined output would be higher than in the baseline, but by only 8 percent by 2001. Government deficits as a percent of GNP would be considerably higher than in the first scenario, as increased unemployment payments, lower revenues, and lower output widen the deficit by 3 to 4 percent of combined GNP relative to baseline for a number of years.

The fifth section explores two policy issues related to German unification. First, given the possibility of persistent deficits, the issue arises as to whether increases in tax rates are desirable. Simulations of an increase in the value-added tax (VAT) are presented. Second, the question of a possible realignment of the currencies participating in the exchange rate mechanism (ERM) of the European Monetary System (EMS) is considered. The scenarios of the previous section suggested that the GEMSU shock, accompanied by a non-accommodating monetary policy by the Deutsche Bundesbank, might lead to appreciation of the deutsche mark in real terms. This would occur via a nominal appreciation against non-ERM currencies (the U.S. dollar, the Japanese yen, etc.) and an increase in the price of German output relative to that of other ERM countries, whose central parities are assumed unchanged relative to the deutsche mark. An alternative scenario replaces the assumption that current ERM parities are fixed with the assumption of a currency realignment. While a realignment could, in and of itself, lower inflation in Germany and strengthen economic activity in other ERM countries, account should also be taken of the effect on the credibility of the "hard-currency" policies pursued by the ERM countries.

A final section sketches some tentative conclusions and discusses some key unresolved questions.

A Global Saving-Investment Perspective

The approach in this chapter is to treat the excess of spending over output in eastern Germany as the main "shock" to the global economy involved in GEMSU. Table 1 presents two sets of estimates of the net import demand in the former GDR that might result from GEMSU.[3] In the first one, which will be termed the "reference case," investment proceeds at a rapid enough rate to raise output per worker in eastern Germany to 80 percent of the level in the western part by 2001. In the second, less optimistic scenario, investment in the east is lower but saving is also lower, and output per worker only reaches 60 percent of western Germany's level in 2001. It is assumed that in the absence of GEMSU, the

---

[3] Estimates taken from Chapter V, Tables 3 and 6.

Table 1. Demands on Global Saving Due to GEMSU: Increased Net Imports of Eastern Germany[1]

(In billions of deutsche mark or U.S. dollars at 1990 prices)

	Reference Scenario (A)		Less Optimistic Scenario (B)	
	In deutsche mark	In U.S. dollars[2]	In deutsche mark	In U.S. dollars[2]
1990	58	34	58	34
1991	127	75	122	72
1992	112	66	110	65
1993	100	59	104	61
1994	92	54	96	56
1995	82	48	88	52
1996	72	42	79	46
1997	60	35	74	44
1998	46	27	67	39
1999	31	18	59	35
2000	17	10	51	30
2001	5	3	43	25

Source: see Chapter V, Tables 3 and 6.
[1] Change in investment-saving balance.
[2] At the deutsche mark–U.S. dollar rate prevailing at the end of 1989.

external position of the GDR would have been roughly in balance, so the figures in Table 1 constitute additional demands on world saving.[4] Table 2 gives estimates of global saving-investment flows for 1989. The latter serve to put the figures for eastern Germany in perspective; the increased demand placed on world saving in any one year is relatively small, less than 2 percent of the world total. In a world of high capital mobility, increased investment can be seen as tapping a global pool of saving, rather than being restricted to a local capital market.

It is useful first to consider the shock to investment in eastern Germany from the point of view of a simple two-region model, where the two regions are Germany and the rest of the world (ROW).[5] For purposes of illustration, Germany here is a united Germany, though it is clearly not appropriate to assume that econometric relationships estimated with data for western Germany also apply to the eastern part. The model is based on three simple hypotheses: (1) saving net of investment depends positively on the (real) interest rate, R; (2) the goods produced in the two regions are imperfect substitutes, hence the demand for each good depends on the relative price, that is, the real exchange rate, ϵ; and (3) prices are perfectly flexible so that output is always equal to potential output, which is constrained by the existing labor force and capital stock. These hypotheses imply that the equilibrium between world saving and investment is given by the intersection between curves SI and SI* in Chart 1. The SI curve describes the combinations of interest rates and real exchange rates at which the desired domestic saving-

investment balance equals net exports; SI* describes the same relationship for the ROW. The SI curve corresponds to combinations of R and ϵ that satisfy the following equation, where S is private saving, I is private investment, N is net exports, and DEF is the general government deficit:

$$S(R, DEF) - I(R) - DEF = N(\epsilon) \qquad (1)$$

Since net saving depends positively on R,[6] and net exports N depend positively on the real exchange rate (where a higher ϵ indicates depreciation), SI is upward sloping. The SI* curve slopes downward because ROW net exports N^* depend negatively on ϵ; moreover, N and N^* are not independent, since one country's exports equal the other country's imports, hence $N = -N^*$.

Chart 1 can be used to analyze the outward shift in the German investment schedule corresponding to increased profit opportunities in the east related to GEMSU; shifts in the saving schedule are ignored for simplicity, though increased consumer spending in eastern Germany might also reduce the German saving rate. The initial equilibrium is at point A. In the short run, the SI curve will shift to the right, while the SI* curve is unchanged.[7] This will have two effects: it will raise world interest rates, and it will lead to an appreciation of Germany's real exchange rate (a fall in ϵ). The new short-run equilibrium is at point B. The appreciation may seem

[4] The baseline also assumes GDP growth of 2 percent in the GDR, and no government borrowing on world capital markets.
[5] The analytical model is discussed in Masson and Knight (1986). In its empirical implementation, discussed below, there are in fact three countries and one remaining region (which implicitly includes the former GDR).

[6] Private saving may also depend on the government deficit—see the discussion below of Ricardian (non)equivalence.
[7] In Chart 1, the same (world) interest rate is assumed to apply to net saving in Germany and in the ROW. This would be consistent with interest parity between the two regions and static real exchange rate expectations. More generally, if the real exchange rate is expected to depreciate (after an initial appreciation), open interest parity would imply lower interest rates in the ROW than in Germany, shifting the SI* curve to the right.

Table 2. Global Saving, Investment, and Government Deficits for 1989

(In billions of U.S. dollars)

	Private Saving[1]	Private Investment	Government Deficit[2]	Current Account Position
United States	835	796	150	−111
Japan	989	917	15	57
Germany, Fed. Rep. of	319	255	11	53
Other industrial countries	1,268	1,172	180	−83
Developing countries	783	691	104	−12
World totals	4,194	3,831	459	−96[3]

Sources: International Monetary Fund, *International Financial Statistics, Government Finance Statistics Yearbook,* 1989 and *World Economic Outlook: A Study by the Staff of the International Monetary Fund,* April 1989.

[1] Calculated residually, so it also includes financial balances of lower levels of government.

[2] Central government.

[3] Current accounts should sum to zero; the figure corresponds to the world current account discrepancy.

counter-intuitive, since it is associated with a decline in a united Germany's current account surplus. It comes about because the increase in investment leads to excess demand for German goods, and a real appreciation is one mechanism by which this excess demand is satisfied, via a crowding out of foreign demand for German goods.[8] Of course, increases in interest rates tend to crowd out investment and stimulate saving within western Germany, also making room for the increased investment in eastern Germany, but western Germany is not made explicit in this simple two-country framework.

A second aspect of GEMSU is the increase in social transfer payments made to residents of eastern Germany. Such transfer payments may lead to a fall in national saving, unless private saving rises one-for-one with government dissaving. The case for the existence of an offset in private saving is that increased deficits today would require tax increases at some point in the future to service (or actually repay) the increased debt. The private sector may anticipate those future taxes and save today in order to provide for them. The existence of a complete offset on private saving—usually termed "Ricardian equivalence"—is unlikely, but evidence exists of at least a partial offset. In Masson and Knight (1986), the offset is 60 percent; in MULTIMOD, the offset is dependent on the baseline values for interest rates and real growth rates, and on the timing of expected future tax increases. In the simulations reported below, government deficits per se have little effect on national saving, interest rates, or output.[9]

[8] If the increased spending fell on other countries' goods to some extent, then the real appreciation of the deutsche mark would be smaller.

[9] In neither of the models does the supply of government debt

Chart 1. Determination of Real Exchange Rate (ε) and World Interest Rate (R)

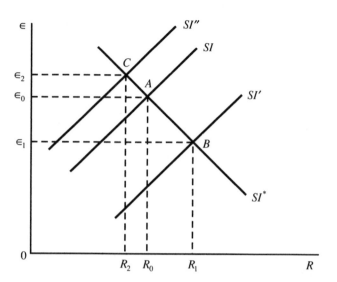

The dynamics of adjustment depend on the speed with which capital accumulation proceeds; the adjustment process would be further complicated by migration of labor and by wealth accumulation. The curves in Chart 1 therefore are conditional on the values of those adjustment variables—capital stocks, labor supplies, and wealth stocks, and possibly on other variables. This dependence can be illustrated in a simple case in which the adjustment process only involves the accumulation of capital. Suppose that GEMSU raises the marginal product of capital (MPK) in Germany, that the rate of investment responds to the gap between the marginal product of capital and the market real interest rate, and that the saving rate is constant. The initial shock will shift the SI schedule to the right, as described above, which raises the real interest rate. The interest rate will be below the MPK in Germany, but above it in the ROW. Higher investment will over time raise the capital stock in Germany, which will tend to shift the SI curve back to the left. Conversely, lower investment in the ROW will reduce the capital stock, shifting the SI* to the right. These shifts will continue until full stock equilibrium is achieved, but the adjustment process may take a considerable amount of time. In general, the movements in interest rates and exchange rates can be expected to be largest in the early stages of GEMSU; as

(relative to supplies of other assets) *directly* affect relative rates of return, as it would do in a portfolio balance model. In portfolio balance models, increased government deficits, by adding to the debt stock, would directly increase the borrowing costs faced by the government because investors would have to be induced to add to their holdings.

Table 3. Germany: Reference Scenario Effects of GEMSU in a Saving-Investment Model

(Deviations from baseline)

	Increase in Real Interest Rate (*In percentage points*)	Real Effective Exchange Rate (*Percent appreciation*)	Change in Unified German Current Account Balance (*In billions of deutsche mark at 1990 prices*)	Memo: Increase in U.S. Real Interest Rate (*In percentage points*)
		(With static exchange rate expectations)		
1990	0.4	2.8	−25	0.4
1991	1.3	8.2	−63	1.3
1992	2.0	11.2	−77	2.0
1993	2.0	5.6	−73	2.0
1994	2.1	5.4	−71	2.1
1995	2.0	4.7	−67	2.0
1996	1.9	3.7	−62	1.9
2000	1.4	0.9	−30	1.4
		(With regressive exchange rate expectations)		
1990	0.7	2.5	−24	0.3
1991	2.2	7.6	−60	1.0
1992	3.5	10.6	−73	1.6
1993	2.9	6.2	−71	1.8
1994	2.8	5.7	−70	1.8
1995	2.6	4.8	−66	1.8
1996	2.4	4.0	−62	1.8
2000	1.3	1.1	−32	1.4

capital accumulation proceeds, exchange rates and interest rates move back to (or close to) their initial equilibrium values.

How much exchange rates move, the size of interest rate increases, and how they are distributed globally depend on a number of features: (1) the size of the shock from a global perspective; (2) interest elasticities of saving and investment; (3) real exchange rate elasticities of net exports; (4) the distribution of increased demand in eastern Germany across countries; (5) the formation of expectations of exchange rate changes; and (6) the speed of the capital accumulation process. The dynamics related to capital accumulation and productivity increases in the east are a crucial feature of the adjustment process, but their likely evolution is very difficult to gauge.

Table 3 presents the results for some variables of simulating in a simple saving-investment model the shock to net imports of eastern Germany given for the reference case in Table 1.[10] The model does not include the east explicitly; consequently, the simulation analyzes the effects of increased demand for the exports of other countries, as well as increased current transfer payments from western Germany to the *ROW* (which implicitly includes the former GDR). These transfers are assumed to cover all noninvestment government spending in eastern Germany. The simulations assume that two thirds of the increase in imports of eastern Germany is directed

to western Germany, with the rest going to the remaining countries on the basis of their historical shares in the imports of the FRG.[11] Two alternative assumptions are made concerning exchange rate expectations. In the top panel of Table 3, exchange rate expectations are static, so that, since open interest parity holds in the model, interest rates increase by the same amount in all countries. It can be seen that the deutsche mark first appreciates against the U.S. dollar in real terms, and then gradually returns to its initial level. In the bottom panel, it is assumed that exchange rate expectations reflect this pattern of gradual regression to its initial level (starting after the second year of the shock, 1992)—with a coefficient equal to 0.2 (that is, in each year the exchange rate is assumed to close 20 percent of the gap between its present level and its assumed constant, long-run equilibrium level).[12] In this simulation, since after the initial shock the deutsche mark is expected to depreciate (which it actually does in the model simulation after 1992), interest parity requires real interest rates to be higher in Germany than elsewhere.

These two sets of results suggest similar qualitative conclusions, though they differ somewhat in their numerical estimates. Under static expectations, GEMSU would cause a rise in real interest rates by 0.4 percentage points in 1990 and a further rise of 1½ percentage points

---

[10] The parameters of this model were estimated using annual data over the period 1961–83 for the United States, Japan, the Federal Republic of Germany (FRG), and a residual rest of the world region; see Masson and Knight (1986).

[11] Data from the GDR's past trade patterns are not considered relevant here.

[12] Knight and Masson (1988) also solve the model with fully model-consistent expectations, finding that for the shocks considered in that paper, the main difference relative to static expectations is the decoupling of interest rates in the various countries.

in 1991–92, while the real effective exchange rate of the deutsche mark would appreciate by 11 percent by 1992, and subsequently depreciate. As a result of this appreciation, the current account surplus of eastern and western Germany combined would decline substantially.[13] Under regressive expectations, real interest rates increase somewhat more in Germany, peaking at 3.5 percentage points above baseline, while in the United States, rates rise more gradually, and to a peak of 1.8 percentage points above baseline. The exchange rate and current account paths are similar in the two cases.

The simulations incorporate only some of the mechanisms that may be important in the adjustment to GEMSU; in particular, they focus on the saving-investment aspects and related capital and wealth accumulation. Other aspects will be considered below: the next section will attempt to quantify the effects of intra-German migration on potential output in the west, while the fourth section of this chapter will simulate both increased investment demand in the east and migration from the east to the west, in a model that allows for stickiness of prices and hence does not constrain actual and potential output to be the same.

Effects of Migration on Potential Output in Western Germany

Another significant aspect of GEMSU has been the re-establishment of free mobility between east and west Germany, resulting in substantial westward migration. The last few months of 1989 saw large population flows from the GDR, and substantial migration continued early in 1990.[14] In scenario A, net migration from eastern to western Germany is assumed to be 320,000 in 1990, 100,000 in 1991, 70,000 in 1992, 40,000 in 1993, and 20,000 a year thereafter.[15] In the less optimistic scenario with lower investment in the east, net migration is assumed to be the same in 1990–91, but to be considerably higher from 1992 onward: 270,000 in that year, 220,000 in 1993, and declining to 90,000 in the year 2001.

Migration can be expected to lead to increases in both aggregate demand and supply in western Germany; the corresponding declines in the east are embodied in higher projected net imports, which are the balance between aggregate supply and demand in that region.[16] Here, the

aggregate supply effects are sketched; the aggregate demand effects are included in the full MULTIMOD simulations discussed below, which include other influences on aggregate demand as well. It is assumed that potential output can be described by a production function that depends on capital and labor with constant returns to scale. For a given capital stock, migration would affect potential output through the induced increase in the labor force, times the marginal product of labor. The labor force increase is the population increase times the participation rate. If labor is paid its marginal product, then the percent increase of potential output is the labor share times the percent increase in the labor force.

Over a longer-term horizon, the capital stock can be expected to increase one-for-one with the labor force. Therefore, potential output should also increase proportionately. Changes in relative factor prices will help to bring this about: increased labor supply will tend to moderate wage increases, and lead to higher employment; higher employment in turn will raise the marginal product of capital and raise investment. In equilibrium, both capital and labor can be expected to increase together, other things being equal. Higher potential output can be expected to moderate the price pressures that result from increased demand generated by GEMSU. In the reference case, potential output calculated in this way is projected to be 1¼ percent higher in western Germany by the year 2001 than it would have been in the absence of migration. In the less optimistic scenario, it is projected to be 3½ percent higher, as a result of the larger migration.

Simulations Using MULTIMOD

MULTIMOD is a global macroeconomic model that includes separate submodels for each of the Group of Seven countries,[17] for the remaining industrial countries as a group, and for the developing countries (divided into capital exporting and capital importing countries). In this model, aggregate demand—which is built up from behavioral equations for consumption, investment, exports and imports, plus exogenous real government spending—determines output in the short run. Capacity utilization, the ratio of actual output to potential output (determined by a production function), can therefore vary. An increase of demand from eastern Germany shows up partly as an increase in demand for German goods, which will to some extent increase output in

---

[13] The joint balance nets out intra-German trade and unilateral transfers between west and east, and hence reflects reduced net exports of western Germany to third countries as well as increased net imports of the east from third countries.

[14] See the discussion in Chapters II and VIII.

[15] Only the migration beginning in 1990 is taken into account in our simulations. During 1989, some 344,000 people emigrated from the GDR to the FRG, most of the emigration occurring between the opening of the border in November 1989 and the end of the year.

[16] It should be noted that effects on output are not offsetting, even if migration merely adds to employment in the west and reduces it in the east. Since productivity is considerably higher in the west, such

migration increases combined output. Moreover, if migration is a reaction to unemployment in the east, and leads to increased employment in the west, there is a further reason for combined output to increase.

[17] The German model is, however, based on data for the FRG before unification; the former GDR is not explicitly included in the model.

western Germany, as well as lead to lower combined German net exports. How much shows up in higher output and how much shows up as higher inflation, depend to a large extent on three factors: (1) the stance of monetary policy, (2) the influence of the level of capacity utilization on inflation, and (3) the interest elasticities of domestic components of demand. These aspects of the model are first briefly discussed, then MULTIMOD simulations of GEMSU are presented.[18]

Clearly, the conduct of monetary policy may be affected by currency union because (among other reasons) the income velocity of money may not be the same in the two parts of Germany. Rather than attempting to quantify those effects here, it is assumed for the purposes of the simulations discussed below that targets would be appropriately adjusted to take into account velocity shifts and other factors that would otherwise affect the relationship between interest rates and economic activity. In other words, the Bundesbank would continue to resist excess demand pressures in the same way as it has in the past, with some smoothing of short-run interest rate fluctuations.

Concerning the effects of an increase in demand on inflation and output, productive capacity is not an absolute constraint on output in MULTIMOD. Instead, the higher is the rate of capacity utilization, the greater are pressures on inflation. In the simulations presented below, the starting point for capacity utilization is high, but it is still well below historical peaks reached in 1972–73 and 1979–80. Moreover, the simulations of GEMSU assume further migration from the east (see the previous section), which tends to increase output capacity.

As the discussion of the GEMSU shock in the section "A Global Saving-Investment Perspective" makes clear, its effects depend importantly on the interest elasticities of saving and investment. The Mark II version of MULTIMOD (see Masson, Symansky, and Meredith (1990)) has quite high elasticities. Some other evidence on Germany and other countries suggests that saving and investment may not be as sensitive to interest rates. The MULTIMOD simulations reported below have been performed using revised equations for consumption and investment that embody lower interest-rate effects than in the original Mark II model, making the results more consistent with this empirical evidence and making the results more comparable to those from the saving-investment model discussed earlier.

The Reference Scenario

The reference case simulation of GEMSU assumes that net imports into eastern Germany increase by amounts

given in the first column of Table 1 above. This increase in demand shows up in the first instance in increased exports by western Germany (two thirds of the amount) and by other countries (the remaining one third, allocated on the basis of historical shares in imports of the FRG). The combined government deficit as reported here includes all GEMSU-related government expenditures, as well as increased interest payments due both to a larger debt stock and to higher interest rates. In the reference case, tax *rates* are assumed to be the same as in the baseline, which does not include GEMSU. However, tax *revenues* are elastic, and increase roughly in proportion to GNP.[19] The simulations also include the projections of migration from the east to the west described above, and the resulting increases of potential output in the west.

The results (Table 4, column 1 and Chart 2) suggest that the stimulus to demand leads to an increase in the rate of growth in western Germany of 0.6 percentage points in 1990 and 1.3 percentage points in 1991. In subsequent years, output *growth* is lower than baseline, because the rate of change of net imports from the east is negative and because of lagged effects of higher interest rates and appreciation of the deutsche mark. Nevertheless, the *level* of output in the west remains above baseline because of favorable supply effects; and output growth of the east and west combined is persistently higher.[20]

Inflation pressures increase, and the rate of change of output prices is higher than in the baseline by about ½ of 1 percentage point on average over 1990–92. Output effects on other ERM countries are negative, but relatively small, while they are slightly positive on non-ERM countries. Both sets of countries are affected to some extent by higher interest rates,[21] while the ERM countries, because of the assumed fixity of their central parities, also experience a real effective appreciation which, combined with a larger interest rate increase, offsets the stimulus from higher exports to eastern Germany. On balance, the reference case suggests that the international effects of GEMSU are not very large, and that increased demand does not put unmanageable strains on German productive capacities. However, higher government spending leads to an increase of 16 percentage points in the combined government debt-GNP ratio by 1999, which thereafter tends to decline back toward its baseline path.

The size of financial market effects is smaller than in the saving-investment model, in good part because of the buffer

---

[18] Details concerning sensitivity of the results to these structural factors are presented in the Appendix.

[19] In addition, the fiscal position benefits over the medium term because of reduced expenditures on West Berlin and other border areas.

[20] In the non-GEMSU baseline, potential output, which assumes no migration from the GDR, grows by about 2¾ percent a year in the FRG and 2 percent in the GDR.

[21] The size of these interest rate effects is of course an important issue; estimates are discussed in the Appendix.

Table 4. Germany: Scenarios of German Unification, 1990–2001

(Deviations from baseline in percent)

	Reference Scenario	Nonlinear Inflation Trade-Off	Scenario B
Combined real GDP			
1990	0.6	0.3	0.6
1991	2.4	2.0	1.6
1992–94	4.2	3.8	2.2
1995–97	8.3	8.4	4.4
2001	14.5	14.5	8.1
Real GDP (western Germany only)			
1990	0.6	0.4	0.6
1991	1.9	1.4	2.0
1992–94	0.7	0.1	1.1
1995–97	0.6	0.8	1.4
2001	0.8	0.8	2.5
Inflation: GDP deflator (percentage points)			
1990	0.2	0.6	0.2
1991	0.7	1.1	0.8
1992–94	0.2	0.1	0.4
1995–97	−0.2	−0.4	−0.1
2001	−0.2	−0.2	−0.1
Real effective exchange rate			
1990	1.5	1.9	1.5
1991	1.8	2.5	1.8
1992–94	2.0	2.5	2.0
1995–97	1.1	0.8	1.2
2001	−0.5	−0.5	−0.2
Real long-term interest rate (percentage points)			
1990	0.7	0.9	0.7
1991	0.8	1.2	0.8
1992–94	0.8	0.9	0.8
1995–97	0.3	0.2	0.4
2001	−0.1	−0.1	0.2
Combined current account balance (percent of GNP)			
1990	−1.3	−1.3	−1.3
1991	−2.7	−2.6	−2.6
1992–94	−2.3	−2.3	−2.6
1995–97	−1.9	−1.9	−2.6
2001	−0.9	−0.8	−2.3
Combined government balance (percent of GNP)[1]			
1990	−2.2	−2.2	−2.2
1991	−4.4	−4.4	−4.8
1992–94	−2.7	−2.8	−3.8
1995–97	−2.1	−2.1	−3.7
2001	−0.6	−0.6	−3.3
Real GDP: other ERM countries			
1990	−0.2	−0.3	−0.2
1991	−0.1	−0.2	−0.0
1992–94	−0.4	−0.4	−0.3
1995–97	−0.2	−0.1	−0.2
2001	0.2	0.2	0.1
Real GDP: other industrial countries			
1990	0.0	0.0	0.0
1991	0.1	0.1	0.1
1992–94	−0.0	−0.0	−0.0
1995–97	0.0	0.0	−0.0
2001	−0.0	−0.0	−0.0

[1] General government, including the Unity Fund and the Trust Fund, on a national accounts basis.

Chart 2. Alternative Scenarios of German Unification: Results for Germany, 1990–2004

(Deviation from baseline)

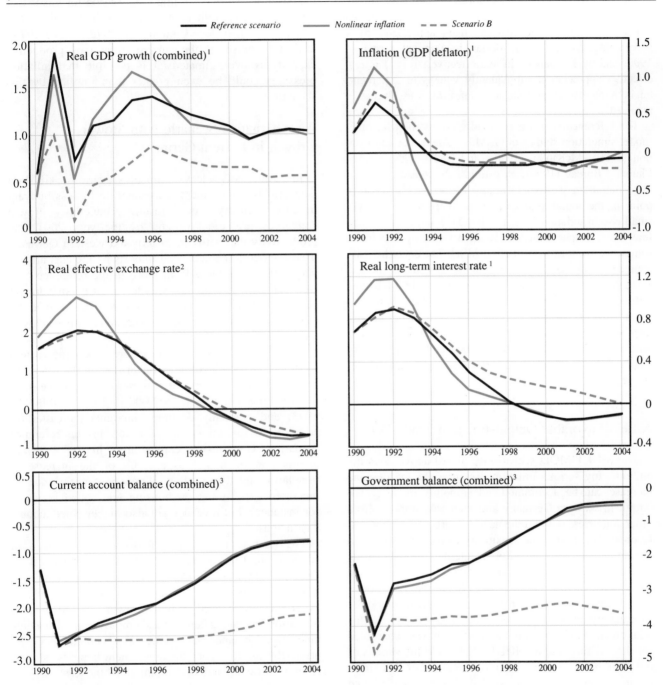

[1] Percentage point difference.
[2] Percentage difference.
[3] Percent of GNP.

role of capacity utilization, which permits aggregate demand to differ from potential output. The effects of GEMSU that result from MULTIMOD simulations are not exceedingly large. Long-term nominal interest rates increase by about 1 percentage point; the deutsche mark appreciates by 4 percent against the U.S. dollar in nominal terms in 1990, and by 1½ percent in real effective terms. The real effective appreciation subsequently widens to 2 percent, but both interest rate and exchange rate effects are ultimately reversed.

The reference scenario is broadly consistent with other model simulation studies of GEMSU. Alexander and Gagnon (1990), McKibbin (1990), and Netherlands, Central Planning Bureau (1990), all estimate that GEMSU would raise output in western Germany by about 1 percentage point in the initial year or two, accompanied by only a small rise in inflation.[22] As in MULTIMOD, after the first few years, output *growth* in western Germany is actually somewhat lower as a result of GEMSU. The deutsche mark appreciates in each of these studies, by more than in MULTIMOD in the first two cited above. In McKibbin (1990), the effect on output in other ERM countries is negative, resulting from the combination of higher interest rates and a joint appreciation with the deutsche mark against third currencies. Similarly, in Alexander and Gagnon (1990) output effects in all other industrial countries taken together are negative.

A Less Favorable Output-Inflation Trade-Off

The MULTIMOD scenario discussed above does not embody any serious inflation pressures, as the demand increase can be accommodated smoothly by increased output in western Germany and increased imports from other countries, without the need for large price changes. In order to examine the sensitivity of this conclusion to the model's inflation equation, an alternative specification was estimated using historical data for the FRG (see Appendix); there is some support for a nonlinear specification in which inflation pressures increase markedly as capacity utilization approaches peak levels.[23] This relationship between output and inflation was substituted for the existing one in MULTIMOD, and the shocks of the reference scenario were rerun. Results of this simulation are reported in column 2 of Table 4 (and plotted in Chart 2 as "Nonlinear Inflation").

Even with the steeper output/inflation trade-off, infla-

tion pressures are not too much greater, and output in western Germany still is higher by 1.4 percent than in the baseline in 1991. An important reason for this is that though capacity utilization is high in the baseline, it is still well short of levels attained in 1972–73 and 1979–80.[24] Of course, if the current margin of productive capacity is overestimated, it is possible that inflation pressures could be even greater than implied by this scenario.

An Alternative Scenario with Slower Growth in Eastern Germany

In an alternative, less optimistic scenario for GEMSU (scenario B), investment is assumed to be less buoyant in east Germany. As a result, productivity growth converges less quickly, and by the year 2001, the productivity gap between eastern and western Germany is still about 40 percent. Net imports by the east are not very different initially from those in the reference case (see Table 1), but the east's trade deficit persists longer because output does not rise as much in the medium term. Correspondingly, income and saving are also lower there.

In scenario B, real incomes are lower in eastern Germany, and emigration is higher than in the reference scenario: there is extra net emigration from the east to the west that amounts to 200,000 in 1992, 180,000 in 1993, and gradually declining amounts thereafter (in addition to the projected migration in the reference scenario). Government expenditures in the west are assumed to be higher as a result of the increase in population relative to the reference scenario (due to increased expenditure on housing and social services, for instance), but revenues are also higher since income has increased.

The results of such a scenario are summarized in column 3 of Table 4 and in Chart 2 (as "Scenario B"). They present a less favorable picture for Germany as a whole, though not for western Germany alone, which experiences increased output growth due to inward migration increasing demand and employment. The combined fiscal balance deteriorates as a percent of GNP, primarily due to higher unemployment benefits, slower revenue growth, and lower output in the east. In this scenario government debt has reached a level 19 percent of combined GNP above baseline by 1995, and 30 percent by 2001. Despite this, effects on financial markets and on other countries are little changed compared to the reference scenario, and inflation effects are also similar.

---

[22] The assumptions behind the various scenarios may differ somewhat, however.

[23] The extent of inflation pressure may also depend on whether demand increases are diffused, or are concentrated in specific sectors where bottlenecks appear. Such effects are not captured in the aggregate specifications used here.

---

[24] For a discussion of alternative estimates of potential output and capacity utilization, see Chapter VII.

Alternative Policy Scenarios

The above simulations are conditional on several assumptions concerning the stance of policy and the economic environment in Europe. In particular, tax rates in Germany were assumed to be unchanged, and existing central parities within the ERM were assumed to be maintained. In this section, possible alternative assumptions are considered: (1) an increase in VAT rates in Germany; and (2) a downward realignment of other ERM currencies against the deutsche mark that also affects the credibility of the commitment of those countries to hard-currency policies.

An Indirect Tax Increase in Western Germany

In the light of the possibility of persistent government debt accumulation in Germany (see, for instance, the less optimistic scenario described above) it is of interest to examine the effects of a tax increase. Because of the comprehensive reform of direct personal taxes, it might be counterproductive to attempt to raise additional revenue from that source to finance GEMSU. Raising VAT rates in Germany would appear to be a more attractive alternative, especially since this would help to harmonize VAT rates in the European Community (EC), German levels being relatively low.

The reference scenario for GEMSU was therefore simulated in MULTIMOD accompanied by an increase in indirect tax receipts of DM 20 billion (about ¾ of 1 percent of GNP), corresponding to increases in VAT rates by a little under 2 points;[25] results are summarized in column 2 of Table 5 (and in Charts 3 and 4 as "Indirect tax increase"). For the purposes of the simulation, the VAT increase is assumed to be imposed only in western Germany, though additional revenue (some DM 3 billion) would also be collected in eastern Germany. The increase in rates is assumed to occur in 1991, and not to have been anticipated beforehand (consequently, the results for 1990 are the same as in column 1). The Bundesbank is assumed to adjust upward its target for M3 to reflect the first-round effect on the GDP deflator of higher indirect taxes.

The additional revenue helps to limit the medium-run budgetary impact of GEMSU: instead of an increase relative to baseline in the government debt ratio of 16 percent of GNP in the year 1999, it increases by only 10 percent in this simulation. However, the tax increase has unfavorable effects on the rate of change of prices. Relative to baseline, the GNP deflator rises 1.7 percentage points faster in 1991

(1 percentage point more than in the reference scenario). Such price increases might kindle fears that inflation would continue; MULTIMOD in fact embodies persistence related to overlapping wage contracts, and as a result inflation is higher in 1992 and 1993 as well. In the context of uncertainty about the effects of GEMSU on inflation, such an increase in indirect taxes would have to be weighed carefully.

An EMS Realignment

The reference case scenario suggests that an initial appreciation of the deutsche mark of about 4 percent against the U.S. dollar might result from GEMSU. With fixed central parities with respect to other currencies participating in the ERM, real appreciation of the deutsche mark results from a combination of nominal appreciation against non-ERM currencies (principally the U.S. dollar and the yen), increases in prices in Germany, and a tendency to deflation in other ERM countries. The tightening of monetary conditions in other ERM countries might be avoided by a realignment vis-à-vis the deutsche mark, also in principle permitting a smoother allocation of the increased demand from eastern Germany among European countries.

Such a scenario, by permitting those countries' currencies to be delinked temporarily from the deutsche mark, would allow them to avoid a short-run real appreciation against non-ERM currencies. The upward realignment of the deutsche mark would also tend to remove some of the short-run pressure on existing capacity in Germany. These favorable effects, however, would have to be balanced against the negative effects of higher inflation in the short run in other ERM countries, and consequently a possible loss of credibility of their commitments to price stability and to hard-currency policies.

In recent years there have been persistent differentials between German interest rates and those of the other members of the ERM, as indicated in Table 6 for France and Italy. It is also apparent that movements in short-term interest differentials have been correlated with the past inflation performance of these countries vis-à-vis the FRG. While the short-term differentials between Germany and other ERM countries have fallen somewhat in recent months, they remain on the order of 2 percentage points for France and 4 percentage points for Italy. This gap runs contrary to what one might expect given a high degree of international capital mobility: if assets denominated in different currencies are otherwise identical, interest rates will differ only to the extent that exchange rates are expected to change over time. In a system of fixed parities where no future realignments are anticipated, nominal interest rate differentials should be small

---

[25] Additional revenue is less than DM 20 billion a year initially, since economic activity is weaker.

Table 5. Scenarios of German Unification Under Alternative Policies, 1990–2001

(Deviations from baseline in percent)

	Reference Scenario	Indirect Tax Increase	EMS Realignment with Credibility Loss
Combined real GDP			
1990	0.6	0.6	0.6
1991	2.4	2.2	2.4
1992–94	4.2	3.9	4.2
1995–97	8.3	8.1	8.2
2001	14.5	14.5	14.5
Real GDP (western Germany only)			
1990	0.6	0.6	0.6
1991	1.9	1.6	1.9
1992–94	0.7	0.3	0.7
1995–97	0.6	0.4	0.5
2001	0.8	0.7	0.8
Inflation: GDP deflator (percentage points)			
1990	0.2	0.2	0.2
1991	0.7	1.7	0.5
1992–94	0.2	0.3	0.3
1995–97	−0.2	−0.3	−0.2
2001	−0.2	−0.2	−0.2
Real effective exchange rate			
1990	1.5	1.5	1.5
1991	1.8	1.6	2.6
1992–94	2.0	1.9	1.8
1995–97	1.1	0.6	0.7
2001	−0.5	−1.3	−0.9
Real long-term interest rate (percentage points)			
1990	0.7	0.7	0.7
1991	0.8	0.9	0.6
1992–94	0.8	0.9	0.7
1995–97	0.3	0.3	0.4
2001	−0.1	−0.2	−0.2
Combined current account balance (percent of GNP)			
1990	−1.3	−1.3	−1.3
1991	−2.7	−2.6	−2.6
1992–94	−2.3	−2.1	−2.3
1995–97	−1.9	−1.6	−1.8
2001	−0.9	−0.5	−0.6
Combined government balance (percent of GNP)[1]			
1990	−2.2	−2.2	−2.2
1991	−4.4	−3.7	−4.4
1992–94	−2.7	−2.0	−2.6
1995–97	−2.1	−1.3	−2.2
2001	−0.6	0.3	−0.7
Real GDP: other ERM countries			
1990	−0.2	−0.2	−0.2
1991	−0.1	−0.1	0.6
1992–94	−0.4	−0.3	−0.1
1995–97	−0.2	0.1	−0.4
2001	0.2	0.3	0.2
Inflation: other ERM countries (percentage points)			
1990	−0.0	−0.1	−0.1
1991	−0.0	−0.1	1.3
1992–94	−0.1	−0.1	1.0
1995–97	0.0	0.2	0.0
2001	0.3	0.3	0.4

[1] General government, including the Unity Fund and the Trust Fund, on a national accounts basis.

Chart 3. Scenarios of German Unification Under Alternative Policy Response: Results for Germany, 1990–2004

(Deviation from baseline)

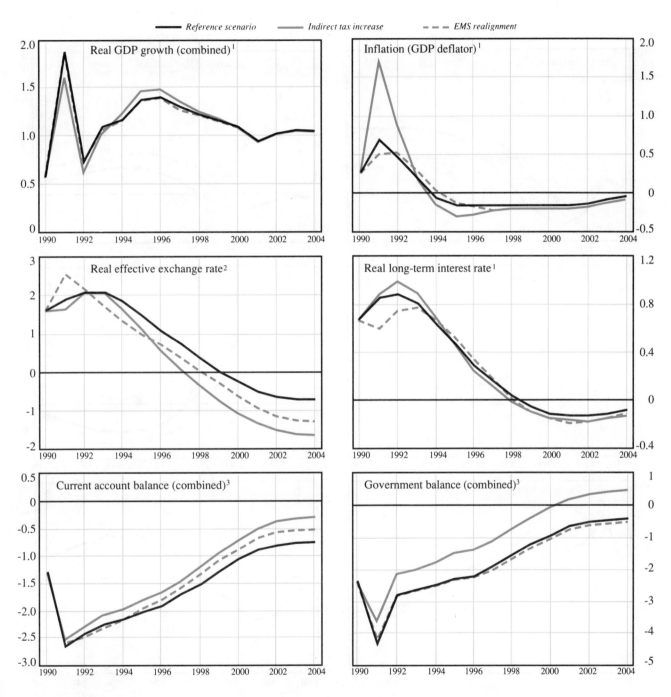

—— Reference scenario	—— Indirect tax increase	- - - EMS realignment

[1] Percentage point difference.

[2] Percentage difference.

[3] Percent of GNP.

Chart 4. Scenarios of German Unification Under Alternative Policy Response: Results for Other ERM Countries, 1990–2004

(Deviation from baseline)

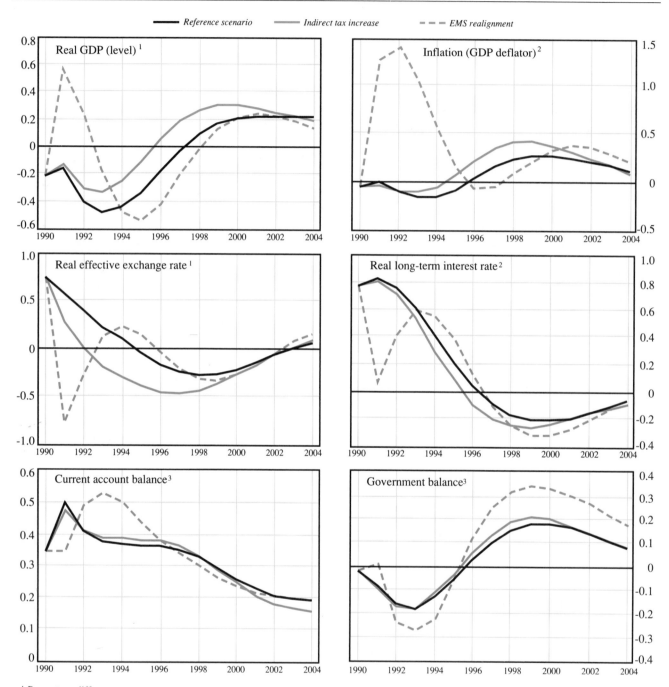

¹ Percentage difference.
² Percentage point difference.
³ Percent of GNP.

Table 6. Recent Interest Rate and Inflation Differentials in the ERM

(Percentage points, annual rates)

	1987	1988	1989	July 1990
France vs. Germany, Fed. Rep. of				
Short-term rate[1]	4.3	3.5	2.5	2.1
Long-term rate	3.6	3.0	1.7	1.9
Inflation[2]	4.1	3.1	2.2	1.8
Italy vs. Germany, Fed. Rep. of				
Short-term rate[1]	7.8	7.3	6.1	3.7[3]
Long-term rate	3.8	4.1	3.6	3.0
Inflation[2]	7.4	5.9	4.9	—
Netherlands vs. Germany, Fed. Rep. of				
Short-term rate[1]	1.9	0.7	0.4	−0.2
Long-term rate	0.5	0.2	0.1	−0.3
Inflation[2]	−0.1	−0.1	−0.6	−0.6

Source: International Monetary Fund, *International Financial Statistics*.

[1] Money market rate.
[2] Average increase in the consumer price index over the previous five years. For July 1990, calculation is relative to the average price level for 1985.
[3] Treasury bill rate for Italy.

since they would be limited by exchange rate movements within the band of admissible fluctuations.[26]

These data raise two questions: (1) does the differential relative to German interest rates reflect expectations of a future exchange rate realignment? and (2) to the extent that this is the case, what would be the impact of a change in market expectations that eliminated the interest rate differential vis-à-vis Germany? Concerning the first issue, there are a number of factors other than expected exchange rate movements that can explain gaps between national interest rates. For example, differences in perceived default risk, tax considerations, and barriers to the flow of financial capital across national boundaries. To the extent that these factors dominate expected exchange rate movements, one would expect the interest differential to move slowly over time consistent with institutional and structural changes. Instead, Table 6 indicates that in the case of France and Italy these differentials have declined over time in line with a

narrowing in inflation differentials. Looked at from a cross-sectional point of view, the gap between the average interest differential for Italy compared to that for France over the last three years approximately equals the inflation gap vis-à-vis the FRG. These data are consistent with the view that the movement in interest differentials over time primarily reflects expected exchange rate changes, where the latter are influenced by inflation differentials. However, the example of the Netherlands (data for which are also reported in Table 6) also suggests that it may take time to establish credibility. Though Dutch inflation performance was better than Germany's (as measured by a five-year moving average), interest rates continued to be higher than those in Germany for several years.

In considering the effects of a realignment, a key issue is the credibility of future exchange rate commitments and anti-inflation policies of other ERM countries. At one extreme, agents might believe that the exchange rate realignment following GEMSU is a "once-and-for-all" event, so that the credibility of a commitment to no further realignments is not called into question. However, in the light of past assurances of several ERM countries that they would not realign, a realignment could seriously undermine the confidence of investors in their commitments to "hard-currency" policies.

Here a realignment scenario is presented in which a depreciation of 4 percent of the other ERM currencies vis-à-vis the deutsche mark occurs in 1991, and has unfavorable effects on expectations of future exchange rate movements and inflation differentials. Specifically, the other EMS currencies are expected to depreciate further against the deutsche mark in the years following the initial realignment, similar to the periodic realignments that were observed in the early years of the EMS. In other words, it is assumed that the hard-earned credibility gains are dissipated by the realignment. Anticipations of further realignments have an unfavorable effect on inflation expectations and price-setting behavior.

A realignment scenario that embodies a temporary loss of policy credibility is shown in column 3 of Table 5 and Charts 3 and 4. Following their initial depreciation in 1991, other ERM currencies are expected to depreciate by a further 1½ percent a year versus the deutsche mark. These expectations turn out to be counter-factual: in the actual simulation, the authorities maintain fixed parities beyond 1991. In subsequent years, as agents incorporate the actual policy stance into their expectations, the unfavorable initial shock is gradually unwound and these economies return to the full credibility path. The realignment combined with the temporary loss of credibility of their anti-inflationary policies produces higher rates of inflation in the short term: the differences relative to the reference scenario average 1.2 percentage points from 1991 to 1993. At the same time, output is above the level in the reference scenario.

[26] At present, for all ERM currencies except the Spanish peseta and the pound sterling, fluctuation margins of 2.25 percent around bilateral central parities apply. Such margins could in principle be consistent with very large three-month interest differentials (as much as 19 percentage points on an annual basis) if, for instance, one currency started at its lower intervention point and the other at its upper intervention point, but the two were expected to switch places over a three-month period (with all other currencies remaining at their central parities). In practice, the starting position inside the band and the position of other ERM currencies will greatly reduce possible bilateral exchange rate changes with unchanged central parities, and the longer the horizon, the smaller the annualized interest differential that is consistent with a given expected appreciation or depreciation.

Concluding Remarks

Given the uncertainties involved in the transition from a centrally planned to a market economy in the former GDR, the model simulations presented above must be seen as only rough quantifications of possible spillover effects of GEMSU onto other countries. In addition to uncertainties concerning the economic policies and the behavior of agents in the united Germany, there are other structural changes underway that may modify these results.

One major structural change is that the economies of EC countries will become increasingly integrated with the achievement of a single market for goods and financial services in 1992. It is likely that with increasing integration, the response of both exports and imports to changes in competitiveness would increase. In effect, goods in different countries become better substitutes, as barriers to trade diminish. This change would tend to distribute increases in demand emerging from the changes in eastern Germany more widely across EC countries, since other countries' goods would be more easily substitutable with German goods. In order to gauge the sensitivity of the simulation results to this development, the import and export elasticities of EC countries with respect to relative prices were increased by roughly a factor of two. Though this distributed demand from eastern Germany more evenly and reduced the magnitude of the real exchange rate response, differences with the reference scenario were relatively slight. It therefore seems reasonable to conclude that the macroeconomic consequences of GEMSU are unlikely to be affected in a major way by increased European integration.

The general picture that emerges from the scenarios is that while additional stimulus from eastern Germany would put upward pressure on capacity in western Germany, with some danger of inflationary tendencies, inflation is unlikely to accelerate markedly and for an extended period of time provided the stance of monetary policy is adjusted appropriately by the Bundesbank. In this respect, the results presented here are similar to those in other studies that use macro models. However, in none of the model simulations has an allowance been made for increased uncertainties in financial, labor, and goods markets. To that extent, then, they may all be too sanguine. A less optimistic scenario was simulated in which productivity gains in the former GDR were smaller, unemployment remained persistently high, and migration from east to west was substantial. Though budget deficits persist in this scenario and the combined output growth of a united Germany is lower, German inflation and effects on other countries are not markedly different. The effects might, however, be considerably more severe if interest rates were directly responsive to the increased supply of government debt.

As for interest rates, simulation of the reference scenario in MULTIMOD suggests that GEMSU might produce an increase of long-term real rates equal to ¾ of 1 percentage point. This is smaller than the increase that occurred in the first few months of 1990, raising the question of whether the market has already discounted these effects of German unification. An alternative tax policy that involves an increase in VAT rates of about 2 percentage points in western Germany leads to a very similar path, with only slightly lower real interest rates—but higher inflation for a few years.

Turning to exchange rates and effects on other countries, the MULTIMOD simulations suggest that the deutsche mark is likely to appreciate in real terms against other currencies as a result of GEMSU. As the value of the deutsche mark relative to the U.S. dollar and the yen has increased since early November 1989 (especially against the former), the market may already have discounted some part of the expected exchange rate effects of unification. All in all, effects on other industrial countries (both ERM and others) would not be large. Again, other studies surveyed reach similar conclusions, as the negative demand effects of higher interest rates and positive stimulus from higher imports of eastern Germany roughly offset.

Appendix

Changes to MULTIMOD and Sensitivity of the Results to Structural Features

This appendix examines the sensitivity of the simulation results to some aspects of the structure of MULTIMOD: it also gives details concerning the way German monetary policy is modeled. The extent to which higher investment demand in eastern Germany can be accommodated in world output markets without putting upward pressure on prices and interest rates depends in large part on two factors: the short-run trade-off between higher output and higher prices, and the sensitivity of private sector spending to changes in real interest rates. These two factors are discussed in turn. The impact of the shock on both western Germany and its trading partners will also be affected by the responsiveness of trade flows to relative price movements. A simulation is presented in which intra-European trade elasticities are assumed to be larger than in the reference case, reflecting the possible effects of greater European economic integration on trade flows. Finally, money demand and the reaction function of the Bundesbank are discussed.

The Price Equation for Germany in MULTIMOD

In MULTIMOD, pressure in output markets is measured by the ratio of actual output to its capacity level. It is assumed that inflation responds linearly to the degree of capacity utilization (CU), that is, a 1 percent increase in CU raises inflation by the same amount relative to its baseline level regardless of the initial amount of slack in the economy. One implication is that there is no absolute constraint on output in the short run: increasing the size of a demand shock will raise effects on output and inflation by proportional amounts.

The linearity of the trade-off between output and inflation in response to a demand shock has, however, been questioned. For instance, if there is a maximum level of output that can be produced in the short run, by implication the trade-off must become rather steep as output approaches this maximum level. Since the tradeoff changes slope, the response of inflation to an increase in demand will depend on the initial level of capacity utilization. Chart 5 shows historical estimates for capacity utilization in the FRG, along with staff projections for the 1990–91 period. The projected utilization rate rises above its historical average in the initial years of GEMSU, suggesting that inflationary pressures could be greater than shown in the reference scenario if the steepness of the price-output trade-off increases as capacity utilization rises above normal levels.

Chart 5. Capacity Utilization Rates in the Federal Republic of Germany, 1970–91[1]

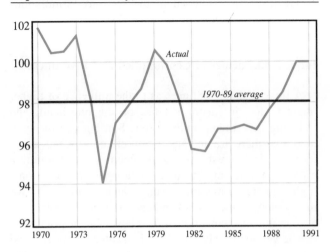

Source: IMF staff estimates.
[1] Projections for 1990 and 1991.

A nonlinear alternative to the existing specification models inflationary pressures as depending on a cubic function of the rate of capacity utilization less a parameter that indicates the level of capacity utilization consistent with no pressure on inflation: $(CU - \beta)^3$. This cubic function was substituted into the equation for German price inflation and the relationship was re-estimated over the 1970–87 period, with the value of β being determined by minimizing the residual sum of squares. Chart 6 illustrates the relationship between inflation and capacity utilization with this cubic specification compared to the existing equation: the output/inflation trade-off with the cubic function is almost twice as steep at the levels of

Chart 6. Alternative Output/Inflation Trade-Offs

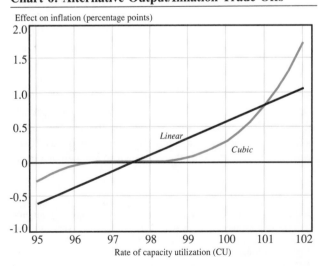

Effect on inflation (percentage points)

Rate of capacity utilization (CU)

capacity utilization estimated to obtain in 1990–91. This increases the response of prices to a demand shock such as GEMSU, as discussed in the section ''Simulations Using MULTIMOD'' in the main text.

Interest Elasticities of Consumption and Investment

A lively debate continues as to the influence of higher interest rates in raising saving, on the one hand, and reducing investment on the other. Some go so far as to deny that there are any significant effects. Indeed, since increases in interest rates cause income and substitution effects on consumption that go in opposite directions, higher interest rates may even reduce saving.[27] As for investment, some studies indicate a stronger link to an accelerator mechanism than to relative factor prices.[28]

The version of MULTIMOD presented in Masson and others (1990) embodies relatively large negative real interest rate effects on consumption (consumption declines in the long run by 6 percent in response to a 1 percentage point increase in real long-term rates) and on investment (consistent with the Cobb-Douglas production function, the elasticity of the desired capital stock with respect to the cost of capital equals −1). Subsequent research on the determinants of consumption and investment in the model has lowered their responsiveness to real interest rates, and this revised version of MULTIMOD was used to perform the simulations in the main text. For investment, the changes involved replacing the existing Cobb-Douglas production function with a constant elasticity of substitution (CES) alternative. The elasticity of substitution between capital and labor is set to one half, compared to the value of unity implied by the Cobb-Douglas specification. This lowers the responsiveness of the capital stock to a rise in interest rates, as the initial decline in the capital-to-output ratio is moderated by an increase in the share of output going to the capital stock. A re-estimation of the consumption function for the industrial countries with updated data and an extended sample period also yielded lower short- and long-run interest-rate effects.

The impact of changes in interest rates on consumption and investment in the old and new versions of MULTIMOD are compared in Table 7: the ranges represent high and low values for the eight industrial regions. It is apparent that interest rate effects are uniformly lower in the new model, with the decrease in the sensitivity of

Table 7. Effects of Changes in Interest Rates on Consumption and Investment in MULTIMOD

(Percent deviation from baseline)

	Effect of a 1 Percentage Point Increase in Real Interest Rates[1]	
	Mark II	New model
Temporary increase		
Year one impact:		
Consumption	−0.11 to −0.23	−0.05 to −0.06
Investment	−0.35 to −0.79	−0.30 to −0.78
Permanent increase		
Year one impact:		
Consumption	−0.56 to −0.58	−0.23 to −0.24
Investment	−1.45 to −4.66	−1.20 to −4.55
Year six impact:		
Consumption	−2.94 to −3.56	−1.33 to −1.97
Investment	−1.78 to −4.85	−1.47 to −4.18

[1] Partial effect holding output and prices constant.

consumption being more pronounced than that of investment.

By making global net saving less elastic with respect to the interest rate, the new model raises the effect on real interest rates, bringing them more in line with the results of the section on ''A Global Saving-Investment Perspective.'' It also produces somewhat less crowding out of domestic demand in the FRG. Here we present an alternative scenario where the interest elasticities of consumption and investment are set at even lower values, defined as one quarter of the MULTIMOD values.

This alternative is compared to the reference scenario in columns 1–2 of Table 8 and in Chart 7. The qualitative results are not surprising: both real output and real interest rates rise by more in the industrial countries the lower are the effects of real interest rates on spending. The German real interest rate peaks at 1.6 percentage points above control, almost twice the effect of the reference scenario. Impacts on output and inflation in Germany are also magnified, causing a greater appreciation in the deutsche mark. While the initial rise in output in the industrial countries is larger with weaker interest rate effects, the result over the longer term is to produce more accentuated cycles in output and prices.

Trade Elasticities

The trade price elasticities in MULTIMOD are typically based on equations for aggregate trade flows estimated over the 1969–87 period: the results are shown in Table 9 for the industrial countries. Import price elasticities range from a low of 0.37 for the United Kingdom to 1.17 for the smaller industrial countries, while the long-run export price elasticity is constrained to a common value for all countries, estimated to equal 0.71. In light of the liberalization of European trade that

---

[27] Contributions to defined-benefit pension plans are an example of a component of saving where income effects dominate; higher interest rates, by increasing earnings from existing assets, allow the payment of given pension benefits at lower contribution rates. See Bernheim and Shoven (1985). The Knight/Masson model used above embodies a negative saving elasticity.

[28] Clark (1979) is a widely cited study of U.S. evidence.

Table 8. Scenarios of German Unification with Alternative Model Parameter Values, 1990–2001

(Deviations from baseline in percent)

	Reference Scenario	Low Interest- Rate Effects	High Trade Elasticities
Combined real GDP			
1990	0.6	1.0	0.6
1991	2.4	2.8	2.3
1992–94	4.2	4.5	4.1
1995–97	8.3	8.2	8.3
2001	14.5	14.6	14.6
Real GDP (western Germany only)			
1990	0.6	1.1	0.6
1991	1.9	2.3	1.8
1992–94	0.7	0.9	0.6
1995–97	0.6	0.5	0.6
2001	0.8	0.9	0.9
Inflation: GDP deflator (percentage points)			
1990	0.2	0.4	0.2
1991	0.7	0.9	0.6
1992–94	0.2	0.3	0.1
1995–97	−0.2	−0.4	−0.1
2001	−0.2	−0.2	−0.1
Real effective exchange rate			
1990	1.5	1.9	1.1
1991	1.8	2.2	1.2
1992–94	2.0	2.3	1.1
1995–97	1.1	1.5	0.4
2001	−0.5	−0.4	−0.3
Real long-term interest rate (percentage points)			
1990	0.7	1.1	0.6
1991	0.8	1.5	0.7
1992–94	0.8	1.6	0.6
1995–97	0.3	0.6	0.2
2001	−0.1	−0.4	−0.1
Combined current account balance (percent of GNP)			
1990	−1.3	−1.3	−1.4
1991	−2.7	−2.7	−2.9
1992–94	−2.3	−2.3	−2.7
1995–97	−1.9	−2.0	−2.3
2001	−0.9	−1.0	−1.0
Combined government balance (percent of GNP)[1]			
1990	−2.2	−2.1	−2.2
1991	−4.4	−4.2	−4.5
1992–94	−2.7	−2.7	−2.7
1995–97	−2.1	−2.3	−2.1
2001	−0.6	−0.6	−0.7
Real GDP: other ERM countries			
1990	−0.2	0.1	−0.1
1991	−0.1	0.2	0.1
1992–94	−0.4	−0.1	−0.1
1995–97	−0.2	−0.1	−0.0
2001	0.2	0.2	0.0
Real GDP: other industrial countries			
1990	0.0	0.2	0.1
1991	0.1	0.4	0.2
1992–94	−0.0	0.1	−0.0
1995–97	0.0	−0.0	−0.0
2001	−0.0	0.0	−0.0

[1] General government, including the Unity Fund and the Trust Fund, on a national accounts basis.

Chart 7. Scenarios of German Unification with Alternative Parameter Values, 1990–2004

(Deviation from baseline)

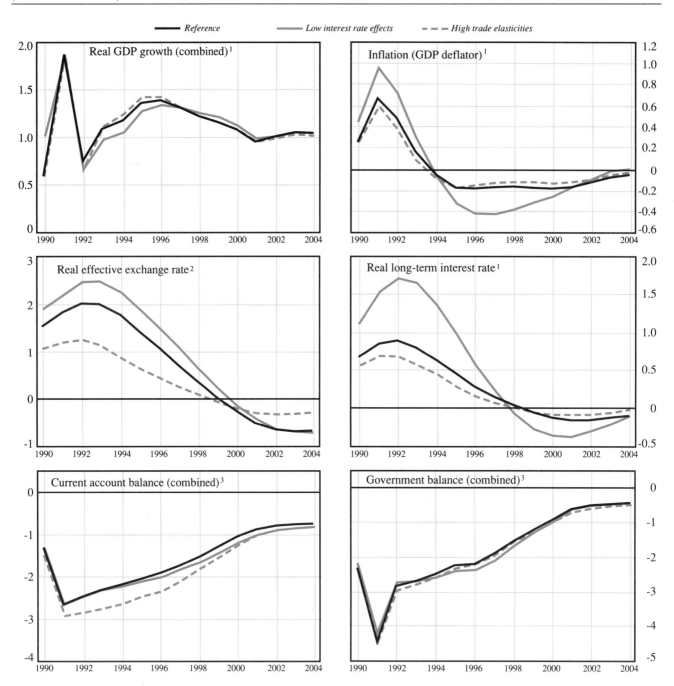

[1] Percentage point difference.
[2] Percentage difference.
[3] Percent of GNP.

Table 9. Long-Run Relative Price Elasticities of Traded Goods in MULTIMOD[1]

(Absolute values)

	Manufactured Imports	Manufactured Exports
United States	1.10	0.71
Japan	0.76	0.71
Germany	0.90	0.71
France	0.72	0.71
United Kingdom	0.37	0.71
Italy	0.40	0.71
Canada	0.45	0.71
Smaller industrial countries	1.17	0.71

Source: Paul Masson, Steven Symansky, and Guy Meredith, *MULTIMOD Mark II: A Revised and Extended Model*, IMF Occasional Paper, No. 71 (Washington: International Monetary Fund, July 1990).

[1] Including nonfactor services, but excluding oil trade and commodity imports from developing countries.

has occurred over this period, these elasticities may understate the sensitivity of trade flows in Europe to relative price movements. Further integration of these markets in conjunction with the proposed integration of Europe in 1992 may also raise the sensitivity of intra-European trade to relative price movements.

In a region with quasi-fixed exchange rates such as the ERM, higher trade price elasticities will tend to increase the positive spillover effects of demand shocks in one country on the output of trade partners. Specifically, the rise in inflation in Germany caused by GEMSU would result in more of the demand stimulus from eastern Germany being directed to other European countries. In order to examine the sensitivity of the simulation results to this effect, the long-run trade price elasticities for the European countries were raised to 2 for both imports and exports.[29] The results for the GEMSU simulation with these parameter values are shown in column 3 of Table 8. Output in western Germany rises by slightly less with higher trade price elasticities, while the negative effect on output in the other ERM countries is almost eliminated. Output in the ERM region as a whole rises with higher trade price elasticities. With higher trade price elasticities, the demand stimulus is weaker in western Germany, limiting the increase in German interest rates and the appreciation of the deutsche mark. Because the other members of the ERM "import" these variables from Germany, monetary conditions in the aggregate ERM region are less contractionary than in the reference scenario.

[29] The adjustment is rather arbitrary. Sufficient data are not available in the MULTIMOD database to obtain estimates of the elasticities for a more recent subperiod. The long-run elasticity of 2 was chosen to reflect the high end of values commonly found in other models that use aggregate trade data.

Money Supply and Demand

It is assumed in the model that Germany, like the United States and Japan, sets short-term interest rates in order to target a monetary aggregate. Money demand determines the actual money stock, and the central bank moves interest rates to bring money demand in line with the money target. In order to accord with the currently targeted aggregate for Germany, a simple demand equation for *M3* was estimated using data for 1964–88 as a function of real GDP, the three-month interest rate *RS*, and the GDP deflator *P*. The following estimates were obtained:

$$\ln(M3/P) = -2.20 + 0.499\ln(Y) - 0.0051\,RS + 0.646\ln(M3/P)_{-1} \quad (A.1)$$
$$(2.6) \quad (2.7) \quad (3.4) \quad (5.2)$$
$$\bar{R}^2 = 0.997 \qquad SER = 0.018$$

The equation passes stability tests starting in 1974, and though there is evidence of residual serial correlation (a Lagrange-Multiplier test is significant at the 5 percent level), this equation was selected because of its simplicity and dynamic stability.

It is assumed that the Bundesbank moves the short-term interest rate, *RS*, in order to hit a target for *M3*, but may not achieve it exactly if the gap between money demand and the target is too large. This is consistent with the existence of a target band, rather than a single value. The Bundesbank's current target is for 4–6 percent growth of *M3*: in the reference scenario, the deviations of *M3* growth from its baseline value peak at 0.7 percent in 1991, which would leave *M3* within the announced target band assuming that the baseline scenario represents growth at the mid-point of the band.

References

Alexander, Lewis S., and Joseph E. Gagnon, "The Global Economic Implications of German Unification," International Finance Discussion Papers, No. 379 (Washington: Board of Governors of the Federal Reserve System, April 1990).

Barro, Robert, "Are Government Bonds Net Wealth?" *Journal of Political Economy*, Vol. 82 (November–December 1974), pp. 1095–1117.

Bernheim, B. Douglas, and John B. Shoven, "Pension Funding and Saving," NBER Working Paper, No. 1622 (Cambridge, Massachusetts: National Bureau of Economic Research, May 1985).

Clark, Peter K., "Investment in the 1970s: Theory, Performance, and Prediction," *Brookings Papers on Economic Activity*: 1 (1979), The Brookings Institution (Washington), pp. 73–113.

Knight, Malcolm D., and Paul R. Masson, "Fiscal Policies, Net Saving, and Real Exchange Rates: The United States, the Federal Republic of Germany, and Japan,'' in *International Aspects of Fiscal Policies*, ed. by J. Frenkel (Chicago: University of Chicago Press, 1988).

Masson, Paul R., and Malcolm Knight, ''International Transmission of Fiscal Policies in Major Industrial Countries,'' *Staff Papers*, International Monetary Fund (Washington), Vol. 33 (September 1986), pp. 387–438.

Masson, Paul R., Steven Symansky, and Guy Meredith, *MULTIMOD Mark II: A Revised and Extended Model*, IMF Occasional Paper, No. 71 (Washington: International Monetary Fund, July 1990).

McKibbin, Warwick, ''Some Global Macroeconomic Implications of German Unification,'' Discussion Papers in International Economics, No. 81 (Washington: The Brookings Institution, May 1990).

Netherlands, Central Planning Bureau, ''Consequences of German Economic Unification,'' Working Paper No. 34A (The Hague, February 1990).

VII

Wage Determination, the Natural Rate of Unemployment, and Potential Output

David T. Coe and Thomas Krueger[1]

The closely related concepts of potential output and the natural rate of unemployment have important policy implications because they describe long-run equilibria in product and labor markets and are important determinants of wage and price developments in the short run. These are now particularly important policy concerns because unification of the two German economies implies a significant increase in demand in west Germany, a demand stimulus that is already apparent in 1990. In the long run, the path of potential output, and hence productivity at potential output, in west Germany will determine the magnitude of the "catch up" that is required for living standards in east Germany to match those in the western part of the country.[2]

Economic developments in the Federal Republic of Germany (FRG) in the 1980s suggest that the relationship between potential output, the natural rate of unemployment, and wage and price inflation may not be straightforward: output expanded steadily after 1982 and, based on most measures, appeared to be at or near capacity in the late 1980s while wage and price inflation was broadly stable;[3] but unemployment rates, after increasing dramatically in the mid-1970s and the early 1980s, remained stuck at historically high levels of about 8 percent until 1988 (Chart 1).

The coexistence of persistent high rates of unemployment, low and stable wage and price inflation, and output that appeared to be at or near capacity would be consistent

Chart 1. Federal Republic of Germany: Output and Unemployment, First Quarter 1968–Fourth Quarter 1989

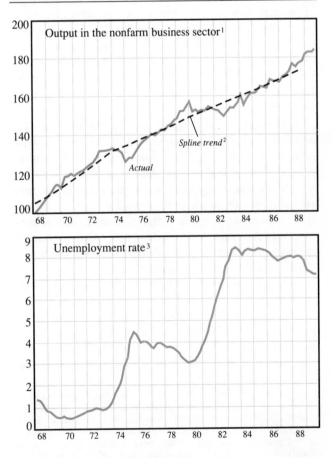

Sources: Statistisches Bundesamt, *Volkswirtschaftliche Gesamtrechnungen*; and authors' estimates.

[1] Seasonally adjusted; actual output in the first quarter of 1968 = 100.

[2] Estimated from the first quarter of 1968 to the fourth quarter of 1988 allowing for changes in trend growth in the first quarter of 1974 and the first quarter of 1980.

[3] Seasonally adjusted; in percent of the labor force.

---

[1] The authors thank Palle S. Andersen and Geoffrey Woglom for helpful comments and suggestions; and Wolfgang Franz, Heinz-Jürgen Scheid, and Wolfgang Scheremet for providing a number of data series.

[2] An estimate of this productivity gap is the starting point for most empirical analyses of the effects of German economic, monetary, and social union; see Chapters IV–VI and the references cited therein.

[3] Capacity utilization in manufacturing in the late 1980s was at its highest level for over a decade; see Commission of the European Communities (1990) and International Monetary Fund (1990), Chart 9.

with the standard Phillips curve model if the natural rate of unemployment was also about 8 percent in the mid-to-late 1980s. It is difficult, however, to identify structural changes in the labor market that would have increased the natural rate of unemployment from less than 1 percent in the 1960s and early 1970s to 7–8 percent in the 1980s.[4] Moreover, the rapid rates of growth and the substantial declines in the unemployment rate in 1989–90 did not appear to be accompanied by significant increases in inflation pressures, suggesting the existence of some excess capacity.

This chapter considers an alternative explanation for the coexistence of persistent high rates of unemployment, stable inflation, and output at capacity, an explanation that focuses on the wage bargaining process and other structural features of the labor market. It is argued that, although there has been some increase in structural unemployment since the early 1970s, the natural rate of unemployment in the FRG was well below the actual unemployment rate for most of the 1980s. But because of the nature of wage bargaining in west Germany, the large gap between the actual and the natural rates of unemployment did not exert ongoing downward pressure on the growth of real wages. In this model, unemployment above the natural rate is consistent with stable wage and price inflation because the level of unemployment has little impact on the growth of wages that are negotiated between employers and employees.

This suggests a distinction between the concept of an equilibrium natural rate of unemployment and a quasi-equilibrium unemployment rate that may be closely related to the actual rate of unemployment, as suggested by the hysteresis hypothesis.[5] Corresponding to these two concepts of equilibrium unemployment are alternative concepts of potential output that differ according to whether labor input is consistent with the quasi-equilibrium rate of unemployment—quasi-potential output—or with the natural rate of unemployment.

Actual output in the FRG may have been near quasi-potential output for much of the 1980s, as suggested by most indicators of capacity utilization. However, a measure of potential output using labor input consistent with the natural rate of unemployment would have indicated that more resources were available to increase

output than suggested by the quasi-equilibrium measure of potential. This does not mean, however, that there were no constraints or "speed limits" on the rapidity with which output could be increased and unemployment reduced from their quasi-equilibrium levels. An obvious constraint was the existing stock of capital, suggesting the possibility of capital-shortage unemployment. But developments in 1989–90 underscore that this is a short-run constraint that is not binding over the medium term, as higher rates of investment can be expected to be forthcoming in response to high rates of capacity utilization and an increase in actual or expected demand.[6]

The objectives of this chapter are threefold. The first is to describe more fully the implications of the alternative models of wage determination noted above. The second objective is to present estimates of potential output and the natural rate of unemployment together with a decomposition of their underlying structural or policy determinants. The third objective is to examine the prospects for potential output and the natural rate of unemployment in light of the additional demand that will be generated by the German economic, monetary, and social union (GEMSU). The chapter concludes with a discussion of the policy implications of the analysis given in the earlier sections.

Wage Determination

In the 1970s and 1980s, unemployment and output developments in many European countries were similar to those depicted for the FRG in Chart 1. This apparent inconsistency with the Phillips curve/natural-rate model led to the development of theoretical labor market models that provided consistent micro-foundations to explain the persistence of involuntary unemployment.[7] One of these models, which distinguishes between insiders and outsiders in wage bargaining at the level of the enterprise, is presented below. This is followed by a discussion of the aggregate wage and unemployment dynamics implied by the target-real-wage-bargaining model—an aggregate model of wage determination consistent in many respects with the insider-outsider model—as opposed to a conventional Phillips curve/natural-rate model.

---

[4] Unemployment in the FRG averaged less than 1 percent in the 15 years to 1974 and was never greater than 2 percent. A number of studies based on estimated Phillips curves have calculated that the nonaccelerating inflation rate of unemployment (the NAIRU) increased to 7–8 percent in the mid-1980s. These estimated increases in the NAIRU were not related to changes in structural aspects of the labor market but reflected increases in unemployment needed to offset the inflation implications of developments such as increases in import prices or secular declines in productivity growth. See, for example, the alternative calculations of the NAIRU presented in Table 8 of Coe (1985), Franz and König (1986), and Franz (1987).

[5] See Blanchard and Summers (1988) and the other papers in Cross (1988).

[6] This point is emphasized in Bean (1989). In the labor market there may also be speed limits to reductions in unemployment if, for example, changes in unemployment have direct impacts on wage growth.

[7] These models, which are not necessarily mutually exclusive, focus on the relationship between employers and employees and include insider-outsider models, implicit contract models, efficiency wage models, union bargaining models, and hysteresis models. See, for example, Oswald (1985), Blanchard and Summers (1988), Carruth and Oswald (1987), Gottfries and Horn (1987), Alogoskoufis and Manning (1988), and Lindbeck and Snower (1988).

An Insider-Outsider Model of Wage Determination

Institutional features of the labor market in west Germany suggest that the unemployed—loosely speaking, the outsiders—have little influence on the wage negotiated by employers and employees—the insiders. Bargaining, for example, is highly centralized and settlements negotiated by unions in key industries or sectors are often extended to include smaller establishments or the nonunionized workforce.[8] Furthermore, unemployment benefits make up a significant portion of lost wage income, and basic benefits (*Arbeitslosenhilfe*) can, in principle, continue indefinitely after eligibility for unemployment insurance has expired, provided a social need exists on the part of the recipient. These features give the employed workforce a degree of market power in the wage negotiation process. The insider-outsider model presented below illustrates how this market power can give rise to persistent involuntary unemployment.[9]

The upper panel of Chart 2 depicts the labor demand and supply curves of a representative firm and the lower panel shows aggregate employment and unemployment under the assumption that the economy is made up of n identical firms. As a point of reference for the discussion to follow, consider initially the case where insiders have no market power. The firm's demand for labor is represented by l^d, the marginal revenue product schedule, and it faces an elastic labor supply curve at the reservation wage (w^r), which reflects, for example, the generosity of the unemployment insurance system. Equilibrium is at A^* with nominal wages equal to the reservation wage (w^r), employment equal to e^*, and aggregate employment equal to E^*. Given the total labor force (L), aggregate unemployment (U^*) is at the natural rate of unemployment. Unemployment is "voluntary," and the natural rate is determined by the reservation wage.

Assume now that the "insiders" (the currently employed) have some market power because it is costly for firms to replace insiders by "outsiders" (the currently unemployed). This turnover cost per employee (c) may be related to severance pay or the ability of insiders to harass or withhold cooperation from new employees.[10] For a given capital stock and technological endowment, the representative firm—which takes output prices, the nominal wages of insiders (w^i), and the reservation wage

Chart 2. Unemployment Persistence in an Insider-Outsider Model

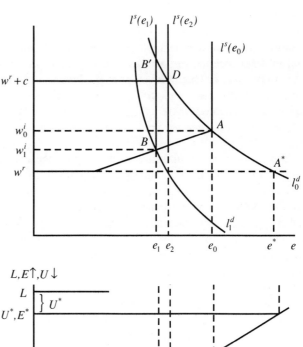

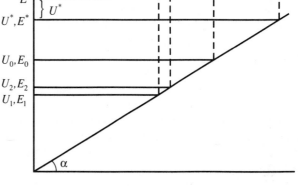

Note.—As discussed in the text, the upper panel shows the labor demand curves (l^d) of a representative firm and the labor supply curves of insiders [$l^s()$]. Assuming identical firms (tan $\alpha = n$), the lower panel shows aggregate employment (E, $E_0 = n e_0$) and (reading down the left axis) unemployment.

of outsiders (w^r) as given—maximizes profits by choosing the labor input of insiders and outsiders. In Chart 2, the corresponding labor demand curves are shown as l^d_0 for insiders and l^d_1 for outsiders, the latter differing from the demand curve for insiders by the turnover cost c.

Insiders will set a wage (w^i) to maximize, for example, their joint wage income. But, because they face some competition for jobs from outsiders, to avoid being replaced by outsiders this wage will not exceed the outsiders' reservation wage by more than the turnover-cost differential. The insiders' labor supply curve ($l^s(\bullet)$) depends on the number of insiders and becomes vertical at the level of insiders engaged in the wage negotiating

---

[8] This feature of the labor market in the FRG is discussed in Burda and Sachs (1987) and Lipschitz and others (1989), p. 32.

[9] A formal derivation of the results in this section is similar to that in Carruth and Oswald (1987). See also the survey article by Oswald (1985) and Lindbeck and Snower (1988).

[10] Sources of this turnover cost, which need not be constant as assumed in Chart 2, are discussed in Lindbeck and Snower (1988), Chapter 3. In general, the results that follow would be similar in the case of firm-specific human capital that depreciates when a worker becomes unemployed.

process, reflecting the assumption that insiders do not take the welfare of outsiders into account. For an initial insider employment of e_0, the resulting labor supply curve for insiders is $l^s(e_0)$. Equilibrium is at A, where the labor demand curve for insiders intersects their labor supply curve. Although current wages exceed the reservation wage of the unemployed, they are unable to find jobs because the turnover cost makes their employment unprofitable. Unemployment at U_0, which is above the natural rate of unemployment, can exist as a quasi-equilibrium because there are no forces in the labor market that would reduce unemployment to the natural rate.

Starting from the equilibrium at A, suppose the economy is subjected to an unanticipated negative demand or supply shock and that, at the time, agents perceive this shock to be permanent.[11] To avoid complicating Chart 2, let the labor demand schedule for insiders shift down from l^d_0 to l^d_1, the previous outsider demand schedule (the new labor demand curve for outsiders is not shown). The new equilibrium is at B, with lower wages ($w^i_1 < w^i_0$), less employment ($E_1 < E_0$), and higher unemployment ($U_1 > U_0$) as some former insiders become unemployed, that is, become outsiders.[12] Once the economy settles at this quasi-equilibrium there are again no forces in the labor market to reduce unemployment either to its previous level or to the natural rate.

Consider now a reversal of the initial shock and a return of the labor demand schedules to their original positions in Chart 2. Insiders would like to move to a new equilibrium like B', but are constrained in their wage demand by outsiders vying for their jobs. To avoid being laid off, insiders will not demand wages higher than ($w^r + c$). At this wage, and given the increased demand for labor, it is profitable for the firm to hire additional workers ($e_2 - e_1$) at the reservation wage. In the following ''period'' these new entrants become insiders and a new equilibrium is reached where all employees receive a wage of ($w^r + c$). The relevant insider labor supply curve becomes $l^s(e_2)$, and D will be the new equilibrium. Even though the exogenous supply conditions have returned to their original levels, unemployment does not return to its pre-shock level ($U_2 > U_0$).[13]

The insider-outsider model highlights how wage bargaining by insiders may result in persistent aggregate unemployment,[14] and also shows how a series of supply

shocks can ratchet-up the unemployment rate, even if the supply shocks are subsequently reversed.[15] Although these implications of the model are consistent with unemployment developments in the FRG in the 1970s and the 1980s, a number of aspects of the model—for example, the membership rules determining the insider and outsider groups—are unrealistic characterizations of aggregate labor market behavior. The aggregate model of wage determination discussed in the next section relies on less extreme assumptions, but has a number of implications—particularly with respect to the persistence of unemployment—that are similar to those of the insider-outsider model.

The Phillips Curve/Natural-Rate Model and the Target-Real-Wage-Bargaining Model

Sargan's (1964) target-real-wage-bargaining model is an aggregate model of wage determination that shares some of the characteristics of the insider-outsider model discussed above.[16] The focus in this alternative to the Phillips curve is on the equilibrium relationship between the *levels* of—as opposed to the changes in—real wages and labor productivity implying that the *growth* of nominal wages will be determined, in part, by a catch-up variable reflecting past deviations of real wages from their target level. This feature of the target-real-wage-bargaining model results in implications for equilibrium unemployment that are very different from those of the standard Phillips curve/natural-rate model. Before presenting a formal nested specification of the two models, the relationship between them is illustrated in the context of the familiar Phillips curve graph.

The top panel of Chart 3 shows the expectations-augmented Phillips curve with a vertical long-run Phillips curve at the natural rate of unemployment (U^*). Demand is represented as a positive relationship between nominal wage inflation (Δw) and unemployment (U).[17] Consider the influence of restrictive monetary policies adopted to reduce wage and price inflation. From an initial equilibrium position of wage inflation at Δw_0 and unemployment

---

[11] A negative demand shock would lower prices for the firm's output, and a negative supply shock would reduce the marginal product of labor. In terms of Chart 2, which has nominal wages on the axis, either shock would shift down the marginal revenue product curve, which is the firm's demand for labor schedule.

[12] Less simple membership rules for the insider and outsider groups would, in general, not affect the qualitative results discussed here.

[13] This would not be the case if the initial equilibrium was a corner solution, that is, if $w^i_0 = (w^r + c)$.

[14] As mentioned before, the insider-outsider model presented here

is one example of a broader class of labor-market models that give qualitatively similar results with regard to the persistence of unemployment. See also Layard and Nickell (1987), who emphasize the distinction between short- as opposed to long-duration unemployment in the determination of aggregate wages, a distinction not unlike that between insiders and outsiders.

[15] Moreover, the insider-outsider model suggests that sizable positive supply shocks might be needed before an economy can be expected to experience a fall in unemployment rates. For example, at B supply shocks that result in an upward shift of the labor demand curve to intersect $l^s(e_1)$ below $w^r + c$ will only lead to higher real wages for insiders (e_1) without any increase in employment.

[16] See also Kuh's (1967) productivity theory of wages.

[17] Dornbusch and Fischer (1981, pp. 429–51) derive a similar aggregate demand curve in terms of inflation and the level of output.

Chart 3. The Phillips Curve/Natural-Rate and Target-Real-Wage-Bargaining Models

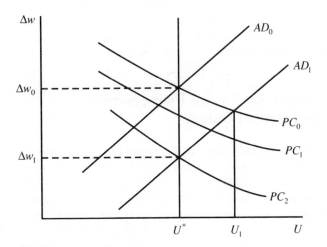

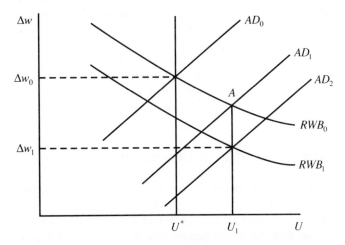

at the natural rate, the more restrictive policies would reduce aggregate demand (AD_0 to AD_1) and increase unemployment to U_1. As the declines in wage inflation are incorporated into inflation expectations, the short-run Phillips curves (PC) shift down, real wages decline, and unemployment falls.[18] This process—which is the mirror image of Friedman's (1968) accelerationist hypothesis—continues until equilibrium is re-established at

the natural rate (U^*) and wage and price inflation is reduced to Δw_1.

In the lower panel of Chart 3, the short-run Phillips curve has been replaced with a real-wage-bargaining curve (RWB). The only difference between the real-wage-bargaining curve and the Phillips curve is that nominal wage growth will now be influenced by an additional catch-up variable reflecting the deviation of real wages from their target level (as shown in the specification of equation (1) below). Just as in the Phillips curve, the real-wage-bargaining curves will shift with changes in expected inflation.

Consider the impact of the same restrictive monetary policies in the target-real-wage-bargaining model. The first-round effects are similar to the Phillips curve model: unemployment increases and nominal wage growth falls as indicated by point A. Real wages also decline with the increase in unemployment as does the target level of real wages. But once the increase in unemployment has been reflected in a reduction in the target level of real wages, the higher level of unemployment does not exert on-going downward pressures on the growth of real wages; because real wages do not decline further, labor demand declines relative to the situation implied by the Phillips curve and AD shifts further down. At the same time, there are ongoing downward pressures on nominal wage growth as the decline in wage inflation gets incorporated into expectations. Consequently, the real-wage-bargaining curves (RWB) shift down until inflation has been reduced to Δw_1.

Although wage and price inflation stabilizes at the same level as in the Phillips curve model, reflecting the same reduction in the growth of money, real wages and unemployment are higher in the target-real-wage-bargaining model due to the market power of the employed labor force. In the target-real-wage-bargaining model, unemployment in excess of the natural rate can exist as a quasi-equilibrium with stable wage and price inflation.[19] If this quasi-equilibrium is disturbed by a positive demand shock, unemployment will decline and inflation will increase. The magnitude of the drop in unemployment depends on the size and nature of the shock, and whether the rise in inflation is permanent or temporary will be determined by the response of monetary policies.

The relationship between the target-real-wage-bargaining model and the Phillips curve model shown in Chart 3 can be expressed in the following wage equation which nests the two models:[20]

---

[18] The aggregate demand curves also shift down with the declines in inflation expectations, giving a clockwise path to the new equilibrium at (Δw_1, U^*); these shifts of the AD curve are not shown in Chart 3. The description given above of the dynamics of a policy-induced disinflationary process is broadly consistent with developments in the United States in the early to mid-1980s, although macroeconomic policies, particularly fiscal policies, were not consistently restrictive and import price developments provided additional stimulus to the disinflation process. Note that the change formulation of the Phillips curve implies that transitory disturbances can have permanent effects on the real wage; this is one of the main theoretical problems with the Phillips curve discussed by Blanchard and Fischer (1989), pp. 542–46.

---

[19] Whether the quasi-equilibrium unemployment rate is above or below the short-run rate U_1 depends on the relative impact of the factors shifting AD_1 and RWB_0.

[20] See Nickell (1988), pp. 215–17 and Coe (1990). Lower-case letters indicate logarithms and $\Delta w = w - w_{-1}$.

$$\Delta w = \Delta p^{exp} + \Delta q^{tr} + \tau_1(U - U^*)$$
$$+ \tau_2(w - p - q^{tr} - \tau_0)_{-1} \quad (1)$$

where $\tau_1 < 0$, $\tau_2 \leq 0$, and τ_0 defines the equilibrium relationship between the level of real wages and trend average labor productivity (q^{tr}). If the final term is absent ($\tau_2 = 0$), the equation is a relatively standard Phillips curve except that trend productivity growth and the natural rate of unemployment are explicitly specified. Including the final term ($\tau_2 < 0$), converts the equation from a growth rate relationship between real wages, productivity, and unemployment, to a level relationship between the same variables. This can be seen in the long-run, stationary steady-state form of equation (1), assuming that $\Delta p^{exp} = \Delta p$:

$$w = p + q^{tr} - (\tau_1/\tau_2)(U - U^*) + \tau_0 \quad (1')$$

Since the level of wages is related to the level of unemployment, the growth of wages is related to changes in unemployment.[21] In this model, the target real wage ($(w - p)^T$) is determined by trend productivity and the labor market gap, which can be thought of as a proxy for the bargaining power of labor:

$$(w - p)^T = q^{tr} - (\tau_1/\tau_2)(U - U^*) + \tau_0.$$

Consider an equilibrium characterized by realized expectations ($\Delta p^{exp} = \Delta p$) and real wages growing the same as trend productivity ($\Delta w - \Delta p = \Delta q^{tr}$). In the Phillips curve model ($\tau_2 = 0$ in equation (1)), it is clear that equilibrium defined in this way requires that unemployment be at the natural rate ($U = U^*$). In the target-real-wage-bargaining model ($\tau_2 < 0$ in equation (1)), a quasi-equilibrium can exist where unemployment is above the natural rate provided that the target level of real wages has been reduced relative to the level of trend productivity; in terms of equation (1), what is required is that the last two terms sum to zero:

$$\tau_1(U - U^*) + \tau_2(w - p - q^{tr} - \tau_0)_{-1} = 0.$$

Empirical tests of the alternative models indicate that aggregate wage developments in west Germany are better described by the target-real-wage-bargaining model than by the Phillips curve/natural-rate model.[22] The persistence of high unemployment in west Germany could therefore be interpreted as a reflection of the nature of aggregate

wage formation rather than as a reflection of a high natural rate of unemployment. But if the natural rate of unemployment in west Germany in the 1980s was not approximately 8 percent, what was it? This issue is addressed in the next section which presents estimates relating the natural rate of unemployment to structural features of the labor market in the FRG.

The Natural Rate of Unemployment and Potential Output

The empirical counterparts to the unobserved concepts of potential output and the natural rate of unemployment have been estimated from a model that exploits the information contained in the relatively well defined and measured wage, price, output, and unemployment data. Equations for wages, prices, multifactor productivity, and unemployment are jointly estimated as a system to ensure that the resulting estimates for potential output and the natural rate of unemployment are consistent, and to incorporate as much relevant information as possible in the estimation procedure.[23] Given the estimated parameters, the natural rate of unemployment and potential output can be calculated as functions of their structural determinants. The model and the estimation results are summarized in the Appendix.

The Natural Rate of Unemployment

The lower panel of Chart 4 shows the estimated natural rate of unemployment. The structural determinants of the natural rate are the age-sex composition of the labor force under the assumption that the higher is the proportion of the labor force which is prime age (25–54 years) and male, the lower is the estimated natural rate; the proportion of the labor force in private sector apprenticeship programs, a unique feature of the labor market in west Germany that contributes to the relatively highly skilled labor force and lowers the natural rate; nonwage labor costs, measured as employers' social security contributions as a percent of total labor compensation, which increase the natural rate; the proportion of the labor force that is unionized, which is a proxy for insider bargaining power and increases the natural rate; and the unemployment insurance replacement ratio, which affects the reservation wage, and hence increases the natural rate.

The natural rate of unemployment is estimated to have

---

[21] Whether the growth of wages is related to the level or the change in unemployment has been suggested as a test for hysteresis; see Coe (1985, 1988), Blanchard and Summers (1988), and Gordon (1990), pp. 1124–46.

[22] See Coe and Krueger (1990).

---

[23] This approach to estimating the natural rate and potential output encompasses many of the methods found in the literature; see the discussion in Adams and Coe (1990) where a similar methodology is applied to the United States.

Table 1. Federal Republic of Germany: The Natural Rate of Unemployment

(In percent of labor force)

	1969–73	1973–75	1975–79	1979–83	1983–88
Change in the unemployment rate	0.4	3.0	−0.8	5.0	−0.3
Change in the natural rate	1.4	1.0	—	−0.2	0.1
Due to:					
Demographics	−0.1	0.1	—	0.3	—
Apprentices	0.1	−0.1	−1.3	−0.3	0.4
Nonwage labor costs	0.7	0.3	0.4	0.3	0.2
Unionization	0.5	0.5	0.8	−0.4	−0.3
Unemployment insurance replacement ratios	0.1	0.2	0.2	−0.2	−0.1
Unemployment rates at end of period					
Actual	1.0	4.0	3.2	8.2	7.8
Natural	2.5	3.5	3.5	3.3	3.4
Difference	−1.5	0.5	−0.3	4.9	4.4

Sources: Statistisches Bundesamt, *Volkswirtschaftliche Gesamtrechnungen;* and authors' estimates.

Chart 4. Federal Republic of Germany: Potential and Quasi-Potential Output and the Natural Rate of Unemployment, First Quarter 1968–Fourth Quarter 1989

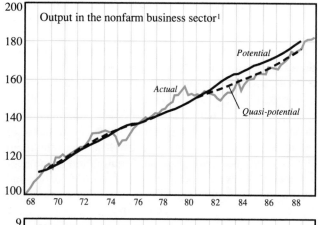

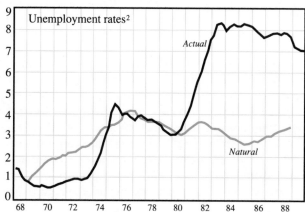

Sources: Statistisches Bundesamt, *Volkswirtschaftliche Gesamtrech-nungen;* and authors' estimates.

[1] Seasonally adjusted; actual output in the first quarter of 1968 = 100.

[2] Seasonally adjusted; in percent of the labor force.

increased steadily from its assumed value of 0.7 percent in 1968 to about 4¼ percent in 1976, and then to have fluctuated between 2½ percent and 3½ percent from 1977–88. Actual rates of unemployment were below the estimated natural rate by about 1¼ percentage points from 1970–73, and followed closely the natural rate after 1975 until the end of the decade. In the 1980s, however, it is estimated that this gap widened considerably and averaged about 5 percentage points from 1983 to 1988.

Table 1 presents a decomposition of the changes in the estimated natural rate of unemployment. The large increases in the natural rate in the early 1970s reflected increases in nonwage labor costs, which rose from about 15 percent of wages and salaries in 1969 to 20 percent in 1975, and in unionization, which increased from 29½ percent of the labor force in 1969 to 32½ percent in 1975. During the late 1970s, the natural rate declined somewhat as the number of apprentices increased from 5 percent of the labor force in 1975 to 6 percent in 1979, although this was partially offset by continued increases in nonwage labor costs (1 percentage point) and unionization (2 percentage points). The natural rate of unemployment is estimated to have averaged about 3¼ percent in the 1980s, reflecting the net effect of some upward pressure from demographic changes, reductions in the share of apprentices in the labor force, and continued increases in nonwage labor costs, offset by reductions in unionization. There was a small increase in unemployment insurance replacement ratios in the mid-to-late 1970s, which tended to increase the estimated natural rate of unemployment somewhat, but this effect was largely reversed in the 1980s.

The 4½ to 5 percentage point gap between the estimated natural rate of unemployment and the actual unemployment rate in the FRG throughout most of the 1980s is striking. It is noteworthy, however, that a number of other studies based on different methodologies arrive at a similar result.

Franz and König (1990) estimate a disequilibrium model and calculate an equilibrium structural unemployment rate that was close to actual rates of unemployment in the 1960s, and then increased to a maximum of 3¾ percent in 1985. The principal determinants of changes in the structural unemployment rate in Franz and König's analysis were nonwage labor costs and, to a much lesser extent, the unemployment insurance replacement ratio, which is consistent with the results presented above. Similarly, Torres and Martin (1990), based on estimated Phillips curves, calculate that the unemployment rate consistent with non-increasing wage inflation in the FRG rose from about 3 percent in the late 1960s to about 4 percent in 1988.[24]

As discussed earlier, the target-real-wage-bargaining model implies that unemployment in excess of the natural rate will result in a downward adjustment of the target real wage relative to labor productivity. Based on the system estimation results, the 5 percentage point gap between the estimated natural rate and the actual unemployment rate that opened from 1980 to 1988 implies a reduction in real compensation relative to productivity at potential ($w - p^c - q^{pot}$) of about 11 percent. During this period, the actual increase in real consumption wages ($w - p^c$) was about 10 percent less than the increase in the estimated labor productivity at potential output (q^{pot}).[25]

Potential Output and Multifactor Productivity

Average output growth in the private nonfarm sector slowed considerably in the FRG over the 1969–88 period. Possible sources of this slowdown are suggested by the growth accounting framework in Table 2, based on a Cobb-Douglas production function with actual income shares used to weight labor and capital inputs.[26]

For the three subperiods identified in the middle of Table 2, all factors contributed to the decline in output growth, although their contributions varied over the different subperiods. Multifactor productivity growth first increased after 1974 before declining sharply in the 1980–88 period, becoming the major ''source'' of the further decline in output growth. A comparison of developments in 1983–88 with developments from the second quarter of 1969 to the first quarter of 1974 is

Table 2. Federal Republic of Germany: Contributions to Output Growth in the Private Nonfarm Sector

(Average annual percentage changes)

	Output	Hours Worked	Capital	Multifactor Productivity
1969:II–1988:IV	2.50	−0.46	1.76	1.20
1969:II–1974:I	4.16	−0.08	2.59	1.65
1974:II–1980:I	2.73	−0.61	1.35	1.99
1980:II–1988:IV	1.41	−0.57	1.56	0.42
1983:I–1988:IV	2.89	−0.08	1.68	1.29

Sources: Statistisches Bundesamt, *Volkswirtschaftliche Gesamtrechnungen*; and authors' estimates.

instructive, since the latter period also began during an early phase of a business cycle upturn (the other subperiods are peak-to-peak). While the contribution of labor was the same in the two periods, the growth of both capital and multifactor productivity was considerably slower in the 1980s expansion.

Based on the system estimation results, the two alternative measures of equilibrium output discussed above—quasi-potential output and potential output—can be calculated. Both measures of potential output are determined by normalized capital and labor inputs and by multifactor productivity. The only difference between the two measures is that for potential output labor input is defined as total manhours consistent with employment at the levels implied by the estimated natural rate of unemployment, whereas for quasi-potential output actual manhours are used.[27] The determinants of multifactor productivity are the stock of research and development (R&D) capital;[28] non-German immigration, which is estimated to have reduced the productivity of labor and thereby reduced potential output per unit of labor; and the integration of the European Community (EC), measured as intra-EC trade as a percent of the GNP of the EC countries, which is assumed to increase efficiency in west Germany.[29]

The upper panel of Chart 4 depicts the time paths of potential, quasi-potential, and actual output in the private nonfarm sector of the FRG. There was little difference between potential and quasi-potential output in the 1970s, reflecting the similar levels of the actual and the natural rates of unemployment. Thereafter, the steep rise in the actual rate of unemployment in contrast to the stability in the estimated natural rate of unemployment is reflected in the opening of a gap between potential output and the

---

[24] In contrast to these results, Jaeger and Parkinson (1990) estimate that the natural rate of unemployment in the FRG in 1988 exceeded 8 percent, the actual rate of unemployment. This result reflects the application of an unobserved-components model that uses capacity utilization to pick up movements in the cyclical component of unemployment. Because the measure of capacity utilization indicates that output was above capacity in 1988, the estimated natural rate of unemployment is, necessarily, above the actual rate of unemployment.

[25] The total impact on real wages from the other variables in the wage level equation roughly summed to zero over this period.

[26] See Maddison (1989) and Englander and Mittelstädt (1988) for international comparisons.

[27] The relationship between potential (y^{POT}) and quasi-potential output (y^{pot}) can be approximated by $y^{POT} \simeq y^{pot} + \lambda(U - U^{NAT})/100$.

[28] See Griliches (1988).

[29] See the discussion about the impact of the unified European market in Baldwin (1989).

Table 3. Federal Republic of Germany: Contributions to Potential and Quasi-Potential Output Growth in the Private Nonfarm Sector

(Annual percentage changes)

	1969:II–1988:IV	1969:II–1974:I	1974:II–1980:I	1980:II–1988:IV	1983:I–1988:IV
Potential output	2.5	3.2	2.1	2.4	2.2
Due to:					
Hours worked	−0.4	−0.8	−0.5	−0.2	−0.4
Capital	1.8	2.4	1.3	1.7	1.8
Multifactor productivity	1.2	1.6	1.3	0.8	0.8
Due to:					
R&D capital	0.6	0.7	0.6	0.6	0.5
Foreign arrivals	0.2	0.3	0.2	0.2	0.2
EC trade share	0.3	0.6	0.4	0.1	0.1
Quasi-potential output	2.4	3.4	2.0	2.1	2.2
Quasi-potential hours worked	−0.6	−0.7	−0.6	−0.4	−0.4
Actual output	2.5	4.2	2.7	1.4	2.9

Sources: Statistisches Bundesamt, *Volkswirtschaftliche Gesamtrechnungen*; and authors' estimates.

lower levels of quasi-potential and actual output. Even though this gap narrowed slightly after 1986 as unemployment rates declined, potential output is estimated to have exceeded actual output by about 2½ percent at the end of 1988; and quasi-potential output is estimated to have been about equal to actual output in 1988.

The annual growth rate of potential output declined by about 1 percent between the early 1970s and the late 1970s, a decline that was even more pronounced in quasi-potential output growth (Table 3). The slowdown in growth reflected primarily a slower pace of capital expansion and a decrease in multifactor productivity growth. Potential output growth increased in the 1980s reflecting increased growth of the capital stock and a slowing in the trend decline of labor input, which were sufficient to offset the continued decline in multifactor productivity growth. During the expansion from 1983 to 1988, however, potential output growth remained about 1 percentage point lower than in the 1969–73 period.

The slowdown in multifactor productivity growth after 1974 contributed significantly to the lower rates of growth of potential and quasi-potential output.[30] The estimation results suggest that this decline was attributable to all of the determinants of multifactor productivity: a decline in the growth of the R&D capital stock, a slowing in the trend reduction in the arrival rate of foreigners in the 1980s, and a smaller contribution from the integration of the EC.

---

[30] A comparison of the growth contributions to potential output with those for actual output (Table 2) reveals differences, not only for hours worked, as could be expected, but also for multifactor productivity. Actual multifactor productivity growth, for example, increased in the second half of the 1970s, whereas multifactor productivity implied by the system estimates did not, suggesting a relatively intensive utilization of factor inputs in this period. During the recession period of 1980–82, this pattern was reversed, and from 1980 to 1988, estimated multifactor productivity at potential output expanded about twice as fast as did actual multifactor productivity.

Prospects for the Natural Rate of Unemployment and Potential Output

Prospects for future developments in the natural rate of unemployment and potential output can be assessed based on assumptions or projections of the likely developments in their determinants. Such an assessment, needless to say, is particularly hazardous at this juncture as it is difficult to gauge the effects of unification on investment and the labor market in west Germany. Nevertheless, it is interesting to consider the possible evolution of potential output in the period to 1995 based on the same growth accounting framework used above.

The estimated natural rate of unemployment has been broadly stable since the mid-1970s, and, for the 1983–88 period, this is also true of the structural determinants of the natural rate. Although unification with the GDR, and the associated movement of labor, may affect some characteristics of the labor force, it seems unlikely that this would have large effects on the natural rate of unemployment. Accordingly, the natural rate of unemployment in west Germany is assumed to remain relatively stable at about 3½ percent over the 1989–95 period.

The future course of potential output depends on developments in factor inputs and in multifactor productivity. The contribution of capital inputs is based on the assumption that the real business fixed investment boom of 1989–90 gradually gives way to more typical annual rates of growth of about 3½ percent. Hours worked by each employee are assumed to decline by 0.2 percent a year. Given a stable natural rate of unemployment, potential employment would rise in line with labor force growth, which is assumed to increase to more than 1 percent a year in 1990–91, reflecting, principally, high immigration from the GDR and from Eastern Europe, and then decline to more normal rates of increase of about ½ of 1 percent a year. Actual rates of

Table 4. West Germany. Potential and Quasi-Potential Output Growth in Private Nonfarm Sector

(Annual percentage changes)

| | 1986–88 | Projections | |
		1989–91	1992–95
Potential output	2.2	3.0	3.0
Due to:			
Hours worked	−0.6	−0.2	—
Capital	2.2	2.5	2.2
Multifactor productivity	0.7	0.7	0.8
Due to:			
R&D capital	0.5	0.6	0.6
Foreign arrivals	0.1	0.1	—
EC trade share	—	—	0.2
Quasi-potential output	2.5	3.2	3.1
Quasi-potential hours worked	−0.3	0.1	0.1
Memorandum items:			
Actual output	2.6	3.7	. . .
GDP	2.6	3.7	. . .
Unemployment rate (end year)	7.8	6.4	. . .
Natural rate of unemployment (end year)	3.5	3.5	. . .

Sources: Statistisches Bundesamt, *Volkswirtschaftliche Gesamtrechnungen*; and authors' estimates.

unemployment—needed to calculate quasi-potential output—are assumed to drop by almost 1½ percentage points from the end of 1988 to 1991 (much of this reduction has already occurred by mid-1990) and then to decline more gradually to about 6 percent in 1994–95.

Multifactor productivity growth is expected to recover only slowly from the relatively low rates of growth at the end of the sample period. Given the strong expansion of actual R&D expenditures in recent years, the contribution of the R&D capital stock to potential output is assumed to increase slightly to equal its average contribution to multifactor productivity growth over the 1969–88 sample period. The impact on multifactor productivity growth in the FRG from the increased integration of the EC was estimated to have declined to zero in the mid-to-late 1980s. With the completion of the unified European market in 1992, it seems reasonable to assume that this will result in some modest contribution to multifactor productivity growth in west Germany, although nothing as large as the estimated impact in the 1970s when intra-EC trade was expanding rapidly. Finally, the trend decline of non-German immigration to west Germany is assumed to continue at a decreasing rate until 1991, with the number of foreign arrivals thereafter constituting a constant fraction of the labor force.

Based on these assumptions, the projected contributions to potential and quasi-potential output growth from 1989 to 1995 are summarized in Table 4, which also reports the estimated contributions to potential output growth in 1986–88, the last three years of the sample period. The annual rate of growth of potential output is projected to increase from 2¼ percent in 1986–88 to 3 percent in 1989–91, reflecting higher contributions from both capital and labor inputs. The slowdown in the trend decline of labor

input is a reflection of substantial increases in the growth of the labor force coupled with a constant natural rate of unemployment. Much of the increased contribution of capital and labor inputs from 1989 to 1991 reflects the robust investment and increased labor force growth that took place in the period up to mid-1990.[31] Quasi-potential output is projected to grow more rapidly than potential output, owing to the decline in the actual unemployment rate over this period. The 2½ percentage point gap by which potential output was estimated to have exceeded actual output in 1988 is reduced to about ¼ of 1 percentage point by 1991 as actual output growth is projected to outpace the growth of potential output by ¾ of 1 percentage point a year. And actual output, which was roughly equal to quasi-potential output in 1988, is projected to exceed quasi-potential output by about 1½ percentage points in 1991.

Potential output growth is projected to remain unchanged at 3 percent a year from 1992 to 1995. A decline in the contribution of capital inputs is offset by increased contributions from labor inputs and multifactor productivity. The halt to the negative contribution of labor inputs that were a feature of the 1970s and the 1980s reflects the projections of higher employment growth. The marginal improvement in multifactor productivity stems from the assumed impact of the unified European market in 1992, partially offset by a leveling off in the reduction in the number of non-German immigrants to west Germany. Since the decline in the unemployment rate is projected to be relatively small after 1991, quasi-potential and potential output are projected to increase at broadly the same rate. Actual output growth is

---

[31] Although the impact on potential output has been attenuated somewhat by the smoothing applied to the determinants of potential output as discussed above.

expected to grow marginally slower than potential output from 1992 to 1995, implying that the gap by which potential output exceeds actual output may increase to about ¾ of 1 percent; actual output is projected to exceed quasi-potential output by about ¾ of 1 percent by the mid-1990s.

Summary and Policy Implications

The results presented above have a number of implications for economic policy in Germany and for the likely effects of economic and monetary unification with the GDR. The output gaps that were estimated for 1988—2½ percent with respect to potential output and zero with respect to quasi-potential output—indicate that there was room for the relatively robust growth and the substantial declines in unemployment that occurred in 1989 and the first half of 1990. The estimation results imply, however, that there would have been some upward pressure on inflation in 1990–91, although this pressure would have been relatively small.[32] To the extent that the growth of quasi-potential output outpaces that of actual output over the next few years, pressures on capacity that built up in 1989–90 will be attenuated.

Perhaps the most important implications derive from the distinction between potential output and quasi-potential output. This distinction is based on two results: first, that the natural rate of unemployment, which is empirically determined by structural aspects of the labor market in west Germany, is about 3½ percent compared with actual rates of unemployment of about 6–7 percent; and second, that aggregate wage determination in west Germany is best characterized by a target-real-wage-bargaining model.

The gap between potential and quasi-potential output in the period to 1995 is a reflection of the high actual unemployment rates that are expected to persist relative to the lower structurally determined natural rate of unemployment. As long as unemployment exceeds the natural rate and actual output is below potential output, there is scope to absorb increases in employment and output without setting in place an ongoing inflationary process. This suggests that some aspects of the constraints on output growth may only be binding in the short run.[33] However, the need for macroeconomic policies to be consistent with medium-term objectives, particularly with regard to price stability and fiscal sustainability, limits the extent to which traditional aggregate demand policies can, by themselves, close the gaps between the actual and the natural rates of unemployment and between quasi-potential and potential output.

The model does point to areas where government policies can increase the supply responsiveness of the west German economy. Policies that improve the qualifications of the labor force, reduce the reservation wage, or increase the bargaining power of outsiders in the wage negotiation process can be expected to restrain real wages, increase actual employment, and lower the natural rate of unemployment. For a given natural rate of unemployment, active labor market policies can contribute to reductions in actual unemployment. Similarly, structural measures aimed at increasing the productivity of capital and labor inputs can raise quasi-potential and potential output, both directly and by stimulating investment. The recent increased flexibility in work arrangements, particularly the greater use of multiple shifts and weekend work, for example, has raised the effective size of the physical capital stock. Finally, the results also suggest that the completion of the unified European market in 1992 and increased expenditures on research and development may stimulate output, raise total factor productivity, and increase the growth of potential output.

---

[32] The upward pressure on inflation in 1989 and 1990 was much less than implied by the estimated growth of potential for 1988 because the robust growth of investment increased productive capacity substantially. In mid-1990, actual output may have exceeded the level of quasi-potential output by about 1 percent implying about ¼ of 1 percentage point upward pressure on inflation. The 1 percentage point decline in the unemployment rate in the year to mid-1990 implied an increase in the level of real wages relative to productivity at potential of about 2 percent. This is consistent with the 1990 wage agreements that suggest some pickup in wage growth.

[33] One such short-run constraint is capital that would normally be expected to respond to actual or expected increases in demand as suggested by the following quote from the May 1990 business survey reported by the Commission of the European Communities (1990), p. 1: "Industrial capacity is virtually fully utilized in the member countries. Despite this, the companies questioned are not expecting serious capacity constraints in the near future. The intention is to increase output further."

Appendix

An Empirical Model of the Natural Rate of Unemployment and Potential Output

This appendix presents a brief description of the model used to estimate the natural rate of unemployment and potential output and summarizes the estimation results. A more complete discussion, including a data appendix, is contained in Coe and Krueger (1990). The variables are defined in Table 5, the specification of the system of equations is given in Table 6, and the estimation results are reported in Table 7.

The first equation in Table 6 is the production function

where the coefficients on labor and capital inputs have been constrained to equal their factor shares. With this constraint, the dependent variable is multifactor productivity which is determined by the stock of research and development capital, a proxy for the impact of foreign arrivals on the "quality" of labor input, a proxy for increased efficiency related to integration among the countries of the EC,[34] and a proxy for the utilization of capital. The multifactor productivity equation, rewritten as an output equation and with some smoothing of the long-run determinants of output, is then used to define potential output as specified at the bottom of Table 6.

[34] See Baldwin (1989).

Table 5.	Federal Republic of Germany: Variable Definitions
y	real output (private nonfarm business sector, NF)
y^{pot}	quasi-potential output (NF)
y^{POT}	potential output (NF)
λ	share of employee compensation in total income (NF)
h	total hours worked (NF)
k	real stock of capital (NF)
rd	real stock of research and development capital
FOR	foreign arrivals as a percent of the labor force[1]
$NFOR$	foreign arrivals less departures as a percent of the labor force[1]
EC	intra-EC trade as a percent of EC GNP
U	unemployment rate
U^{TR}	trend unemployment rate (spline)
U^{NAT}	the natural rate of unemployment
w	hourly compensation per employee (NF)
p^c	implicit deflator for private consumption expenditures
p	implicit output deflator (NF)
p^m	implicit deflator for imports of goods and services
p^x	implicit deflator for exports of goods and services
p^o	price of oil
q	output per hour (NF)
q^{pot}	labor productivity at quasi-potential output (NF)
$NWLC$	nonwage labor costs as a percent of total wages and salaries
DEM	impact on the unemployment rate of changing labor force shares
APP	apprentices as a percent of the labor force
$UNION$	union members as a percent of the labor force
$UIRR$	unemployment insurance replacement ratio

[1] Foreign arrivals exclude ethnic Germans (*Aussiedler* and *Übersiedler*). When ethnic German immigration was included in the regressions, the coefficients were generally insignificant; this may in part have resulted from the relatively low variability in these series over most of the sample period.

Table 6. Equation Specification[1]

1. Production function

$$y - \lambda h - (1 - \lambda)k = \alpha_0 + \alpha_1 rd + \alpha_2 \Theta^8(L)FOR + \alpha_3 EC + \alpha_4(U - U^{TR}) + \epsilon^y$$

2. Wage level

$$w = \beta_0 + \beta_1 p^c + \beta_2 q^{pot} + \beta_3 (U - U^{NAT}) + \beta_4(p^c - p) + \beta_5 NWLC + \beta_6 NFOR + \epsilon^w$$

3. Wage growth

$$\Delta w = \gamma_1 \Delta p^c + \gamma_2 \Theta^4(L)\Delta q + \gamma_3 \Delta(p^c - p) + \gamma_4 \Delta(p^c - p)_{-1} + \gamma_5 \Delta(U - U^{NAT})$$
$$+ \gamma_6 \Delta\Delta(U - U^{NAT})_{-1} + \gamma_7 \epsilon^w_{-1} + \epsilon^{\Delta w}$$

4. Price inflation

$$\Delta p = \delta_1(\Theta^{12}(L)\Delta w - \Delta q^{pot}) + \delta_2(\Delta p^m - \Delta p^m_{-2}) + \delta_3(y - y^{pot})_{-1} + \epsilon^p$$

5. Unemployment rate change

$$\Delta(U - DEM) = \psi_1 \Delta(y - y^{pot}) + \psi_2 \Delta(y - y^{pot})_{-1} + \psi_3 \Delta(p^o - p)_{-3} + \psi_4 \Delta(p^x - p^m)$$
$$+ \psi_5 \Delta APP + \psi_6 \Delta APP_{-1} + \psi_7 \Delta APP_{-2} + \psi_8 \Delta NWLC_{-1} + \psi_9 \Delta UNION*UIRR_{-2}$$
$$+ \psi_{10}\Delta(U - DEM)_{-1} + \epsilon^U$$

Memorandum:

The following expressions for quasi-potential output (y^{pot}), labor productivity at quasi-potential output (q^{pot}), and the natural rate of unemployment (U^{NAT}) must be substituted into the above equations:

$$y^{pot} = \lambda \mathbf{h} + (1 - \lambda)\mathbf{k} + \alpha_0 + \alpha_1 \mathbf{rd} + \alpha_2 \mathbf{FOR} + \alpha_3 \mathbf{EC}$$

$$q^{pot} = (\lambda - 1)\mathbf{h} + (1 - \lambda)\mathbf{k} + \alpha_0 + \alpha_1 \mathbf{rd} + \alpha_2 \mathbf{FOR} + \alpha_3 \mathbf{EC}$$

$$U^{NAT} = 0.7 + \Sigma\Delta DEM + ((\psi_5 + \psi_6 + \psi_7)/(1 - \psi_{10}))\Sigma\Delta APP + (\psi_8/(1 - \psi_{10}))\Sigma\Delta NWLC$$

$$+ (\psi_9/(1 - \psi_{10}))\Sigma\Delta UNION*UIRR$$

where the variables in bold print in the first two expressions have been smoothed and labor input is consistent with actual rates of unemployment.

[1] The estimated equations also include a number of dummy variables which are specified in Coe and Krueger (1990). $\Theta^n(L)$ represents an n-quarter moving average lag operator.

Equation 2 in Table 6 determines the equilibrium level of wages and corresponds to equation (1′) in the main text. In addition to the variables discussed in the context of equation (1′), the level of wages is determined by the difference between consumer and output prices,[35] nonwage labor costs and the net immigration of non-German foreigners. Equation 3 in Table 6 determines the growth of wages and corresponds to equation (1) in the text.[36] The lagged residual from the levels equation (ϵ^w_{-1}) is included as an error-correction term in the wage growth equation and corresponds to the final term in equation (1) discussed in the main text.

The fourth equation in Table 6 determines output price inflation as a variable markup on the growth of unit labor costs with the markup depending on the gap between actual and potential output, and, temporarily, on changes in import prices.

The final equation in Table 6 distinguishes between cyclical and structural unemployment. Changes in cyclical unemployment are determined by changes in the output gap, real oil prices, and the terms of trade. Changes in structural unemployment are determined by the number of apprentices as a percent of the labor force—which affects the quality of the labor force—nonwage labor costs, unionization, and unemployment insurance replacement ratios. The long-run, steady-state relationship between unemployment and its structural determinants is used to determine the natural rate of unemployment as specified at the bottom of Table 6.

Since potential output and the natural rate of unemployment are unobserved, the three expressions given at the bottom of Table 6 must be substituted into each of the five equations. With these substitutions, the system is internally consistent, includes no proxies for trend output or trend productivity growth, and the relationship between the actual and the natural rate of unemployment is explicitly incorporated into the two wage equations.[37] These substitutions give rise to a large number of

[35] This is approximately equal to the terms of trade and implies that wages are indexed to a weighted average of the two prices.

[36] Both the level and the change specifications of the wage equation are included in the system to take advantage of the relationship between the unemployment gap and the equilibrium level of wages, as well as the relationship between changes in the unemployment gap and short-run changes in wages.

[37] A proxy for the quasi-equilibrium unemployment rate (U^{TR}) appears in the production function and is set equal to the unemployment rate ($U = U^{TR}$) in the expression for potential output.

Table 7. Three-Stage Least Squares Estimation Results[1]

	Equation				
	1	2	3	4	5
	$\alpha_0 =$ 0.022 (0.02)	$\beta_0 =$ −0.243 (0.02)	$\gamma_1 =$ 1.593 (0.18)	$\delta_1 =$ 1.0 (const.)	$\psi_1 =$ −0.011 (0.003)
	$\alpha_1 =$ 0.129 (0.009)	$\beta_1 =$ 1.0 (const.)	$\gamma_2 =$ 0.351 (0.22)	$\delta_2 =$ −0.069 (0.02)	$\psi_2 =$ −0.004 (0.002)
	$\alpha_2 =$ −0.064 (0.007)	$\beta_2 =$ 1.0 (const.)	$\gamma_3 =$ −2.399 (0.52)	$\delta_3 =$ 0.281 (0.12)	$\psi_3 =$ 0.002 (0.0006)
	$\alpha_3 =$ 0.012 (0.002)	$\beta_3 =$ −0.022 (0.001)	$\gamma_4 =$ −2.336 (0.45)		$\psi_4 =$ −0.013 (0.005)
	$\alpha_4 =$ 0.022 (0.002)	$\beta_4 =$ −0.002 (0.0007)	$\gamma_5 =$ −5.626 (1.78)		$\psi_5 =$ −3.495 (0.59)
		$\beta_5 =$ −0.014 (0.001)	$\gamma_6 =$ 4.990 (1.88)		$\psi_6 =$ −5.835 (0.99)
		$\beta_6 =$ −0.005 (0.0008)	$\gamma_7 =$ −0.350 (0.07)		$\psi_7 =$ −2.712 (0.59)
					$\psi_8 =$ 0.066 (0.02)
					$\psi_9 =$ 0.267 (0.08)
					$\psi_{10} =$ 0.705 (0.06)
R^2	0.984	0.999	0.692	0.499	0.805
SEE	0.009	0.011	3.116	2.391	0.105
DW (Durbin h)	1.014	1.381	2.388	1.458	(2.785)

[1] The following variables were considered to be endogenous in addition to the dependent variables: output prices, unemployment, and the level and change of output and consumer prices. The instruments were all exogenous and predetermined variables, lagged values of all endogenous variables, and the current and two lags of the logarithm of M2.

nonlinear parameter restrictions across the five-equation system. Because of the simultaneous nature of the system, and given that the errors can be expected to be correlated across the five equations, the system has been estimated using nonlinear three-stage least squares. The estimation results are presented in Table 7.

References

Adams, Charles, and David T. Coe, "A Systems Approach to Estimating the Natural Rate of Unemployment and Potential Output for the United States," *Staff Papers*, International Monetary Fund, Vol. 37 (June 1990), pp. 232–93.

Alogoskoufis, George S., and Alan Manning, "On the persistence of unemployment," *Economic Policy*, Vol. 3 (October 1988), pp. 428–69.

Baldwin, Richard, "The Growth Effects of 1992," *Economic Policy*, Vol. 4 (October 1989), pp. 247–81.

Bean, Charles, "Capital shortages and persistent unemployment," *Economic Policy*, Vol. 4 (April 1989), pp. 11–53.

Blanchard, Olivier J., and Stanley Fischer, *Lectures on Macroeconomics* (Cambridge: MIT Press, 1989).

Blanchard, Olivier J., and Lawrence H. Summers, "Hysteresis and the European Unemployment Problem," in *Unemployment, Hysteresis of the Natural Rate Hypothesis*, ed. by Rod Cross (New York: Basil Blackwell, 1988).

Burda, Michael, and Jeffrey Sachs, "Institutional Aspects of High Unemployment in the Federal Republic of Germany," NBER Working Paper No. 2241 (Cambridge: National Bureau of Economic Research, May 1987).

Carruth, Alan A., and Andrew J. Oswald, "On Union Preferences and Labour Market Models: Insiders and Outsiders," *Economic Journal*, Vol. 97 (June 1987), pp. 431–45.

Coe, David T., "Nominal Wages, the NAIRU and Wage Flexibility," *OECD Economic Studies*, No. 5 (Autumn 1985), pp. 87–126.

———, "Hysteresis Effects in Aggregate Wage Equations," in *Unemployment, Hysteresis and the Natural Rate Hypothesis*, ed. by Rod Cross (New York: Basil Blackwell, 1988).

———, "Insider-Outsider Influences on Industry Wages," *Empirical Economics*, Vol. 15, Issue 2 (1990), pp. 163–83.

Coe, David T. and Thomas Krueger, "Why is Unemployment So High at Full Capacity? The Persistence of Unemployment, the Natural Rate, and Potential Output in the Federal

Republic of Germany," IMF Working Paper No. 90/101 (October 1990).

Commission of the European Communities, *European Economy*, Supplement B, "Business and Consumer Survey Results," No. 5 (May 1990).

Cross, Rod, ed., *Unemployment, Hysteresis and the Natural Rate Hypothesis* (New York: Basil Blackwell, 1988).

Dornbusch, Rudiger, and Stanley Fischer, *Macroeconomics* (New York: McGraw Hill, 2nd ed., 1981).

Englander, Steven A., and Axel Mittelstädt, "Total Factor Productivity: Macroeconomic and Structural Aspects of the Slowdown," *OECD Economic Studies*, No. 10 (Spring 1988), pp. 7–56.

Franz, Wolfgang, "Hysteresis, Persistence, and the NAIRU: An Empirical Analysis for the Federal Republic of Germany," in *The Fight Against Unemployment*, ed. by Richard Layard and Lars Calmfors (Cambridge: MIT Press, 1987).

———, and Heinz König, "The Nature and Causes of Unemployment in the Federal Republic of Germany since the 1970s: An Empirical Investigation," *Economica* (Supplement, 1986), pp. S219–44.

———, "A Disequilibrium Approach to Unemployment in the Federal Republic of Germany," *European Economic Review*, Vol. 34 (May 1990), pp. 413–22.

Friedman, Milton, "The Role of Monetary Policy," *American Economic Review*, Vol. 58 (March 1968), pp. 1–17.

Gordon, Robert J., "What is New-Keynesian Economics?" *Journal of Economic Literature*, Vol. 28 (September 1990), pp. 1115–71.

Gottfries, Nils, and Henrik Horn, "Wage formation and the persistence of unemployment," *Economic Journal*, Vol. 97 (December 1987), pp. 877–84.

Griliches, Zvi, "Productivity Puzzles and R&D: Another Nonexplanation," *Journal of Economic Perspectives*, Vol. 2 (Fall 1988), pp. 9–21.

International Monetary Fund, *World Economic Outlook: A Survey by the Staff of the International Monetary Fund* (October 1990).

Jaeger A., and M. Parkinson, "Testing for Hysteresis in Unemployment: An Unobserved Components Approach," *Empirical Economics*, Vol. 15, (1990), pp. 185–98.

Kuh, Edwin, "A Productivity Theory of Wage Levels—An Alternative to the Phillips Curve," *Review of Economic Studies*, Vol. 34 (October 1967), pp. 333–60.

Layard, Richard, and Stephen Nickell, "The Labor Market," in *The Performance of the British Economy*, ed. by Rudiger Dornbusch and Richard Layard (Oxford: Clarendon Press, 1987).

Lindbeck, Assar, and Dennis Snower, *The Insider-Outsider Theory of Employment and Unemployment* (Cambridge: MIT Press, 1988).

Lipschitz, Leslie, Jeroen Kremers, Thomas Mayer, and Donogh McDonald, *The Federal Republic of Germany: Adjustment in a Surplus Country,* Occasional Paper No. 64 (International Monetary Fund, January 1989).

Maddison, Angus, *The World Economy in the 20th Century*, Development Centre of the Organization for Economic Cooperation and Development (Paris, 1989).

Nickell, Stephen, "The Supply Side and Macroeconomic Modeling," in *Empirical Macroeconomics for Interdependent Economies*, ed. by Ralph Bryant and others (Washington: The Brookings Institution, 1988).

Oswald, Andrew J., "The Economic Theory of Trade Unions: An Introductory Survey," *Scandinavian Journal of Economics*, Vol. 87 (1985), pp. 160–93.

Sargan, J.D., "Wages and Prices in the United Kingdom: A Study in Econometric Methodology," in *Econometric Analysis for National Economic Planning*, Colston Papers, Vol. 16, ed. by Peter Hart and others (London: Butterworths, 1964).

Solow, Robert M., "Technical Change and the Aggregate Production Function," *Review of Economics and Statistics,* Vol. 39 (August 1957), pp. 312–20.

Torres, Raymond, and John P. Martin, "Measuring Potential Output in the Seven Major OECD Countries," *OECD Economic Studies*, No. 14 (Spring 1990), pp. 127–49.

VIII

Immigration into West Germany
Historical Perspectives and Policy Implications

Thomas Mayer

The political changes that have taken place in Eastern European countries since the mid-1980s have facilitated increased emigration from these countries, particularly of ethnic and religious minorities. A considerable proportion of these emigrants have been ethnic Germans who have moved to the Federal Republic of Germany (FRG). In addition, the political collapse of the German Democratic Republic (GDR) in 1989 paved the way for another wave of immigration into the FRG.

The scale of recent immigration has given rise to concerns about its economic and political effects in west Germany. The purpose of this chapter is to provide some historical perspective on immigration into west Germany, discuss the outlook for the next few years, and assess some of the likely economic effects and the appropriate policy response.

Historical Perspectives[1]

Migration of ethnic Germans from Eastern European countries and the eastern parts of the German Reich began with the retreat of the defeated German army at the end of World War II. At the beginning of the war, 9.6 million Germans lived in those eastern parts of the German Reich that, after the war, were outside the boundaries of the GDR (East Prussia, East Pomerania, East Brandenburg, and Silesia). A further 8.8 million ethnic Germans lived in other areas of eastern and southeastern Europe (for example, the U.S.S.R., Hungary, and Romania). Beginning in June 1945, many of these Germans were expelled and by the end of 1950, the number of ethnic Germans living outside the FRG and the GDR had fallen to 4.2 million; about 4.1 million had moved to the GDR and some 8 million to the FRG.

During the 1950s and 1960s, significant immigration from Eastern European countries continued, although on a much reduced scale (Table 1). Immigration from the GDR, on the other hand, picked up until east Germany closed its borders to the west in 1961. Thus, between 1950 and August 13, 1961, the day the Berlin wall was erected, 2.6 million people moved from the GDR to the FRG; after the closure of the border between the GDR and the FRG, the number of immigrants dropped markedly, with only 264,000 crossing from east to west Germany in the rest of the 1960s. Between 1970 and 1986, immigration averaged 57,000 persons a year. In the aftermath of the political changes in Eastern European countries, immigration gathered steam in 1987 and strengthened further in 1989, with the surge in immigration from the GDR. Thus, between 1950 and the end of 1989, the FRG received more than 5½ million immigrants from the east; about 2 million immigrated from the Eastern European countries and the rest from the GDR. These immigrants came in addition to the 8 million people who had moved to the territory of the FRG in 1945–49.

Immigration from Eastern European countries is expected to continue at a high level over the next few years as it has been estimated that there are 3–4 million people in these countries who are of German descent.[2] There could also be sizable further immigration from east Germany during the time of structural change and adjustment to a market economy. An important question is whether migration from east Germany to west Germany will continue until the wage gap between the two parts of Germany has been substantially closed. Since it is expected that it will take at least 10–15 years until labor productivity in east Germany reaches the level prevailing in west Germany, some have argued that wage subsidies will be needed in order to stem the flow of emigration and prevent an economic collapse in the east. Both assumptions—that only wage equalization can stop

---

[1] For additional details on immigration flows, see Statistisches Bundesamt (1989).

[2] See Deutsches Institut der Wirtschaft (1989), p. 201.

Table 1. Federal Republic of Germany: Immigration from the East and Macroeconomic Developments

	From Eastern European Countries	From GDR	Total	Unemployment Rate[1]	Growth of Real GNP Per Head
1950–59	439,714	2,203,107	2,642,821	7.8	6.7
1960–69	221,516	618,345[2]	839,861	1.3	3.9
1970–79	355,381	148,695	504,076	3.3	2.9
1980–89	984,087	547,455	1,531,542	8.4	1.8
1980	52,071	12,763	64,834	4.8	1.1
1981	69,455	15,433	84,888	7.3	−0.2
1982	48,170	13,208	61,378	9.1	−0.9
1983	37,925	11,343	49,268	9.5	2.3
1984	36,459	40,974	77,433	9.4	3.7
1985	38,968	24,912	63,880	9.4	2.2
1986	42,788	26,178	68,966	8.9	2.2
1987	78,523	18,958	97,481	9.2	1.5
1988	202,673	39,832	242,505	8.5	3.1
1989	377,055	343,854	720,909	8.0	2.9
Total	2,000,698	3,517,602	5,518,300	. . .	. . .

Sources: Statistisches Bundesamt, *Wirtschaft und Statistik*, September 1989, pp. 584–85, and Bundesanstalt für Arbeit, *Arbeitsmarkt in Zahlen*.

[1] Unemployed in percent of the dependent labor force in December of each year; not seasonally adjusted.

[2] Of this, 345,590 persons immigrated from the GDR between the beginning of 1960 and August 13, 1961 when the GDR authorities closed the border.

the flow of migration and that wage equalization should be achieved in the short to medium term through subsidy payments—need to be examined.

To put the existing wage gap between east and west Germany in perspective, it is useful to examine wage differentials that exist between regions of west Germany. Table 2 presents, for a variety of industries, a comparison of hourly wages of male blue-collar workers in the Länder of west Germany; this comparison shows that, in 1988, wages varied within industries by up to 35 percent of earnings in low-paying regions.[3] Owing to differences in the economic structure of the Länder, GDP per capita showed an even larger regional spread; in the richest area it was more than twice that in the poorest area (Chapter IV, Table 1). However, this latter comparison is somewhat distorted by the rather small but densely populated city states (Berlin, Bremen, and Hamburg). If these city states are excluded, the difference between the highest and lowest GDP per capita was reduced to 35 percent of the level in the poorest region. Moreover, it is also likely that income comparisons between the Länder are affected by government transfer payments.

Since these wage and income differentials have not given rise to large-scale migration within the FRG, it is clear that there are other factors that discourage migration. These

seem to include home ownership; differences in the cost of living, particularly housing; family ties; and the attachment to certain regions. Thus with political unification, the implementation of comprehensive economic reforms and the end of special social benefits granted to GDR immigrants under FRG law in the past, the factors that militate against migration should be felt more clearly.[4]

But what should be the response of economic policy if migration remains large? Wage subsidies would boost wages in the east but would also run the risk of becoming entrenched and creating a distorted economic structure, inflexible in responding to market signals. Moreover, feasible subsidies would not be sufficient to discourage many of those determined to leave because of better job prospects in the west. An alternative scheme to discourage migration by linking distribution of public property to long-term residency in the former GDR was also suggested at the time GEMSU was being designed.

It is clear that migration of skilled workers from east to west would have adverse effects on the east German economy. In the context of a unified Germany, the rationale behind the economic policy response to migration from east

---

[3] Differences in purchasing power, however, are likely to have been smaller as prices for nontradable goods, such as housing and personal services, also differ significantly across regions.

[4] In principle, the prospects for relatively large wage increases in line with increases in productivity should dampen incentives for emigration of those holding jobs in east Germany. Moreover, social security payments in west Germany to people migrating from east Germany are now based on their past earnings in east Germany, discouraging migration of those without good job prospects in the west.

Table 2. Federal Republic of Germany: Regional Distribution of Earnings of Blue-Collar Workers, 1988

(Federal Republic of Germany = 100)

	Chemical Industry	Machinery Industry	Textiles Industry	Food and Beverages
Baden-Württemberg	94.1	102.7	103.0	102.1
Bavaria	90.9	97.9	99.8	99.3
Berlin (West)	—	105.5	92.5	105.7
Bremen	80.7	103.1	89.8	108.6
Hamburg	97.0	112.5	118.7	105.6
Hesse	103.0	100.3	107.0	97.5
Lower Saxony	91.1	96.3	95.8	97.4
North Rhine-Westphalia	102.6	98.9	100.0	101.2
Rhineland-Palatinate	106.3	98.3	94.5	97.5
Saarland	86.1	100.8	87.9	97.9
Schleswig-Holstein	93.8	99.7	90.7	96.5
Difference between highest and lowest earnings (in percent of lowest earnings)	31.7	16.9	35.0	12.5

Source: Bundesministerium für Wirtschaft, "Das regionale Lohnkostengefälle in der Bundesrepublik Deutschland," Beilage zum Monatsbericht 11/89.

Germany should also take into account the effects on the west German economy. Indeed, irrespective of what happens to population flows between east and west Germany, significant immigration into west Germany from Eastern European countries is likely to continue for a number of years, as the economic outlook for these countries remains relatively less favorable. Economic policy will therefore have to take account of sizable immigration. It is on the effects of immigration in west Germany and the appropriate policy response that the remainder of this chapter focuses.

Effects of Immigration and Policy Response

In the history of the FRG, large-scale immigration from the east has generally coincided with phases of strong growth (see Table 1). Absorption of the immigrants on the labor market has therefore rarely been a problem. During the 1950s, when immigration totaled more than 2½ million people, growth of real GNP per capita averaged 6¾ percent and the unemployment rate declined from 11½ percent of the dependent labor force to 2½ percent. During the 1960s, a further 840,000 people moved to the FRG, but unemployment dropped to a historical low and real GNP per capita grew at an average rate of 4 percent. Reflecting, inter alia, the effects of the first oil shock in 1974, growth fell to just under 3 percent on average in the 1970s and unemployment increased to 3¼ percent; at the same time, immigration declined to about 500,000 people. During the first eight years of the 1980s, immigration continued at a slightly faster annual rate than in the 1970s, while growth was low and unemployment high by historical

standards. In contrast, the surge in immigration in 1988–89 was accompanied by more rapid growth and a decline in unemployment.

One should be cautious, however, in interpreting this apparent inverse relationship between economic activity and immigration. Migration can occur for reasons that are unrelated to the economic environment, such as changes in the political climate of the country that the migrant is leaving or changes in the receptiveness of the area to which the migrant is traveling, but it can also be encouraged by favorable economic developments in the recipient country. Migration can also influence economic performance in the recipient country; for example, the apparently inverse relationship between economic growth and immigration that can be observed in the past has prompted the argument that immigrants have helped to lower structural unemployment in west Germany by removing bottlenecks in the labor market.[5] This would seem to be supported by the recent experience. Data on arrivals of and unemployment of immigrants from Eastern European countries and east Germany suggest that the majority of immigrants have found employment[6] (Table 3) and, moreover, the overall unemployment rate has fallen. But the successful integration of immigrants seems also to have been helped by the favorable economic climate that existed during these years and the moderate wage increases embodied in multiyear contracts agreed upon in 1987–88.

[5] See Walter (1988).

[6] In June 1990, about 235,000 immigrants from east Germany and Eastern Europe were unemployed, equivalent to 14 percent of the total number of immigrants (including those not in the labor force) between January 1985 and June 1990.

Table 3. Federal Republic of Germany: Migration and Unemployment

(In thousands)

	Immigration from Eastern Europe			Immigration from GDR			Total Arrivals	Unemployed Immigrants	
		Unemployed			Unemployed				
	Arrivals	Absolute	Change	Arrivals	Absolute	Change	Arrivals	Absolute	Change
1984	36,459	33,452[1]	−2,084[2]	40,974	—	—	77,433	—	—
1985	38,968	30,326[1]	−3,126[2]	24,912	6,244[1]	—	63,880	36,570[1]	—
1986	42,788	29,831[1]	−495[2]	26,178	6,910[1]	666[2]	68,966	36,741[1]	171[2]
1987	78,523	36,579[1]	6,748[2]	18,958	5,966[1]	−944[2]	97,481	42,545[1]	5,804[2]
1988	202,673	72,747[1]	36,168[2]	39,832	10,483[1]	4,517[2]	242,505	83,230[1]	40,685[2]
1989	377,055	111,806[1]	39,059[2]	343,854	45,309[1]	34,826[2]	720,909	157,115[1]	73,885[2]
Jan.	23,523	85,459	...	4,627	13,917	...	28,150	99,376	...
Feb.	22,510	87,798	2,339	5,008	15,162	1,245	27,518	102,960	3,584
Mar.	25,381	88,209	411	5,671	16,300	1,138	31,052	104,509	1,549
Apr.	25,454	86,108	−2,101	5,887	17,138	838	31,341	103,246	−1,263
May	24,751	88,517	2,409	10,642	19,893	2,755	35,393	108,410	5,164
June	29,574	92,613	4,096	12,428	22,929	3,036	42,002	115,542	7,132
July	33,432	99,384	6,771	11,707	25,930	3,001	45,139	125,314	9,772
Aug.	41,169	106,603	7,219	20,959	31,859	5,929	62,128	138,462	13,148
Sept.	35,922	111,806	5,203	33,255	45,309	13,450	69,177	157,115	18,653
Oct.	35,697	115,413	3,607	57,024	61,698	16,389	92,721	177,111	19,996
Nov.	41,611	120,544	5,131	133,429	119,892	58,194	175,040	240,436	63,325
Dec.	38,031	132,069	11,525	43,221	129,147	8,030	81,252	261,216	20,780
1990									
Jan.	38,189	137,454	5,385	73,729	132,064	2,917	111,918	269,518	8,302
Feb.	33,835	138,426	972	63,893	140,091	8,027	97,728	278,517	8,999
Mar.	36,579	135,552	−2,874	46,241	131,881	−8,210	82,820	267,433	−11,084
Apr.	32,731	135,810	258	24,615	114,107	−17,774	57,346	249,917	−17,516
May	37,222	134,523	−1,287	19,217	100,378	−13,729	54,439	234,901	−15,016
June	53,499	144,521	9,998	10,689	90,286	−10,092	64,188	234,807	−94
July[3]	49,254	162,451	17,930	...	84,359	−5,927	...	246,810	12,003

Source: Bundesanstalt für Arbeit, *Arbeitsmarkt in Zahlen.*

[1] September.

[2] Change from September of the previous year.

[3] From July 1990, data on immigration from the GDR was not collected.

The likely continuation of sizable immigration in the coming years raises the question of what policies should be adopted to facilitate the absorption of immigrants in the labor market.[7] In the following analysis, a computable general equilibrium model is used to investigate this question. The model is comparative-static and belongs to the type of so-called Johansen models. It follows closely the version developed by Dixon and others (1982) and is described in detail in Mayer (1989).[8]

The simulation exercise assumes an inflow of about 700,000 people into west Germany in 1990—400,000 from Eastern Europe and 300,000 from east Germany. Assuming a participation rate of about 52 percent,[9] this would lead to an increase in the labor force by 364,000 people or 1¼ percent from its 1989 level.[10] The simulations trace the effects of different policy responses to this inflow. In policy scenario 1, it is assumed that trade unions resist any decline in real wages. In this case, it would not be possible for the new immigrants to find work immediately and they would have to receive unemployment compensation. The second

---

[7] The Deutsches Institut der Wirtschaft (1989) examined the implications of immigration by ethnic Germans on the finances of the social security system and concluded that, owing to the favorable age structure of immigrants, there will be positive effects in the medium to long term.

[8] The model emphasizes the role of relative prices and substitution possibilities in explaining trade flows and the commodity composition of domestic production and demand. The essential postulates governing producer and consumer behavior are profit and utility maximization. The model distinguishes four productive sectors (one producing basic goods such as agricultural products and energy, the second producing traditional tradable goods such as steel, ships, textiles, and clothing, the third producing all remaining tradables, and the fourth producing nontradables such as personal and financial services); four categories of final demand (investment, government consumption, private consumption, and exports), satisfied either from domestic sources or from imports; and three primary inputs (labor, capital, and land). It is

numerically specified using a 1984 input-output table for the FRG and parameter estimates culled from the literature. Some important assumptions are (1) capital and land are fixed factors of production in each sector; (2) investment does not add to the productive capital stock in the current period; (3) markups in foreign trade are proportional and constant; and (4) the nominal exchange rate does not change.

[9] In 1989, about 52 percent of the immigrants from Eastern Europe were ready and willing to take up work and the same participation rate is expected for 1990. Recent evidence suggests that the participation rate of immigrants from east Germany, after higher rates in earlier years, is now converging to the rate of other immigrants.

[10] This illustrative exercise abstracts from the lags between immigration flows and increases in the labor force, lags that are due to the need for immigrants to take German language classes or enroll in training programs.

133

scenario assumes that unions resist cuts in nominal wages. The immediate effect of this wage policy on the employment of new immigrants is the same as in the first scenario, that is, they will not find jobs upon arrival. The second-round effects, however, are likely to differ as real wages react to changes in the price level. In the third and fourth scenarios, it is assumed that real wages adjust to allow the increase in the labor force to be absorbed; thus, unemployment does not increase in response to the flow of immigration. Scenarios 3 and 4, however, differ both from each other and from the first two scenarios in their assumptions about the stance of monetary and fiscal policy during the period of labor inflow. In scenarios 1 and 2, immigration leads to an increase in government transfers in the form of unemployment compensation; this gives rise to a corresponding increase in nominal private consumption.[11] Real government consumption remains unchanged and monetary policy accommodates the resulting changes in nominal incomes and absorption. In scenarios 3 and 4, on the other hand, it is assumed that fiscal and monetary policy stabilize, respectively, nominal domestic absorption or the external balance of the economy, while the labor force increases.[12]

The key elements of the simulations are presented in Table 4. The results in columns 1–4 indicate percentage deviations of the listed variables from the values they would have attained in the absence of immigration and the assumed policy responses after all domestic and international effects have worked their way through the economy. The analysis is comparative-static in character and the results are of course contingent on the numerous model assumptions and the chosen parameter values. The purpose of the exercise is merely to illustrate the effects of migration under different policy scenarios after an appropriate adjustment period of perhaps one to two years, and not to make forecasts of the likely outcome.

The assumed increase in government transfers and nominal private consumption in response to the inflow of 364,000 workers under scenario 1 (fixed real wages) raises prices and induces a small expansion of output.[13] The additional demand in the form of real private consumption and investment exceeds the increase in output so that real exports decrease, imports increase, and the external surplus declines slightly. Employment increases but only by a small amount, leaving in the event some 336,000 of the 364,000 new workers still unemployed after adjustment is completed.

---

[11] On the basis of average unemployment compensation payments, government expenditures (in the form of transfers) are assumed to increase by DM 7 billion or 0.7 percent of the total government expenditures in 1989. Under the assumption that there are no savings out of unemployment compensation, nominal private consumption is expected to increase by 0.6 percent from its 1989 level.

[12] The reason for differences among the scenarios in the macroeconomic policy stance will become apparent from the discussion below.

[13] The real wage is fixed in terms of the consumption basket. With domestic demand and prices rising, the terms of trade improve and the real product wage declines, allowing a rise in employment.

The money supply expands to accommodate domestic demand and the government deficit rises owing to higher transfers and nominal government consumption that are only partly offset by increased government revenue. The rise in domestic demand benefits primarily production of nontraded goods; heavier demand for basic goods and tradables is met by a reduction in exports and an increase in imports.

In scenario 2, unions are satisfied with maintaining nominal wages. In the first round, real (consumption) wages decline by the amount that consumer prices increase in response to higher consumption (induced by increased government transfers). The decline in the real product wage is thus greater than in scenario 1 and this allows a slightly stronger second-round output response with a somewhat more favorable outcome for inflation. The decline in exports is smaller than in the previous scenario, but imports increase at about the same rate, as higher demand for inputs by domestic industries offsets lower demand for imported consumption goods. Output and employment rise in all sectors, but the expansion is largest for nontradable goods, where the additional demand cannot be satisfied from external sources. Reflecting the stronger output response, there is a larger increase in employment than in scenario 1, but about 281,000 of the new immigrant workers remain unemployed after adjustment is completed.

With flexible nominal and real wages and macroeconomic policies directed at maintaining nominal domestic absorption, real wages fall by 0.8 percent to absorb the rise in the labor force and output is boosted by almost the same amount (scenario 3). Reflecting lower production costs, consumer prices decline by 0.6 percent from the level they would have reached otherwise and real domestic absorption increases. Lower product prices improve the competitiveness of German industries so that exports rise. Imports grow by a smaller amount, since the effects of higher total demand are largely offset as demand shifts from imports to domestic goods in response to the fall in the price of domestic output relative to baseline. Reflecting the decline in the terms of trade, real income increases by slightly less than output. Moreover, the decline in the terms of trade offsets the increase in real net exports, and the external balance evaluated at foreign currency prices weakens slightly. In fact, the change in the foreign balance is so small that macroeconomic policies directed at stabilizing the external position of the economy rather than domestic demand have broadly similar effects (scenario 4).

Against the background of high immigration, wage bargaining by unions could, broadly speaking, pursue two alternative objectives. It could aim at maintaining the real or nominal wage level of job holders or it could aim at maximizing aggregate labor income. Real wage flexibility, though lowering wage income of job holders, would result in higher aggregate labor income (scenarios 3 and 4). Real wage flexibility would also be preferable from a macro-

Table 4. West Germany: Economic Effects of Immigration—Main Simulation Results

(Deviations from baseline in percent)

	Scenarios			
	1	2	3	4
Macroeconomic results				
Output	0.1	0.2	0.7	0.8
Terms of trade	0.1	—	−0.7	−0.9
Real income	0.1	0.2	0.5	0.4
Real labor income	0.1	0.2	0.4	0.3
Real capital income	0.1	0.2	0.5	0.4
Real private consumption	0.3	0.4	0.6	0.5
Real public consumption	—	—	0.6	0.5
Real investment	0.2	0.3	0.6	0.5
Real exports	−0.3	−0.1	0.7	0.9
Real imports	0.2	0.2	0.1	—
External balance[1,2]	−0.1	−0.1	−0.1	—
Employment	0.1	0.3	1.2	1.2
Consumer prices	0.3	0.2	−0.6	−0.9
Real wages	—	−0.2	−0.8	−0.9
Broad money	1.0	1.2	0.5	—
Government budget balance[1]	−0.3	−0.2	—	—
Sectoral results				
Output				
Basic goods	—	0.1	0.3	0.4
Traded goods I	−0.1	0.1	0.9	1.0
Traded goods II	—	0.2	0.8	0.8
Nontraded goods	0.2	0.3	0.7	0.6
Employment				
Basic goods	—	0.2	0.8	0.9
Traded goods I	−0.1	0.1	1.1	1.3
Traded goods II	0.1	0.3	1.3	1.4
Nontraded goods	0.3	0.4	1.1	1.0

[1] In percent of GDP.

[2] Evaluated at foreign currency prices.

economic view as it would have a more favorable effect on inflation, unemployment, and government finances.[14]

The key question therefore is the objective function of unions. The findings in Chapter VII would suggest that unions in the FRG have tended to represent the insiders in the labor market, that is, those already employed. Large-scale migration can erode some of the bargaining power of insiders by lowering the wages asked by outsiders in the labor market. However, to the extent that the power of insiders is due to structural rigidities under the influence of the Government, there is a role for the Government in promoting greater flexibility. Elements of the legal structure in Germany that increase the cost of labor turnover or that extend a wage agreement to groups or sectors not party to the agreement should be examined carefully in this light.[15] It is clear why insiders in the labor market might be concerned about high levels of immigration. However, it

is worth noting that, to the extent that labor stays in the east and capital moves from west to east, there will be downward pressures on wages in west Germany, though these perhaps would materialize over a longer time period.

Concluding Remarks

The discussion in this chapter leads to a number of broad conclusions: First, wage and income differentials between different regions of west Germany suggest that it may not be necessary to completely eliminate wage differentials between west and east Germany in the near future in order to slow the flow of migrants to a more sustainable level for the east German economy. Second, historically, periods of high immigration have tended to coincide with high growth and low unemployment in the FRG. This experience and the present strength of the west German economy suggest that a continuation of the flow of immigration of the order of magnitude experienced in 1988–89 should not pose an insurmountable problem. Third, to enhance the prospect that the favorable experience with the absorption of immigrants will continue, structural policies should be used to reduce im-

[14] This comparison of scenarios 1 and 2 with scenarios 3 and 4 is not materially distorted by differences in the assumed stance of macroeconomic policy; indeed, if the policy stance in scenarios 1 and 2 had been to maintain nominal absorption, there would have been no decline in the real product wage and hence no increase in output and employment.

[15] See Lipschitz and others (1989), Section IV for a discussion of the structural features of the labor market in west Germany.

pediments to wage flexibility in the economy. Indeed, the greater the ease with which immigrants are absorbed in the labor market, the better placed Germany will be to cope with the surge in demand resulting from unification.

References

Deutsches Institut der Wirtschaft, *Die Integration deutscher Aussiedler: Perspektiven für Bundesrepublik Deutschland* (Cologne, 1989).

Dixon, P.B., B.R. Parameter, J. Sutton, and D. Vincent, *ORANI—A Multisectoral Model of the Australian Economy* (Amsterdam and New York: North-Holland, 1982).

Lipschitz, Leslie L., Jeroen Kremers, Thomas Mayer, and Donogh McDonald, *The Federal Republic of Germany: Adjustment in a Surplus Country*, IMF Occasional Paper, No. 64 (Washington: International Monetary Fund, January 1989).

Mayer, Thomas, "Economic Structure, the Exchange Rate, and Adjustment in the Federal Republic of Germany: A General Equilibrium Approach," *Staff Papers*, International Monetary Fund (Washington), Vol. 36 (June 1989), pp. 435–63.

Statistisches Bundesamt, *Wirtschaft und Statistik* (Wiesbaden), September 1989, pp. 582–89.

Walter, N., "Demographic Factors and Economic Momentum—Wave of Corporate Start-Ups in Germany Imminent," Deutsche Bank, *Bulletin* (Frankfurt), October 1988.

IX

Implications of Unification for Saving and Investment in West Germany

Donogh McDonald

Background

Substantial resources will be needed to rebuild the economy of east Germany. Over time, as productivity rises, a growing proportion of these resources is likely to come from domestic (i.e., east German sources). But, in the early years of German economic, monetary, and social union (GEMSU), it is likely that net saving in east Germany will be negative. From the perspective of the German economy as a whole, the large external surplus that has existed in the western part of the country will be more than adequate to finance resource needs in the eastern part. But the redirection of this surplus will have implications both for west Germany and the rest of the world. The transmission of demand shock associated with GEMSU to the rest of the world, which has been analyzed in Chapter VI, will depend, inter alia, on the extent to which the west German economy is able to generate additional resources for investment in the east, that is, over and above its existing surplus of saving. In examining this last issue, there are three important questions concerning how the west German economy responds to GEMSU: How much additional output will be stimulated? How will saving respond? And what will be the reaction of investment? Some of the important considerations bearing on the first question were analyzed in Chapters VII and VIII. Taking an assumed scenario for the effects of GEMSU on output, interest rates, and other macroeconomic variables, this chapter uses econometric estimates of saving and investment behavior in west Germany to look at aspects of the second and third questions. In addition, the influence of changes in government saving is examined closely, in order to evaluate the potential role for budgetary measures in generating additional saving at the national level.

The broad conclusion is that higher saving in west Germany rather than reduced investment is the most likely source of additional resources that could be chan-neled to east Germany. However, particularly in the early years, the rise in saving, while far from insignificant, will be small in relation to the prospective net import demand of east Germany.[1] Initially, the boost to saving will come largely from higher output. A shift in the distribution of income away from labor (relative to baseline) is likely to occur more gradually but has potential to be a relatively important source of additional saving. Quantification of the effects of GEMSU on income shares is, however, rather difficult at this stage. As regards the role for policy, the econometric work indicates that perhaps 60 percent of any change in government saving is offset, in the short term, by adjustments in private saving, but that this offset is reduced to about one fourth in the third year and is negligible in the longer term. On investment, the simulations suggest that, in the early years of GEMSU, capital spending by businesses will be negatively influenced by a rise in real interest rates, but that these negative effects are likely to be offset by the boost given by faster growth. On balance, therefore, changes in business investment in west Germany are unlikely to free resources for capital formation in the east.

The Effects of GEMSU on Saving Behavior in West Germany

Econometric Estimates

A marked rise in national saving in west Germany since 1982 has been the principal factor in the emergence of a large current account surplus (Chart 1 in Chapter I). A previous study (McDonald (1989)), seeking to

---

[1] See Chapter V for some scenarios for the net import demand of east Germany.

Table 1. Federal Republic of Germany: Equations for the National Saving Rate (s_n)[1]

Equation	Period	const	*labsh*	*tot*	g_y	s_g	$s_n(-1)$	SEE	ρ	D-W	$\overline{R}^2$	Influence of s_g	
												Third year	Long run
1.1	1962–89	−0.106 (1.31)	−0.260 (4.96)	0.238 (2.09)	0.311 (5.70)	0.305 (3.66)	0.673 (16.07)	0.0050	−0.443		0.982	0.65	0.93
1.2	1965–89	−0.080 (1.01)	−0.272 (5.34)	0.219 (1.99)	0.295 (5.25)	0.302 (3.39)	0.683 (17.40)	0.0048	−0.492		0.981	0.65	0.95
1.3	1970–89	−0.116 (1.23)	−0.240 (4.37)	0.241 (2.12)	0.309 (4.56)	0.329 (3.59)	0.652 (15.18)	0.0048	−0.478		0.971	0.68	0.95
1.4	1962–85	−0.137 (1.31)	−0.216 (2.51)	0.333 (1.90)	0.312 (5.02)	0.318 (3.09)	0.668 (13.38)	0.0054	−0.432		0.982	0.67	0.96
1.5	1962–89	−0.140 (1.30)	−0.234 (3.12)	0.301 (2.08)	0.332 (4.79)	0.375 (3.49)	0.614 (10.96)	0.0056		2.37	0.980	0.75	0.97
1.6	1965–89	−0.101 (0.91)	−0.248 (3.34)	0.284 (1.99)	0.303 (4.19)	0.396 (3.43)	0.617 (11.16)	0.0055		2.52	0.978	0.79	1.03
1.7	1970–89	−0.173 (1.49)	−0.212 (2.93)	0.297 (2.22)	0.351 (4.32)	0.402 (3.54)	0.606 (9.55)	0.0051		2.29	0.976	0.79	1.02
1.8	1962–85	−0.216 (1.53)	−0.141 (1.15)	0.380 (1.72)	0.345 (4.45)	0.401 (3.54)	0.608 (9.55)	0.0059		2.30	0.980	0.79	1.02

Source: Author's estimates.

[1] Variable definitions are as follows: s_n is the net national saving divided by net national product; g_y is the real rate of growth of net national product; s_g is general government saving divided by net national product; *labsh* is the share of labor in net national product; and *tot* is the gain in the terms of trade divided by the previous year's net national product. The equations are estimated by ordinary least squares. The numbers in parentheses are t-statistics; SEE is the standard error of the estimate; ρ is the first-order autocorrelation coefficient; D-W is the Durbin-Watson statistic; and $\overline{R}^2$ is calculated based on original levels, not levels as transformed by the autocorrelation adjustment.

explain this, developed a model that tracked saving quite well, both in and out of sample, including the sharp change in direction that took place after 1982. The model—which related the net national saving rate (s_n) to the growth rate of real NNP (g_y),[2] gains in the terms of trade (*deltot*), the labor share in NNP (*labsh*), and government saving in relation to NNP (s_g)—forms the basis of the analysis in this chapter.[3]

Two sets of estimation results are reported in Table 1: the first (equations 1.1 to 1.4) incorporates a correction for first-order autocorrelation, while the second (equations 1.5 to 1.8) does not. The second set of equations produces higher standard errors, reflecting the omission of the autocorrelation correction; the point estimates also seem somewhat less stable to the eye. What is striking about the estimates in Table 1, however, is the degree of parameter stability across the various sample periods, even for the second set of equations.[4] This stability is

all the more notable when one considers the major shifts in the behavior of some of the explanatory variables in the sample period, particularly in s_g and *labsh* (Chart 1). The overall results are consistent with the good in-sample and out-of-sample tracking ability of the model found in McDonald (1989).

In view of the large fiscal demands that are to emerge in the course of GEMSU and the debate concerning the need for new budgetary measures, Table 1 provides additional information on the influence of the fiscal variable showing the estimated three-year effect of a change in s_g as well as the long-run effect. Again, the stability across the various sample subperiods is notable. The broad picture that emerges from the first set of equations (1.1 to 1.4) is that, in the first year, about 30 percent of an increase in s_g is transmitted to s_n, with the rest offset as the private sector adjusts its saving behavior. As time passes, the effect on s_n gets larger; in the third year, s_n has increased by about two thirds of the increase in s_g and in the long run by almost all of the rise in s_g. The equations without autocorrelation correction produce an estimate of the effect of s_g, which is higher both on impact (close to 40 percent) and after three years (three fourths) but not dramatically different. While the short-run offset in the private sector to changes in s_g reported in equations 1.1 to 1.8 might seem Ricardian in nature, the results appear to be more consistent with a Keynesian interpretation. The weaker influence of changes in s_g in the short run may well reflect the slow adaptation of

---

[2] NNP is net national product.

[3] A notable feature of the model is the role played by the distribution of income and the terms of trade, following ideas originating, respectively, in Kaldor (1955) and Laursen and Metzler (1951).

[4] The levels of the parameter estimates, however, differ to some extent between the two sets of equations. The somewhat greater variability in the estimated coefficient on *deltot* than for the other variables should be seen in the context of the less precisely estimated coefficients (high standard errors relative to coefficient size): within each set of equations, the various coefficient estimates for *deltot* are not significantly different from one another. Similarly, the coefficient on *labsh* in equation 1.8 is not significantly different from the estimates in equations 1.5–1.7.

Chart 1. Federal Republic of Germany: Factors Influencing National Saving, 1961–89

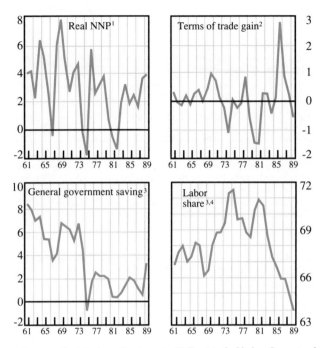

Source: Statistisches Bundesamt, *Volkswirtschaftliche Gesamtrechnungen*.

[1] Percent change in real net national product (NNP).

[2] In percent of previous year's NNP.

[3] In percent of NNP.

[4] Adjusted for shifts in employment between dependent employment and self-employment.

private consumption to changes in disposable income;[5] as time passes, however, with lower disposable income, private agents find that maintaining consumption at the expense of their financial position becomes less feasible and/or less desirable and the adjustment of private consumption is intensified. It is, nevertheless, surprising to find that in the long run almost the entire change in the government saving rate gets absorbed in the national saving rate.

While tests do not indicate a problem with serial correlation in equations 1.5–1.8,[6] the relatively high value for the first-order autocorrelation coefficient in equations 1.1–1.4 suggests the desirability of exploring alternative lag patterns for the lagged dependent variable. In Table 2, equation 2.1, an additional lag of the dependent variable is added to equation 1.5. The estimated parameter on s_g is only a little larger in the short run and essentially the same in the medium and long

run. Estimates over different subperiods (one of which is reported as equation 2.2) show this model producing lower overall standard errors than is the case for the equations in Table 1. There is, however, less parameter stability across estimation periods. Moreover, over some subperiods, the long-run effects of changes in government saving are implausibly high.[7]

A feature of the equations that have been reported thus far is that the same pattern of adjustment is forced on all variables; to see how this might have affected the estimated coefficient on s_g, the lagged value of s_g was added to equations 1.5 and 2.1 and the results are reported as equations 2.3 and 2.4. This had little material effect on the fit of the equations.

On balance, therefore, it would seem that, other things being constant, about 40 percent of a change in government saving might get reflected in national saving in the short run, with the effect rising to about three fourths in the third year. However, in the short run, other variables are likely to be influenced by changes in budgetary policy in a way that dampens the effect of s_g on s_n. In particular, budgetary measures to increase government saving may not only reduce g_y but also shift the distribution of income toward labor.[8] They might also produce a terms of trade loss. Over the medium and long term, however, there is no reason to expect that the other explanatory variables will be influenced significantly by a change in s_g. Finally, in interpreting the estimate on s_g, one should consider the possibility that private saving responds differently, depending on the nature of the change in government saving. It seems plausible, for example, that the effects, particularly in the short term, of changes in government consumption (i.e., direct current expenditure on goods) might be somewhat different than for other elements of the fiscal balance, with, for example, a decline in government consumption having a much greater effect on national saving than an increase in taxes. An attempt to identify such a differential influence in the econometric work was, however, not successful.

Simulation of the Effects of GEMSU on Saving

All of the explanatory variables that appear in the equations reported in Tables 1 and 2 are likely to be affected by GEMSU. In this chapter, the saving model discussed above is simulated under assumptions as to how GEMSU might affect these variables. The illustrative

[5] In part, this process is likely to depend on the perceived permanence of the change in s_g; no attempt has been made in the econometric work to distinguish between temporary and permanent budgetary developments.

[6] A Lagrange-multiplier test rejects the presence of serial correlation of first and higher orders.

[7] In some cases the short-run effect of s_g is in the region of one half, for example in equation 2.2 in Table 2, but this is associated generally with unacceptably high estimates for the long-run effect of s_g.

[8] In the short run, profits tend to absorb a large share of fluctuations in income.

Table 2. Federal Republic of Germany: Additional Equations for the National Saving Rate (s_n)[1]

Equation	Period	labsh	tot	g_y	s_g	$s_g(-1)$	$s_n(-1)$	$s_n(-2)$	SEE	D-W	$\overline{R^2}$	Influence of s_g	
												Third year	Long run
2.1	1962–89	−0.316	0.289	0.296	0.418		0.408	0.192	0.0048	1.93	0.985	0.74	1.05
		(4.55)	(2.34)	(4.88)	(4.49)		(4.89)	(3.01)					
2.2	1965–89	−0.374	0.241	0.228	0.524		0.338	0.249	0.0040	2.43	0.988	0.89	1.27
		(6.10)	(2.33)	(4.11)	(5.89)		(4.40)	(4.26)					
2.3	1962–89	−0.208	0.348	0.293	0.432	−0.166	0.692		0.0056	2.59	0.980	0.66	0.86
		(2.67)	(2.31)	(3.76)	(3.62)	(1.08)	(7.55)						
2.4	1962–89	−0.294	0.326	0.257	0.461	−0.129	0.475	0.186	0.0048	2.15	0.985	0.68	1.00
		(4.01)	(2.51)	(3.94)	(4.47)	(0.97)	(4.37)	(2.91)					

Source: Author's estimates.

[1] Variable definitions are as follows: s_n is the net national saving divided by net national product; g_y is the real rate of growth of net national product; s_g is general government saving divided by net national product; labsh is the share of labor in net national product; and tot is the gain in the terms of trade divided by the previous year's net national product. The equations are estimated by ordinary least squares. The estimate for the constant term is not reported. The numbers in parentheses are t-statistics; SEE is the standard error of the estimate; D-W is the Durbin-Watson statistic; and R^2 is calculated based on original levels, not levels as transformed by the autocorrelation adjustment.

baseline scenario adopted is as follows: (1) the labor share in net national product recovers somewhat over the coming years, returning to its 1987 level by 1995;[9] (2) net output grows by 3½ percent in 1990 and by 2¾ percent a year subsequently; (3) the terms of trade are constant; and (4) government saving, in percent of NNP, changes little from its 1990 level.[10]

Table 3 presents, in the form of deviations from baseline, an alternative scenario for these variables reflecting considerations of how they might be affected by the process of GEMSU:[11]

(1) The expansion of output is initially faster than under the baseline, owing to the surge in demand from east Germany: growth is boosted by ¾ of 1 percentage point in 1990 and by 1 percent in 1991. Subsequently, growth falls a little below baseline, as the demand impulse from east Germany lessens and the effects of higher real interest rates and the appreciated exchange rate continue to pass through to other components of demand. The level of output remains above baseline throughout the scenario.

(2) The higher rate of return to capital and the closer links with the labor market in east Germany are likely to put downward pressure on the labor share in west Germany. Thus, this scenario assumes that, instead of recovering somewhat over the next few years, the labor share stays broadly unchanged before starting to rise toward its longer run level in the second half of the 1990s.

[9] This represents a relatively moderate recovery compared with the sharp decline that occurred in the 1980s; see Chapter II, section on "Employment, Wages, and Prices".

[10] The calculations of the effects of GEMSU on saving reported below are not, however, very sensitive to the choice of baseline.

[11] The alternative scenario outlined in Table 3 is designed to reflect broadly some of the macroeconomic effects of GEMSU simulated in the different scenarios in Chapter VI. It should be noted, however, that the savings and investment functions used here are different from those in the model used to generate the simulation output in Chapter VI.

(3) The large increase in demand for west German goods is expected to result in a real appreciation of the deutsche mark, producing a terms of trade gain. As the demand shock subsides, the terms of trade gain is likely to be reversed. The illustrative scenario used here assumes a 2 percent gain in the terms of trade gain in 1990–92, which then unwinds gradually in the following years.

It should be stressed that the alternative scenario is purely illustrative, as there are many uncertainties concerning how GEMSU will affect west Germany, including any effects it might have on saving behavior. Nevertheless, it can be used to give some sense of the possible response of saving.

Table 3. West Germany: Assumptions for the Effects of GEMSU on Selected Variables

(Relative to baseline)

	Growth Rate of Net National Product[1]	Change in Terms of Trade[1]	Real Long-Term Interest Rate[1]	Labor Share[2]
1990	0.7	1.5	0.7	−0.5
1991	1.0	0.3	0.8	−1.0
1992	−0.2	0.3	0.8	−1.5
1993	−0.2	—	0.7	−2.0
1994	−0.2	−0.5	0.7	−2.0
1995	−0.1	−0.5	0.5	−1.5
1996	—	−0.5	0.3	−1.0
1997	—	−0.4	0.1	−0.5
1998	—	−0.2	—	—
1999	—	−0.2	—	—
2000	—	—	—	—

[1] Percentage points.
[2] Percent of net national product.

Table 4.   West Germany: Effects of GEMSU on Net National Saving[1]

(Deviations from baseline, in billions of 1990 deutsche mark)

	1990	1991	1992	1993	1994	1995	1996	1997	1998	1999	2000
Higher growth	7	16	10	5	3	2	2	2	3	3	3
Lower labor share	2	7	12	18	22	23	20	16	10	6	4
Changes in terms of trade	3	3	2	2	—	−1	−1	−1	−2	−2	−2
Higher growth, lower labor share, and changes in terms of trade	12	25	24	26	25	23	21	17	11	7	5
Memorandum items:											
Effect of measures to increase government saving (1 percent of NNP)	8	13	17	20	21	23	24	25	26	26	27
Effect of higher growth scenario on the level of NNP	14	36	32	29	25	23	24	24	25	26	27

Source: Author's calculations, based on assumptions in Table 3.
[1] Excluding fiscal transfers to east Germany.

The simulations of saving under the assumptions of Table 3 are presented in Table 4 using the coefficients in equation 1.5.[12] The broad conclusion is that the boost to saving coming from higher output is significant, representing close to one half of the increase in the level of NNP in west Germany in 1991 (relative to the baseline); however, it still represents a relatively small share of the possible resource demands from east Germany and, moreover, subsides after 1991. The stimulus to saving from the changes in the terms of trade is relatively small and is reversed as the increase in the terms of trade unwinds.[13] The calculations would suggest that, over the medium term, changes in the labor share have the greatest potential for stimulating saving, though it should be stressed that the calculations are sensitive to the assumed scale of the effect of GEMSU on the labor share. Given the lags in the adjustment of saving behavior (a high value for the lagged dependent variable) and the assumption that changes in labor share resulting from GEMSU are spread over a number of years, the implications for saving of these changes materialize gradually, reaching a peak in the mid-1990s. Putting all three variables together (the effects on growth, the terms of trade, and the labor share), one sees that the boost to saving amounts to over 1 percent of NNP a year in the period 1991–95; by the mid-1990s, it is due almost entirely to the assumed path of the labor share.

The discussion up to now has not focused on how GEMSU could affect national saving in west Germany through its effect on government saving. While transfers to east Germany are likely to reduce government saving,[14] it is questionable whether this will have a major influence on consumption in west Germany as it does not affect the income streams (including public goods) of private individuals.[15] Thus, it would seem inappropriate to mechanically include in the simulation changes in s_g due to these transfers.[16] A memorandum item in Table 4, however, shows how national saving might be expected to adjust if new budgetary measures (affecting income streams in west Germany) were enacted to boost government saving by 1 percent of NNP per annum. While a large part of the increased government saving is initially offset in the private sector, the induced change in national saving would over time represent a significant source of additional saving.

The Effects of GEMSU on Investment in West Germany

Econometric Estimates

The effects of GEMSU on investment are examined using a study of machinery and equipment investment reported in McDonald (1988). While this focused only on machinery and equipment, it may be a good basis for discussing the likely effects on business sector investment.[17] In 1989, however, the business sector accounted

[12] Using one of the other estimated equations does not produce calculations that are markedly different.

[13] A change in the terms of trade has no long-term effect on the level of saving (expressed in terms of domestic output); however, a change in output growth does have a long-term effect as it results in a higher level of output.

[14] For illustrative purposes, it is assumed that the fiscal accounts in east and west Germany remain completely separate, except for transfers.

[15] As noted earlier, the results of the study of saving suggest that slow adjustment to changes in income (rather than "Ricardian" influences) may be the principal factor underlying the pattern of private saving adjustment to changes in government saving.

[16] National saving declines one for one with the increase in government transfers to east Germany but this fall in saving directly supplies part of the external resource needs of east Germany. If increased government transfers from west to east Germany were to increase private saving in the west, in the short run, (as would be suggested by a mechanical application of the econometric estimates), additional resources would be freed for use in east Germany.

[17] Machinery and equipment investment represents two thirds of total business sector investment.

Table 5.   Federal Republic of Germany: Equations for Machinery and Equipment Investment[1]

Equation	Period	$\ln(r/p)_{-1}$	$\ln(Y/K)_{-1}$	$\Delta\Delta lnY$	$\Delta lnY(-2)$	D74	D8384	D8687	$(I/K)_{-1}$	SEE	$\bar{R}^2$	D-W (Chi-sq,(1))	σ
6.1	1965–76	−0.065 (2.77)	0.108 (2.38)	0.159 (4.46)	0.094 (1.81)	−0.007 (2.68)			0.397 (2.98)	0.0030	0.945	1.44 (1.96)	0.60
6.2	1965–80	−0.069 (4.47)	0.113 (3.80)	0.156 (5.26)	0.103 (3.03)	−0.007 (4.00)			0.340 (3.39)	0.0027	0.945	1.58 (1.27)	0.61
6.3	1965–85	−0.066 (5.48)	0.112 (4.94)	0.157 (6.53)	0.108 (3.86)	−0.007 (4.72)	0.007 (3.03)		0.318 (4.22)	0.0024	0.953	1.60 (1.84)	0.59
6.4	1965–89	−0.045 (5.36)	0.090 (4.41)	0.141 (5.83)	0.117 (4.18)	−0.007 (4.41)	0.007 (3.01)		0.362 (4.91)	0.0025	0.941	1.51 (3.87)	0.50
6.5	1965–89	−0.060 (6.30)	0.109 (5.39)	0.144 (6.40)	0.103 (3.90)	−0.007 (4.87)	0.007 (3.12)	−0.004 (2.72)	0.321 (4.57)	0.0024	0.950	1.52 (2.83)	0.55

Source: Author's estimates.

[1] The dependent variable is I/K. Variables are as follows: I is real gross investment in machinery and equipment by the private sector; K is the real net stock of machinery and equipment at the beginning of the period; r/p is the user cost of capital relative to the GNP deflator; Y is real GNP; D74 is a dummy to capture the effects of the first oil shock on investment; D8384 is a dummy to capture the effects of the temporary investment scheme for machinery and equipment that was introduced in 1982 and expired at the end of 1983; D8687 is a dummy to capture the "export pessimism" of 1986–87; the estimated coefficients on the seasonal dummy and constant are not reported. The estimate of the elasticity of substitution is presented in the last column. The numbers in parentheses are t-statistics. The Chi-square test in the second last column is for first-order correlation. The critical value at the 5 percent level is 3.84. A delta sign Δ in front of a variable denotes a first derivative and two deltas denotes a second difference. Equations are estimated with semiannual data, using ordinary least squares. The estimate for the constant term is not reported. R^2 is calculated based on original levels, not levels as transformed by the autocorrelation adjustment.

for only 63 percent of total fixed investment, with government (11 percent) and residential construction (26 percent) also being significant components. Estimates for the equation explaining machinery and equipment investment, using semiannual data, are presented in Table 5. The dependent variable is gross fixed investment divided by the net capital stock and this is related to the output-capital ratio, the user cost of capital, and accelerator terms to capture short-run cyclical effects on investment.[18] The coefficient estimates are relatively stable up to 1985 (the time span explored in the original study), but the model has more difficulty in 1986–87, a period of almost unprecedented slow growth in exports; as a result of this slow export growth, there was significant business sector pessimism, particularly in parts of the manufacturing sector dependent on exports. Adding a dummy variable for the four observations in 1986–87 improves the fit and results in parameter estimates closer to those for the earlier estimation period.

Simulation of the Effects of GEMSU on Investment

To illustrate possible effects of GEMSU on machinery and equipment investment, the investment equation described above has been simulated on the basis of the following assumptions: (1) Output growth follows the path laid out in Table 3; (2) the real interest rate rises by about ¾ of 1 percentage point in 1990–94 and then falls back gradually toward the baseline level;[19] and (3) the price of investment goods rises by 1 percent relative to other goods.

Table 6 shows the effects of these alternative assumptions relative to a baseline for machinery and equipment investment which assumes a constant real cost of capital and the baseline growth pattern assumed for the saving simulations. The broad conclusion is that in the early years the output-accelerator effects offset the investment dampening effects originating in the higher cost of capital.[20] It would thus seem that lower business sector investment in west Germany is unlikely to be an important source of increased resources for investment in east Germany. It is also clear that assuming a sharper rise in interest rates and in the prices of capital goods would moderate this conclusion but not fundamentally alter it.

With regard to government investment, while some areas for economy might be found in light of the high infrastruc-

---

[18] The theoretical basis for the model is discussed in McDonald (1988). Essentially, investment is determined by the difference between the actual capital-output ratio and the desired capital-output ratio (which is related to the user cost of capital), with the speed of adjustment being influenced by cyclical factors.

[19] It is assumed that the increase in the required yield on internal funds of enterprises is one half of the increase in the cost of external funds, assuming that the marginal effective tax rate is about half. This assumption on the change in the cost on internal funds also seems reasonable in light of sample magnitude of these variables: in the 1980s, the proxy for the internal cost of funds (the dividend yield) was about one half of the real bond rate. Moreover, for the large number of small and medium-sized firms in Germany, the link of investment decisions to yields in the capital market may not be particularly tight.

[20] In the long run, investment is higher due to the increased level of output. With the same capital-output ratio as under the baseline, there is higher gross investment, particularly to offset higher depreciation.

Table 6. West Germany: Effects of GEMSU on Gross Machinery and Equipment Investment[1]

(Deviations from baseline, in billions of 1990 deutsche mark)

	Effect of Higher Growth	Effect of Higher Cost of Capital[2]	Combined Growth and Cost of Capital Effects
1990	—	—	—
1991	4	−2	2
1992	4	−4	—
1993	2	−3	−1
1994	—	−2	−2
1995	—	−1	−1
1996	—	—	—
1997	1	1	1
1998	1	1	1
1999	1	1	1
2000	1	1	2

Source: Author's calculations.

[1] Based on assumptions in Table 3.

[2] Higher real interest rates and relative price of investment goods that are subsequently reversed.

tural demands in the east, it is also likely that the authorities will have to make additional investments to improve infrastructure in areas in west Germany close to the former border between the FRG and the GDR (particularly to enhance infrastructural links with the east) and to respond to demand resulting from immigration. Thus, the scope for a significant fall in investment to provide additional resources for east Germany would seem to rest with residential homebuilding; however, given that residential construction is only one fourth of total investment, the impact would have to be quite large to have a marked effect. Moreover, increased immigration in 1990–91 can be expected to have a positive influence on residential construction activity.

References

Kaldor, Nicholas, "Alternative Theories of Distribution," *Review of Economic Studies*, Vol. 23 (1955), pp. 83–100.

Laursen, Svend, and Lloyd A. Metzler, "Flexible Exchange Rates and the Theory of Employment," *Review of Economics and Statistics*, Vol. 32 (November 1950), pp. 281–99.

McDonald, Donogh, "An Econometric Analysis of Machinery and Equipment Investment in Germany" (unpublished; Washington: International Monetary Fund, 1988).

———, "The German Current Account from a Saving-Investment Perspective," (unpublished; Washington: International Monetary Fund, 1989).

X

Monetary and Financial Issues in German Unification

Garry J. Schinasi, Leslie Lipschitz, and Donogh McDonald

This chapter examines some of the issues that arise in the process of integrating the monetary and financial system of the former German Democratic Republic (GDR) into that of the Federal Republic of Germany (FRG). The topic is divided into three broad areas: an analysis of the currency conversion, an examination of difficulties that will be faced in conducting monetary policies in the new environment, and issues related to the restructuring of the financial system and its prospective performance at a microeconomic level.

The conversion of GDR marks into deutsche mark was a monetary event and thus, in principle, should not have a long-lasting effect on the real economy. However, the conversion process will influence inflation, current payments (such as wages) in the very short run, and the distribution of wealth between debtors and creditors. For east Germany, the conversion rate has important implications for the distribution of wealth: between the State and households on one level, and within the old state sector (comprising the Government, the banking system, and the state enterprises) on another. Under the old system, households were financial creditors (through their savings deposits), while the State was a net financial debtor; obviously the redenomination of the creditor and debtor positions affects both. Within the old state sector, the distribution of financial positions is important because the economic reform entails a breaking up of this sector into a banking system and an enterprise system that are independent of government. The financial solidity of the banking system and the burden of debt on the enterprise sector are the key considerations in this context.

Monetary control will be more difficult. The Deutsche Bundesbank is determined to maintain a low-inflation stable financial environment. A combination of higher fiscal deficits, rapidly rising demand, and an anti-inflationary monetary policy would create tensions in most circumstances; given the limited guidance as to how the demand for money and credit will evolve in east Germany, the conduct of monetary policy will be even more challenging in the present circumstances.

At a microeconomic level, it is important that the restructuring of the east German financial system transform it quickly into an efficient channel of intermediation. Given that the financial market is open to the participation of banks from west Germany and other countries and is subject to the same laws and regulations that govern the financial markets in west Germany, the efficiency of the financial system is unlikely to be limited by its structure. The principal concern is to ensure that bank lending and deposit policies are responsive to market signals, economic incentives, and a proper evaluation of risks and returns. In particular, it is important that lending decisions are consistent with an efficient distribution of resources and are not determined by a perception that the Trust Fund (*Treuhandanstalt*) or the Government will stand behind certain preferred credits.

Mechanics of the Conversion

Following the announcement of currency union, there was widespread debate on the conversion rate. Some considered a rate of M 1 = DM 1 to be appropriate, as it was judged to be the rate that would set starting wages in the GDR relative to those in the FRG in line with relative productivity levels.[1] Others suggested conversion rates ranging as high as the prevailing free-market rate.[2] There was also some discussion of a schedule of conversion rates varying by type of asset and liability, as was done in the conversion of reichsmark to deutsche mark in 1948.[3]

The broad outlines of two official proposals were made public before agreement was reached by the two Gov-

---

[1] See the discussion of wage and productivity levels in the GDR in Chapter III, section on "Economic Background."

[2] In December 1988, the market rate in West Berlin averaged M 7.75 = DM 1. In January 1990, it was about M 7 = DM 1. The mark appreciated following the announcement of currency union to M 5.75 = DM 1 in February and to M 2.75 = DM 1 in June 1990.

[3] For a discussion of the 1948 currency conversion see Thomas Mayer and Günther Thumann, "Radical Currency Reform: Germany, 1948," *Finance & Development* (Washington), March 1990, pp. 6–8.

ernments: the Bundesbank's proposal and a proposal that emerged from the Government in Bonn.[4] The Bundesbank proposal, published on April 2, 1990, called for a conversion rate of M 2 = DM 1 for all assets and liabilities denominated in marks, except for bank accounts up to M 2,000 per person, which would be converted at the rate of M 1 = DM 1. Other important features of the proposal were as follows: participation in GDR state properties would compensate holders of bank accounts in excess of M 2,000 for the less favorable conversion rate; the Bundesbank would have full control over monetary policy in the GDR; the GDR would adopt FRG banking law, with banks from the FRG and abroad allowed to set up establishments in the GDR; and interest rates and foreign currency transactions would be fully liberalized. Current payments would also be converted at the rate of M 2 = DM 1, but wages and pensions would be adjusted to compensate for subsidies removed before currency union and for the introduction of social security contributions.

The Bonn proposal, announced on April 23, 1990, differed somewhat concerning the treatment of savings deposits and current payments. It called for a rate of M 1 = DM 1 for currency and deposits up to M 4,000 for each individual and a rate of M 2 = DM 1 for the remaining balances; a rate of M 2 = DM 1 for all other assets and liabilities denominated in marks; and a rate of M 1 = DM 1 for wages and pensions, with no compensation for the removal of subsidies.

On May 2, 1990 the Governments of the GDR and the FRG announced a jointly agreed plan for currency conversion that would take effect on July 1, 1990. Financial claims and liabilities of permanent residents and enterprises would be converted at M 2 = DM 1. However, as an exception to this general formula, individuals would be allowed to convert limited sums at a more favorable rate of M 1 = DM 1, according to the following schedule: M 2,000 for persons under 14 years; M 4,000 for persons of 14 to 58 years; and M 6,000 for persons 59 years and older. Wages, salaries, stipends, rents, leases, and other maintenance payments would be converted at M 1 = DM 1, with wages and salaries set initially at their gross levels as of May 1. GDR pensioners would be provided the same benefits in relation to earnings as in the FRG.[5] Deposits in marks held by persons with residence outside of the GDR would be converted at M 2 = DM 1 if acquired up to December 31, 1989, and at M 3 = DM 1 if acquired between January 1, 1990 and June 30, 1990. The official exchange rate between the mark and the deutsche mark, which was used chiefly for tourism, was changed from M 3 = DM 1 to M 2 = DM 1 on May 2, 1990.

The consolidated balance sheet for the banking system of the GDR as of June 30, 1990 was not available at the time of writing. However, the balance sheet implications of the conversion agreement can be approximated from the position at the end of May (Table 1). As of that date, financial assets with a book value of M 447 billion were on the books of the various financial institutions in the GDR. Credit to enterprises amounted to DM 232 billion (52 percent of assets), balanced in part by enterprise deposits of DM 57 billion. Credit to the housing sector totaled DM 103 billion. On the liability side of the balance sheet, the largest single item was deposits of households totaling M 182 billion (40 percent of total liabilities). The other key liability for the conversion process was the liability position of the State Bank to future exporters—the *Richtungskoeffizienten* (RIKOs), see below— reflecting the difference between the official exchange rate and the exchange rate used in foreign trade.

Table 1 shows the results of applying the conversion rates to the balance sheet at the end of May. On this basis, the banking system would have had assets with a book value of DM 246 billion and a net worth of DM 23 billion (9½ percent of total assets). It is useful to describe the key elements of the conversion of assets and liabilities.

Liabilities

Taking into account the favorable conversion rate for a portion of household deposits, the average conversion rate for GDR mark deposits was about M 1.6 = DM 1. For foreign currency liabilities, market rates were applied as far as possible, while equity capital was converted at M 1 = DM 1. However, the average overall conversion rate was M 1.8 = DM 1. This reflected the nonconversion—that is, a writing down to zero—of the RIKO fund.

The RIKO fund can be interpreted as a reserve to help finance future export activities of GDR enterprises. The valuation of the fund resulted from an internal accounting system involving an official exchange rate and a more depreciated commercial rate. The difference between the two exchange rates was in essence a tax on importers and a subsidy to exporters.[6] The surplus in the fund

---

[4] See Box 1 in Chapter III.

[5] In line with lower wage levels in the GDR, pension payments would be lower in the GDR.

[6] There are two ways of viewing the operations of the RIKO fund. That presented here starts with the assumption that the actual exchange rate between the deutsche mark, the valuta mark, and the GDR mark was DM 1 = VM 1 = M 1, but that hard-currency trade was subject in effect to export subsidies and import taxes that were paid out or received by the RIKO fund. Alternatively, one might see the actual exchange rate at DM 1 = VM 1 = M 4.4 with exporters receiving M 1 directly and M 3.4 through the RIKO fund for each DM 1 of exports. In either case the change in the exchange system meant that the RIKO fund became obsolete, and, since there were no actual claimants on it, it could be used to help bridge the asymmetry between the conversion of assets and liabilities.

Table 1. German Democratic Republic: Consolidated Balance Sheet of the Credit System Before and After Currency Conversion

(Based on figures for May 31, 1990; in billions of marks and deutsche mark)

Assets	In Marks	Conversion Rate	In Deutsche Mark	Liabilities	In Marks	Conversion Rate	In Deutsche Mark
Domestic credit	397.4		180.7	Domestic deposits	249.0	M 1.6 = DM 1[1]	156.6
Enterprises	231.7	M 2 = DM 1	115.8	Enterprises	57.0[2]	M 2.05 = DM 1	27.8
Housing	102.6	M 2 = DM 1	51.3				
Consumers	2.5	M 2 = DM 1	1.3	Households	182.1	M 1.48 = DM 1[1]	123.4[3]
Government	60.6[4]	M 2 = DM 1	12.3	Government	10.8	M 2 = DM 1	5.4
Foreign assets	45.0		36.3	Foreign liabilities	56.1		55.6
State-trading countries	17.4	M 2 = DM 1	8.7	State-trading countries	1.1	M 2 = DM 1	0.6
Other	27.6	M 1 = DM 1	27.6	Other	55.0	M 1 = DM 1	55.0
				Currency in circulation	13.6	M 2 = DM 1	6.8
Participations	1.1	M 1 = DM 1	1.1				
Other assets	3.1	M 2 = DM 1	1.5	Other liabilities	127.0		27.0
				Equity	23.4	M 1 = DM 1	23.4
Subtotal	446.6	M 2.03 = DM 1[1]	219.6	RIKOs	96.4	—	—
				Other	7.2	M 2 = DM 1	3.6
Equalization claims	—	—	26.4				
Total	446.6	M 1.81 = DM 1[1]	246.0	Total	446.6	M 1.81 = DM 1[1]	246.0

Sources: Deutsche Bundesbank; and authors' calculations.

[1] Average conversion rate.

[2] A small part was deposited after December 31, 1989 by nonresidents and was therefore converted at M 3 = DM 1.

[3] M 2,000 million for each of 3.2 million residents under age 14, plus M 4,000 million for each of 10.1 million residents between ages 14 and 58, plus M 6,000 for each of 3 million residents over age 58, are all converted at M 1 = DM 1; the remaining deposits are converted at M 2 = DM 1.

[4] Of this, M 31.2 billion constituted credits to the Government for the revaluation of *Richtungskoeffizienten*—RIKOs (see text) and M 4.9 billion was a credit to the Government for the minting of coins and currency during the conversion of 1948. Thus, only M 24.5 billion was actually converted.

reflected past trade deficits with hard-currency trading partners. Unlike deposit liabilities, there were no actual claimants on the RIKO fund. On conversion day, the deutsche mark became the legal tender of the GDR and the need for these cumbersome accounting procedures disappeared. Accordingly, the RIKO fund was used partly to balance some of the credit outstanding to Government (due to revaluation of foreign currency liabilities) and partly to finance other aspects of the conversion process. In effect, it was not converted into deutsche mark.

Assets

The average conversion rate on domestic credit of the banking system was about M 2.2 = DM 1. This was above the conversion rate of M 2 = DM 1 because of the special treatment of the above-mentioned credit outstanding to the Government. Of the total claims on Government of DM 60½ billion, only M 24½ million was actually converted. Most of the balance reflected credit extended to the Government associated with revaluations of the RIKO fund[7]—consistent with the treatment of this

fund, these credits were not converted. With hard-currency foreign assets valued at market exchange rates, the overall conversion rate on the asset side was M 2 = DM 1. Given that the average conversion rate was more depreciated on the asset side than on the liability side, an infusion of capital from the Government was required to balance assets and liabilities. These equalization claims (*Ausgleichsforderungen*) were estimated at DM 26½ billion on the basis of the May balance sheet.[8] This sum did not represent a measure of the insolvency of the banking system; rather it reflected the infusion necessary to maintain equity and reserve funds (converted in this initial stage at the rate of M 1 = DM 1) at the preconversion level. The banking system was technically insolvent, however, as, without equalization claims, the gap between the liability and asset sides would have been larger than the converted value of equity.[9] The process of conversion will not be completed

---

[7] From time to time, the RIKO fund was revalued in line with

changes in the commercial exchange rate. The Government absorbed the valuation losses, sometimes through budgetary contributions but more recently through borrowing from the State Bank.

[8] The mechanics of the equalization claims and the establishment of the Equalization Fund are described below.

[9] Interpretation in a normative sense is, however, hazardous. First, the insolvency reflected the arbitrary asymmetric conversion rate. Second, the distribution of assets and liabilities within the state sector had had little economic meaning under the former system.

Table 2. Estimates of the Money Supply in Germany Under Various Conversion Proposals

(In billions of marks and deutsche mark)

	In Marks	In Deutsche Mark			
		At M 1 = DM 1	Bundesbank proposal	Bonn proposal	Agreed plan
GDR					
Currency	13.6	13.6	6.8[1]	6.8[1]	6.8[1]
Total deposits[2]	235.7	235.7	134.2	150.5	150.3
One-to-one (M 1 = DM 1)	—	—	32.6[3]	65.2[4]	64.8[5]
Two-to-one (M 2 = DM 1)	—	—	101.6	85.3	85.5
Estimate of M3	249.3	249.3	141.0	157.3	157.1
FRG					
M3 (May 31, 1990)		1,221.9	1,221.9	1,221.9	1,221.9
Estimate of combined M3		1,471.2	1,362.9	1,379.2	1,379.0
Percent increase in deutsche mark M3 owing to conversion		20.4	11.5	12.9	12.9

Sources: Consolidated Balance Sheet of the GDR Banking System, May 31, 1990 provided by the Deutsche Bundesbank; Deutsche Bundesbank, *Monthly Report*; and authors' calculations.

[1] Converted at M 2 = DM 1.

[2] Excludes insurance company deposits of M 14.2 billion.

[3] Assumes that the population of 16.3 million residents each had a M 2,000 deposit which was converted at M 1 = DM 1. All other deposits are assumed to have been converted at M 2 = DM 1.

[4] Assumes that each resident had a deposit of M 4,000 which was converted at M 1 = DM 1. All other deposits are assumed to have been converted at M 2 = DM 1.

[5] Assumes that each resident between the ages of 14 and 58 (10.1 million) had a deposit of M 4,000, that each resident under 14 years of age (3.2 million) had a deposit of M 2,000, and that each resident age 59 or older (3 million) had a deposit of M 6,000, and that these deposits were converted at M 1 = DM 1. All other deposits are assumed to have been converted at M 2 = DM 1.

until the initial balance sheets of the banks and the enterprises can be closely evaluated; what is described above represents only the first stage. The status of enterprise debt, in particular, is still uncertain, both as to its value and the extent to which it will be borne by the enterprises themselves. The size of the equalization fund and the starting equity position of the banking system will thus not be determined until the end of 1990 or early 1991.

The Implications of the Conversion Rate

Effects on Liquidity

The money supply in the GDR was determined initially by the rate at which marks were converted into deutsche mark. Table 2 examines how the conversion rate would have influenced M3 in the GDR and in the unified German economy on the basis of the balance sheet position of the banking system at the end of May.[10] At a conversion rate of M 1 = DM 1 for currency in circulation and all domestic deposit liabilities of the banking system, M3 in Germany would have been

roughly 20 percent above the level of M3 in the FRG. Under the Bundesbank proposal, M3 after unification would have been 11½ percent higher than M3 in the FRG before unification, while under the Bonn proposal it would have been 13 percent higher, the same increase as under the plan actually implemented.

Assuming underlying productivity at about one third of the level in the FRG, output in the GDR was about one tenth of the level in the FRG. Thus, if one assumed velocity of M3 in the GDR similar to that in the FRG, the actual terms of the currency conversion seemed unlikely to produce a dangerous increase in liquidity. It was thought that even if velocity in east Germany turned out to be higher than in west Germany, there was not much basis for concern. Bank deposits in the GDR represented the entire financial holdings of households at the time of conversion; it was reasonable to expect, therefore, that a significant part of the deposits of households would be shifted into higher-yielding non-monetary assets that would become available after July 1. In this context, it is interesting to note that the ratio of households' financial assets to income in the FRG in the late 1950s and early 1960s was similar to that in the GDR in recent years. Moreover, in view of the uncertainties about short-term employment and income prospects, it seemed likely that households would be quite cautious in their expenditure behavior in the immediate aftermath of currency union.

---

[10] M3 in the GDR was approximated by the sum of currency in circulation held by individuals and total domestic deposits.

Implications for the Labor Market

While the actual rate of conversion is unlikely to have had much influence on the equilibrium real wage in the GDR, it did set the initial wage rate. Actual GDR wage rates at the end of May 1990 were converted at a rate of M 1 = DM 1 on July 1. As such, the conversion rate influenced starting demand and supply conditions, migration decisions, and the initial cost of the social safety net.

One might have expected the extent and duration of this influence to depend on a number of economic factors: for instance, the degree of flexibility in wage formation, the initial level of wages relative to the equilibrium level, and the rate of change of productivity. To the extent that nominal wages were inflexible downward over an extended period, setting initial wages too high could have had adverse supply effects in the economy, with ramifications for unemployment and government finances. However, on the basis of the evidence available prior to GEMSU, it did not appear that the average level of wages was initially pitched too high. First, wage levels relative to the FRG seemed to be roughly proportional to relative productivity levels.[11] Moreover, it was thought likely that productivity would rise fast in the early stages of GEMSU as labor dishoarding occurred. The level of wages would not greatly affect the dishoarding of surplus labor, although it would, perhaps, influence the absorption of dishoarded labor into other activities.[12]

Developments in the opening months of GEMSU have called into question earlier judgments on relative productivity levels and the pace of dishoarding. However, the clearest indication that the conversion rate was not, in the event, of great consequence in the labor market was the pronounced upward pressure on wages immediately after the currency union. Wage demands seem to have been determined more by aspirations for parity with west Germany (and possibly by a belief that the Government would protect employment) than by any realistic economic assessment.

Distributional Effects

Central to the currency conversion were its distributional effects. Two aspects of this are interesting to explore. First, did the currency conversion in itself represent a direct subsidy to the GDR? It is popularly supposed that the Bundesbank simply swapped deutsche mark for marks so that, to the extent that the rate of exchange was not an equilibrium one, there was a subsidy involved. In fact there was no such exchange. The Bundesbank did not take mark notes on its books in return for the supply of deutsche mark-denominated base money to the GDR. Rather the banks in the GDR, having called in all the cash in the economy, simply redenominated assets and liabilities in deutsche mark. To the extent that deutsche mark cash was then needed for cash withdrawals, deutsche mark were borrowed from the Bundesbank at the discount or the Lombard rate. Thus, the currency conversion, in itself, did not represent a subsidy to the GDR. Indeed, the Bundesbank gained seignorage through the supply of reserve money to banks in the GDR.

Second, the currency conversion did influence the distribution of wealth between households and the State. The mechanics of this process are clearest if, as a simplification, one thinks of the GDR as being made up of two sets of agents: households, whose wealth consists entirely of financial assets, and the State which is a net debtor in financial terms (largely the counterpart to household net financial assets) but which owns all of the real assets in the economy. The difference between the value of real assets and the net financial liabilities of the State reflects the equity position of the State. At this level, the conversion rate can be seen as determining the distribution of the net worth of the GDR between the financial wealth of households and the net worth of the State.[13] But, as there is no objective way of deciding upon the correct distribution of wealth, these distributional considerations do not provide any useful criteria for determining the appropriate exchange rate.[14]

A number of other considerations may have entered into the determination of the appropriate conversion rate. First, caution was needed to ensure that the overall level of liquidity provided was appropriate. This liquidity constraint could have been circumvented by effecting the conversion partially in the form of nonmonetary assets (as was, for example, suggested in the Bundesbank proposal), but nonmonetary wealth might also have influenced spending decisions. To the extent that the conversion rate was determined mainly by liquidity considerations, any unwanted distributional effects could easily have been altered by fiscal mechanisms. Second, the architects of GEMSU may have believed that the private rate of time discount was high relative to the social one,[15] and that it was therefore desirable for the

---

[11] See Chapter III, section on "Economic Background."

[12] Given the shortage of capital and the inevitable mismatch of skills in the labor market, the extent to which lower wages would have eased the unemployment situation in the short run is not clear.

[13] It is, of course, impossible to estimate the net worth of the State with any confidence at the present juncture because of uncertainties about the value of its holdings of land and industrial capital.

[14] Indeed, if one saw the net worth of the State as being ultimately attributable to households, one could argue that the distribution of wealth between the two is unimportant; this, however, would be an extreme view.

[15] Particularly given concerns about an impatience for rising consumption levels in the GDR after many years of living standards far below those in the FRG.

State itself to marshal resources to restructure the economy. Third, the national wealth would depend, inter alia, upon how efficiently assets were managed; it is possible that views on the conversion rate were influenced by an assessment of how efficiently the State would manage the assets entrusted to it. In the final analysis it is likely that the choice of the conversion rate was determined chiefly by a desire to maintain a reasonable amount of wealth and liquidity at the level of households on the one hand, without stimulating excessive consumption or crippling the finances of the State on the other.

The conversion process, aside from its effect on household wealth and the overall financial position of the State, redistributed the net financial debtor position of the State between its various components—banks, the Government, and the producing enterprises. For example, changing the conversion rate from M 2 = DM 1 to M 3 = DM 1 (while still retaining a rate of M 1 = DM 1 for a portion of household savings) would have increased the value of producing enterprises (by reducing their debt) and hence the value of the State's equity position in these enterprises. Offsetting this, however, there would have been a drop in the net worth of state-owned banks or an increase in the capital infusion needed to maintain the equity position of the banking system. In principle, therefore, there would not have been any net effect on the Government's financial position.

One should not interpret the foregoing analysis as implying that the actual distribution of the State's net financial position is irrelevant. In particular, to the extent that the separation of institutional responsibility, especially the enterprise sector from the Government, is strictly maintained, the level of debt left on the books of enterprises is likely to be an important practical determinant (next to their underlying competitiveness) of whether they are able to survive the transition and how easily they can be privatized. In particular, enterprise debt levels that are too high would prejudice the ability of enterprises to raise financing and would divert earnings from investment to debt service.[16]

Monetary Control During the Early Stages of GEMSU

The track record and recent statements of the Bundesbank leave little doubt about its determination to keep inflation under control. With higher fiscal deficits and strong demand pressures, however, one can imagine circumstances under which monetary policy would come under pressure in the period ahead. Moreover, in guiding monetary policy, the Bundesbank will face technical challenges related to uncertainties about how to implement monetary policy in east Germany.

Thus far, the Bundesbank has monitored monetary developments separately in west and east Germany. In the west, it has not departed from its traditional methods of operating (see Box 1), with its primary focus on keeping monetary growth in line with potential output and an acceptable inflation rate. Initially, statistics in the west may not be greatly distorted by money held in the east, although it will be difficult to identify the geographic distribution of currency holdings. As the two economies become more integrated, however, segregated monetary statistics and monetary management will become less reliable.

In the early stages of GEMSU, with monetary targeting only in the west and a single currency with free capital flows between east and west, the money supply in the east will be determined by demand. In normal circumstances this should not pose an inflation risk—after all, for the smaller countries participating in the exchange rate mechanism of the European Monetary System, whose currencies are effectively pegged to the deutsche mark, the situation is not very different.

In the case of east Germany, however, there are two important differences. First, a substantial increase in certain prices—chiefly for services—may be warranted as part of the unwinding of distorted relative prices in the GDR. Monetary conditions will accommodate this and it may be difficult to distinguish these relative price changes from general inflation pressures. Second, normal credit extension by banks, in line with the production decisions of enterprises and reasonable expectations about inflation, would not constitute a problem; but credit extended under government guarantees to fund unrealistic wage increases by enterprises with very short life expectancies could result in a monetary expansion that is out of line with real developments. This second mechanism is largely a "fiscal" as opposed to a "monetary" problem—the government guarantees are the essence of the problem.

It is difficult to see any alternative to the approach followed by the Bundesbank in the first stage of unification. There is no reasonable basis for determining how much liquidity to supply to the east German market. Traditional indicators are of little use: there is no sound statistical base, and no basis for extrapolating the demand for money or the behavior of velocity from historical relationships. The relative scale of the two economies, however, is such that errors in the provision of liquidity

---

[16] It is worth noting that the distribution of debt between various components of the State had little to do with economic fundamentals. It reflected the arbitrary nature of the pricing system under central planning and the role of enterprises as the major source of government revenue.

Box 1. Monetary Policy Instruments and Procedures in the FRG[1]

Overall Strategy

After the final breakdown of the Bretton Woods system of fixed exchange rates in early 1973, domestic anchors had to be found to limit monetary expansion in individual countries. In late 1974, the Bundesbank introduced a target for monetary growth through 1975. The Bundesbank chose central bank money (CBM), comprising currency in circulation and banks' required reserves on domestic deposits (measured at constant 1974 reserve ratios), as its target aggregate. CBM served as the target aggregate through 1987, but in 1988 the Bundesbank shifted to announcing targets for broad money (M3). The Bundesbank's experience of using monetary targets to anchor inflation and inflation expectations has been successful; while targets (or target ranges) were exceeded in some years (owing, inter alia, to turbulence in foreign exchange markets), the targets themselves provided a clear and transparent point of reference for an anti-inflationary monetary policy that was widely accepted.

In setting its monetary targets, the Bundesbank seeks to accommodate not *current* real growth but the rate of growth of productive potential and a minimal (and acceptable) rate of inflation. This means that monetary developments provide stabilizing feedback to the real economy: if actual growth exceeds potential, monetary conditions tighten, while if growth falls below potential, monetary conditions ease. This method of setting monetary targets requires the Bundesbank to estimate potential growth and to determine an "acceptable" and achievable rate of price inflation. Consumer price inflation has averaged less than 3½ percent in the period since monetary targeting began, despite some major global bouts of inflation. In the cyclical upswing from 1983–89, consumer price inflation has averaged only 1¾ percent.

The Bundesbank's Instruments

The Bundesbank uses both interest rate and liquidity policy instruments to influence money and credit market conditions and the reserve position of the banking system. These mechanisms accommodate two key features of financial markets in the FRG: the dominant role of the universal commercial banking system, which represents the main channel of transmission of monetary policy, and the almost exclusive reliance of banks on the interbank money market for short-term money management.

The Bundesbank uses its interest rate instruments, chiefly the Lombard rate and the discount rate, to establish upper and lower bounds, respectively, for the movement of short-term interest rates over a time horizon measured in months.[2] Over a shorter time horizon, measured in weeks, the interest rate on repurchase transactions influences the rates in the short-term interbank money market more directly. The interest rate corridor established by the discount and Lombard rates is used by the Bundesbank to signal its intentions regarding the general stance of monetary policy; within this corridor, the repurchase rate is used to determine the center of gravity of money market rates.

Within the established interest rate band, the Bundesbank employs its liquidity instruments to vary the ease, predictability, and timing with which reserves are made available to the banking system. Because the FRG does not have a well-developed short-term market for securities, the Bundesbank has relied on supplementary instruments known as "reversible assistance measures." These measures take the form of short-term bilateral transactions between the Bundesbank and the commercial banks in the money, foreign exchange, and long-term securities markets. The Bundesbank also injects reserves into the system by shifting federal government deposits into the money market for short periods.

Since 1985, open market transactions under repurchase agreements in fixed-interest securities (repurchase agreements) have been the Bundesbank's main instrument for influencing bank liquidity, as well as short-term money market rates, on a week-to-week basis. Such transactions are short-term agreements, which usually run for one or two months.

For day-to-day fine-tuning of bank liquidity and short-term interest rates, the Bundesbank uses its other reversible assistance measures. From an operational point of view, the day-to-day management of money market conditions is guided by operating constraints on the level and structure of key interest rates and the development of the banking system's liquidity position. The monetary authorities monitor key balance sheet indicators of the banks' liquidity position—including unutilized rediscount quotas, indebtedness to the Lombard facility, and net liability positions resulting from "fine-tuning" operations.

---

[1] For further discussion, see Deutsche Bundesbank, *The Deutsche Bundesbank: Its Monetary Policy Instruments and Functions* (Frankfurt, 1989); Deutsche Bundesbank, "The Longer-Term Trend and Control of the Money Stock," in *Monthly Report* (Frankfurt), January 1985, pp. 13–26; and Hermann-Josef Dudler, "The Implementation of Monetary Objectives in Germany—Open Market Operations and Credit Facilities," in *Central Bank Views on Monetary Targeting*, ed. by Paul Meek (New York: Federal Reserve Bank of New York, 1983).

[2] The Lombard facility is a borrowing facility for exceptional financing with an administered interest rate (the Lombard rate). While there are no explicit ceilings on Lombard credit, the Bundesbank discourages the use of Lombard credit by an individual bank continuously, in large amounts, or over long periods. The Lombard facility is designed to offer liquidity at a penalty rate; the rate on overnight money in the interbank market, the call-money rate, is usually below the Lombard rate. The discount window offers a rate below both the Lombard rate and market rates. The quantity of borrowing at the discount window is limited by quotas that are generally fully utilized. The Bundesbank also has established an intervention rate at which it offers short-term treasury bills, usually with a maturity of three days. This rate places a lower bound on the call-money rate, above the discount rate. Thus, the call-money rate is bounded from above by the Lombard rate and from below by the interest rate offered by the Bundesbank on short-term treasury bill transactions.

to the east are unlikely to have any major effect on the German economy as a whole.[17]

At a technical level, even access by banks to Bundesbank resources initially presented problems insofar as banks did not have financial instruments eligible for refinancing. To solve this problem, the Bundesbank Act was amended to allow east German banks temporary access to the discount window and to the Lombard facility against equalization claims and single signature paper (i.e., banks' own IOUs).[18] Pending the issuance of equalization claims, liquidity operations by the Bundesbank have been exclusively against single signature paper.

Structural Reform of the East German Banking System

The Banking System in the Centrally Planned Economy

As in the other socialist countries, the banking system of the GDR had to contribute to the execution of the central plan. Accordingly, it was organized as a one-tier system with the State Bank (*Staatsbank*) at the head and a few commercial and a larger number of savings banks at the lower levels. The State Bank was the "central organ of the Council of Ministers for the implementation of the monetary and credit policy issued by the party and the government."[19] In this regard, it served as both a central bank and a commercial bank. As a central bank, it had the exclusive right to issue bank notes and coins and, with the agreement of the Council of Ministers, to set the official exchange rate between foreign currencies and the mark, the rate between foreign currencies and the valuta mark (the unit of account for foreign trade), and the domestic rate between the valuta mark and the mark.[20] The commercial banking activities of

the State Bank consisted of serving the state-owned enterprises and the *Kombinate* in industry, construction, transportation, and domestic trade. In order to execute this function, the State Bank maintained 41 branches.

The commercial banking activities of the State Bank were supplemented by a number of state-owned and cooperative banks. Among the former were the Deutsche Aussenhandelsbank AG (DABA), the Deutsche Handelsbank AG (DHB),[21] and the Bank für Landwirtschaft und Nahrungsgüterwirtschaft (BLN). DABA and DHB were the designated special institutions for all international trade and financial transactions of the GDR; BLN was the state-owned bank for the agricultural sector. The cooperative banks comprised the *Genossenschaftsbanken für Handwerk und Gewerbe* (GHG) and the *Bauerliche Handelsgenossenschaften* (BHG). The former served the crafts and trade sector, while the latter provided banking services to farmers.

The municipal and county savings banks (*Stadt- und Kreissparkassen*) together with railways and postal banks (*Reichsbahn- und Postsparkassen*) had the function of collecting the monetary savings of the population and passing them on to the commercial banks and the commercial arm of the State Bank as a source of funding for their lending business. About 80 percent of private sight and savings deposits were held at the savings banks. The remainder was distributed over the BLN, GHG, BHG, as well as the railways and postal banks.

The Banking Reform of March 1990

On March 6, 1990, the GDR parliament, in preparation for GEMSU, passed a law (*Gesetz über die Änderung des Gesetzes über die Staatsbank der DDR*) that replaced the one-tier, socialist banking system by a two-tier system compatible with that of the FRG. The State Bank gave up its commercial banking activities but remained the central bank of the GDR. The larger part of the commercial branch of the State Bank was used to create the Deutsche Kreditbank AG, and the smaller East Berlin operation (Stadtkontor Ost) was transformed into the Berliner Stadtbank AG. The central operation of the BLN was used to create the Genossenschaftsbank Berlin der DDR, while the branches of the BLN together with the BHG were merged into rural cooperative banks (*Genossenschafts- und Raiffeisenbanken*); the GHG formed the nucleus of the *Volksbanken*, the cooperative banks for the crafts and trade sector.[22] The municipal and

---

[17] Moreover, there is nothing to prevent the Bundesbank reacting to any disturbing inflationary tendencies in the east by tightening monetary conditions in the west—there is room within the target range for discretionary action and the Bundesbank's concern, after all, is with inflation in all of Germany. The Bundesbank has not yet announced its monetary policy intentions for 1991.

[18] As in the west, each bank has been assigned a rediscount quota. In total, these amount to DM 25 billion. The banks have access to additional funds from the Lombard facility.

[19] See *Gesetz über die Staatsbank der DDR*, December 19, 1974.

[20] The system seems to have been logically inconsistent in that cross-restrictions between these exchange rates did not always hold. For example, the official exchange rate between the deutsche mark and the mark, as well as the rate between the deutsche mark and the valuta mark, were both 1:1. In 1989, however, the internal rate between the valuta mark and the mark for hard-currency trade was VM 1 = M 4.4. A fund was created at the State Bank (RIKO fund) to finance differences between the official and the internal exchange rates (see above and Chapter III).

[21] In order to facilitate business with Western countries, the GDR Government had given DHB and DABA the status of *Aktiengesellschaften*, that is, joint-stock companies, already at the time they were founded in 1956 and 1966, respectively.

[22] The Genossenschaftsbank Berlin was created as the head organization for the local *Genossenschafts- und Raiffeisenbanken*, as well as the *Volksbanken*.

county savings banks remained. The organization of the GDR commercial banking system and the constitution of its components as universal banks set up a structure similar to that of the banking system in the FRG.

At the time of the reorganization, however, ownership of the GDR commercial banking system remained with the State or the cooperatives. The State Bank was given more than 80 percent of the shares in both the Deutsche Kreditbank AG and the Berliner Stadtbank AG, which were both constituted as joint-stock companies.[23] The State Bank was also the main shareholder in DABA and DHB (also both organized as joint-stock companies), which, in addition to their commercial activities, continued to perform the functions of a house bank for the external trade companies engaged in trade with member countries of the Council for Mutual Economic Assistance (CMEA).[24] In contrast to the above-mentioned banks, the Genossenschaftsbank Berlin and the savings banks (*Stadt- und Kreissparkassen*) were organized as public corporations.[25] The *Genossenschafts- und Raiffeisenbanken* and the *Volksbanken* continued to be organized as cooperatives.

The Equalization Fund and Equalization Claims

The establishment of a two-tier banking system compatible with that of the FRG was an important prerequisite for the currency conversion that took place on July 1. Since the assets of most banks were converted into deutsche mark at a lower rate than the liabilities, in order to maintain the equity of the banks, the assets of the banking system had to be topped up with claims issued by the Equalization Fund, that is, the equalization claims discussed above. The Equalization Fund, in turn, covered its liabilities by claims against the State Bank and the GDR Government. Reflecting the structure of their assets and liabilities on the day of conversion, however, individual banks were affected differently by the currency conversion.

On July 1, 1990, the State Bank ceased to exist as a central bank. It nevertheless continued to perform an important role as a "money market bank" linking the savings deposits of the population held at the savings, postal, and cooperative banks to the business and housing credits extended by the Kreditbank. Since an important liability, the RIKO fund, was eliminated in conversion, and since it had no deposits that were converted at parity,

the State Bank registered a gain from currency conversion (after converting its equity position at the rate of M 1 = DM 1) and was allocated a corresponding liability to the Equalization Fund (Chart 1).

All other major banks suffered conversion losses and had to be given claims on the Equalization Fund. Since the savings and cooperative banks held the lion's share of the population's sight and savings deposits, part of which was converted at parity, their conversion losses, and hence equalization claims, were the largest. Banks holding foreign liabilities (DABA and DHB) also incurred substantial conversion losses as their liabilities to Western countries had to be valued at market rates while their assets had to be converted at a rate of M 2 = DM 1.[26]

Based on calculations using data from end May 1990, the Bundesbank estimated that the GDR banking system would have gross claims of about DM 57 billion on the Equalization Fund. These would be offset in part by liabilities of the State Bank to the Equalization Fund so that the net claim on the Government by the Fund was estimated at about DM 26½ billion. A preliminary calculation, as well as an allocation, of equalization claims, would be made as soon as the end-June balance sheets became available. A final calculation would be made only after east German companies had published their opening balance sheets in deutsche mark, the distribution of enterprise debt was decided, and banks had evaluated their portfolios incorporating this information.

Developments in East German Banking After GEMSU

As mentioned above, the commercial operations of the GDR banking system were placed with the newly created Deutsche Kreditbank (DKB) in March 1990. Subsequently, the DKB entered into joint ventures with the two largest west German commercial banks. Deutsche Bank invested DM 1 billion in a joint venture with DKB that encompasses 122 of the DKB's branches and 8,500 of its employees. Dresdner Bank also entered into a joint venture with DKB covering 72 branches of DKB with an original investment of DM 150 million effective July 1, 1990. An additional investment of DM 350 million was made in September 1990, which increased the Dresdner Bank's stake in the joint venture from 49 percent to 85 percent. At that time, Dresdner Bank also had 35 branches in the GDR which it had established *de novo*, including its original headquarters in Dresden.

---

[23] The remainder of the equity interest was acquired by state-owned enterprises and *Kombinate*.

[24] DABA, in particular, remained the designated bank for transactions with the two CMEA banks—the International Bank for Economic Cooperation (IBWZ) and the International Investment Bank (IIB) that are located in Moscow.

[25] This form of ownership is also common for savings banks in the FRG.

[26] Reflecting the allocation of responsibilities that existed in the one-tier banking system, the State Bank, the DABA, and the DHB had undertaken foreign borrowing on behalf of the Government. The authorities decided to leave the foreign liabilities after conversion with the banks that had incurred them and to give the banks offsetting claims on the Equalization Fund.

Chart 1. German Democratic Republic: Simplified Outline of the Banking System and Interbank Relations at the Time of the Currency Conversion[1]

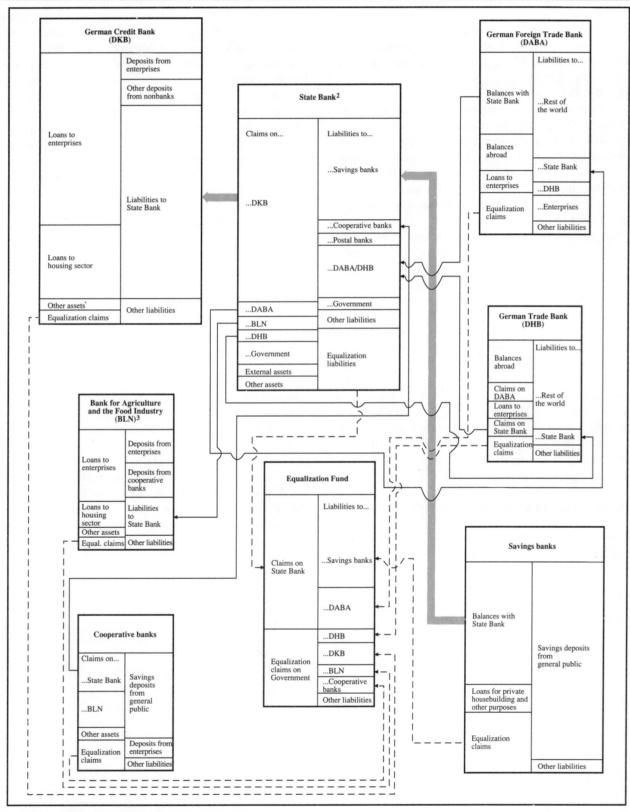

Source: Deutsche Bundesbank, *Monthly Report*, July 1990, p. 17.

[1] Excluding the Bundesbank. The joint venture banks established since the currency conversion, and the restructuring of the GDR banking system effected since then, are not included.

[2] Now known as State Bank Berlin.

[3] Now known as Cooperative Bank Berlin.

The Westdeutsche Landesbank, another FRG bank, has entered into a joint venture with the Deutsche Aussenhandelsbank (DABA), taking over 200 branches and approximately 1,200 employees. The joint venture is called the Deutsche Industrie- und Handelsbank (DIHB). Likewise, the Berliner Handels- und Frankfurter Bank (BHF) has taken a 64 percent stake in the Deutsche Handelsbank (DHB).

In contrast to the other large FRG banks operating in east Germany, the Commerzbank decided not to engage in joint ventures with former GDR banks; instead it adopted the strategy of opening new branches in the east. Commerzbank expects to have 50 branches operating in east Germany by the end of 1990; as of the end of September, its east German operations had total assets of about DM 6 billion, with about 80,000 customers and DM 2 billion in deposits.

There are also a number of non-German banks operating in east Germany: Citicorp has established representative offices in East Berlin, Dresden, and Leipzig; Salomon Brothers and Barclays Bank have offices in East Berlin; and the Bank of Tokyo has received permission to establish a branch in East Berlin.

Savings institutions, which are generally owned by municipalities in west Germany, will be similarly structured in the east. As of mid-October, there were 4,000 branches of savings banks (*Spaarkassen*), with 20,000 employees, which accounted for about 80 percent of total deposits in east Germany. Like in west Germany, there were also a number of cooperative banks (*Genossenschaftsbanken*): 95 in urban areas and 272 in rural areas catering to the agricultural community.

Role of Banks in Economic Reconstruction

The central position of the banking system in the allocation of resources gives it a key role in the transformation of the east German economy. The March banking system reform initiated the refashioning of the GDR's banking system to this end. The establishment of the necessary institutional structure has been embodied in the State Treaty on GEMSU. In particular, after July 1, financial markets in the GDR were opened to external competition both in terms of cross-border business and the participation of external banks (i.e., from the FRG and other countries) in the domestic market. Furthermore, laws regulating financial markets in the FRG were adopted by the GDR although, in certain circumstances, they could be applied more flexibly than in the FRG.[27]

It will no doubt take some time before banks in east Germany operate as efficiently as those in the west. The principal concern about the operations of the banking system, however, would seem to be that the incentives facing banks in their lending decisions are appropriate. Credits to enterprises extended before July 1, 1990 appear to have an implicit guarantee from the Trust Fund or the Government. But for new credits, and given the desire not to distort the allocation of credit by government intervention, the situation is more difficult. Uncertainties about the underlying competitive position of enterprises are likely to persist for some time. Banks will therefore be extremely cautious in extending new credits without government guarantees, at least until decisions are made on the allocation of existing enterprise debt and on enterprise balance sheets. In the period July–September, the Trust Fund was authorized to guarantee working capital loans to enterprises up to a total of DM 30 billion. A significant portion of these guarantees, at least in the first tranche of DM 10 billion in July, was allocated to enterprises that are unlikely to survive the transition to a market economy. It now appears likely that the system of guaranteeing working capital credits will be continued through the first quarter of 1991.

A second consideration relates to the next step of balance sheet reorganization that will occur with the valuation of enterprise debts and perhaps also the redistribution of these debts. The redistribution of assets and liabilities within the state sector may have important consequences for the success of the restructuring effort as it will influence assessments of the creditworthiness of individual enterprises. It is important that as a result of this process, viable economic entities not be excessively burdened with debt related to decisions under the previous system.

---

[27] For example, the Banking Supervisory Office in the FRG could, under certain circumstances, grant exemption from the banking law to east German banks.

XI

The System of Public Finance in the German Democratic Republic and the Challenges of Fiscal Reform

Günther Thumann

Despite some similarities reflecting common historical roots, in many respects the fiscal system of the German Democratic Republic (GDR) differed fundamentally from that of the Federal Republic of Germany (FRG), both in role and in scope. In the FRG, fiscal policy is geared toward supporting market processes within a social market economy. It is democratically controlled with a federative structure that offers considerable fiscal autonomy to the lower levels of government. In the former GDR, fiscal planning played a pervasive role in the context of a command economy, essentially uncontrolled by the people and burdened with complex and at times conflicting political objectives. It was highly centralized, granting little if any fiscal autonomy to the lower levels of government.

Unification of the two German economies required, among a host of other tasks, a fundamental reform of the fiscal system, involving the adoption in east Germany of the fiscal system of the FRG. Details of fiscal reform were spelled out in the State Treaty, which constituted the legal basis for German economic, monetary, and social union (GEMSU). The Unification Treaty (which dealt with political union) had further consequences for the fiscal system in east Germany, the most obvious of which was the elimination of a separate central government.

This chapter describes the major features of the fiscal system of the GDR prior to GEMSU, identifies the crucial elements of the reform process, and discusses some implications for budgetary developments.

Outline of the Fiscal System in the GDR Prior to GEMSU

Institutional Framework

Fiscal planning was regarded as an integral part of central planning. In combination with banking it formed the sphere of financial planning, the counterpart of material planning, and was assessed by the success with which it steered decisions toward those prescribed by the central economic plan, the *Volkswirtschaftsplan*. The fiscal plan in the form of the state budget comprised the central government, the governments of the counties (*Bezirke*) and the local authorities (*Kreise* and *Gemeinden*), and the social insurance system. In addition, the state enterprise sector, although not itself part of the budget, had a major influence on the size and the structure of revenue and expenditure.

In line with the principle of "democratic centralism," budgetary planning and control were carried out "top-down." The Ministry of Finance, backed by the Ministerial Council, issued plans to all levels of government. The county and local authorities had little autonomy in raising revenue and were dependent on revenue-sharing arrangements over which they had hardly any influence. Although the People's Chamber formally voted each year on the budget law, the budget was in essence determined by the executive. Any broader political discussion was effectively prevented, partly because of the lack of transparency in the way the state budget was presented.

Fiscal Structure

Overview

Both general government revenue and expenditure tended over time to rise faster than net material product (NMP), bringing the shares of revenue and expenditure to 99 percent each in 1988, from 91 percent in 1983. Revenue, which, according to published data, usually exceeded expenditure by a small margin, relied heavily on receipts from the state-owned enterprises; in 1988, these receipts accounted for more than three fourths of state revenue. Taxes on wages and social security contributions amounted to less than 4 percent and 7 percent, respectively, of total revenue. About 5 percent of revenue was recorded as "other revenue," with no identification as to its source. The expenditure accounts also lacked transparency. The lion's share of expenditure appears to have been allocated to social welfare and "economic development," the latter principally in the form of subsidies and transfers to state-owned enterprises (Table 1).

In 1988, revenue from the state-owned enterprises fell below the budgeted figure but, owing to unplanned receipts in the category of other revenue, overall revenue exceeded target. Expenditure also rose faster than expected, yet a small surplus was recorded as usual. The 1989 budget was set up in accordance with earlier practice. Not least because of the mass exodus of people during the second half of 1989, the reported budgetary results deviated from the plan to a larger extent than had been typical. The Annual Report of the *Staatsbank* (State Bank) for 1989 noted a deficit of M 6 billion, equivalent to about 2 percent of NMP. No budget for 1990 was prepared prior to GEMSU. In the first half of 1990, government institutions were instructed to follow the plan laid out for 1989. With higher expenditure, for example, on the recently introduced unemployment benefits, and lower revenue, because of the decline in output,

the deficit in the first half of 1990 is believed to have amounted to at least M 20 billion.

The major items of the fiscal accounts are described in some detail below, looking first at revenue and expenditure of the territorial authorities and then at the social insurance system.

Revenue of the Territorial Authorities

Political considerations dominated revenue policy in the GDR. Levies and taxes were aimed at a politically ordained allocation of resources and distribution of income. The fiscal burden on business was high, whereas households were taxed comparatively lightly. Business taxes were negotiable, which introduced an element of arbitrariness into the tax system. Indirect taxes played a limited role in financing expenditure; this was, however, more a reflection of the size of the state budget in relation to economic activity than an indication of the level of tax rates. The major components of revenue are presented in Table 2.

There were four main categories of receipts from state-owned enterprises:

- *The net profit levy* was determined by the Government in the context of the central plan.[1] In an accounting sense, it represented dividends paid by the enterprises to their shareholder, the State, and in 1988 accounted for 17 percent of revenue.[2]

- *The production fund and trade fund levies* represented taxes on capital at a rate normally of 6 percent. Reduced rates could be stipulated by the Ministerial Council. In 1988, these levies made up 12 percent of revenue.

- The so-called *contribution to social funds*, introduced in 1984, was in effect a tax on labor inputs at a rate of up to 70 percent of wages and salaries and represented 14 percent of revenue in 1988. Its use was not restricted to social purposes.

- *Product-specific levies* were turnover taxes on consumption goods, with rates varying by product; the average rate exceeded 50 percent.[3] "Luxury" items carried a particularly high tax burden, while basic goods were practically exempt. These levies amounted to 17 percent of revenue in 1988.

Table 1.   German Democratic Republic: State Budget

(In billions of marks)

	1987	1988
Revenue	260.4	269.7
Levies and taxes from		
state-owned enterprises	202.1	205.9
Wage tax and other direct taxes		
Of which:	20.1	20.8
Wage tax	9.6	10.0
Private business taxes	4.0	4.2
Social security contributions,		
fees, and other tax-like revenue	29.4	30.3
Of which:		
Social security contributions	18.3	18.8
Other revenue	8.9	12.6
Expenditure	260.2	269.5
"Economic development"	85.3	94.0
Research and development, investment,		
and transport	17.2	20.0
Social policy	150.3	155.1
Housing	29.1	30.2
Price subsidies	49.3	49.8
Education	14.9	15.5
Health	16.3	17.8
Social security	35.2	36.3
Other	5.5	5.6
Other expenditure	7.4	0.4
Balance	0.3	0.2

Source: Staatliche Zentralverwaltung für Statistik der DDR, *Statistisches Jahrbuch der DDR, 1989.*

[1] The profits of a state-owned enterprise did not reflect market conditions. Heavily influenced by the decisions of the central planners, the size of an enterprise's profit was not an appropriate indicator of its competitiveness.

[2] In the national accounts of the FRG, revenue of the territorial authorities from entrepreneurial activity and wealth amounted to 2½ percent of revenue in 1988.

[3] A large number of individual tax rates existed but details were not made public.

Table 2. German Democratic Republic: Revenue of the Territorial Authorities

	1987		1988	
	In billions of marks	In percent of total	In billions of marks	In percent of total
Levies on the state-owned companies	202.1	83.5	205.9	82.1
Industry and service sectors	188.3	77.8	193.5	77.1
Of which:				
Production and trade fund levies	28.4	11.7	30.0	12.0
Net profit levy	39.2	16.2	43.6	17.4
Contribution to social funds	34.1	14.1	35.2	14.0
Product-specific levies	43.0	17.7	43.1	17.2
Agriculture and food	13.8	5.7	12.5	5.0
Taxes and levies paid by cooperatives and private businesses	8.9	3.7	9.2	3.7
Cooperatives and craftsmen	2.7	1.1	2.8	1.1
Consumer cooperatives	2.2	0.9	2.1	0.9
Private craftsmen and other private business	4.0	1.6	4.2	1.7
Wage tax	9.6	4.0	10.0	4.0
Other taxes	1.6	0.7	1.7	0.7
Car tax	0.5	0.2	0.5	0.2
Local authority taxes	0.4	0.2	0.4	0.2
Inheritance, land purchase, and other taxes	0.7	0.3	0.7	0.3
Contributions to the social welfare system	11.1	4.6	11.5	4.6
Other receipts[1]	8.9	3.7	12.6	5.0
Total revenue	242.1	100.0	250.9	100.0

Source: Staatliche Zentralverwaltung für Statistik der DDR, *Statistisches Jahrbuch der DDR, 1989.*

[1] Mostly unidentified.

Business outside the state sector, which included cooperatives, the self-employed, and small-scale private companies, was subject to a complicated system of taxation with regulations varying by the type of business. The cooperatives and some of the professions were treated favorably but private companies faced prohibitively high average tax rates, with marginal rates up to almost 100 percent. Although an onerous burden on individual businesses, revenue from nonstate-owned business was of limited budgetary importance,[4] reflecting the small size of this sector following the nationalizations of 1972.

The system of wage taxation in the GDR was structurally similar to that in the FRG, although average tax rates were much lower. Rates differed according to family status and specific circumstances. For a married income earner with two children, wage income below M 332 a month was exempt from wage tax. On incomes between M 332 and M 1,400, the marginal tax rate increased up to 20 percent and remained at this level for higher incomes. The structure of tax allowances and exemptions was complex, and reduced rates applied to certain types of income (for example, overtime pay, premiums, and shift and weekend work). The average tax rate on gross wage and salary income was 8½ percent in 1988, compared with 18 percent in the FRG.[5] Taxes on wages and salaries accounted for 4 percent of total revenue in 1988, compared with 27½ percent in the FRG.

Other taxes, which made a relatively minor contribution to revenue, included a wealth tax, an inheritance tax, a land purchase tax, a lottery tax, a car tax, and a number of taxes levied by the local authorities (e.g., a land tax, dog license fees, and a tax on leisure and cultural activities).[6] Revenue of the territorial authorities also included contributions and fees for various goods and services provided by the state welfare system, which accounted for about 5 percent of revenue in 1988.

Expenditure of the Territorial Authorities

The classification of spending in the budget rendered its analysis even more difficult than in the case of

---

[4] Taxes from the nonstate-owned business sector amounted to only 3½ percent of revenue in 1988.

[5] The FRG calculation is based on compensation of employees in the national accounts.

[6] Similar taxes, though with a higher relative yield, exist in the FRG.

Table 3. German Democratic Republic: Expenditure of the Territorial Authorities[1]

	1987		1988	
	In billions of marks	In percent of total	In billions of marks	In percent of total
Subsidies and transfers to				
state-owned enterprises	85.3	37.9	94.0	40.3
Agriculture and food	10.8	4.8	9.4	4.0
Of which:				
Investment	0.2	0.1	0.3	0.1
Interest subsidies	0.2	0.1	0.2	0.1
Price subsidies	3.8	1.7	4.6	2.0
Product development	1.0	0.4	0.8	0.4
Other sectors	74.5	33.1	84.5	36.3
Consumer price subsidies	49.3	21.9	49.8	21.4
Other welfare expenditure	69.2	30.8	72.6	31.1
Housing	29.1	12.9	30.2	12.9
Health care	16.3	7.2	17.8	7.6
Education	18.4	8.2	19.0	8.2
Cultural activities	5.5	2.4	5.6	2.4
Investment and maintenance expenditure	13.8	6.1	16.5	7.1
Investment	8.1	3.6	10.4	4.5
Maintenance of roads, railways, etc.	5.7	2.5	6.1	2.6
Other expenditure	7.4	3.3	0.3	0.1
Total expenditure	225.0	100.0	233.2	100.0

Source: Staatliche Zentralverwaltung für Statistik der DDR, *Statistisches Jahrbuch der DDR, 1989.*

[1] Excluding transfer payments to the social security system of M 16.9 billion in 1987 and M 17.5 billion in 1988.

revenue. The largest category of expenditure was transfers and subsidies to nonagricultural state-owned enterprises, which accounted for over 36 percent of total expenditure in 1988 (Table 3). It included contributions to finance research and development and investment projects, and subsidies for intermediate inputs, but no quantitative breakdown was published. Setting-off the levies and taxes paid by the enterprises against the transfers they received, they were substantial net contributors to the budget. State-owned agricultural enterprises received even higher transfers per employee than the other state-owned enterprises,[7] with, in 1988, about half of the total amount of M 9½ billion used to subsidize intermediate inputs for agricultural production. On balance, however, agricultural enterprises made a net contribution to the budget.

Subsidies on consumer goods amounted to M 50 billion in 1988, or 21 percent of expenditure. These subsidies aimed at stabilizing prices for basic consumer goods and services.[8] As basic consumer goods were also largely exempt from product-specific taxes, their prices could be kept

unrealistically low.[9] Public investment (excluding housing) accounted for a comparatively small share of expenditure as did the maintenance of roads, railways, and waterways. The current inadequate state of public infrastructure indicates the low priority that was given to this category of expenditure. Public housing, on the other hand, was a high-priority area, with budgetary expenditure amounting to 11 percent of NMP. At the end of 1989, the housing sector (including privately owned housing) carried a debt of M 108 billion.[10]

Social Insurance

The social insurance system in the GDR was monolithic, in contrast to the complex structure found in the FRG. More than 90 percent of the population was organized in an institution known as the "Social Insurance of Blue and White Collar Workers at the Free German Trade Union (FDGB)." The remainder, mostly professionals, self-employed, and farmers were organized in

---

[7] Agricultural state-owned enterprises included food processing enterprises.

[8] The bulk of these subsidies—64 percent in 1988—related to food, and another 24 percent was for basic manufactured consumer goods. Subsidies on transportation (10 percent), drinking water (1 percent), and services (1 percent) accounted for the remainder.

[9] Subsidies on consumer goods rose significantly, from about 13 percent of retail turnover in 1980 to almost 35 percent in 1988. On the other hand, product-specific taxes declined in relative terms—from about 38 percent of retail turnover in 1980 to 34 percent in 1988. As a result, the net revenue yield fell quite sharply and was negative in 1988.

[10] Part of the interest and amortization payments on this debt was financed by the state budget (M 4 billion in 1988).

the "State Insurance of the GDR." Both institutions ran a mandatory insurance system and a voluntary supplementary system.[11]

As in the FRG, the social security system in the GDR was unfunded. Contributions to the system, which were not distinguished by type of insurance, were mandatory and paid by both employees and employers. In addition, a voluntary system was introduced in 1971, which provided supplementary benefits. In 1988, the social security contributions of employees amounted to about 6 percent of gross income from employment and those of the employers to about 7½ percent.[12] Contribution rates and income limits above which earnings were not subject to taxation had remained more or less unchanged since the 1950s, except for the introduction of the voluntary system in 1971;[13] with benefits rising much faster than contributions, the deficit of the social insurance system widened markedly. In 1988, about half of expenditure was financed out of transfers from the territorial authorities (Table 4).

Benefits of the GDR social insurance system fell into four categories: pensions, health care, family-related benefits, and poverty assistance. Pensions were by far the most important category, accounting for more than half of total expenditure. Unlike in the FRG, pensions in the GDR were not adjusted annually to keep them in line with wage and salary developments. Instead, discretionary adjustments were made at intervals of several years. The increase in pensions in December 1989 raised the monthly statutory old age pension from M 378 to M 447 and the disability pension from M 404 to M 482.[14] The maximum monthly old age pension amounted to M 510 under the mandatory system; those who participated in the voluntary system (about one third of old age pensioners) received on average an additional M 60 a month. The minimum pension was M 330 a month. Taking into account the December 1989 increase, the average old age pension was equivalent to about 45 percent of net wages in the GDR, compared with about 50 percent in the FRG.[15]

[11] Starting in 1971, individuals could—on a voluntary basis—make an additional contribution to the social security system that entitled them to higher pension benefits (retirement, survivors', disability, and orphans' pensions).

[12] See "Quantitative Aspects of Economic and Financial Reform in the GDR," Deutsches Institut für Wirtschaftsforschung, Economic Bulletin (Berlin), vol. 27(5), July 1990.

[13] In the case of the mandatory system, employees paid a rate of 10 percent and employers a rate of 12.5 percent on monthly incomes of up to M 600. Contributions to the voluntary system were 10 percent of the monthly income in excess of M 600 for both employees and employers. There was no upper income limit for contributions to the voluntary system from blue collar and white collar workers but for the self-employed the limit was M 1,200.

[14] Individuals who had earned the average wage and had contributed for a specified number of years were eligible for the statutory pension.

[15] The FRG system guarantees a worker about 70 percent of his or her previous net earnings after 45 years of employment. The average is significantly lower than 70 percent, mainly because women typically accumulate lower claims on the pension insurance system and receive smaller pensions.

Table 4. German Democratic Republic: Revenue of the Social Insurance System

	1987		1988	
	In billions of marks	In percent of total	In billions of marks	In percent of total
Contributions	18.3	52.1	18.8	51.9
Employees	8.1	23.1	8.3	23.0
Employers	10.2	29.0	10.5	28.9
Transfers from the territorial authorities	16.9	47.9	17.5	48.1
Total revenue	35.2	100.0	36.3	100.0

Source: Staatliche Zentralverwaltung für Statistik der DDR, Statistisches Jahrbuch der DDR, 1989.

Table 5. German Democratic Republic: Expenditure of the Social Insurance System

	1987		1988	
	In billions of marks	In percent of total	In billions of marks	In percent of total
Pensions	17.1	48.5	17.2	47.4
Medical care	15.0	42.7	15.8	43.6
Medical services	7.2	20.4	7.5	20.5
Sick pay	4.4	12.6	4.6	12.8
Medicines	3.4	9.7	3.7	10.3
Family assistance	2.1	6.0	2.2	6.2
Maternity benefits	0.9	2.4	0.9	2.4
Infant care	0.8	2.2	0.8	2.3
Child sickness	0.5	1.4	0.6	1.5
Other benefits[1]	0.8	2.4	0.9	2.4
Administrative	0.1	0.4	0.1	0.4
Total expenditure	35.2	100.0	36.3	100.0

Source: Staatliche Zentralverwaltung für Statistik der DDR, Statistisches Jahrbuch der DDR, 1989.

[1] Including poverty assistance.

Health care expenditure covered benefits in kind (mostly medical services), medicines, and transfer payments. The latter consisted of sick pay, which was granted for up to 78 weeks at a rate of 90 percent of previous earnings. Medical services and medicines were provided free to the user; in 1988, they accounted for 30 percent of social insurance expenditure (Table 5). Family benefits included transfers to mothers, allowances for childbirth, benefits for children, and interest-free credit to young families.[16] Poverty assistance, which—as in the FRG—was subject to a means test, played only a minor role according to official data. Poverty assistance was lower than the minimum pension; as virtually all old people received at least the minimum

[16] Allowances for childbirth were M 1,000 for each child and children's benefits were between M 50 and M 150 a year. The interest-free credits were often later converted into grants.

pension and as open unemployment was practically non-existent, demand for regular poverty assistance was limited.

Structural Aspects of Fiscal Reform

Institutional Changes

Plans for the reform of the system of public finance in the GDR were worked out by a joint commission of experts established by the Governments of the FRG and the GDR; these plans became a central part of the State Treaty on GEMSU. The new fiscal system that emerged in the GDR after July 1, 1990, was, except for certain transitional arrangements, practically identical to that of the FRG.[17] This implied a fundamental change in the role of government in the GDR. Most importantly, the state-owned company sector was removed from the system of government finances and was to be restructured and privatized as quickly as possible.[18] The monolithic social insurance system of the GDR was also separated from the state budget and broken up into its component parts, essentially the pension, health insurance, and accident insurance funds. The remaining elements of the government finances initially were left with the GDR Government and the local authorities. At the time of political unification, central government functions in east Germany were merged with those of the Federal Government of the FRG. The newly formed Länder[19] and the local authorities would perform the same functions as their counterparts in west Germany. They would not, however, participate in the revenue-sharing arrangements that exist between the Federal Government and the Länder of west Germany. These arrangements would have to be renegotiated.[20]

Revenue and Expenditure Reform

Territorial Authorities

On the revenue side, probably the most pressing task was the reform of the tax system in east Germany, not least because of the immense burden that it imposed on the enterprise sector under the former system. Besides the need for generating revenue, other important goals were to create a stable tax structure and to establish a system of uniform tax treatment across individuals and enterprises. The task of reforming the tax system was resolved pragmatically. The State Treaty on GEMSU stipulated that, from July 1, 1990, essentially all FRG tax laws would be applied in the GDR[21] with the temporary exception of the income tax and certain business taxes, which would be governed by simplified schemes until the end of 1990.[22] Customs duties would be regulated in line with the customs law and the Common Customs Tariff of the European Community (EC).[23] Contributions and fees for public services would be harmonized with the system in the FRG.[24]

Given that in the early stages of GEMSU, incomes in east Germany were likely to be much smaller than in the west, it was expected that the yield (relative to GDP) of direct taxes would be low, reflecting the interaction of a progressive income tax system with exemption levels attuned to conditions in west Germany. Initially, the main source of revenue was likely to be indirect taxes; indeed, in view of the high share of consumption in GDP that was expected for a number of years, the potential yield (relative to GDP) would be higher than in west Germany. Tax collections related to the expenditure of east German residents in west Germany would, of course, not be registered as revenue in east Germany; this, however, would be of little material interest in the context of the government finances of Germany as a whole. Collections in east Germany might also be affected by administrative difficulties during the early stages of GEMSU.

The level and structure of government expenditure in east Germany have also changed radically. Expenditure of the social insurance system, the state-owned enterprises, the public railways, the postal system, and the public housing corporation has been removed from the budget.[25] Subsidies have been largely abolished or have

---

[17] See, in particular, Articles 1, 11, 18, 26 and Annexes II–IV of the State Treaty on GEMSU.

[18] In addition, the State Treaty stipulated that the railways (Deutsche Reichsbahn) and post and telecommunications (Deutsche Post) would be operated as special funds.

[19] The five Länder that existed prior to 1952—Brandenburg, Mecklenburg-West Pomerania, Saxony, Saxony-Anhalt, and Thuringia.

[20] Initially, 85 percent of the resources of the German Unity Fund would be directed to the Länder of east Germany. See the discussion in Chapter II, section on ''Fiscal Implications of GEMSU.''

[21] See Articles 30 and 31 and Annex IV (III) of the State Treaty. The possibility of deviating from FRG tax regulations in certain cases was provided if such deviations could be justified by circumstances (see Annex IV (II-(2) of the Treaty). Although perhaps attractive from a theoretical perspective, it would not have been feasible to introduce a tax system in the east that was significantly different from that in the FRG, particularly in view of the impending political unification.

[22] Until the end of 1990, the individual income tax would be paid solely according to Class I (single taxpayers) of the FRG wage tax code, including a child allowance. Given the comparatively low incomes in the GDR, the full application of the FRG wage tax code would have yielded very little revenue. To give companies time to adjust, corporation, trade and wealth taxes would be paid under the tax rules that had been introduced by the Modrow Government in March 1990. The tax bases, however, would be calculated to conform with FRG accounting rules. From January 1, 1991 all income and profit taxes would be levied in accordance with FRG regulations.

[23] See Article 30 of the State Treaty.

[24] See Article 26(3) of the State Treaty.

[25] See Article 26(2) of the State Treaty.

been earmarked for reduction.[26] The need for substantial cuts in personnel expenditure in the public services has also been identified; reportedly public service in the GDR was about twice as labor-intensive as its counterpart in the FRG.[27] On the other hand, given that infrastructural needs were severely neglected in the past, these are likely to become a major priority for expenditure in the years ahead.

Social Insurance

The State Treaty on GEMSU envisaged a social security system in east Germany corresponding to the west German system, that is, the establishment of separate pension, health, unemployment, and accident insurance institutions.[28] With political unification, the systems in the two parts of Germany will be merged but a date for this has not yet been set. In the interim, the four constituent parts of the social insurance system in east Germany are being administered by a single institution, but with separate revenue and expenditure accounts maintained for each type of insurance. Benefits are linked to insured earnings, and primarily financed by contributions, paid half by the employee and half by the employer.[29] Contribution rates and the income ceilings for compulsory insurance cover are the same as in west Germany.[30] Those with incomes in excess of the ceilings may join professional schemes outside the compulsory system.

The pension law that applied in the GDR has been adapted to the pension insurance law of the FRG.[31] The supplementary and special pension schemes of the GDR were discontinued on July 1, 1990, with accrued claims transferred to the new system. Initial pension levels and future adjustments are linked to the development of net wages and salaries in east Germany.

Introduction of the health insurance law of the FRG implies that the institutional diversity found in west Germany will develop in east Germany over time. Medical expenses and sick pay of the insured are funded by the medical insurance system in line with the present FRG legislation. The health insurance contributions of pensioners are covered by the pension insurance fund. Outlays for investment in inpatient and outpatient facilities in the health service are financed from the budgets of the territorial authorities.

The unemployment insurance system in east Germany has been required, since July 1, 1990, to abide by the Employment Promotions Act of the FRG. In addition to paying unemployment benefits and assistance, the system is also responsible for conducting an active labor market policy, including vocational training and retraining. The State Treaty on GEMSU stipulated that in the transitional phase, the special labor market situation in east Germany would be taken into account.[32] For instance, regulations with regard to short-time work are being applied more liberally than in west Germany until mid-1991.

Social assistance is now provided in line with the Social Assistance Act of the FRG, with the cost borne by the east German local authorities. The amounts involved are expected to be small initially, since practically all the unemployed will be covered for some time under the unemployment insurance system and pensions will in most cases be above the level provided by social assistance, which is based on a means test.

Financial Framework for the Fiscal Reforms

Besides stipulating how the revenue and expenditure systems of east Germany were to be reformed, the State Treaty on GEMSU provided a financial framework for the management of the public finances in east Germany. In particular, borrowing by the territorial authorities of the GDR would be limited to DM 10 billion in the second half of 1990 and DM 14 billion in 1991. They would receive additional financing from the German Unity Fund amounting to DM 22 billion in the second half of 1990 and DM 35 billion in 1991. The Federal Government would also provide DM 3 billion to the GDR Government in the second half of 1990 and a further DM 3 billion in 1991 to cover initial imbalances in the social security funds. The state budget for the second half of 1990, which was passed by the GDR parliament on July 22, 1990, was consistent with these financing constraints (Table 6). The budget projected revenue of DM 29½ billion. DM 25 billion would be in the form of taxes, of

---

[26] For instance, subsidies for industrial goods, agricultural products, and food were eliminated, except where they were in line with EC regulations. Subsidies on transportation, energy for private households, and housing were to be phased out progressively as incomes rose.

[27] Information on the size of the civil service was not published in the GDR. The number of employees in the so-called nonproducing sector was reported to be 1.8 million in 1988, a large part of which probably worked in the government sector. According to the Deutsches Institut für Wirtschaftsforschung, over 1.1 million workers were employed in public sector jobs, excluding the army and the security forces and the health service. See "Quantitative Aspects of Economic and Financial Reform in the GDR," Deutsches Institut für Wirtschaftsforschung, *Economic Bulletin* (Berlin), Vol. 27(5), July 1990.

[28] See Article 18(2) of the State Treaty.

[29] See Article 18(1) of the State Treaty. Accident insurance contributions are paid by the employer only.

[30] Contribution rates for both employers and employees in the FRG in 1990 are 9.35 percent of gross wage and salary income for pension insurance, 2.15 percent for unemployment insurance, and 6.45 percent for health insurance.

[31] In contrast to arrangements prior to May 18, 1990, entitlements earned in east Germany will not be changed when a person transfers his or her residence to west Germany (Article 20(7) of the State Treaty). Because of income differentials between east and west Germany, this acts as a disincentive to westward migration.

---

[32] See Article 19 of the State Treaty.

Table 6. East Germany: Central Government Budget in the Second Half of 1990

(In billions of deutsche mark)

	Original Budget[1]	Revised Estimates[1]
Total expenditure	**64.2**	**81.8**
Public services	9.8	. . .
Education, science, and research	4.0	. . .
Social welfare	6.4	. . .
Of which:		
Child benefits	2.5	. . .
Housing	1.3	. . .
Food, agriculture, and forestry	4.4	. . .
Energy, water, and mining	1.1	. . .
Transportation and communications	4.9	. . .
Transfers	26.1	. . .
To other levels of government	19.5	. . .
To pension fund	3.6	. . .
To unemployment insurance	2.0	. . .
To health insurance	0.9	. . .
Subsidies (excluding agriculture)	6.2	. . .
Export subsidies (CMEA)	2.0	. . .
Public transport	1.3	. . .
Energy	2.9	. . .
Interest	2.9	. . .
Across-the-board expenditure cut	−3.4	. . .
Other (including contingency reserves)	1.7	. . .
Total revenue	**29.4**	**22.8**
Taxes	24.8	17.7
Value-added tax	10.2	. . .
Excise taxes	5.5	. . .
Lump-sum company tax	6.0	. . .
Wage tax	2.1	. . .
Other	1.0	. . .
Other revenue	4.7	5.2
Financial balance	**−34.8**	**−59.0**
Financing	34.8	−59.0
Transfers from German Unity Fund	22.0	. . .
Transfers from Federal Government	2.8	. . .
for start-up financing of:		
Pensions	0.8	. . .
Unemployment insurance	2.0	. . .
Borrowing by GDR Government	10.0	. . .

Source: Bundesministerium der Finanzen.

[1] Passed by the parliament of the GDR on July 22, 1990.

[2] As estimated in the proposals for the third supplementary budget for the FRG, September 1990.

which two thirds would be generated by value-added and excise taxes. Expenditure was budgeted at DM 64 billion. On an annual basis, this represented only about half of expenditure prior to GEMSU; the separation of social security and public enterprises from the state budget, as well as expenditure cuts, accounted for the reduction in expenditure.

Establishing a budget for the immediate post-GEMSU period was severely hampered by many uncertainties. On the revenue side, it was difficult to project economic developments in east Germany and there were questions about how efficiently the tax collection system would work. On the expenditure side, the lack of transparency in the old accounting system was a major problem. Moreover, the

likely financial needs of the social insurance funds were difficult to anticipate.

Problems in these and other areas substantially affected budgetary developments in the second half of 1990. It was officially recognized in August that fiscal imbalances in east Germany would not be contained within the limits prescribed by the State Treaty. In September 1990, revised estimates were published along with the proposals for the third supplementary budget of the FRG. In the revised estimates, expenditure was 28 percent higher than budgeted earlier and revenue about 22 percent lower. These adjustments resulted in a projected deficit of DM 59 billion, compared with DM 35 billion in the original budget. On the expenditure side, about half of the increase was accounted for by transfers to the social insurance funds (Table 7). The budget had assumed that some 430,000 people would be receiving unemployment benefits on average in the second half of 1990, of which 270,000 would be fully unemployed; in September, however, the number of unemployed and part-time workers totaled 2.2 million, with 20 percent of these fully unemployed.[33] Moreover, benefits were larger than expected, owing to the size of wage increases in east Germany. In the area of health expenditure, costs had risen because of higher salaries and because of a shift in the use of medicines away from those produced in east Germany toward more expensive west German products. Pension expenditure was also higher, since a decision to increase benefits was reached after the budget had been formulated. On the other hand, the income of the social security funds had been lower than anticipated, as firms with liquidity problems had been unable to remit payroll taxes. Lower employment had also reduced receipts, though this had been offset by higher wages.

Expenditure on subsidies was also expected to be greater than in the budget. Energy and transportation subsidies had increased, in part because of the rise in oil prices but also because of higher consumption than anticipated: for example, large purchases of consumer durables had boosted demand for electricity. Subsidies to agriculture would exceed the budgeted amount, as a result of the difficulties being experienced in this sector following the lifting of restrictions on imports; moreover, the estimate of subsidies related to supporting exports to member countries of the Council for Mutual Economic Assistance (CMEA) had also been increased. Of the other components of expenditure, the biggest overrun would be in transfers to local governments.

The financial framework set by the State Treaty also covered the operations of the public Trust Fund. In particular, the treaty limited borrowing by the Trust Fund to DM 7 billion in the second half of 1990 and a further DM 10 billion in 1991, these funds were to be used in the

---

[33] The cost of an additional 100,000 fully unemployed people has been estimated at DM ½ billion in the second half of 1990.

Table 7. East Germany: Sources of Expenditure Overruns in the Budget for the Second Half of 1990

(In billions of deutsche mark)

	Original Budget	Change	New Estimate
Total expenditure	64.2	17.7	81.8
Principal factors increasing expenditure			
Transfers to social security	5.1	8.9	14.0
Transfers to local government	19.5	3.1	22.6
Agriculture			
Market regulation	1.5	1.2	2.7
Structural adjustment	2.0	0.8	2.8
Subsidies			
Energy	2.9	1.2	4.1
Rents	0.6	1.1	1.7
CMEA trade	2.0	0.6	2.6
Early retirement benefits	0.1	0.3	0.4
Wages and salaries	. . .	0.8	0.8
Defense	3.8	0.4	4.2
Transport investment	2.1	0.5	2.6
Principal factors reducing expenditure			
General contingency	1.4	−1.0	0.4
Interest	2.9	−0.5	2.5

Source: Bundesministerium der Finanzen, *Pressemitteilung*, September 28, 1990.

restructuring of the enterprise sector. In addition, the Trust Fund was authorized to guarantee liquidity loans to enterprises.

In the first months of GEMSU, the Trust Fund focused on the severe liquidity crunch being faced by enterprises. With questions of property rights unresolved, the initial balance sheets of enterprises yet to be finalized, and great uncertainty about the underlying competitive position of firms, banks were reluctant to take lending risks. Against this background, the Trust Fund guaranteed working capital loans to firms; in July, these guarantees, which amounted to about DM 10 billion, were granted across the board at a rate of about 40 percent of the requests from enterprises. Additional guarantees of some DM 20 billion were provided in August and September and authorization was given to extend liquidity guarantees until March 1991. In August–September the Trust Fund began to scrutinize liquidity requests to ensure that guarantees were more closely related to the needs of firms and their longer-term prospects.

Thus, in the early months of GEMSU, the efforts to keep enterprises operational diverted the attention of the Trust Fund, to some extent, from its work related to rationalization, restructuring, and privatization. Decisions on the disposition of publicly owned enterprises were made on a case-by-case basis and concerns about employment and the social impact were weighed, along with financial and efficiency considerations. Thus, in the case of privatization, not only financial offers but also the investment and employment intentions of the purchasing firms were taken

into account. In the case of liquidation, action was delayed until the social consequences of closing the firms concerned had been evaluated. Through mid-August, 12 companies had been privatized, which yielded total receipts of some DM 70 million. Since then the pace of privatization has quickened. By early October, 30 firms had been privatized, yielding DM 1 billion; 80 percent of these receipts arose from the privatization of the electricity generating companies.

Implications of GEMSU for the Course of Public Finances in East Germany

With political unification, the scope of separate fiscal institutions in east Germany has been greatly reduced; for example, a separate central government budget for east Germany will not be produced in 1991. However, assuming a separate fiscal sector (including central government functions) is a useful analytical tool as it enables us to examine how the fiscal situation in Germany might be influenced by unification.

The new fiscal system in east Germany raises a number of important issues for the conduct of fiscal policy. First, the flexibility of government finances is quite limited, given the adoption in east Germany of the most important elements of the fiscal structures that govern taxation and social security in west Germany; this limits the extent to which policies can be adjusted to circumstances in the east. Second, the fiscal situation in east Germany is extremely difficult to project, owing in part to insufficient information on the starting conditions but even more to the uncertainties as to how economic conditions will evolve, particularly over the next few years. The inflexibility in the budget reinforces the vulnerability of the fiscal situation to macroeconomic developments.[34] For example, the links with the economic and social system of west Germany place a floor on the provision of services. Infrastructure services will have to be improved rapidly, independent of economic developments in east Germany. Similarly, the cost of social benefits, in particular medical services, will be strongly influenced by the quality of services in the west. Moreover, if links with the labor market in west Germany develop rapidly and if wages rise at a fast pace as a result, expenditure on pensions and other social welfare programs will be higher at the same time that increased unemployment would reduce contributions relative to expenditure.

The links between labor markets in east and west Germany may also induce pressures for measures to boost wages in east Germany, for instance, through investment subsidies and other incentives for business.

---

[34] Compare, for example, the fiscal outcomes in scenarios A and B in Chapter V.

However, in this case the ability of the Government to resist should, in principle, be greater as there are good arguments for limiting the extent to which the Government tries directly to influence investment and employment decisions in the private sector.[35] In other respects, too, one should not exaggerate the inflexibility of the budgetary situation. This is particularly the case if one takes as starting point the budgetary position in the second half of 1990, a period when expenditure was heavily influenced by pre-GEMSU budgetary policies. For example, while many subsidies have been abolished, important ones remain in the areas of energy, transportation, and housing. Eliminating these subsidies is a crucial step in bringing relative prices in line with the availability of resources. The Government intends to phase these out as quickly as possible. The main constraint is a concern for living standards of the less affluent, but such concerns can also be dealt with through direct income transfers. There is also room for economies in personnel expenditure; the public service of the former GDR was reportedly twice as labor-intensive as that in the FRG. Political unification will greatly reduce central government employment in the unified Germany, as the increased employment of the Federal Government will absorb only a limited number of former employees of the GDR central government. However, one should bear in mind that the scope of the central government of the GDR was much broader than that of the FRG. How much reduction in government employment takes place with unification will, thus, depend on the employment practices of the newly reconstituted Länder in east Germany. Over time, the speed with which employment is rationalized both at the Länder and municipality levels will influence not only the government finances but also the pace at which productivity rises toward west German levels.

A key feature of the fiscal reform has been the separation of various components of the state sector. When interpreting the macroeconomic effects of fiscal developments, one should bear in mind that this institutional change has had fundamental implications for government revenue, in view of the historical reliance of the government finances in the east on revenue from the state-owned enterprises. In particular, to the extent that larger government deficits in the east (compared with deficits that prevailed under the old system) are matched by an increase in retained earnings of the enterprises that no longer have to pass their profits on to the Government, the macroeconomic consequences are attenuated. The enterprises would be able to finance investment to a greater extent from internal resources, and government borrowing would take the place of borrowing previously carried out by the enterprises. Of course, the key question is enterprise profitability. It is likely that in the early stages of GEMSU, the labor share in income will be rather large, but, assuming that enterprises place emphasis on efficiency criteria, significant profits should in due course emerge at an aggregate level.

The extent to which publicly owned firms earn profits will also be important for the net worth of the public sector. It is likely that the highest profitability will be outside the state-owned sector, accruing to new private businesses and those public enterprises that are privatized early.[36] But, to the extent that the Trust Fund emphasizes efficiency, profits should also recover in the enterprises it oversees; this would boost future receipts from privatization and enable a reduction of part of the increases in public debt that occur in the interim. Nevertheless, questions remain about the financial prospects of the Trust Fund. The borrowing authority granted to the Trust Fund in the State Treaty on GEMSU (see above) was subsequently raised to DM 25 billion in the period to the end of 1991. It is also likely that, in the course of 1991, calls will be made on guarantees given by the Trust Fund to banks for liquidity credits extended to enterprises in the second half of 1990. Moreover, great uncertainty remains about the future proceeds from privatization, the costs of paying compensation to people whose assets were expropriated by the GDR Government, and the financial obligations that may result from the environmental cleanup and the resolution of the "old debt" of state-owned enterprises. There is a danger that overburdening the Trust Fund could endanger its core activities, that is, the restructuring and privatization of enterprises.

---

[35] See the discussion in Chapter XII.

[36] Most of the enterprises privatized at an early stage are likely to be already in a position to compete effectively with foreign producers.

XII

The Role of Fiscal and Structural Policies in German Unification
Lessons from the Past

Thomas Mayer

The process of German economic, monetary, and social union (GEMSU) raises many questions about the role for economic policy, both in influencing the overall degree of resource use in the economy and in pursuing an efficient allocation of resources. This chapter analyzes these questions against the background of past experience with economic policy in the Federal Republic of Germany (FRG). Three major periods of economic policymaking can be distinguished in the FRG: from 1948 until about the mid-1960s, a period of strongly market-oriented policies associated with Ludwig Erhard; from the mid-1960s to perhaps the early 1980s, a period of Keynesian policies associated with Karl Schiller; and, since the early 1980s, a revival of Erhardian ideas.[1]

The Period of Liberalism: Financing the Essential Government Tasks

Economic policy in the FRG formally began in 1948 with the merger of the U.S., British, and French occupation zones into one united economic area and the currency reform.[2] The conceptual framework that governed economic policy, however, was developed much earlier, in the writings of Ludwig Erhard and others, before and during World War II. The writings of these economists reflected a reverence for market forces as the best guide to economic decision making.[3] The main task

of economic policy was, therefore, to provide a secure and unobtrusive legal and financial framework within which markets could operate efficiently.

Ordnungspolitik, as this policy has been called, allocated clearly defined tasks to each aspect of economic policy, that is, monetary, fiscal, and structural policy. The main task of monetary policy was to ensure stability of prices and the currency. This required the establishment of a strong and independent central bank that was legally bound to pursue these objectives. Thus, the central bank's commitment to these objectives could not be overruled by the government. Fiscal policy was charged with the role of providing a tax system that generated enough revenue (with as little distortion of market signals as possible) to finance expenditures for the classical tasks of government. There was no room in this concept for fiscal demand management policies and, in fact, the general government accounts were in surplus during the 1950s and the first half of the 1960s (see Chart 11 in Chapter II). Structural policies were seen as passive rather than active: the objective was to provide an economic structure that rewarded competitiveness and facilitated structural adjustment in response to market forces. Strong antitrust laws and laws that ensured fair competition were essential to this objective.[4]

---

[1] See Leslie Lipschitz and Thomas Mayer, "Accepted Economic Paradigms Guide German Policies," *IMF Survey* (Washington), November 28, 1988, pp. 370–74.

[2] See, for example, Thomas Mayer and Günther Thumann, "Radical Currency Reform: Germany, 1948," *Finance & Development* (Washington), March 1990, pp. 6–8.

[3] In a paper written in 1943–44 ("The Economic Needs of Postwar Germany"), Erhard emphasized the role of the private sector in the reconstruction effort as follows: "the State's economic power and initiative are bound by strictly circumscribed limits so that trade and industry will be largely left to their own devices in finding ways of providing a new basis for Germany's economic life by establishing a new gross national product. The private sector of the economy will enjoy a fresh opportunity to demonstrate its skill and it must seize

this opportunity in order to refute the criticism sometimes directed against it. Entrepreneurs will once more have to resolve the problem of producing for a market without any purchasing power i.e. devoid of sure sales." See *Standard Texts of the Social Market Economy: Two Centuries of Discussion* (Stuttgart; New York: Gustav Fischer, 1982), p. 7.

[4] Walter Eucken, in an essay written in 1952 ("A Policy for Establishing a System of Free Enterprise"), described this policy in the following words: "The fundamental principle not only calls for abstinence from certain economic acts such as government subsidies, the establishment of mandatory State monopolies, a general freeze on prices, prohibitions of imports etc. Nor is it enough simply to prohibit cartels, for instance. The principle is not primarily negative in nature. There is, rather, a need for a positive economic policy aimed at developing the marketing structure of unrestricted competition and thus at realizing the fundamental principle. This is also a field in which the competitive system differs entirely from the policy of laissez-faire, which in substance did not admit of any positive system of economic regulation." Ibid. p. 116.

This description of economic policy should not be taken to suggest that the system was one of virtually unbridled market forces. Indeed, economic policy was constrained by social policy that ensured consensus between the so-called social partners, organized labor and capital. In this sense, there was government intervention to influence market forces. But the intervention was not ad hoc or unpredictable; social policy consisted of a set of rules—similar to the rest of the institutional and legal framework of the economic system—that set the bounds within which market forces could operate. In the thinking of the postwar German ''Ordo-liberal'' economists, the role of social policy was important, if not vital, to the success of economic policy. This view had historical roots. In postwar Germany, the memory of the close cooperation of big industry with the Nazi regime was still vivid. It was believed that the involvement of labor in industrial management, through workers' councils and economically strong trade unions, was essential to the well-being of the young democracy and for economic prosperity. On economic grounds, social policy was seen as helping to overcome the traditional antagonism between capital and labor so as to foster a social environment conducive to a smoothly functioning economy.[5] The main instruments of social policy were the establishment of comprehensive unemployment, health, and pension systems, as well as institutional regulations that allowed for the representation of labor in the main areas of industry.

The combination of a market-oriented economic policy with an active social policy came to be known as *Soziale Marktwirtschaft* (social market economy).[6] The execution of this policy was fairly straightforward. Once the economic framework was in place, the Ministry of Economics, headed by Erhard, took over the role of the guardian of its principles. Day-to-day management was not required, and the Ministry concentrated on basic policy issues and occasional modifications of the policy framework when these were needed because of economic developments. The other economic policy institutions, the Ministry of Finance and the Deutsche Bundesbank, had an essentially supportive role. To play this role was, however, not always easy. Monetary policy, for example, was often caught between domestic considerations and the external constraints imposed by the Bretton Woods system of fixed exchange rates, as the German target for inflation often differed from those of trading partner countries. In most cases, the record suggests that external constraints prevailed over domestic objectives.[7]

The rejection of the notion that economic policy should try to steer economic developments was reflected in the relatively small size of government during the 1950s and early 1960s. In 1955, the share of government revenue in GNP was 35 percent (more than 10 percentage points below the share in the mid-1980s, see Table A15 in Chapter II). The share of government expenditures in GNP was only 30 percent (almost 20 percentage points below that reached 30 years later), and the government accounts registered a considerable surplus.

The noninterventionist paradigm of the 1950s and early 1960s, supported by a favorable economic environment, was associated with a buoyant economy: real per capita GNP growth averaged close to 7 percent through the 1950s; unemployment declined from almost 2 million in 1950 to 300,000 in 1960; inflation was below 2 percent on average during 1950–60; share prices rose manyfold in the 1950s; and real interest rates on government bonds averaged about 4½ percent during 1955–60.

The Period of Keynesianism: Restoring Internal Equilibrium

In the early 1960s, the Social Democratic Party (SPD) moved from the left toward the political center. In the area of economic policy, the old, more socialist philosophy was replaced by a moderate Keynesianism. When the SPD formed a government with the Christian Democrats (CDU) in 1966, the ground was laid for the application of these ideas. At the same time, there was also something of an international consensus on Keynesian policies.

---

[5] In 1944, in ''The Guiding Principles of the Liberal Programme,'' Wilhelm Röpke wrote, ''If left to itself, a market economy is dangerous and indefensible because it reduces people to a thoroughly unnatural existence which they then cast aside together with the free market which has become hateful. In other words, the market economy requires a firm framework, which we may conveniently refer to in short as the anthropological-sociological framework. If this framework breaks down, then it is no longer possible to have a free market. In other words, market economy is not everything. It has a special place in a healthy and efficient society where it is indispensable and where it must remain pure and undiluted.'' Ibid. p. 190.

[6] In 1947, Alfred Müller-Armack spelled out the theoretical foundations of the social market economy in ''The Social Aspect of the Economic System'' as follows: ''We would therefore be well advised to look for a new system which will harmonize both the social aims of our time and the most fundamental tenets of business practice and the science of political economy. Such a synthesis can only be achieved by the re-establishment of a genuine market economy. This new market economy must distinguish itself from the liberal market economy of the 19th century which, like the system of central control, is a thing of the past, by virtue of its social objectives. We must build a 'Social Market Economy'.'' Ibid. p. 17.

[7] In the mid-1960s, for example, a major battle took place within the so-called Grand Coalition between the CDU/CSU and the SPD over the question of a revaluation of the deutsche mark. The SPD, led by Karl Schiller, the Minister of Economics, argued that a revaluation was needed to dampen inflationary pressures caused by the sizable balance of payments surpluses. Chancellor Kiesinger (CDU) rejected the request. The exchange rate remained unchanged until the end of the 1960s when a new SPD/FDP government was elected.

The main proponent of Keynesian policies in Germany at this time was Karl Schiller. In contrast to the "Ordoliberal" school, he argued for active demand management policies by the Government with a view to maintaining full employment in the economy. Given the limited scope for independent monetary action in the fixed exchange rate system of the time, the obvious instrument was fiscal policy. The "mini-recession" of 1967 provided the first test case for the application of these policies. After strong growth in 1964–65, the economy had weakened in the course of 1966 and had fallen into mild recession in 1967. Schiller interpreted this development in the following way: "The absence of . . . a coordination between fiscal and monetary policy as well as between actions of the government bodies on the one hand and the autonomous social forces on the other hand was responsible . . . for the deepest recession in the Federal Republic in the post war period in 1966–67."[8] The Government reacted with deficit spending and so contributed to a strong economic rebound in the following year. At the same time, a law was enacted that was intended to provide a framework for the regular application of demand management policies (*Gesetz zur Förderung der Stabilität und des Wachstums der Wirtschaft* or "stability law".)[9]

The law stated that fiscal policy at all levels of government (federal, state, and municipal) should be directed at maintaining price stability, a high level of employment, external balance, and appropriate economic growth. These four objectives were to be taken into account when budgets were drafted. But the law also provided instruments—such as expenditure freezes, public borrowing ceilings, and additional government expenditures—to adjust fiscal policy between budgets. Private investment could be stimulated through investment premiums, or it could be dampened through limitations on depreciation allowances. A particularly powerful instrument under the stability law was the so-called tax regulator. Under this provision, prepayments of income taxes could be changed and, if necessary, income and corporation taxes could be raised or reduced by up to 10 percent. All of these instruments could be implemented fairly quickly by the Federal Government provided both houses of parliament agreed.

Although the tax regulator under the stability law has been rarely used since its introduction,[10] the spirit of the law influenced fiscal policy during most of the 1970s. Prime examples of Keynesian policies were the Government's reactions to the first oil price shock in 1974 and the program that it undertook at the time of the May 1978 Bonn economic summit. At this summit meeting of the heads of state or government of the Group of Five countries, Germany and Japan committed themselves to more expansionary fiscal policies, while the United States promised greater fiscal restraint; the objective was for policies in Germany and Japan to support economic growth and, combined with those in the United States, to redress the trade imbalances that had emerged among the major industrial countries. A stimulatory fiscal package, based chiefly on public construction, was introduced with the budget for 1979. However, this investment program, though countercyclical in intention, was not so in effect. Indeed, the increase in public construction in 1979–80 reinforced a boom in private construction and the subsequent drop in public construction coincided with a fall in private construction activity.

The 1967 "mini-recession" had been handled in a textbook manner,[11] but subsequent episodes of fine-tuning showed up a basic flaw: postrecession efforts at demand management proved incapable of reining back fiscal deficits.[12] Thus, fiscal deficits and public debt rose during the 1970s and early 1980s to levels unprecedented in postwar Germany as policymakers struggled to deal with an unfavorable external environment (see Chart 11 in Chapter II). In this process, the structure of revenues and expenditures changed substantially (see below). Moreover, as a result of the increase in the share of expenditure on entitlements and debt service, the room for discretionary spending diminished sharply. In the event, these developments contributed to the fall of the SPD/FDP government.

The Revival of Erhardian Ideas

Attempts at "Consolidation"

The second oil price shock in 1979 coincided with the stimulatory effects of the internationally coordinated

---

[8] Karl Schiller, "Konjunkturpolitik auf dem Wege zu einer Affluent Society," Kieler Vorträge No. 54 (Kiel, 1968), p. 8 (translated).

[9] Schiller gave the following characterization of the Stability Law: "The tool box of demand management possibilities provided by this law is indeed extraordinarily rich; in fact, it is probably the most modern tool box available. But . . . this law is not a panacea. It provides . . . instruments to counter a recession or dampen an overheating of the economy. But it does not, for instance, provide instruments to boost unsatisfactory economic growth." See ibid., p. 9 (translated).

[10] The tax regulator was used in 1970 and 1971 to raise DM 2¼ billion and DM 3¾ billion, respectively, in additional taxes to withdraw stimulus from the economy. Of this, DM 5¾ billion was repaid in 1972 and DM ¼ billion in 1973, shortly before the rise in oil prices triggered a recession.

[11] After deficits in 1967–68, the federal budget ran surpluses in 1969–70 when economic activity was strong (see Chart 11 in Chapter II).

[12] Schiller, who became "Super" Minister of Finance and Economics in 1971, resigned in 1972 mainly because he was concerned about this inability to control deficits in the aftermath of cyclical downturns and recoveries.

economic action of 1978 and led to a sharp worldwide increase in inflation. In the FRG, higher oil prices together with the rapid, policy-induced, growth of domestic demand produced, in 1980, the largest external current account deficit in postwar history. At the same time, an international consensus began to emerge that forces had to be concentrated on fighting inflation and that the old recipes of demand management would not help put the world economy back on its feet. In a major change of fiscal policy in 1981, Chancellor Schmidt gave priority to the reduction of fiscal deficits over demand stimulation of the economy, but he did not find the full support of his party in this endeavor. Otto Lambsdorff, the FDP Minister of Economics at this time, explained in a now famous "U-turn" paper (*Wendepapier*) why he thought it was impossible to pursue the appropriate economic policies within the then government.[13] This triggered the end of the SPD/FDP Government and the move of the FDP into a coalition with the CDU/CSU in October 1982. The disenchantment with the interventionist paradigm, which had set in already in 1980–81, was then endorsed by the 1983 elections. The new CDU/CSU/FDP coalition won a majority on an economic platform committed to a more limited role for government and a greater reliance on market forces.

The new Government saw the lax fiscal policies of the previous years as the main problem. The increase in the share of government revenue, expenditure, and of the deficit in GNP in the course of the 1970s (see Table A15 in Chapter II) was believed to have deprived the private sector of the resources it needed to contribute to healthy economic growth and a reduction of unemployment. In addition, an overly generous social policy—with social transfers equivalent to 18 percent of GNP in 1982—was believed to have contributed to the high rate of unemployment by pushing up wage costs and suppressing incentives to work. Also, the micro-management of industry by the Government, through rules, regulations, direct subsidies, and incentives, was held responsible for structural rigidities in the economy and a general inability to adjust to the new international environment; these rigidities, which were seen as a broader European problem, were dubbed "Eurosclerosis."[14] In short, there was a widely held view that government interference in the economy had proved counterproductive and that it was necessary to "pare down the state to the core of its sovereign activities, which it will then be able to carry out all the more reliably."[15]

The new economic strategy contained a number of implications for structural and fiscal policies. The task of structural policy was to attack the rigidities present in the economy with a view to speeding up adjustment. In particular, labor market rigidities that had increased significantly over the previous decade were to be eased; subsidies to ailing industries were to be curtailed; many areas of industry were to be deregulated; and important state enterprises were to be privatized. The task of fiscal policy was to "consolidate" the government finances and to pursue medium-term objectives—the Government was loath to set any targets on variables such as real growth, unemployment, or external balances and disavowed the stop-and-go policies of the past. There was a quantitative and a qualitative aspect to consolidation. The term "quantitative consolidation" meant the reduction of government expenditure, revenue, and the budget deficit relative to GNP; "qualitative consolidation" meant the reform of the tax system and a restructuring of government expenditure away from current spending toward investment. Given the complexity of the program, the politicians thought that a gradual implementation was appropriate. In the first step, the most detrimental rigidities in the labor market would be eliminated and government spending and budget deficits would be curtailed. This was expected to create more room for maneuver for both fiscal and structural policies so that, in the second step, the "qualitative" consolidation of government finances and the deregulation of the economy could follow.

During its first legislative period, the Government was indeed successful in improving the state finances. The share of general government expenditures in GNP declined from 49¾ percent in 1981–82 to 47 percent in 1986. This made possible a narrowing of the general government deficit from about 3½ percent of GNP in 1981–82 to 1¼ percent of GNP in 1986 and a lowering of the share of general government revenues in GNP from 46¼ percent to 45½ percent over the same period. There was a significant cutback in social expenditures by the government as well; the share of these outlays in GNP fell from 17¾ percent in 1981–82 to 16 percent in 1986, despite a rise in the unemployment rate. Also, labor market legislation in 1984–86 limited the trade unions' negotiating power in labor

---

[13] O. Lambsdorff, "Konzept für eine Politik zur Uberwindung der Wachstumsschwäche und zur Bekämpfung der Arbeitslosigkeit" (mimeographed; Bonn, 1982).

[14] See, for example, Herbert Giersch, "Eurosclerosis," *Kiel Discussion Papers* No. 112 (Kiel, 1985).

[15] See Bundesministerium für Wirtschaft, *Jahreswirtschaftsbericht 1987*, p. 21 (translated). In December 1985, the Federal Ministry of Finance

described the role of fiscal policy in more detail: "In an economic system based on free enterprise, economic growth is not so much the aim as the result of market processes. The task of the public sector is not to realize the highest possible growth rates at the cost of unwarrantable fiscal policy measures, but to ensure that economic activity can develop unhindered and is provided with sufficient incentive. The price signals transmitted by the market must reach the recipients . . . with as little distortion as possible. Sound public finances will increase the confidence of markets in the dependability of policies. Well-ordered public budgets are thus an important basis for long-term decisions . . . and part of the foundation of an efficient free-market system." See Bundesministerium der Finanzen, *Tasks and Objectives of a New Fiscal Policy: The Limits to Public Indebtedness* (1985), p. 19.

disputes, improved the conditions for the hiring of youths and part-time workers, and increased the flexibility of labor contracts.[16]

Relatively little progress, however, was made in the areas of qualitative consolidation of government expenditures, privatization of state enterprises, and deregulation of the economy. Contrary to the authorities' intentions, the share of subsidy payments in total expenditures increased from 3¾ percent to 4½ percent between 1981–82 and 1986; only a small part of the privatization program was carried out; and the process of deregulation was slow.

On the other hand, soon after some progress in quantitative consolidation became visible, the objective of reducing and reforming taxes gained momentum. In 1985, a DM 20 billion (1 percent of GNP) tax reform package was enacted. It was aimed chiefly at providing relief for families with children and at reducing marginal tax rates and it was to be implemented in two parts: DM 11 billion from 1986 and DM 8½ billion from 1988. After being returned to office in January 1987, the ruling coalition agreed upon a larger package of tax reform and reduction (coupled with a reining-back of tax preferences) that became fully effective in 1990 (see Table A16 in Chapter II).

International Concerns: Tackling the External Surplus

A prominent feature of the present economic upswing in the FRG has been the emergence of a large external surplus. This was the result, first, of export-led growth in 1984–85 and, second, of the large terms of trade gains in 1986–87 in the wake of the appreciation of the deutsche mark and the fall in oil prices. Following the Plaza Agreement in the fall of 1985 in which the Group of Five countries committed themselves to work toward a controlled depreciation of the U.S. dollar, greater pressure was put on the FRG to adopt policies that would boost domestic demand. An expansion of domestic demand in countries with external surpluses was considered desirable to take up the slack in the world economy that was expected to result from a reduction in U.S. net imports. These considerations temporarily influenced the conduct of economic policy in the FRG.

In 1986–87, fiscal policy turned expansionary, though this was more the result of the tax reform already enacted than a response to international pressures. The response of fiscal policy to the macroeconomic environment was, however, more evident in decisions taken in 1987–88. At a meeting of the Group of Six in early 1987 (the Louvre Accord), the German authorities agreed to bring

forward DM 5 billion of the tax cuts envisaged for 1990 to 1988, raising the size of the tax cut already scheduled from DM 8½ billion to almost DM 14 billion (¾ of 1 percent of GNP). This, it was thought, would help bolster domestic demand and contribute both to stronger growth and a more rapid reduction of the current account surplus. Against the backdrop of turbulence in financial markets in the latter part of 1987, the Federal Government decided in December 1987 to take further fiscal action to support economic growth. The measures included additional loans to municipalities and medium-sized enterprises and an increase in investment by the Federal Postal System. Later, in January 1988, when confronted with an unexpected shortfall in revenues due to lower-than-expected profit transfers from the Bundesbank and higher-than-envisaged transfers to the European Community (EC) budget, the Government decided not to take offsetting measures and to tolerate a temporary rise in the deficit. As a result of these decisions, the federal deficit widened, from its narrowest point in 1985, by almost DM 13 billion to DM 36 billion (1¾ percent of GNP) in 1988. Deficits at the other levels of government rose too: thus, the general government deficit increased to DM 45 billion (2 percent of GNP).

The expansionary fiscal policy stance, combined with an accommodating monetary policy, contributed to rapid growth of domestic demand in 1986–88. The progress in external adjustment, however, was limited. The reduction in the real external balance that took place in 1986–87 was more than offset by improvements in the terms of trade, so that the external current account surplus increased substantially. When the terms of trade stabilized in 1988, real exports rebounded and prevented the current account surplus from declining.

On the Eve of GEMSU

In 1989, fiscal policy returned to the consolidation of government finances. A DM 8 billion increase in indirect taxes, enacted in 1988, together with fiscal drag, resulted in a negative fiscal impulse from the revenue side. This contractionary impulse was reinforced by a withdrawal of stimulus from the expenditure side at the general government level as the savings from a reform of the health system more than offset higher expenditures of the territorial authorities. As a consequence of this and the buoyant economy, the general government accounts showed a surplus for the first time in 15 years; the deficit of the territorial authorities declined to its 1985 level; and the federal deficit fell to its lowest point during the present upswing. Thus, following slippages in 1986–88, quantitative consolidation seemed to be back on track. The prospect of somewhat higher deficits in 1990 did not imply a permanent weakening in the quantitative consolidation effort since the increase in deficits was

---

[16] For more information on this and the following see Leslie Lipschitz and others, *The Federal Republic of Germany: Adjustment in a Surplus Country*, IMF Occasional Paper, No. 64 (Washington: International Monetary Fund, January 1989).

expected to be temporary and reflected a major step toward qualitative consolidation of government finances.[17]

Progress in the area of qualitative consolidation, on the other hand, continued to fall short of the Government's objectives. There were achievements in tax reform, privatization of federal government holdings in private industry, reform of the public health and pension insurance systems, and in reducing some of the rigidities in the labor market. Further reforms in business taxation[18] were also planned, but in other areas, such as privatization,[19] subsidy reduction,[20] and deregulation,[21] much remained to be done.

Against this background, the question arises as to what extent GEMSU will affect the future course of fiscal policy, in particular whether qualitative consolidation can be completed and how the goal of quantitative consolidation will be affected.

Fiscal and Structural Policies in GEMSU

From the fiscal perspective, GEMSU came at a very favorable time. Government finances in 1989 were in a strong position and several major fiscal reforms had been successfully implemented. As a result, there was scope for fiscal support of the economic unification process. While this was fortunate, there was also the danger that the by and large satisfactory state of government finances could invite overly generous fiscal support.

For 1990, budgetary decisions in the FRG were originally determined by the Government's medium-term fiscal program that foresaw the implementation of the third and largest part of the three-step program of tax reform and reduction with effect from January 1, 1990 (see footnote 17). But the changing political and economic environment soon began to leave its imprint on fiscal policy.[22] During 1990, the Bundestag enacted three supplementary federal budgets primarily aimed at supporting the economic unification process; additional borrowing related to east Germany totaled some DM 33 billion. Moreover, the Federal Government and the Länder established an extrabudgetary fund (German Unity Fund) with a total endowment of DM 115 billion to provide assistance to the GDR Government in 1990–94.[23] Of the total, DM 95 billion would be raised in the capital market (including DM 20 billion in 1990) and DM 20 billion would come from the federal budget.[24]

As the economic integration of the two economies proceeds, additional pressures on government budgets seem likely. Many of the requests for government assistance will be justified with the need to support economic adjustment in east Germany.[25] However, as the experience in the FRG during the 1970s and 1980s has demonstrated, there is the risk that financial support for economic adjustment tends to extend the adjustment period and in the event to become entrenched.[26] The experience of the 1950s and 1960s, on the other hand, suggests that adjustment can occur quite efficiently when the Government limits its involvement in the economy.

The following points seem to be of particular importance. First, rapid economic adjustment and growth can be successfully achieved without subsidies to industries—in 1955, real per capita GNP growth reached a high of 10½ percent, while subsidy payments reached a low of only ¼ of 1 percent of GNP, one tenth of their level of the mid-1980s. In fact, as the experience in later years has demonstrated, subsidies may well be counterproductive

---

[17] On January 1, 1990, the third step of tax reform took effect that included an estimated reduction in income taxes by DM 39 billion, coupled with a reduction in tax preferences equivalent to DM 14 billion (Table A16 in Chapter II). The tax reform package of 1990 thus implied a net tax cut of DM 25 billion, bringing total net tax relief granted in the 1986–90 tax reform program to about DM 50 billion (2½ percent of GNP). For a more detailed discussion of the tax reform see Lipschitz and others, ibid.

[18] Although tax reform provided some tax relief for businesses (inter alia through a reduction of the top marginal rates of income and corporation taxes), the Government intended to implement a business sector tax reform in the next legislative period in time for the completion of the EC internal market at the end of 1992.

[19] The Federal Government had completed its privatization program but little privatization had occurred at the state and municipal levels.

[20] In 1989, subsidy payments as defined in the national accounts still stood at 2 percent of GNP, slightly above their level of 1982. Subsidies of the territorial authorities as defined in the Federal Government's biannual subsidy report stood at 3½ percent of GNP; federal subsidies alone were equal to 1½ percent of GNP. Despite the reduction of tax exemptions—a part of the 1990 tax reform package—federal subsidies were budgeted to decline by only 6 percent in 1990.

[21] In the restructuring of the Federal Postal System that took place in 1989, the supply of some telecommunication services was partly liberalized. An initiative to liberalize shop-opening hours resulted in the possibility of an extension of opening hours by two and one half hours on each Thursday with an unchanged weekly maximum. Further deregulation activities still await preparation of a report by the Deregulation Commission (now scheduled for 1991). See footnote 55 in Chapter II for additional information on the Deregulation Commission.

[22] See Chapter II, section on "Fiscal Implications of GEMSU."

[23] The prime purpose of keeping the bulk of transfers to the GDR off-budget was to facilitate continuation of the present system of financial relations between the Federal Government and the Länder, as well as between the Länder, until the end of 1994.

[24] The contribution from the federal budget is expected to be financed by a reduction in "the costs of division" of Germany (see below).

[25] There are significant incentives for investment in east Germany which are outlined in footnote 54 of Chapter III. In addition, the public Trust Fund (Treuhandanstalt) in east Germany has been given authority to borrow (in anticipation of revenues from privatization of government assets) to support the structural adjustment of east German enterprises. The borrowing authority was initially set at DM 7 billion in 1990 and DM 10 billion in 1991 and was subsequently raised to DM 25 billion over the period to end-1991.

[26] A case in point is the coal mining industry where subsidies have been paid over many years. In 1988, subsidies per employee were estimated at DM 63,300 while labor costs per employee were DM 60,400. Total subsidies in 1988 were estimated at DM 12 billion (½ of 1 percent of GNP).

because they reduce the pressures for adjustment and thus tend to preserve existing economic structures. Second, although a social safety net is important to increase the public acceptance of economic restructuring, care should be taken to limit the adverse effects of social transfers on the flexibility of the labor market. It is noteworthy that in 1955 social transfers relative to GNP amounted to only a little more than two thirds of their 1985 value. Third, policymakers should be careful that the pursuit of equity through the tax system is balanced against efficiency losses that might ensue. Direct taxes, which have grown markedly since the 1950s, may, if excessive, seriously impair work incentives. However, in interpreting the experience of the 1950s, one needs also to bear in mind that circumstances and expectations at that time differed substantially from those that now constitute the environment for GEMSU.

The question arises: Should fiscal policy be used to moderate some of the demand pressures emanating from GEMSU, including those related to budgetary assistance to east Germany? A review of the historical experience urges caution in using fiscal policy for demand management. The problem lies not so much in the principle of demand management—indeed, gains from well-designed and timely policies are likely—but rather with the practical problems of implementation. There is, of course, the usual problem of timing—because of lags in implementation, policies designed to be anticyclical can turn out procyclical—this was evident from the experience of the FRG in the late 1970s. Moreover, even when implemented, there can be significant lags before policies have their full effect— evidence presented in Chapter IX indicates, for example, that the effect of increased government saving on national saving may be offset to quite a large extent by reductions in private saving, at least initially. But more fundamentally, there is a danger that the measures used to achieve stabilization objectives have long-run adverse effects on the structure of the budget and the allocation of resources in the economy: the microeconomic effects of tax and expenditure changes may not be given much attention in the face of pressing stabilization objectives, and tax changes which generate revenue initially for stabilization purposes can, in the long run, fuel ill-considered expenditure programs.

In the event that fiscal measures are needed to offset some of the expansionary effects of GEMSU, the first priority should be to take actions that were already warranted on microeconomic grounds before GEMSU. In the case of the FRG, there are a number of government subsidy programs that fit into this category, including those related to the "costs of division." In 1990, the territorial authorities are estimated to support West Berlin and the areas negatively affected by the inner-German border by about DM 27 billion in the form of transfers and tax exemptions (DM 13 billion in direct transfers from the Federal Government to the West Berlin budget and DM 14 billion in subsidies for enterprises and workers active in Berlin and the other areas).[27] Clearly, with the lifting of the inner-German border, the rationale for this support will disappear. The phasing-out of these tax preferences and transfers would go part of the way toward financing the integration of the east German economy into the expanded Federal Republic. There are, moreover, numerous other subsidies and transfers the reduction of which would make economic sense even without GEMSU.

Considerations outlined above suggest that the Government should be very cautious in tailoring new taxes simply to the financing needs of GEMSU: if new taxes are unavoidable, they should, at least, be consistent with the Government's ongoing tax reform program. Moreover, to the extent that the adverse effects of GEMSU on government finances are projected to be temporary, it might be unwise to allow revenue increases to become embedded in the fiscal structure. However, a tax measure perceived as temporary may result in a particularly large offset in private saving behavior.

The case against a tax increase in the FRG rests on the rise in the deficit being limited and temporary and the spillover effects of rapid demand growth in east Germany remaining manageable. It is clear, however, that the outlook for the government finances in east Germany is highly uncertain and that one could envisage large fiscal imbalances being sustained for some time. It may also turn out that past experience, on which model calculations of the effects of GEMSU are based, is a poor guide given the unprecedented character of the unification process. These factors argue for a close monitoring of developments in Germany and their international effects. Should persistent and sizable fiscal imbalances seem likely, policymakers should be ready to take decisive action.

---

[27] In addition, the territorial authorities are estimated to spend about DM 7½ billion and the social security system roughly DM 5½ billion to ease the consequences of the division of Germany.